WEST-E / PRAXIS II
0049
0089

Middle Level Humanities
Teacher Certification Exam

By: Sharon Wynne, M.S
Southern Connecticut State University

"And, while there's no reason yet to panic, I think it's only prudent that we make preparations to panic."

XAMonline, INC.
Boston

Copyright © 2007 XAMonline, Inc.

All rights reserved. No part of the material protected by this copyright notice may be reproduced or utilized in any form or by any means, electronic or mechanical, including photocopying, recording or by any information storage and retrievable system, without written permission from the copyright holder.

To obtain permission(s) to use the material from this work for any purpose including workshops or seminars, please submit a written request to:

XAMonline, Inc.
21 Orient Ave.
Melrose, MA 02176
Toll Free 1-800-509-4128
Email: info@xamonline.com
Web www.xamonline.com
Fax: 1-781-662-9268

Library of Congress Cataloging-in-Publication Data

Wynne, Sharon A.
    Middle Level Humanities 0049, 0089 Teacher Certification / Sharon A. Wynne. -2nd ed.
    ISBN 978-1-58197-556-7
    1. Middle School Humanities 0049, 0089.   2. Study Guides.   3. WEST
    4. Teachers' Certification & Licensure.   5. Careers

Disclaimer:

The opinions expressed in this publication are the sole works of XAMonline and were created independently from the National Education Association, Educational Testing Service, or any State Department of Education, National Evaluation Systems or other testing affiliates.

Between the time of publication and printing, state specific standards as well as testing formats and website information may change that is not included in part or in whole within this product. Sample test questions are developed by XAMonline and reflect similar content as on real tests; however, they are not former tests. XAMonline assembles content that aligns with state standards but makes no claims nor guarantees teacher candidates a passing score. Numerical scores are determined by testing companies such as NES or ETS and then are compared with individual state standards. A passing score varies from state to state.

Printed in the United States of America

WEST-E/PRAXIS II: Middle Level Humanities 0049, 0089
ISBN: 978-1-58197-556-7

TEACHER CERTIFICATION STUDY GUIDE

Table of Contents

MIDDLE SCHOOL LANGUAGE ARTS

DOMAIN I.   **READING AND LITERATURE**

Competency 1.0   Identifying major works and authors of literature appropriate for adolescents 1

Competency 2.0   Interpreting, paraphrasing, and comparing various types of texts, including fiction, poetry, essays, and other nonfiction ... 7

Competency 3.0   Identifying and analyzing figurative language and other literary elements 15

Competency 4.0   Identifying patterns, structures, and characteristics of literary forms and genres 25

Competency 5.0   Situating and interpreting texts within their historical and cultural contexts 35

Competency 6.0   Recognizing various strategic approaches to and elements of teaching reading and textual interpretation 48

DOMAIN II.   **LANGUAGE AND LINGUISTICS**

Competency 7.0   Understanding elements of traditional grammar 57

Competency 8.0   Understanding various semantic elements 68

Competency 9.0   Understanding subjects relating to the analysis and history of English 71

DOMAIN III.   **COMPOSITION AND RHETORIC**

Competency 10.0   Understanding strategies for teaching writing and theories of how students learn to write 76

Competency 11.0   Recognizing individual and collaborative approaches to teaching writing 86

Competency 12.0   Knowledge of various tools and response strategies for assessing student writing 88

Competency 13.0   Recognizing, understanding, and evaluating rhetorical features of writing and organizational strategies 90

MID. LEVEL HUMANITIES

TEACHER CERTIFICATION STUDY GUIDE

DOMAIN IV.   LITERARY ANALYSIS

Competency 14.0   Describe and give examples of the use of one or two specified literary element(s) present in the stimulus 95

Competency 15.0   Discuss how the author's use of the literary element(s) contributes to the overall meaning and/or effectiveness of the text.. 95

DOMAIN V.   RHETORICAL ANALYSIS

Competency 16.0   Identify and describe and/or give examples of the use of one or more rhetorical elements in the stimulus 97

Competency 17.0   Discuss the degree to which the use of the rhetorical element(s) is effective in conveying the author's point and contributing to the overall meaning of the text 98

Sample Test: Middle School Language Arts 99

Answer Key: Middle School Language Arts 115

Rationales with Sample Questions: Middle School Language Arts 116

MIDDLE SCHOOL SOCIAL STUDIES

DOMAIN VI.   UNITED STATES HISTORY

COMPETENCY 18.0 PHYSICAL GEOGRAPHY OF NORTH AMERICA 145

Skill 18.1   Demonstrate knowledge of North America's location in the world, and of the continent's rivers, lakes, and important land features....... 145

Skill 18.2   Demonstrate knowledge of broad climate patterns and physiographic regions 146

COMPETENCY 19.0 NATIVE AMERICAN PEOPLES 149

Skill 19.1   Demonstrate knowledge of Native American tribes living in the various regions of North America 149

Skill 19.2   Demonstrate understanding of the political, economic, social, and cultural life of Native American peoples... 149

TEACHER CERTIFICATION STUDY GUIDE

COMPETENCY 20.0 EUROPEAN EXPLORATION AND COLONIZATION 152

Skill 20.1 Identify the major explorers and the reasons for European exploration 152

Skill 20.2 Demonstrate understanding of the consequences of early contacts between Europeans and Native Americans 153

Skill 20.3 Demonstrate knowledge of colonization by various European powers 154

Skill 20.4 Demonstrate knowledge of the establishment and growth of the English colonies, including their political, economic, social, and cultural organization and institutions 157

COMPETENCY 21.0 ESTABLISHING A NEW NATION (1776–1791) 159

Skill 21.1 Demonstrate understanding of the American Revolution, including its causes, leaders, events, and results 159

Skill 21.2 Demonstrate knowledge of the Declaration of Independence and other revolutionary documents 160

Skill 21.3 Demonstrate knowledge of the first government of the United States under the Articles of Confederation 163

Skill 21.4 Demonstrate understanding of the process of writing and adopting the Constitution and the Bill of Rights 166

COMPETENCY 22.0 EARLY YEARS OF THE NEW NATION (1791–1829) 168

Skill 22.1 Demonstrate understanding of political development, including early presidential administrations, establishment of the federal judiciary, and inception and growth of political parties 168

Skill 22.2 Demonstrate understanding of foreign policy issues, including the Louisiana Purchase, the War of 1812, and the Monroe Doctrine 170

Skill 22.3 Demonstrate understanding of economic development, including Hamilton's economic plan, tariffs, and changes in agriculture, commerce, and industry 173

Skill 22.4 Demonstrate understanding of social and cultural development in this period, including immigration and the frontier, family life and the role of women, religious life, and nationalism and regionalism 174

MID. LEVEL HUMANITIES

TEACHER CERTIFICATION STUDY GUIDE

COMPETENCY 23.0 CONTINUED NATIONAL DEVELOPMENT (1829–1850S) 178

Skill 23.1   Demonstrate understanding of political development, including Jacksonian Democracy, the nullification crisis, Manifest Destiny, the Mexican War and Cession, and the Oregon Territory 178

Skill 23.2   Demonstrate knowledge of geographic expansion, including the development of the transportation network and the displacement of Native Americans 180

Skill 23.3   Demonstrate knowledge of industrialization, including technological and agricultural innovations, and the early labor movement 181

Skill 23.4   Demonstrate understanding of social and cultural developments, such as changes in the role of women in society, and reform movements 184

COMPETENCY 24.0 CIVIL WAR ERA (1850–1870S) 186

Skill 24.1   Demonstrate knowledge of the growth of sectionalism and of attempts at political compromise 186

Skill 24.2   Demonstrate knowledge of the abolitionist movement, including the roles of African Americans and women in the movement 188

Skill 24.3   Demonstrate understanding of the failure of political institutions in the 1850s 190

Skill 24.4   Demonstrate knowledge of the Civil War (1861–1865), including its causes, leaders, and major events 192

Skill 24.5   Demonstrate knowledge of the Reconstruction period, including the various plans for Reconstruction, the new amendments to the Constitution, and the Compromise of 1877 195

COMPETENCY 25.0 EMERGENCE OF THE MODERN UNITED STATES (1877–1900) 200

Skill 25.1   Demonstrate understanding of United States expansion and imperialism, including the displacement of Native Americans, the development of the West, and international involvement 200

Skill 25.2   Demonstrate understanding of the process of industrialization and of the political, economic, and social changes associated with industrialization in this period 202

MID. LEVEL HUMANITIES

Skill 25.3	Demonstrate understanding of the causes and consequences of urban development in this period	203
Skill 25.4	Demonstrate understanding of political, cultural, and social movements	204

COMPETENCY 26.0 PROGRESSIVE ERA THROUGH THE NEW DEAL (1900–1939) 206

Skill 26.1	Demonstrate knowledge of political, economic, and social developments	206
Skill 26.2	Demonstrate understanding of the causes of United States participation in the First World War and of the consequences at home and abroad	207
Skill 26.3	Demonstrate knowledge of political, economic, social, and cultural life in the "Roaring Twenties"	210
Skill 26.4	Demonstrate knowledge of political, economic, and social developments during the Great Depression and the New Deal	211

COMPETENCY 27.0 THE SECOND WORLD WAR AND THE POSTWAR PERIOD (1939–1963) 219

Skill 27.1	Demonstrate understanding of the causes of United States participation in the Second World War and of the consequences at home and abroad	219
Skill 27.2	Demonstrate understanding of domestic and foreign developments during the Cold War	221
Skill 27.3	Demonstrate knowledge of political, economic, social, and cultural life in the 1950s	226

COMPETENCY 28.0 RECENT DEVELOPMENTS (1960S–PRESENT) 227

Skill 28.1	Demonstrate understanding of political developments, including the war in Vietnam, the "imperial presidency," and the new conservative movement	227
Skill 28.2	Demonstrate understanding of economic developments, including changes in industrial structure, the growth of the budget deficit, the impact of deregulation, and energy and environmental issues	230

Skill 28.3	Demonstrate understanding of major social movements and of social policy initiatives	232
Skill 28.4	Demonstrate understanding of the social and cultural effects of changes in the American family and in the ethnic composition of the United States population in this period	232
Skill 28.5	Demonstrate understanding of international relations, including United States relations with the Soviet Union and its successor states and the changing role of the United States in world political and economic affairs	234

DOMAIN VII. WORLD HISTORY

COMPETENCY 29.0 PREHISTORY TO 1400 CE 236

Skill 29.1	Demonstrate knowledge of human society before approximately 3000 BCE	236
Skill 29.2	Understand the development of city civilizations 3000–1500 BCE	237
Skill 29.3	Demonstrate knowledge of ancient empires and civilizations 1700 BCE–500 CE	239
Skill 29.4	Understand the decline of classical civilizations and changes 500–1400 CE	245

COMPETENCY 30.0 WORLD HISTORY: 1400 TO 1914 251

Skill 30.1	Demonstrate understanding of emerging global-wide interactions 1400-1800 CE	251
Skill 30.2	Demonstrate knowledge of political and industrial revolutions 1750-1914	252

COMPETENCY 31.0 1914 TO THE PRESENT 271

Skill 31.1	Evaluate conflicts, ideologies, and changes in the twentieth century	271
Skill 31.2	Understand contemporary trends 1991 to the present	277

DOMAIN VIII. GOVERNMENT/CIVICS

COMPETENCY 32.0 BASIC POLITICAL CONCEPTS 278

Skill 32.1 Demonstrate understanding of why government is needed 278

Skill 32.2 Demonstrate knowledge of political theory 279

Skill 32.3 Demonstrate understanding of political concepts such as legitimacy, power, authority, and responsibility 281

Skill 32.4 Demonstrate understanding of various political orientations 283

COMPETENCY 33.0 UNITED STATES POLITICAL SYSTEM 288

Skill 33.1 Demonstrate understanding of the constitutional foundation of the United States government, including knowledge of the basic content and structure of the United States Constitution, and of the processes of constitutional interpretation and amendment 288

Skill 33.2 Demonstrate knowledge of the functions and powers of the legislative, executive, and judicial branches of government, and of the relationships among them 293

Skill 33.3 Demonstrate knowledge of the formation and operation of political institutions not established by the Constitution, such as political parties and interest groups, and of the role of the media and public opinion in American political life 294

Skill 33.4 Demonstrate understanding of the relationship among federal, state, and local governments 301

Skill 33.5 Demonstrate understanding of political behavior at both the individual and group levels, including elections and other forms of political participation 302

COMPETENCY 34.0 OTHER FORMS OF GOVERNMENT 306

Skill 34.1 Demonstrate understanding of the structures of various forms of government 306

COMPETENCY 35.0 INTERNATIONAL RELATIONS 308

Skill 35.1 Demonstrate knowledge of the functions and powers of international organizations, such as the United Nations 308

TEACHER CERTIFICATION STUDY GUIDE

DOMAIN IX.   GEOGRAPHY

COMPETENCY 36.0   THEMES 310

Skill 36.1   Identify relative and absolute location and the physical and human characteristics of "place" 310

Skill 36.2   Demonstrate understanding of human-environment interactions 312

Skill 36.3   Identify significant types of movement such as migration, trade, and the spread of ideas 314

COMPETENCY 37.0   MAP SKILLS 316

Skill 37.1   Read and interpret various types of maps 316

Skill 37.2   Determine distance, direction, latitude, longitude, and the location of physical features 319

Skill 37.3   Recognize and describe spatial patterns 321

Skill 37.4   Use a legend or key 321

COMPETENCY 38.0   PHYSICAL GEOGRAPHY 322

Skill 38.1   Demonstrate knowledge of landforms and water, climate, and vegetation and natural resources 322

Skill 38.2   Demonstrate understanding of human impact on the environment 325

COMPETENCY 39.0   HUMAN GEOGRAPHY 327

Skill 39.1   Demonstrate knowledge of human geography, including cultural geography; economic geography; political geography; and population geography 327

COMPETENCY 40.0   REGIONAL GEOGRAPHY 329

Skill 40.1   Demonstrate knowledge of the geography of the major regions of the world 329

TEACHER CERTIFICATION STUDY GUIDE

DOMAIN X.   ECONOMICS

COMPETENCY 41.0 MICROECONOMICS I 331

Skill 41.1   Understand the definition of economics and identify the factors of production and explain how they are used 331

Skill 41.2   Demonstrate understanding of scarcity, choice, and opportunity cost 332

Skill 41.3   Demonstrate knowledge and application of the production possibilities curve to illustrate efficiency, unemployment, and tradeoffs 333

Skill 41.4   Demonstrate knowledge of economic systems: be able to list and describe the characteristics of free-market capitalism, socialism, and mixed models 334

Skill 41.5   Demonstrate understanding of the concepts of absolute and comparative advantage, free trade, and the impacts of trade barriers such as tariffs and quotas 335

Skill 41.6   Demonstrate understanding of property rights, incentives, and the role of markets 337

Skill 41.7   Demonstrate understanding of the supply and demand model and its application in the determination of equilibrium price in competitive markets 338

Skill 41.8   Demonstrate understanding of market surpluses and shortages 339

Skill 41.9   Demonstrate understanding of the role of government and the impact of price ceilings, price floors, and taxes on market outcomes 340

Skill 41.10   Demonstrate understanding of the concept of market failure and public policy 342

COMPETENCY 42.0 MICROECONOMICS II 344

Skill 42.1   Demonstrate knowledge of types of market structure and the characteristics and behavior of firms in perfect competition, monopoly, oligopoly, and monopolistic competition 344

Skill 42.2	Demonstrate understanding of factor markets and the determination of income distributions and the returns to factors of production	345

COMPETENCY 43.0 MACROECONOMICS I 347

Skill 43.1	Demonstrate understanding of gross domestic product and its components	347
Skill 43.2	Demonstrate understanding of how unemployment is measured and its causes and consequences	348
Skill 43.3	Demonstrate understanding of inflation and its causes and consequences	349

COMPETENCY 44.0 MACROECONOMICS II 351

Skill 44.1	Demonstrate understanding of national income determination using aggregate demand and aggregate supply analysis	351
Skill 44.2	Demonstrate understanding of fiscal policy and its instruments: taxes and government spending and their impact on the federal budget deficits and national debt	352
Skill 44.3	Demonstrate understanding of the Federal Reserve System and monetary policy	353
Skill 44.4	Demonstrate understanding of the major concepts in international finance and investment	354
Skill 44.5	Demonstrate understanding of the determinants of long run economic growth	355
Skill 44.6	Demonstrate understanding of current national and international issues and controversies	356

DOMAIN XI. SOCIOLOGY AND ANTHROPOLOGY

COMPETENCY 45.0 SOCIALIZATION 357

Skill 45.1	Demonstrate understanding of the role of socialization in society and of positive and negative sanctions in the socialization process	357

COMPETENCY 46.0 PATTERNS OF SOCIAL ORGANIZATION 358

Skill 46.1 Demonstrate knowledge of folkways, mores, laws, beliefs, and values 358

Skill 46.2 Demonstrate understanding of social stratification 359

COMPETENCY 47.0 SOCIAL INSTITUTIONS 360

Skill 47.1 Demonstrate understanding of the roles of the following social institutions and of their interactions: the family, education, government, religion, and the economy 360

COMPETENCY 48.0 THE STUDY OF POPULATIONS 362

Skill 48.1 Demonstrate knowledge of populations, including the impact on society of changes in population growth and distribution, migration, and immigration 362

COMPETENCY 49.0 MULTICULTURAL DIVERSITY 363

Skill 49.1 Define the concepts of ethnocentrism and cultural relativity 363

Skill 49.2 Demonstrate knowledge of variation in race, ethnicity, and religion 364

Skill 49.3 Demonstrate understanding of the prevalence and consequences of discrimination and prejudice 366

Skill 49.4 Demonstrate understanding of the concept of pluralism 367

COMPETENCY 50.0 SOCIAL PROBLEMS 368

Skill 50.1 Demonstrate understanding of major contemporary social problems 368

COMPETENCY 51.0 HOW CULTURES CHANGE 370

Skill 51.1 Demonstrate understanding of how cultures change 370

Bibliography 371

Sample Test: Middle School Social Studies 373

Answer Key: Middle School Social Studies 400

Rationales with Sample Questions: Middle School Social Studies 401

TEACHER CERTIFICATION STUDY GUIDE

Great Study and Testing Tips!

What to study in order to prepare for the subject assessments is the focus of this study guide but equally important is *how* you study.

You can increase your chances of truly mastering the information by taking some simple, but effective steps.

Study Tips:

1. Some foods aid the learning process. Foods such as milk, nuts, seeds, rice, and oats help your study efforts by releasing natural memory enhancers called CCKs (*cholecystokinin*) composed of *tryptophan*, *choline*, and *phenylalanine*. All of these chemicals enhance the neurotransmitters associated with memory. Before studying, try a light, protein-rich meal of eggs, turkey, and fish. All of these foods release the memory enhancing chemicals. The better the connections, the more you comprehend.

Likewise, before you take a test, stick to a light snack of energy boosting and relaxing foods. A glass of milk, a piece of fruit, or some peanuts all release various memory-boosting chemicals and help you to relax and focus on the subject at hand.

2. Learn to take great notes. A by-product of our modern culture is that we have grown accustomed to getting our information in short doses (i.e. TV news sound bites or USA Today style newspaper articles.)

Consequently, we've subconsciously trained ourselves to assimilate information better in neat little packages. If your notes are scrawled all over the paper, it fragments the flow of the information. Strive for clarity. Newspapers use a standard format to achieve clarity. Your notes can be much clearer through use of proper formatting. A very effective format is called the *"Cornell Method."*

> Take a sheet of loose-leaf lined notebook paper and draw a line all the way down the paper about 1-2" from the left-hand edge.
>
> Draw another line across the width of the paper about 1-2" up from the bottom. Repeat this process on the reverse side of the page.

Look at the highly effective result. You have ample room for notes, a left hand margin for special emphasis items or inserting supplementary data from the textbook, a large area at the bottom for a brief summary, and a little rectangular space for just about anything you want.

MID. LEVEL HUMANITIES

TEACHER CERTIFICATION STUDY GUIDE

3. Get the concept then the details. Too often we focus on the details and don't gather an understanding of the concept. However, if you simply memorize only dates, places, or names, you may well miss the whole point of the subject.

A key way to understand things is to put them in your own words. If you are working from a textbook, automatically summarize each paragraph in your mind. If you are outlining text, don't simply copy the author's words.

Rephrase them in your own words. You remember your own thoughts and words much better than someone else's, and subconsciously tend to associate the important details to the core concepts.

4. Ask Why? Pull apart written material paragraph by paragraph and don't forget the captions under the illustrations.

Example: If the heading is "Stream Erosion", flip it around to read "Why do streams erode?" Then answer the questions.

If you train your mind to think in a series of questions and answers, not only will you learn more, but it also helps to lessen the test anxiety because you are used to answering questions.

5. Read for reinforcement and future needs. Even if you only have 10 minutes, put your notes or a book in your hand. Your mind is similar to a computer; you have to input data in order to have it processed. *By reading, you are creating the neural connections for future retrieval.* The more times you read something, the more you reinforce the learning of ideas.

Even if you don't fully understand something on the first pass, *your mind stores much of the material for later recall.*

6. Relax to learn so go into exile. Our bodies respond to an inner clock called biorhythms. Burning the midnight oil works well for some people, but not everyone.

If possible, set aside a particular place to study that is free of distractions. Shut off the television, cell phone, and pager and exile your friends and family during your study period.

If you really are bothered by silence, try background music. Light classical music at a low volume has been shown to aid in concentration over other types. Music that evokes pleasant emotions without lyrics is highly suggested. Try just about anything by Mozart. It relaxes you.

MID. LEVEL HUMANITIES

7. **Use arrows not highlighters.** At best, it's difficult to read a page full of yellow, pink, blue, and green streaks. Try staring at a neon sign for a while and you'll soon see that the horde of colors obscure the message.

A quick note, a brief dash of color, an underline, and an arrow pointing to a particular passage is much clearer than a horde of highlighted words.

8. **Budget your study time.** Although you shouldn't ignore any of the material, *allocate your available study time in the same ratio that topics may appear on the test.*

TEACHER CERTIFICATION STUDY GUIDE

Testing Tips:

1. <u>Get smart, play dumb.</u> Don't read anything into the question. Don't make an assumption that the test writer is looking for something else than what is asked. Stick to the question as written and don't read extra things into it.

2. <u>Read the question and all the choices *twice* before answering the question.</u> You may miss something by not carefully reading, and then re-reading both the question and the answers.

If you really don't have a clue as to the right answer, leave it blank on the first time through. Go on to the other questions, as they may provide a clue as to how to answer the skipped questions.

If later on, you still can't answer the skipped ones . . . ***Guess.*** The only penalty for guessing is that you *might* get it wrong. Only one thing is certain; if you don't put anything down, you will get it wrong!

3. <u>Turn the question into a statement.</u> Look at the way the questions are worded. The syntax of the question usually provides a clue. Does it seem more familiar as a statement rather than as a question? Does it sound strange?

By turning a question into a statement, you may be able to spot if an answer sounds right, and it may also trigger memories of material you have read.

4. <u>Look for hidden clues</u>. It's actually very difficult to compose multiple-foil (choice) questions without giving away part of the answer in the options presented.

In most multiple-choice questions you can often readily eliminate one or two of the potential answers. This leaves you with only two real possibilities and automatically your odds go to Fifty-Fifty for very little work.

5. <u>Trust your instincts.</u> For every fact that you have read, you subconsciously retain something of that knowledge. On questions that you aren't really certain about, go with your basic instincts. **Your first impression on how to answer a question is usually correct.**

6. <u>Mark your answers directly on the test booklet</u>. Don't bother trying to fill in the optical scan sheet on the first pass through the test.

Just be very careful not to miss-mark your answers when you eventually transcribe them to the scan sheet.

7. <u>Watch the clock!</u> You have a set amount of time to answer the questions. Don't get bogged down trying to answer a single question at the expense of 10 questions you can more readily answer.

MID. LEVEL HUMANITIES

DOMAIN I. READING AND LITERATURE

Competency 1.0 Identifying major works and authors of literature appropriate for adolescents.

Prior to twentieth century research on child development and child/adolescent literature's relationship to that development, books for adolescents were primarily didactic. They were designed to be instructive of history, manners, and morals.

Middle Ages

As early as the eleventh century, Anselm, the Archbishop of Canterbury, wrote an encyclopedia designed to instill in children the beliefs and principles of conduct acceptable to adults in medieval society. Early monastic translations of the *Bible* and other religious writings were written in Latin, for the edification of the upper class. Fifteenth century hornbooks were designed to teach reading and religious lessons. William Caxton printed English versions of *Aesop's Fables*, Malory's *Le Morte d'Arthur* and stories from Greek and Roman mythology. Though printed for adults, tales of adventures of Odysseus and the Arthurian knights were also popular with literate adolescents.

Renaissance

The Renaissance saw the introduction of the inexpensive chapbooks, small in size and 16-64 pages in length. Chapbooks were condensed versions of mythology and fairy tales. Designed for the common people, chapbooks were imperfect grammatically but were immensely popular because of their adventurous contents. Though most of the serious, educated adults frowned on the sometimes-vulgar little books, they received praise from Richard Steele of *Tatler* fame for inspiring his grandson's interest in reading and pursuing his other studies.

Meanwhile, the Puritans' three most popular reads were the *Bible*, John Foxe's *Book of Martyrs*, and John Bunyan's *Pilgrim's Progress*. Though venerating religious martyrs and preaching the moral propriety which was to lead to eternal happiness, the stories of the *Book of Martyrs* were often lurid in their descriptions of the fate of the damned. Not written for children and difficult reading even for adults, *Pilgrim's Progress* was as attractive to adolescents for its adventurous plot as for its moral outcome. In Puritan America, the *New England Primer* set forth the prayers, catechisms, *Bible* verses, and illustrations meant to instruct children in the Puritan ethic. The seventeenth-century French used fables and fairy tales to entertain adults, but children found them enjoyable as well.

Seventeenth century

The late seventeenth century brought the first concern with providing literature that specifically targeted the young. Pierre Perrault's *Fairy Tales*, Jean de la Fontaine's retellings of famous fables, Mme. d'Aulnoy's novels based on old folktales, and Mme. de Beaumont's "Beauty and the Beast" were written to delight as well as instruct young people. In England, publisher John Newbury was the first to publish a line for children. These include a translation of Perrault's *Tales of Mother Goose; A Little Pretty Pocket-Book*, "intended for instruction and amusement" but decidedly moralistic and bland in comparison to the previous century's chapbooks; and *The Renowned History of Little Goody Two Shoes*, allegedly written by Oliver Goldsmith for a juvenile audience.

Eighteenth century

By and large, however, into the eighteenth century adolescents were finding their reading pleasure in adult books: Daniel Defoe's *Robinson Crusoe*, Jonathan Swift's *Gulliver's Travels*, and Johann Wyss's *Swiss Family Robinson*. More books were being written for children, but the moral didacticism, though less religious, was nevertheless ever present. The short stories of Maria Edgeworth, the four-volume *The History of Sandford and Merton* by Thomas Day, and Martha Farquharson's twenty-six volume *Elsie Dinsmore* series dealt with pious protagonists who learned restraint, repentance, and rehabilitation from sin. Two bright spots in this period of didacticism were Jean Jacques Rousseau's *Emile* and *The Tales of Shakespeare*, Charles and Mary Lamb's simplified versions of Shakespeare's plays. Rousseau believed that a child's abilities were enhanced by a free, happy life, and the Lambs subscribed to the notion that children were entitled to more entertaining literature in language comprehensible to them.

Nineteenth century

Child/adolescent literature truly began its modern rise in nineteenth century Europe. Hans Christian Andersen's *Fairy Tales* were fanciful adaptations of the somber revisions of the Grimm brothers in the previous century. Andrew Lang's series of colorful fairy books contain the folklores of many nations and are still part of the collections of many modern libraries. Clement Moore's "A Visit from St. Nicholas" is a cheery, non-threatening child's view of the "night before Christmas." The humor of Lewis Carroll's books about Alice's adventures, Edward Lear's poems with caricatures, Lucretia Nole's stories of the Philadelphia Peterkin family, were full of fancy and not a smidgen of morality. Other popular Victorian novels introduced the modern fantasy and science fiction genres: William Makepeace Thackeray's *The Rose and the Ring*, Charles Dickens' *The Magic Fishbone*, and Jules Verne's *Twenty Thousand Leagues Under the Sea*. Adventure to exotic places became a popular topic: Rudyard Kipling's *Jungle Books*, Verne's *Around the World in Eighty Days*, and Robert Louis Stevenson's *Treasure Island* and *Kidnapped*. In 1884, the first English translation Johanna Spyre's *Heidi* appeared.

North America was also finding its voices for adolescent readers. American Louisa May Alcott's *Little Women* and Canadian L.M. Montgomery's *Anne of Green Gables* ushered in the modern age of realistic fiction. American youth were enjoying the articles of Tom Sawyer and Huckleberry Finn. For the first time children were able to read books about real people just like themselves.

Twentieth century

The literature of the twentieth century is extensive and diverse, and as in previous centuries much influenced by the adults who write, edit, and select books for youth consumption. In the first third of the century, suitable adolescent literature dealt with children from good homes with large families. These books projected an image of a peaceful, rural existence. Though the characters and plots were more realistic, the stories maintained focus on topics that were considered emotionally and intellectually proper. Popular at this time were Laura Ingalls Wilder's Little House on the Prairie Series and Carl Sandburg's biography *Abe Lincoln Grows Up*. English author J.R.R. Tolkien's fantasy *The Hobbit* prefaced modern adolescent readers' fascination with the works of Piers Antony, Madelaine L'Engle, and Anne McCaffery.

These classic and contemporary works combine the characteristics of multiple theories. Functioning at the concrete operations stage (Piaget), being of the "good person," orientation (Kohlberg), still highly dependent on external rewards (Bandura), and exhibiting all five needs previously discussed from Maslow's hierarchy, these eleven to twelve year olds should appreciate the following titles, grouped by reading level. These titles are also cited for interest at that grade level and do not reflect high-interest titles for older readers who do not read at grade level. Some high interest titles will be cited later.

Reading level 6.0 to 6.9

Barrett, William. *Lilies of the Field*
Cormier, Robert. *Other Bells for Us to Ring*
Dahl, Roald. *Danny, Champion of the World; Charlie and the Chocolate Factory*
Lindgren, Astrid. *Pippi Longstocking*
Lindbergh, Anne. *Three Lives to Live*
Lowry, Lois. *Rabble Starkey*
Naylor, Phyllis. *The Year of the Gopher, Reluctantly Alice*
Peck, Robert Newton. *Arly*
Speare, Elizabeth. *The Witch of Blackbird Pond*
Sleator, William. *The Boy Who Reversed Himself*

For seventh and eighth grades

Most seventh and eight grade students, according to learning theory, are still functioning cognitively, psychologically, and morally as sixth graders. As these are not inflexible standards, there are some twelve and thirteen year olds who are much more mature socially, intellectually, and physically than the younger children who share the same school. They are becoming concerned with establishing individual and peer group identities that presents conflicts with breaking from authority and the rigidity of rules. Some at this age are still tied firmly to the family and its expectations while others identify more with those their own age or older. Enrichment reading for this group must help them cope with life's rapid changes or provide escape and thus must be either realistic or fantastic depending on the child's needs. Adventures and mysteries (the Hardy Boys and Nancy Drew series) are still popular today. These preteens also become more interested in biographies of contemporary figures rather than legendary figures of the past.

<u>Reading level 7.0 to 7.9</u>
Armstrong, William. *Sounder*
Bagnold, Enid. *National Velvet*
Barrie, James. *Peter Pan*
London, Jack. *White Fang*, *Call of the Wild*
Lowry, Lois. *Taking Care of Terrific*
McCaffrey, Anne. The *Dragonsinger* series
Montgomery, L. M. *Anne of Green Gables* and sequels
Steinbeck, John. *The Pearl*
Tolkien, J. R. R. *The Hobbit*
Zindel, Paul. *The Pigman*

<u>Reading level 8.0 to 8.9</u>
Cormier, Robert. *I Am the Cheese*
McCullers, Carson. *The Member of the Wedding*
North, Sterling. *Rascal*
Twain, Mark. *The Adventures of Tom Sawyer*
Zindel, Paul. *My Darling, My Hamburger*

For ninth grade

Depending upon the school environment, a ninth grader may be top-dog in a junior high school or underdog in a high school. Much of his social development and thus his reading interests become motivated by his peer associations. He is technically an adolescent operating at the early stages of formal operations in cognitive development. His perception of his own identity is becoming well-defined and he is fully aware of the ethics required by society. He is more receptive to the challenges of classic literature but still enjoys popular teen novels.

Reading level 9.0 to 9.9

Brown, Dee. *Bury My Heart at Wounded Knee*
Defoe, Daniel. *Robinson Crusoe*
Dickens, Charles. *David Copperfield*
Greenberg, Joanne. *I Never Promised You a Rose Garden*
Kipling, Rudyard. *Captains Courageous*
Mathabane, Mark. *Kaffir Boy*
Nordhoff, Charles. *Mutiny on the Bounty*
Shelley, Mary. *Frankenstein*
Washington, Booker T. *Up From Slavery*

For tenth - twelfth grades

All high school sophomores, juniors and seniors can handle most other literature except for a few of the very most difficult titles like *Moby Dick* or *Vanity Fair*. However, since many high school students do not progress to the eleventh or twelfth grade reading level, they will still have their favorites among authors whose writings they can understand. Many will struggle with assigned novels but still read high interest books for pleasure. A few high interest titles are listed below without reading level designations, though most are 6.0 to 7.9.

Bauer, Joan. *Squashed*
Borland, Hal. *When the Legends Die*
Danzinger, Paula. *Remember Me to Herald Square*
Duncan, Lois. *Stranger with my Face*
Hamilton, Virginia. *The Planet of Junior Brown*
Hinton, S. E. *The Outsiders*
Paterson, Katherine. *The Great Gilly Hopkins*

Teachers of students at all levels must be familiar with the materials offered by the libraries in their own schools. Only then can she guide her students into appropriate selections for their social age and reading level development.

Adolescent literature, because of the age range of readers, is extremely diverse. Fiction for the middle group, usually ages ten/eleven to fourteen/fifteen, deals with issues of coping with internal and external changes in their lives. Because children's writers in the twentieth century have produced increasingly realistic fiction, adolescents can now find problems dealt with honestly in novels.

Teachers of middle/junior high school students see the greatest change in interests and reading abilities. Fifth and sixth graders, included in elementary grades in many schools, are viewed as older children while seventh and eighth graders are preadolescent. Ninth graders, included sometimes as top dogs in junior high school and sometimes as underlings in high school, definitely view themselves as teenagers. Their literature choices will often be governed more by interest than by ability; thus, the wealth of high-interest, low readability books that have flooded the market in recent years. Tenth through twelfth graders will still select high-interest books for pleasure reading but are also easily encouraged to stretch their literature muscles by reading more classics.

Because of the rapid social changes, topics that once did not interest young people until they reached their teens - suicide, gangs, homosexuality - are now subjects of books for even younger readers. The plethora of high-interest books reveals how desperately schools have failed to produce on-level readers and how the market has adapted to that need. However, these high-interest books are now readable for younger children whose reading levels are at or above normal. No matter how tastefully written, some contents are inappropriate for younger readers. The problem becomes not so much steering them toward books that they have the reading ability to handle but encouraging them toward books whose content is appropriate to their levels of cognitive and social development. A fifth-grader may be able to read V.C. Andrews book *Flowers in the Attic* but not possess the social/moral development to handle the deviant behavior of the characters. At the same time, because of the complex changes affecting adolescents, the teacher must be well versed in learning theory and child development as well as competent to teach the subject matter of language and literature.

Competency 2.0 **Interpreting, paraphrasing, and comparing various types of texts, including fiction, poetry, essays, and other nonfiction.**

Paraphrasing is the art of rewording text. The goal is to maintain the original purpose of the statement while translating it into your own words. Your newly generated sentence can be longer or shorter than the original. Concentrate on the meaning, not on the words. Do not change concept words, special terms, or proper names. There are numerous ways to effectively paraphrase:

- Change the key words' form or part of speech. Example: "American news **coverage** is frequently **biased** in favor of Western views," becomes "When American journalists **cover** events, they often display a Western **bias**."
- Use synonyms of "relationship words." Look for relationship word, such as **contrast, cause,** or **effect,** and replace it with a word that conveys a similar meaning, thus creating a different structure for your sentence. Example: "**Unlike** many cats, Purrdy can sit on command," becomes "Most cats are not able to be trained, **but** Purrdy can sit on command."
- Use synonyms of phrases and words. Example: "The Beatnik writers were relatively unknown at **the start of the decade**," becomes "**Around the early 1950s**, the Beatnik writers were still relatively unknown."
- Change passive voice to active voice or move phrases and modifiers. Example: "Not to be outdone by the third graders, the fourth grade class added a musical medley to their Christmas performance," becomes "The fourth grade class added a musical medley to their Christmas performance to avoid being showed up by the third graders."
- Use reversals or negatives that do not change the meaning of the sentence. Example: "That burger chain is only found in California," becomes "That burger chain is not found on the east coast."

Literary Techniques to Evaluate

- **Ambiguity:** Ambiguity is any writing whose meaning cannot be determined by its context. Ambiguity may be introduced accidentally, confusing the readers and disrupting the flow of reading. If a sentence or paragraph jars upon reading, there is lurking ambiguity. It is particularly difficult to spot your own ambiguities, since authors tend to see what they mean rather than what they say.
- **Connotation:** Connotation refers to the ripple effect surrounding the implications and associations of a given word, distinct from the denotative, or literal meaning. For example, "Good night, sweet prince, and flights of angels sing thee to thy rest," refers to a burial. Connotation is used when a subtle tone is preferred. It may stir up a more effective emotional response than if the author had used blunt, insensitive diction.

- **Symbolism:** Also referred to as a sign, a symbol designates something which stands for something else. In most cases, it is standing for something that has a deeper meaning than its literal denotation. Symbols can have personal, cultural, or universal associations. An understanding of symbols can be used to unearth a meaning the author might have intended but not expressed, or even something the author never intended at all.
- **Rhythm:** Writing can be compared to dancing, in that it is a balance between words and flow. Rhythm refers to the harmony between the words chosen and the smoothness, rapidity, or disjointedness of the way those words are written. Sentences that are too long may disrupt the rhythm of a piece. Reading text out loud is an easy way to impart understanding of literary rhythm.
- **Rhyme:** Writing with rhyme can be especially effective on reader response. Think about the success Dr. Seuss had with his rhyming style. Rhyme is tricky though; used ineffectively or unnecessarily, it can break up the entire rhythm of the piece or fog the reader's understanding of it. Rhyme should be used when it is purely beneficial to the format of the piece. Make sure it is not forcing you to use more words than needed, and that each verse is moving the story forward.
- **Diction:** Diction is simply the right word in the right spot for the right purpose. The hallmark of a great writer is precise, unusual, and memorable diction.
- **Imagery:** Imagery involves engaging one or more of your five senses in your writing. An author might use imagery to give the reader a greater, more real picture of the scene they are trying to depict. Imagery may conjure up a past experience that the reader had (the smell of the ocean, the feeling of their childhood blanket) thereby enriching their mental picture of the scene.

Reading literature involves a reciprocal interaction between the reader and the text.

Types of responses

Emotional

The reader can identify with the characters and situations so as to project himself into the story. The reader feels a sense of satisfaction by associating aspects of his own life with the people, places, and events in the literature. Emotional responses are observed in a reader's verbal and non-verbal reactions - laughter, comments on its effects, and retelling or dramatizing the action.

Interpretive

Interpretive responses result in inferences about character development, setting, or plot; analysis of style elements - metaphor, simile, allusion, rhythm, tone; outcomes derivable from information provided in the narrative; and assessment of the author's intent. Interpretive responses are made verbally or in writing.

Critical

Critical responses involve making value judgments about the quality of a piece of literature. Reactions to the effectiveness of the writer's style and language use are observed through discussion and written reactions.

Evaluative

Some reading response theory researchers also add a response that considers the readers considerations of such factors as how well the piece of literature represents its genre, how well it reflects the social/ethical mores of society, and how well the author has approached the subject for freshness and slant.

Middle school readers will exhibit both emotional and interpretive responses. Naturally, making interpretive responses depends on the degree of knowledge the student has of literary elements. A child's being able to say why a particular book was boring or why a particular poem made him sad evidences critical reactions on a fundamental level. Adolescents in ninth and tenth grades should begin to make critical responses by addressing the specific language and genre characteristics of literature. Evaluative responses are harder to detect and are rarely made by any but a few advanced high school students. However, if the teacher knows what to listen for, she can recognize evaluative responses and incorporate them into discussions.

For example, if a student says, "I don't understand why that character is doing that," he is making an interpretive response to character motivation. However, if he goes on to say, "What good is that action?" he is giving an evaluative response that should be explored in terms of "What good should it do and why isn't that positive action happening?"

At the emotional level, the student says, "I almost broke into a sweat when he was describing the heat in the burning house." An interpretive response says, "The author used descriptive adjectives to bring his setting to life." Critically, the student adds, "The author's use of descriptive language contributes to the success of the narrative and maintains reader interest through the whole story." If he goes on to wonder why the author allowed the grandmother in the story to die in the fire, he is making an evaluative response.

TEACHER CERTIFICATION STUDY GUIDE

Levels of response

The levels of reader response will depend largely on the reader's level of social, psychological, and intellectual development. Most middle school students have progressed beyond merely involving themselves in the story enough to be able to retell the events in some logical sequence or describe the feeling that the story evoked. They are aware to some degree that the feeling evoked was the result of a careful manipulation of good elements of fiction writing. They may not explain that awareness as successfully as a high school student, but they are beginning to grasp the concepts and not just the personal reactions. They are beginning to differentiate between responding to the story itself and responding to a literary creation.

Fostering self-esteem and empathy for others and the world in which one lives

All-important is the use of literature as bibliotherapy that allows the reader to identify with others and become aware of alternatives, yet not feeling directly betrayed or threatened. For the high school student the ability to empathize is an evaluative response, a much desired outcome of literature studies. Use of these books either individually or as a thematic unit of study allows for discussion or writing. The titles are grouped by theme, not by reading level.

ABUSE:

Blair, Maury and Brendel, Doug. *Maury, Wednesday's Child*

Dizenzo, Patricia. *Why Me?*

Parrot, Andrea. *Coping with Date Rape and Acquaintance Rape*

NATURAL WORLD CONCERNS:

Caduto, M. and Bruchac, J. *Keeper's of Earth*

Gay, Kathlyn. *Greenhouse Effect*

Johnson, Daenis. *Fiskadaro*

Madison, Arnold. *It Can't Happen to Me*

EATING DISORDERS:

Arnold, Caroline. *Too Fat, Too Thin, Do I Have a Choice?*

DeClements, Barthe. *Nothing's Fair in Fifth Grade*

Snyder, Anne. *Goodbye, Paper Doll*

FAMILY

Chopin, Kate. *The Runner*

Cormier, Robert. *Tunes for Bears to Dance to*

Danzinger, Paula. *The Divorce Express*

Neufield, John. *Sunday Father*

Okimoto, Jean Davies. *Molly by any Other Name*

Peck, Richard. *Don't Look and It Won't Hurt*

Zindel, Paul. *I Never Loved Your Mind*

STEREOTYPING:

Baklanov, Grigory. (Trans. by Antonina W. Bouis) *Forever Nineteen*

Kerr, M.E. *Gentle Hands*

Greene, Betty. *Summer of My German Soldier*

Reiss, Johanna. *The Upstairs Room*

Taylor, Mildred D. *Roll of Thunder, Hear Me Cry*

Wakatsuki-Houston, Jeanne and Houston, James D. *Farewell to Manzanar*

SUICIDE AND DEATH:

Blume, Judy. *Tiger Eyes*

Bunting, Eve. *If I Asked You, Would You Stay?*

Gunther, John. *Death Be Not Proud*

Mazer, Harry. *When the Phone Rings*

Peck, Richard. *Remembering the Good Times*

Richter, Elizabeth. *Losing Someone You Love*

Strasser, Todd. *Friends Till the End*

Cautions

There is always a caution when reading materials of a sensitive or controversial nature. The teacher must be cognizant of the happenings in the school and outside community to spare students undue suffering. A child who has known a recent death in his family or circle of friends may need to distance himself from classroom discussion. Whenever open discussion of a topic brings pain or embarrassment, the child should not be further subjected. Older children and young adults will be able to discuss issues with greater objectivity and without making blurted, insensitive comments. The teacher must be able to gauge the level of emotional development of her students when selecting subject matter and the strategies for studying it. The student or his parents may consider some material objectionable. Should a student choose not to read an assigned material, it is the teacher's responsibility to allow the student to select an alternate title. It is always advisable to notify parents if a particularly sensitive piece is to be studied.

Drawing Conclusions from a Text

A common fallacy in reasoning is the *post hoc ergo propter hoc* ("after this, therefore because of this") or the false-cause fallacy. These occur in cause/effect reasoning, which may either go from cause to effect or effect to cause. They happen when an inadequate cause is offered for a particular effect; when the possibility of more than one cause is ignored; and when a connection between a particular cause and a particular effect is not made.

An example of a *post hoc*: Our sales shot up thirty-five percent after we ran that television campaign; therefore the campaign caused the increase in sales. It might have been a cause, of course, but more evidence is needed to prove it.

An example of an inadequate cause for a particular effect: An Iraqi truck driver reported that Saddam Hussein had nuclear weapons; therefore, Saddam Hussein is a threat to world security. More causes are needed to prove the conclusion.

An example of ignoring the possibility of more than one possible cause: John Brown was caught out in a thunderstorm and his clothes were wet before he was rescued; therefore, he developed influenza the next day because he got wet. Being chilled may have played a role in the illness, but Brown would have had to contract the influenza virus before he would come down with it whether or not he had gotten wet.

An example of failing to make a connection between a particular cause and an effect assigned to it. Anna fell into a putrid pond on Saturday; on Monday she came down with polio; therefore, the polio was caused by the pond. This, of course, is not acceptable unless the polio virus is found in a sample of water from the pond. A connection must be proven.

Comparing Texts

Fiction is the opposite of fact, and, simple as that may seem, it's the major distinction between fictional works and nonfictional works. The earliest nonfiction came in the form of cave-paintings, the record of what prehistoric man caught on hunting trips. On the other hand, we don't know that some of it might be fiction—that is, what they would like to catch on future hunting trips. Cuneiform inscriptions, which hold the earliest writings, are probably nonfiction, about conveying goods such as oxen and barley and dealing with the buying and selling of these items. It's easy to assume that nonfiction, then, is pretty boring, since it simply serves the purpose of recording everyday facts. Fiction, on the other hand, is the result of imagination and is recorded for the purpose of entertainment. If a work of nonfiction endures beyond its original time, it tends to be viewed as either exceptionally well made or perfectly embodying the ideas, manners, and attitudes of the time when it was produced.

Some (not all) types of nonfiction:
- Almanac
- Autobiography
- Biography
- Blueprint
- Book report
- Diary
- Dictionary
- Documentary film
- Encyclopedia
- Essay
- History
- Journal
- Letter
- Philosophy
- Science book
- Textbook
- User manual

These can also be called genres of nonfiction—divisions of a particular art according to criteria particular to that form. How these divisions are formed is vague. There are actually no fixed boundaries for either fiction or nonfiction. They are formed by sets of conventions and many works cross into multiple genres by way of borrowing and recombining these conventions.

Some genres of fiction (not all):

- Action-adventure
- Crime
- Detective
- Erotica
- Fantasy
- Horror
- Mystery
- Romance
- Science fiction
- Thriller
- Western

A *bildungsroman* (from the German) means "novel of education" or "novel of formation" and is a novel that traces the spiritual, moral, psychological, or social development and growth of the main character from childhood to maturity. Dickens' *David Copperfield* (1850) represents this genre as does Thomas Wolfe's *Look Homeward Angel* (1929).

A work of fiction typically has a central character, called the protagonist, and a character that stands in opposition, called the antagonist. The antagonist might be something other than a person. In Stephen Crane's short story, *The Open Boat*, for example, the antagonist is a hostile environment, a stormy sea. Conflicts between protagonist and antagonist are typical of a work of fiction, and climax is the point at which those conflicts are resolved. The plot has to do with the form or shape that the conflicts take as they move toward resolution. A fiction writer artistically uses devices labeled characterization to reveal character. Characterization can depend on dialogue, description, or the attitude or attitudes of one or more characters toward another.

Enjoying fiction depends upon the ability of the reader to suspend belief, to some extent. The reader makes a deal with the writer that for the time it takes to read the story, his/her own belief will be put aside, replaced by the convictions and reality that the writer has written into the story. This is not true in nonfiction. The writer of nonfiction declares in the choice of that genre that the work is reliably based upon reality. The *MLA Style Manual*, for instance, can be relied upon because it is not the result of someone's imagination.

Competency 3.0 Identifying and analyzing figurative language and other literary elements.

It's no accident that **plot** is sometimes called action. If the plot does not *move*, the story quickly dies. Therefore, the successful writer of stories uses a wide variety of active verbs in creative and unusual ways. If a reader is kept on his/her toes by the movement of the story, the experience of reading it will be pleasurable. That reader will probably want to read more of this author's work. Careful, unique, and unusual choices of active verbs will bring about that effect. William Faulkner is a good example of a successful writer whose stories are lively and memorable because of his use of unusual active verbs. In analyzing the development of plot, it's wise to look at the verbs. However, the development of believable conflicts is also vital. If there is no conflict, there is no story. What devices does a writer use to develop the conflicts, and are they real and believable?

Character is portrayed in many ways: description of physical characteristics, dialogue, interior monologue, the thoughts of the character, the attitudes of other characters toward this one, etc. Descriptive language depends on the ability to recreate a sensory experience for the reader. If the description of the character's appearance is a visual one, then the reader must be able to *see* the character. What's the shape of the nose? What color are the eyes? How tall or how short is this character? Thin or chubby? How does the character move? How does the character walk? Terms must be chosen that will create a picture for the reader. It's not enough to say the eyes are blue, for example. What blue? Often the color of eyes is compared to something else to enhance the readers' ability to visualize the character. A good test of characterization is the level of emotional involvement of the reader in the character. If the reader is to become involved, the description must provide an actual experience—seeing, smelling, hearing, tasting, or feeling.

Dialogue will reflect characteristics. Is it clipped? Is it highly dialectal? Does a character use a lot of colloquialisms? The ability to portray the speech of a character can make or break a story.

The kind of person the character is in the mind of the reader is dependent on impressions created by description and dialogue. How do other characters feel about this one as revealed by their treatment of him/her, their discussions of him/her with each other, or their overt descriptions of the character. For example, "John, of course, can't be trusted with another person's possessions." In analyzing a story, it's useful to discuss the devices used to produce character.

Setting may be visual, temporal, psychological, or social. Descriptive words are often used here also. In Edgar Allan Poe's description of the house in "The Fall of the House of Usher" as the protagonist/narrator approaches it, the air of dread and gloom that pervades the story is caught in the setting and sets the stage for the story. A setting may also be symbolic, as it is in Poe's story, where the house is a symbol of the family that lives in it. As the house disintegrates, so does the family.

The language used in all of these aspects of a story—plot, character, and setting—work together to create the **mood** of a story. Poe's first sentence establishes the mood of the story: "During the whole of a dull, dark, and soundless day in the autumn of the year, when the clouds hung oppressively low in the heavens, I had been passing alone, on horseback, through a singularly dreary tract of country; and at length found myself, as the shades of the evening drew on, within view of the melancholy House of Usher."

Essential terminology and literary devices germane to literary analysis include alliteration, allusion, antithesis, aphorism, apostrophe, assonance, blank verse, caesura, conceit, connotation, consonance, couplet, denotation, diction, epiphany, exposition, figurative language, free verse, hyperbole, iambic pentameter, inversion, irony, kenning, metaphor, metaphysical poetry, metonymy, motif, onomatopoeia, octava rima, oxymoron, paradox, parallelism personification, quatrain, scansion, simile, soliloquy, Spenserian stanza, synecdoche, terza rima, tone, and wit.

The more basic terms and devices, such as alliteration, allusion, analogy, aside, assonance, atmosphere, climax, consonance, denouement, elegy, foil, foreshadowing, metaphor, simile, setting, symbol, and theme are defined and exemplified in the English 5-9 Study Guide.

Antithesis: Balanced writing about conflicting ideas, usually expressed in sentence form. Some examples are expanding from the center, shedding old habits, and searching never finding.

Aphorism: A focused, succinct expression about life from a sagacious viewpoint. Writings by Ben Franklin, Sir Francis Bacon, and Alexander Pope contain many aphorisms. "Whatever is begun in anger ends in shame" is an aphorism.

Apostrophe: Literary device of addressing an absent or dead person, an abstract idea, or an inanimate object. Sonneteers, such as Sir Thomas Wyatt, John Keats, and William Wordsworth, address the moon, stars, and the dead Milton. For example, in William Shakespeare's *Julius Caesar*, Mark Antony addresses the corpse of Caesar in the speech that begins: "O, pardon me, thou bleeding piece of earth, That I am meek and gentle with these butchers! Thou art the ruins of the noblest man That ever lived in the tide of times. Woe to the hand that shed this costly blood!"

Blank Verse: Poetry written in iambic pentameter but unrhymed. Works by Shakespeare and Milton are epitomes of blank verse. Milton's Paradise Lost states, "Illumine, what is low raise and support, That to the highth of this great argument I may assert Eternal Providence And justify the ways of God to men."

Caesura: A pause, usually signaled by punctuation, in a line of poetry. The earliest usage occurs in *Beowulf*, the first English epic dating from the Anglo-Saxon era. 'To err is human, // to forgive, divine' (Pope).

Conceit: A comparison, usually in verse, between seemingly disparate objects or concepts. John Donne's metaphysical poetry contains many clever conceits. For instance, Donne's "The Flea" (1633) compares a flea bite to the act of love; and in "A Valediction: Forbidding Mourning" (1633) separated lovers are likened to the legs of a compass, the leg drawing the circle eventually returning home to "the fixed foot."

Connotation: The ripple effect surrounding the implications and associations of a given word, distinct from the denotative, or literal meaning. For example, "Good night, sweet prince, and flights of angels sing thee to thy rest," refers to a burial.

Consonance: The repeated usage of similar consonant sounds, most often used in poetry. "Sally sat sifting seashells by the seashore" is a familiar example.

Couplet: Two rhyming lines of poetry. Shakespeare's sonnets end in heroic couplets written in iambic pentameter. Pope is also a master of the couplet. His *Rape of the Lock* is written entirely in heroic couplets.

Denotation: What a word literally means, as opposed to its connotative meaning. For example, "Good night, sweet prince, and flights of angels sing thee to thy *rest*" refers to sleep.

Diction: The right word in the right spot for the right purpose. The hallmark of a great writer is precise, unusual, and memorable diction.

Epiphany: The moment when the proverbial light bulb goes off in one's head and comprehension sets in.

Exposition: Fill-in or background information about characters meant to clarify and add to the narrative; the initial plot element which precedes the buildup of conflict.

Figurative Language: Not meant in a literal sense, but to be interpreted through symbolism. Figurative language is made up of such literary devices as hyperbole, metonymy, synecdoche, and oxymoron. A synecdoche is a figure of speech in which the word for part of something is used to mean the whole; for example, "sail" for "boat," or vice versa.

Free Verse: Poetry that does not have any predictable meter or patterning. Margaret Atwood, E. E. Cummings, and Ted Hughes write in this form.

Hyperbole: Exaggeration for a specific effect. For example, "I'm so hungry that I could eat a million of these."

Iambic Pentameter: The two elements in a set five-foot line of poetry. An iamb is two syllables, unaccented and accented, per foot or measure. Pentameter means five feet of these iambs per line or ten syllables.

Inversion: A typical sentence order to create a given effect or interest. Bacon's and Milton's work use inversion successfully. Emily Dickinson was fond of arranging words outside of their familiar order. For example in "Chartless" she writes "Yet know I how the heather looks" and "Yet certain am I of the spot." Instead of saying "Yet I know" and "Yet I am certain" she reverses the usual order and shifts the emphasis to the more important words.

Irony: An unexpected disparity between what is written or stated and what is really meant or implied by the author. Verbal, situational, and dramatic are the three literary ironies. Verbal irony is when an author says one thing and means something else. Dramatic irony is when an audience perceives something that a character in the literature does not know. Irony of situation is a discrepancy between the expected result and actual results. Shakespeare's plays contain numerous and highly effective use of irony. O. Henry's short stories have ironic endings.

Kenning: Another way to describe a person, place, or thing so as to avoid prosaic repetition. The earliest examples can be found in Anglo-Saxon literature such as *Beowulf* and "The Seafarer." Instead of writing King Hrothgar, the anonymous monk wrote, great Ring-Giver, or Father of his people. A lake becomes the swans' way, and the ocean or sea becomes the great whale's way. In ancient Greek literature, this device was called an "epithet."

Metaphysical Poetry: Verse characterization by ingenious wit, unparalleled imagery, and clever conceits. The greatest metaphysical poet is John Donne.

Henry Vaughn and other 17th century British poets contributed to this movement as in *Words*, "I saw eternity the other night, like a great being of pure and endless light."

Metonymy: Use of an object or idea closely identified with another object or idea to represent the second. "Hit the books" means "go study." Washington, D.C. means the U.S. government and the White House means the U.S. President.

Motif: A key, oft-repeated phrase, name, or idea in a literary work. Dorset/Wessex in Hardy's novels and the moors and the harsh weather in the Bronte sisters' novels are effective use of motifs. Shakespeare's *Romeo and Juliet* represents the ill-fated young lovers' motif.

Onomatopoeia: Word used to evoke the sound in its meaning. The early Batman series used *pow, zap, whop, zonk* and *eek* in an onomatopoetic way.

Octava rima: A specific eight-line stanza of poetry whose rhyme scheme is abababcc. Lord Byron's mock epic, *Don Juan*, is written in this poetic way.

Oxymoron: A contradictory form of speech, such as jumbo shrimp, unkindly kind, or singer John Mellencamp's "It hurts so good."

Paradox: Seemingly untrue statement, which when examined more closely proves to be true. John Donne's sonnet "Death Be Not Proud" postulates that death shall die and humans will triumph over death, at first thought not true, but ultimately explained and proven in this sonnet.

Parallelism: A type of close repetition of clauses or phrases that emphasize key topics or ideas in writing. The psalms in the King James Version of the *Bible* contain many examples.

Personification: Giving human characteristics to inanimate objects or concepts. Great writers, with few exceptions, are masters of this literary device.

Quatrain: A poetic stanza composed of four lines. A Shakespearean or Elizabethan sonnet is made up of three quatrains and ends with a heroic couplet.

Scansion: The two-part analysis of a poetic line. Count the number of syllables per line and determine where the accents fall. Divide the line into metric feet. Name the meter by the type and number of feet. Much is written about scanning poetry. Try not to inundate your students with this jargon; rather allow them to feel the power of the poets' words, ideas, and images instead.

Soliloquy: A highlighted speech, in drama, usually delivered by a major character expounding on the author's philosophy or expressing, at times, universal truths. This is done with the character alone on the stage.

Spenserian Stanza: Invented by Sir Edmund Spenser for usage in *The Fairie Queene*, his epic poem honoring Queen Elizabeth I. Each stanza consists of nine lines, eight in iambic parameter. The ninth line, called an alexandrine, has two extra syllables or one additional foot.

Sprung Rhythm: Invented and used extensively by the poet, Gerard Manley Hopkins. It consists of variable meter, which combines stressed and unstressed syllables fashioned by the author. See "Pied Beauty" or "God's Grandeur."

Stream of Consciousness: A style of writing which reflects the mental processes of the characters expressing, at times, jumbled memories, feelings, and dreams. "Big time players" in this type of expression are James Joyce, Virginia Woolf, and William Faulkner.

Terza Rima: A series of poetic stanzas utilizing the recurrent rhyme scheme of aba, bcb, cdc, ded, and so forth. The second-generation Romantic poets - Keats, Byron, Shelley, and, to a lesser degree, Yeats - used this Italian verse form, especially in their odes. Dante used this stanza in *The Divine Comedy*.

Tone: The discernible attitude inherent in an author's work regarding the subject, readership, or characters. Swift's or Pope's tone is satirical. Boswell's tone toward Johnson is admiring.

Wit: Writing of genius, keenness, and sagacity expressed through clever use of language. Alexander Pope and the Augustans wrote about and were themselves said to possess wit.

Poetic Elements

Slant Rhyme: Occurs when the final consonant sounds are the same, but the vowels are different. Occurs frequently in Irish, Welsh, and Icelandic verse. Examples include: green and gone, that and hit, ill and shell.

Alliteration: Alliteration occurs when the initial sounds of a word, beginning either with a consonant or a vowel, are repeated in close succession. Examples include: Athena and Apollo, Nate never knows, People who pen poetry.

Note that the words only have to be close to one another: Alliteration that repeats and attempts to connect a number of words is little more than a tongue-twister.

The function of alliteration, like rhyme, might be to accentuate the beauty of language in a given context, or to unite words or concepts through a kind of repetition. Alliteration, like rhyme, can follow specific patterns. Sometimes the consonants aren't always the initial ones, but they are generally the stressed syllables.

Alliteration is less common than rhyme, but because it is less common, it can call our attention to a word or line in a poem that might not have the same emphasis otherwise.

Assonance: If alliteration occurs at the beginning of a word and rhyme at the end, assonance takes the middle territory. Assonance occurs when the vowel sound within a word matches the same sound in a nearby word, but the surrounding consonant sounds are different. "Tune" and "June" are rhymes; "tune" and "food" are assonant. The function of assonance is frequently the same as end rhyme or alliteration; all serve to give a sense of continuity or fluidity to the verse. Assonance might be especially effective when rhyme is absent: It gives the poet more flexibility, and it is not typically used as part of a predetermined pattern. Like alliteration, it does not so much determine the structure or form of a poem; rather, it is more ornamental.

Imagery can be described as a word or sequence of words that refers to any sensory experience—that is, anything that can be seen, tasted, smelled, heard, or felt on the skin or fingers. While writers of prose may also use these devices, it is most distinctive of poetry. The poet intends to make an experience available to the reader. In order to do that, he/she must appeal to one of the senses. The most-often-used one, of course, is the visual sense. The poet will deliberately paint a scene in such a way that the reader can see it. However, the purpose is not simply to stir the visceral feeling but also to stir the emotions. A good example is "The Piercing Chill" by Taniguchi Buson (1715-1783):

> The piercing chill I feel:
>   My dead wife's comb, in our bedroom,
>   Under my heel . . .

In only a few short words, the reader can feel many things: the shock that might come from touching the corpse, a literal sense of death, the contrast between her death and the memories he has of her when she was alive. Imagery might be defined as speaking of the abstract in concrete terms, a powerful device in the hands of a skillful poet.

A **symbol** is an object or action that can be observed with the senses in addition to its suggesting many other things. The lion is a symbol of courage; the cross a symbol of Christianity; the color green a symbol of envy. These can almost be defined as metaphors because society pretty much agrees on the one-to-one meaning of them. Symbols used in literature are usually of a different sort. They tend to be private and personal; their significance is only evident in the context of the work where they are used. A good example is the huge pair of spectacles on a sign board in Fitzgerald's *The Great Gatsby*. They are interesting as a part of the landscape, but they also symbolize divine myopia.

A symbol can certainly have more than one meaning, and the meaning may be as personal as the memories and experiences of the particular reader. In analyzing a poem or a story, it's important to identify the symbols and their possible meanings.

Looking for symbols is often challenging, especially for novice poetry readers. However, these suggestions may be useful: First, pick out all the references to concrete objects such as a newspaper, black cats, etc. Note any that the poet emphasizes by describing in detail, by repeating, or by placing at the very beginning or ending of a poem. Ask yourself, what is the poem about? What does it add up to? Paraphrase the poem and determine whether or not the meaning depends upon certain concrete objects. Then ponder what the concrete object symbolizes in this particular poem. Look for a character with the name of a prophet who does little but utter prophecy or a trio of women who resemble the Three Fates. A symbol may be a part of a person's body such as the eye of the murder victim in Poe's story *The Tell-Tale Heart* or a look, a voice, or a mannerism.

Some things a symbol is not: an abstraction such as truth, death, and love; in narrative, a well-developed character who is not at all mysterious; the second term in a metaphor. In Emily Dickenson's *The Lightning is a yellow Fork*, the symbol is the lightning, not the fork.

An **allusion** is very much like a symbol, and the two sometimes tend to run together. An allusion is defined by Merriam Webster's *Encyclopedia of Literature* as "an implied reference to a person, event, thing, or a part of another text." Allusions are based on the assumption that there is a common body of knowledge shared by poet and reader and that a reference to that body of knowledge will be immediately understood. Allusions to the Bible and classical mythology are common in western literature on the assumption that they will be immediately understood. This is not always the case, of course. T. S. Eliot's *The Wasteland* requires research and annotation for understanding. He assumed more background on the part of the average reader than actually exists. However, when Michael Moore on his web page headlines an article on the war in Iraq: "Déjà Fallouja: Ramadi surrounded, thousands of families trapped, no electricity or water, onslaught impending," we understand immediately that he is referring first of all to a repeat of the human disaster in New Orleans although the "onslaught" is not a storm but an invasion by American and Iraqi troops.

The use of allusion is a sort of shortcut for poets. They can use an economy of words and count on meaning to come from the reader's own experience.

Figurative language is also called figures of speech. If all figures of speech that have ever been identified were listed, it would be a very long list. However, for purposes of analyzing poetry, a few are sufficient.
1. Simile: Direct comparison between two things. "My love is like a red-red rose."
2. Metaphor: Indirect comparison between two things. The use of a word or phrase denoting one kind of object or action in place of another to suggest a comparison between them. While poets use them extensively, they are also integral to everyday speech. For example, chairs are said to have "legs" and "arms" although we know that it's humans and other animals that have these appendages.

3. Parallelism: The arrangement of ideas in phrases, sentences, and paragraphs that balance one element with another of equal importance and similar wording. An example from Francis Bacon's *Of Studies:* "Reading maketh a full man, conference a ready man, and writing an exact man."
4. Personification: Human characteristics are attributed to an inanimate object, an abstract quality, or animal. Examples: John Bunyan wrote characters named Death, Knowledge, Giant Despair, Sloth, and Piety in his *Pilgrim's Progress.* The metaphor of an arm of a chair is a form of personification.
5. Euphemism: The substitution of an agreeable or inoffensive term for one that might offend or suggest something unpleasant. Many euphemisms are used to refer to death to avoid using the real word such as "passed away," "crossed over," or nowadays "passed."
6. Hyperbole: Deliberate exaggeration for effect or comic effect. An example from Shakespeare's *The Merchant of Venice*:

   > Why, if two gods should play some heavenly match
   > And on the wager lay two earthly women,
   > And Portia one, there must be something else
   > Pawned with the other, for the poor rude world
   > Hath not her fellow.

7. Climax: A number of phrases or sentences are arranged in ascending order of rhetorical forcefulness. Example from Melville's *Moby Dick*:

   > All that most maddens and torments; all that stirs up the lees of things; all truth with malice in it; all that cracks the sinews and cakes the brain; all the subtle demonisms of life and thought; all evil, to crazy Ahab, were visibly personified and made practically assailable in Moby Dick.

8. Bathos: A ludicrous attempt to portray pathos—that is, to evoke pity, sympathy, or sorrow. It may result from inappropriately dignifying the commonplace, elevated language to describe something trivial, or greatly exaggerated pathos.
9. Oxymoron: A contradiction in terms deliberately employed for effect. It is usually seen in a qualifying adjective whose meaning is contrary to that of the noun it modifies such as wise folly.
10. Irony: Expressing something other than and particularly opposite the literal meaning such as words of praise when blame is intended. In poetry, it is often used as a sophisticated or resigned awareness of contrast between what is and what ought to be and expresses a controlled pathos without sentimentality. It is a form of indirection that avoids overt praise or censure. An early example: the Greek comic character Eiron, a clever underdog who by his wit repeatedly triumphs over the boastful character Alazon.

11. Alliteration: The repetition of consonant sounds in two or more neighboring words or syllables. In its simplest form, it reinforces one or two consonant sounds. Example: Shakespeare's Sonnet #12:
    When I do count the clock that tells the time.
    Some poets have used more complex patterns of alliteration by creating consonants both at the beginning of words and at the beginning of stressed syllables within words. Example: Shelley's "Stanzas Written in Dejection Near Naples"
    The City's voice itself is soft like Solitude's
12. Onomatopoeia: The naming of a thing or action by a vocal imitation of the sound associated with it such as buzz or hiss or the use of words whose sound suggests the sense. A good example: from "The Brook" by Tennyson:
    I chatter over stony ways,
    In little sharps and trebles,
    I bubble into eddying bays,
    I babble on the pebbles.
13. Malapropism: A verbal blunder in which one word is replaced by another similar in sound but different in meaning. Comes from Sheridan's Mrs. Malaprop in *The Rivals* (1775). Thinking of the geography of contiguous countries, she spoke of the "geometry" of "contagious countries."

Poets use figures of speech to sharpen the effect and meaning of their poems and to help readers see things in ways they have never seen them before. Marianne Moore observed that a fir tree has "an emerald turkey-foot at the top." Her poem makes us aware of something we probably had never noticed before. The sudden recognition of the likeness yields pleasure in the reading. Figurative language allows for the statement of truths that more literal language cannot. Skillfully used, a figure of speech will help the reader see more clearly and to focus upon particulars. Figures of speech add many dimensions of richness to our reading and understanding of a poem; they also allow many opportunities for worthwhile analysis. The approach to take in analyzing a poem on the basis of its figures of speech is to ask the question: What does it do for the poem? Does it underscore meaning? Does it intensify understanding? Does it increase the intensity of our response?

Competency 4.0   Identifying patterns, structures, and characteristics of literary forms and genres.

The major literary genres include allegory, ballad, drama, epic, epistle, essay, fable, novel, poem, romance, and the short story.

Allegory: A story in verse or prose with characters representing virtues and vices. There are two meanings, symbolic and literal. John Bunyan's *The Pilgrim's Progress* is the most renowned of this genre.

Ballad: An *in medias res* story told or sung, usually in verse and accompanied by music. Literary devices found in ballads include the refrain, or repeated section, and incremental repetition, or anaphora, for effect. Earliest forms were anonymous folk ballads. Later forms include Coleridge's Romantic masterpiece, "The Rime of the Ancient Mariner."

Drama: Plays – comedy, modern, or tragedy - typically in five acts. Traditionalists and neoclassicists adhere to Aristotle's unities of time, place and action. Plot development is advanced via dialogue. Literary devices include asides, soliloquies and the chorus representing public opinion. Greatest of all dramatists/playwrights is William Shakespeare. Other dramaturges include Ibsen, Williams, Miller, Shaw, Stoppard, Racine, Moliére, Sophocles, Aeschylus, Euripides, and Aristophanes.

Epic: Long poem usually of book length reflecting values inherent in the generative society. Epic devices include an invocation to a Muse for inspiration, purpose for writing, universal setting, protagonist and antagonist who possess supernatural strength and acumen, and interventions of a God or the gods. Understandably, there are very few epics: Homer's *Iliad* and *Odyssey*, Virgil's *Aeneid*, Milton's *Paradise Lost*, Spenser's *The Fairie Queene*, Barrett Browning's *Aurora Leigh*, and Pope's mock-epic, *The Rape of the Lock*.

Epistle: A letter that is not always originally intended for public distribution, but due to the fame of the sender and/or recipient, becomes public domain. Paul wrote epistles that were later placed in the Bible.

Essay: Typically a limited length prose work focusing on a topic and propounding a definite point of view and authoritative tone. Great essayists include Carlyle, Lamb, DeQuincy, Emerson and Montaigne, who is credited with defining this genre.

Fable: Terse tale offering up a moral or exemplum. Chaucer's "The Nun's Priest's Tale" is a fine example of a *bete fabliau* or beast fable in which animals speak and act characteristically human, illustrating human foibles.

Legend: A traditional narrative or collection of related narratives, popularly regarded as historically factual but actually a mixture of fact and fiction.

Myth: Stories that are more or less universally shared within a culture to explain its history and traditions.

Novel: The longest form of fictional prose containing a variety of characterizations, settings, local color and regionalism. Most have complex plots, expanded description, and attention to detail. Some of the great novelists include Austin, the Brontes, Twain, Tolstoy, Hugo, Hardy, Dickens, Hawthorne, Forster, and Flaubert.

Poem: The only requirement is rhythm. Sub-genres include fixed types of literature such as the sonnet, elegy, ode, pastoral, and villanelle. Unfixed types of literature include blank verse and dramatic monologue.

Romance: A highly imaginative tale set in a fantastical realm dealing with the conflicts between heroes, villains and/or monsters. "The Knight's Tale" from Chaucer's *Canterbury Tales*, *Sir Gawain and the Green Knight* and Keats' "The Eve of St. Agnes" are prime representatives.

Short Story: Typically a terse narrative, with less developmental background about characters. May include description, author's point of view, and tone. Poe emphasized that a successful short story should create one focused impact. Considered to be great short story writers are Hemingway, Faulkner, Twain, Joyce, Shirley Jackson, Flannery O'Connor, de Maupassant, Saki, Edgar Allen Poe, and Pushkin.

Types of Drama

Comedy: The comedic form of dramatic literature is meant to amuse, and often ends happily. It uses techniques such as satire or parody, and can take many forms, from farce to burlesque. Examples include Dante Alighieri's *The Divine Comedy,* Noel Coward's play *Private Lives,* and some of Geoffrey Chaucer's *Canterbury Tales* and William Shakespeare's plays.

Tragedy: Tragedy is comedy's other half. It is defined as a work of drama written in either prose or poetry, telling the story of a brave, noble hero who, because of some tragic character flaw, brings ruin upon himself. It is characterized by serious, poetic language that evokes pity and fear. In modern times, dramatists have tried to update its image by drawing its main characters from the middle class and showing their nobility through their nature instead of their standing. The classic example of tragedy is Sophocles' *Oedipus Rex*, while Henrik Ibsen and Arthur Miller epitomize modern tragedy.

Drama: In its most general sense, a drama is any work that is designed to be performed by actors onstage. It can also refer to the broad literary genre that includes comedy and tragedy. Contemporary usage, however, denotes drama as a work that treats serious subjects and themes but does not aim for the same grandeur as tragedy.

Drama usually deals with characters of a less stately nature than tragedy. A classical example is Sophocles' tragedy *Oedipus Rex,* while Eugene O'Neill's *The Iceman Cometh* represents modern drama.

Dramatic Monologue: A dramatic monologue is a speech given by an actor, usually intended for themselves, but with the intended audience in mind. It reveals key aspects of the character's psyche and sheds insight on the situation at hand. The audience takes the part of the silent listener, passing judgment and giving sympathy at the same time. This form was invented and used predominantly by Victorian poet Robert Browning.

Tempo

Interpretation of dialogue must be connected to motivation and detail. During this time, the director is also concerned with pace and seeks a variation of tempo. If the overall pace is too slow, then the action becomes dull and dragging. If the overall pace is too fast, then the audience will not be able to understand what is going on, for they are being hit with too much information to process.

Dramatic Arc

Good drama is built on conflict of some kind — an opposition of forces or desires that must be resolved by the end of the story. The conflict can be internal, involving emotional and psychological pressures, or it can be external, drawing the characters into tumultuous events. These themes are presented to the audience in a narrative arc that looks roughly like this:

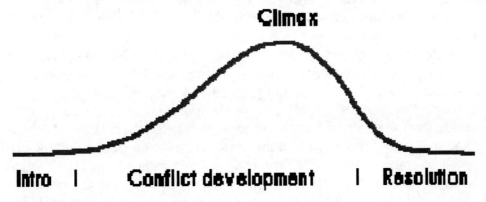

a) Following the Arc

Although any performance may have a series of rising and falling levels of intensity, in general the opening should set in motion the events which will generate an emotional high toward the middle or end of the story. Then, regardless of whether the ending is happy, sad, bittersweet, or despairing, the resolution eases the audience down from those heights and establishes some sense of closure. Reaching the climax too soon undermines the dramatic impact of the remaining portion of the performance, whereas reaching it too late rushes the ending and creates a jarringly abrupt end to events.

Types of Nonfiction

Biography: A form of nonfictional literature, the subject of which is the life of an individual. The earliest biographical writings were probably funeral speeches and inscriptions, usually praising the life and example of the deceased. Early biographies evolved from this and were almost invariably uncritical, even distorted, and always laudatory. Beginning in the 18th century, this form of literature saw major development; an eminent example is James Boswell's *Life of Johnson*, which is very detailed and even records conversations. Eventually, the antithesis of the grossly exaggerated tomes praising an individual, usually a person of circumstance, developed. This form is denunciatory, debunking, and often inflammatory. A famous modern example is Lytton Strachey's *Eminent Victorians* (1918).

Autobiography: A form of biography, but it is written by the subject himself or herself. Autobiographies can range from the very formal to intimate writings made during one's life that were not intended for publication. These include letters, diaries, journals, memoirs, and reminiscences. Autobiography, generally speaking, began in the 15th century; one of the first examples is one written in England by Margery Kempe. There are four kinds of autobiography: thematic, religious, intellectual, and fictionalized. Some "novels" may be thinly disguised autobiography, such as the novels of Thomas Wolfe.

Informational books and articles: Make up much of the reading of modern Americans. Magazines began to be popular in the 19th century in this country, and while many of the contributors to those publications intended to influence the political/social/religious convictions of their readers, many also simply intended to pass on information. A book or article whose purpose is simply to be informative, that is, not to persuade, is called exposition (adjectival form: expository). An example of an expository book is the *MLA Style Manual*. The writers do not intend to persuade their readers to use the recommended stylistic features in their writing; they are simply making them available in case a reader needs such a guide. Articles in magazines such as *Time* may be persuasive in purpose, such as Joe Klein's regular column, but for the most part they are expository, giving information that television coverage of a news story might not have time to include.

Newspaper accounts of events: Expository in nature, of course, a reporting of a happening. That happening might be a school board meeting, an automobile accident that sent several people to a hospital and accounted for the death of a passenger, or the election of the mayor. They are not intended to be persuasive although the bias of a reporter or of an editor must be factored in. A newspapers' editorial stance is often openly declared, and it may be reflected in such things as news reports. Reporters are expected to be unbiased in their coverage and most of them will defend their disinterest fiercely, but what a writer *sees* in an event is inevitably shaped to some extent by the writer's beliefs and experiences.

Characteristics of Poetry

The greatest difficulty in analyzing narrative poetry is that it partakes of many genres. It can have all the features of poetry: meter, rhyme, verses, stanzas, etc., but it can have all the features of prose, not only fictional prose but also nonfictional. It can have a protagonist, characters, conflicts, action, plot, climax, theme, and tone. It can also be a persuasive discourse and have a thesis (real or derived) and supporting points. The arrangement of an analysis will depend to a great extent upon the peculiarities of the poem itself.

In an epic, the conflicts take place in the social sphere rather than a personal life, and it will have a historical basis or one that is accepted as historical. The conflict will be between opposed nations or races and will involve diverging views of civilization that are the foundation of the challenge. Often it will involve the pitting of a group that conceives of itself as a higher civilization against a lower civilization and, more often than not, divine will determines that the higher one will win, exerting its force over the lower, barbarous, and profane enemy. Examples are the conflict of Greece with Troy, the fates of Rome with the Carthaginian and the Italian, the Crusaders with the Saracen, or even of Milton's Omnipotent versus Satan. In analyzing these works, protagonist and antagonist need to be clearly identified, the conflicts established, the climax and an outcome that sets the world right in the mind of the writer clearly shown .

At the same time, the form of the epic as a poem must be considered. What meter, rhyme scheme, verse form, and stanza form have been chosen to tell this story. Is it consistent? If it varies, where does it vary and what does the varying do for the poem/story? What about figures of speech? Is there alliteration or onomatopoeia? Etc.

The epic is a major literary form historically although it had begun to fall out of favor by the end of the seventeenth century. There have been notable efforts to produce an American epic, but they always seem to slide over into prose. The short story and the novel began to take over the genre. Even so, some would say that *Moby Dick* is an American epic.

Narrative poetry has been very much a part of the output of modern American writers totally apart from attempts to write epics. Many of Emily Dickenson's poems are narrative in form and retain the features that we look for in the finest of American poetry. The first two verses of "A Narrow Fellow in the Grass" illustrate the use of narrative in a poem:

> A narrow fellow in the grass
> Occasionally rides;
> You may have met him—did you not?
> His notice sudden is.

The grass divides as with a comb,
A spotted shaft is seen;
And then it closes at your feet
And opens further on. . . .

This is certainly narrative in nature and has many of the aspects of prose narrative. At the same time, it is a poem with rhyme, meter, verses, stanzas, etc. and can be analyzed as such.

Types of Poetry

The sonnet is a fixed-verse form of Italian origin, which consists of 14 lines that are typically five-foot iambics rhyming according to a prescribed scheme. Popular since its creation in the thirteenth century in Sicily, it spread at first to Tuscany, where it was adopted by Petrarch. The Petrarchan sonnet generally has a two-part theme. The first eight lines, the octave, state a problem, ask a question, or express an emotional tension. The last six lines, the sestet, resolve the problem, answer the question, or relieve the tension. The rhyme scheme of the octave is abbaabba; that of the sestet varies.

Sir Thomas Wyatt and Henry Howard, Earl of Surrey, introduced this form into England in the sixteenth century. It played an important role in the development of Elizabethan lyric poetry, and a distinctive English sonnet developed, which was composed of three quatrains, each with an independent rhyme-scheme, and it ended with a rhymed couplet. A form of the English sonnet created by Edmond Spenser combines the English form and the Italian. The Spenserian sonnet follows the English quatrain and couplet pattern but resembles the Italian in its rhyme scheme, which is linked: abab bcbc cdcd ee. Many poets wrote sonnet sequences, where several sonnets were linked together, usually to tell a story. Considered to be the greatest of all sonnet sequences is one of Shakespeare's, which are addressed to a young man and a "dark lady" wherein the love story is overshadowed by the underlying reflections on time and art, growth and decay, and fame and fortune.

The sonnet continued to develop, more in topics than in form. When John Donne in the seventeenth century used the form for religious themes, some of which are almost sermons, or on personal reflections ("When I consider how my light is spent"), there were no longer any boundaries on the themes it could take.

That it is a flexible form is demonstrated in the wide range of themes and purposes it has been used for—all the way from more frivolous concerns to statements about time and death. Wordsworth, Keats, and Elizabeth Barrett Browning used the Petrarchan form of the sonnet. A well-known example is Wordsworth's "The World Is Too Much With Us." Rainer Maria Rilke's Sonnette an Orpheus (1922) is a well-known twentieth-century sonnet.

Analysis of a sonnet should focus on the form—does it fit a traditional pattern or does it break from tradition? If so, why did the poet choose to make that break?

Does it reflect the purpose of the poem? What is the theme? What is the purpose? Is it narrative? If so, what story does it tell and is there an underlying meaning? Is the sonnet appropriate for the subject matter?

The limerick probably originated in County Limerick, Ireland, in the 18th century. It is a form of short, humorous verse, often nonsensical, and often ribald. Its five lines rhyme aabbaa with three feet in all lines except the third and fourth, which have only two. Rarely presented as serious poetry, this form is popular because almost anyone can write it.

Analysis of a limerick should focus on its form. Does it conform to a traditional pattern or does it break from the tradition? If so, what impact does that have on the meaning? Is the poem serious or frivolous? Is it funny? Does it try to be funny but does not achieve its purpose? Is there a serious meaning underlying the frivolity?

A cinquain is a poem with a five-line stanza. Adelaide Crapsey (1878-1914) called a five-line verse form a cinquain and invented a particular meter for it. Similar to the haiku, there are two syllables in the first and last lines and four, six, and eight in the middle three lines. It has a mostly iambic cadence. Her poem, "November Night," is an example:

> Listen…
> With faint dry sound
> Like steps of passing ghosts,
> the leaves, frost-crisp'd, break from the trees
> And fall.

Haiku is a very popular unrhymed form that is limited to seventeen syllables arranged in three lines thus: five, seven, and five syllables. This verse form originated in Japan in the seventeenth century where it is accepted as serious poetry and is Japan's most popular form. Originally, it was to deal with the season, the time of day, and the landscape although as it has come into more common use, the subjects have become less restricted. The imagist poets and other English writers used the form or imitated it. It's a form much used in classrooms to introduce students to the writing of poetry.

Analysis of a cinquain and a haiku poem should focus on form first. Does the haiku poem conform to the seventeen-syllables requirement and are they arranged in a five, seven, and five pattern? For a cinquain, does it have only five lines? Does the poem distill the words so as much meaning as possible can be conveyed? Does it treat a serious subject? Is the theme discernable? Short forms like these seem simple to dash off; however, they are not effective unless the words are chosen and pared so the meaning intended is conveyed. The impact should be forceful, and that often takes more effort, skill, and creativity than longer forms. This should be taken into account in their analysis.

Fables, Folk Tales, Fairy Tales, and Mythology

Literary allusions are drawn from classic mythology, national folklore, and religious writings that are supposed to have such familiarity to the reader that he can recognize the comparison between the subject of the allusion and the person, place, or event in the current reading. Children and adolescents who have knowledge of proverbs, fables, myths, epics, and the *Bible* can understand these allusions and thereby appreciate their reading to a greater degree than those who cannot recognize them.

Fables and folktales

This literary group of stories and legends was originally orally transmitted to the common populace to provide models of exemplary behavior or deeds worthy of recognition and homage.

In fables, animals talk, feel, and behave like human beings. The fable always has a moral and the animals illustrate specific people or groups without directly identifying them. For example, in Aesop's *Fables,* the lion is the "King" and the wolf is the cruel, often unfeeling, "noble class." In the fable of "The Lion and the Mouse" the moral is that "Little friends may prove to be great friends." In "The Lion's Share" it is "Might makes right." Many British folktales - *How Robin Became an Outlaw* and *St. George - Slaying of the Dragon* - stress the correlation between power and right.

Classical mythology

Much of the mythology that produces allusions in modern English writings is a product of ancient Greece and Rome because these myths have been more liberally translated. Some Norse myths are also well known. Children are fond of myths because those ancient people were seeking explanations for those elements in their lives that predated scientific knowledge just as children seek explanations for the occurrences in their lives. These stories provide insight into the order and ethics of life as ancient heroes overcome the terrors of the unknown and bring meaning to the thunder and lightning, to the changing of the seasons, to the magical creatures of the forests and seas, and to the myriad of natural phenomena that can frighten mankind. There is often a childlike quality in the emotions of supernatural beings with which children can identify. Many good translations of myths exist for readers of varying abilities, but Edith Hamilton's *Mythology* is the most definitive reading for adolescents.

Fairy tales

Fairy tales are lively fictional stories involving children or animals that come in contact with super-beings via magic. They provide happy solutions to human dilemmas. The fairy tales of many nations are peopled by trolls, elves, dwarfs, and pixies, child-sized beings capable of fantastic accomplishments.

Among the most famous are "Beauty and the Beast," "Cinderella," "Hansel and Gretel," "Snow White and the Seven Dwarfs," "Rumplestiltskin," and "Tom Thumb." In each tale, the protagonist survives prejudice, imprisonment, ridicule, and even death to receive justice in a cruel world.

Older readers encounter a kind of fairy tale world in Shakespeare's *The Tempest* and *A Midsummer Night's Dream*, which use pixies and fairies as characters. Adolescent readers today are as fascinated by the creations of fantasy realms in the works of Piers Anthony, Ursula LeGuin, and Anne McCaffrey. An extension of interest in the supernatural is the popularity of science fiction that allows us to use current knowledge to predict the possible course of the future.

Angels (or sometimes fairy godmothers) play a role in some fairy tales, and Milton in Paradise Lost and Paradise Regained also used symbolic angels and devils.

Biblical stories provide many allusions. Parables, moralistic like fables but having human characters, include the stories of the Good Samaritan and the Prodigal Son. References to the treachery of Cain and the betrayal of Christ by Judas Iscariot are oft-cited examples.

American folk tales

American folktales are divided into two categories.

Imaginary tales, also called tall tales (humorous tales based on non-existent, fictional characters developed through blatant exaggeration)

> John Henry is a two-fisted steel driver who beats out a steam drill in competition.

> Rip Van Winkle sleeps for twenty years in the Catskill Mountains and upon awakening cannot understand why no one recognizes him.

> Paul Bunyan, a giant lumberjack, owns a great blue ox named Babe and has extraordinary physical strength. He is said to have plowed the Mississippi River while the impression of Babe's hoof prints created the Great Lakes.

Real tales, also called legends (based on real persons who accomplished the feats that are attributed to them even if they are slightly exaggerated)

> For more than forty years, Johnny Appleseed (John Chapman) roamed Ohio and Indiana planting apple seeds.
>
> Daniel Boone - scout, adventurer, and pioneer - blazed the Wilderness Trail and made Kentucky safe for settlers.
>
> Paul Revere, an colonial patriot, rode through the New England countryside warning of the approach of British troops.
>
> George Washington cut down a cherry tree, which he could not deny, or did he?

Competency 5.0 Situating and interpreting texts within their historical and cultural contexts.

American Literature

Local Color is defined as the presenting of the peculiarities of a particular locality and its inhabitants. This genre began to be seen primarily after the Civil War although there were certainly precursors such as Washington Irving and his depiction of life in the Catskill Mountains of New York. However, the local colorist movement is generally considered to have begun in 1865, when humor began to permeate the writing of those who were focusing on a particular region of the country. Samuel L. Clemens (Mark Twain) is best-known for his humorous works about the southwest such as *The Notorious Jumping Frog of Calaveras County*. The country had just emerged from its "long night of the soul," a time when death, despair, and disaster had preoccupied the nation for almost five years. It's no wonder that the artists sought to relieve the grief and pain and lift spirits nor is it surprising that their efforts brought such a strong response. Mark Twain is generally considered to be not only one of America's funniest writers but one who also wrote great and enduring fiction.

Other examples of local colorists who used many of the same devices are Harriet Beecher Stowe, Bret Harte, George Washington Cable, Joel Chandler Harris, and Sarah Orne Jewett.

Slavery

The best-known of the early writers who used fiction as a political statement about slavery is Harriet Beecher Stowe, author of *Uncle Tom's Cabin.* This was her first novel, and it was published first as a serial in 1851 then as a book in 1852. It brought an angry reaction from people living in the South.

This antislavery book infuriated Southerners. However, Stowe, herself, had been angered by the 1850 Fugitive Slave Law that made it legal to indict those who assisted runaway slaves. It also took away rights not only of the runaways but also of the free slaves. She intended to generate a protest of the law and slavery. It was the first effort to present the lives of slaves from their standpoint.

The novel is about three slaves, Tom, Eliza, and George who are together in Kentucky. Eliza and George are married to each other but have different masters. They successfully escape with their little boy, but Tom does not. Although he has a wife and children, he is sold, ending up finally with the monstrous Simon Legree, where he dies at last. Stowe cleverly used depictions of motherhood and Christianity to stir her readers. When President Lincoln finally met her, he told her it was her book that started the war.

Many writers used the printed word to protest slavery. Some of them include:
- Frederick Douglas
- William Lloyd Garrison
- Benjamin Lay, a Quaker
- Connecticut theologian Jonathan Edward
- Susan B. Anthony

Immigration

This has been a popular topic for literature from the time of the Louisiana Purchase in 1804. The recent *Undaunted Courage* by Stephen E. Ambrose is ostensibly the autobiography of Meriwether Lewis but is actually a recounting of the Lewis and Clark expedition. Presented as a scientific expedition by President Jefferson, the expedition was actually intended to provide maps and information for the opening up of the west. A well-known novel of the settling of the west by immigrants from other countries is *Giants in the Earth* by Ole Edvart Rolvaag, himself a descendant of immigrants.

Civil Rights

Many abolitionists were also early crusaders for civil rights. However, the 1960s movement focused attention on the plight of the people who had been "freed" by the Civil War in ways that brought about long overdue changes in the opportunities and rights of African Americans. David Halberstam, who had been a reporter in Nashville at the time of the sit-ins by eight young black college students that initiated the revolution, wrote *The Children*, published in 1998 by Random House, for the purpose of reminding Americans of their courage, suffering, and achievements. Congressman John Lewis, Fifth District, Georgia, was one of those eight young men who has gone on to a life of public service. Halberstam records that when older black ministers tried to persuade these young people not to pursue their protest, John Lewis responded: "If not us, then who? If not now, then when?"

Some examples of protest literature:
- James Baldwin, *Blues for Mister Charlie*
- Martin Luther King, *Where Do We Go from Here?*
- Langston Hughes, *Fight for Freedom: The Story of the NAACP*
- Eldridge Cleaver, *Soul on Ice*
- Malcolm X, *The Autobiography of Malcolm X*
- Stokely Carmichael and Charles V. Hamilton, *Black Power*
- Leroi Jones, *Home*

Vietnam

An America that was already divided over the civil rights movement faced even greater divisions over the war in Vietnam. Those who were in favor of the war and who opposed withdrawal saw it as the major front in the war against communism. Those who opposed the war and who favored withdrawal of the troops believed that it would not serve to defeat communism and was a quagmire.

Catch-22 by Joseph Heller was a popular antiwar novel that became a successful movie of the time. *Authors Take Sides on Vietnam*, edited by Cecil Woolf and John Bagguley is a collection of essays by 168 well-known authors throughout the world. *Where is Vietnam?* edited by Walter Lowenfels consists of 92 poems about the war.

Many writers were publishing works for and against the war, but the genre that had the most impact was rock music. Bob Dylan was an example of the musicians of the time. His music represented the hippie aesthetic and brilliant, swirling colors and hallucinogenic imagery and created a style that came to be called psychedelic. Some other bands that originated during this time and became well-known for their psychedelic music, primarily about the Vietnam War in the early years, are the Grateful Dead, Jefferson Airplane, Big Brother, Sly and the Family Stone. In England, the movement attracted the Beatles and the Rolling Stones.

Immigration

John Steinbeck's *Cannery Row* and *Tortilla Flats* glorifies the lives of Mexican migrants in California. Amy Tan's *The Joy Luck Club* deals with the problems faced by Chinese immigrants.

Leon Uris' *Exodus* deals with the social history that led to the founding of the modern state of Israel. It was published in 1958, only a short time after the Holocaust. It also deals with attempts of concentration camp survivors to get to the land that has become the new Israel. In many ways, it is the quintessential work on immigration—causes and effects.

British Literature

The reign of Elizabeth I ushered in a renaissance that led to the end of the medieval age. It was a very fertile literary period. The exploration of the new world expanded the vision of all levels of the social order from royalty to peasant, and the rejection of Catholicism by many in favor of a Christianity of their own opened up whole new vistas to thought and daily life. The manufacture of cloth had increased, driving many people from the countryside into the cities, and the population of London exploded, creating a metropolitan business center. Printing had been brought to England by William Caxton in the 1470s, and literacy increased from 30% in the 15th century to over 60% by 1530. These seem dramatic changes, and they were, but they were occurring gradually.

The Italian renaissance had a great influence on the renaissance in England, and early in the 16th century most written works were in Latin. It was assumed that a learned person must express his thoughts in that language. However, there began to emerge a determination that vernacular English was valuable in writing, and it began to be defended. Elizabeth's tutor, Roger Ascham, for example, wrote in English.

Luther's thesis in 1517, which brought on the Reformation—an attempt to return to pure Christianity—brought on the breakup of western Christendom and eventually the secularization of society and the establishment of the king or queen as the head of this new/old church. This also brought about a new feeling that being religious was also being patriotic; it promoted nationalism.

The ascension of Elizabeth to the throne also followed a very turbulent period regarding succession, and she ruled for 45 peaceful years, which allowed arts and literature to flourish. Although she, herself, was headstrong and difficult, she happened to have very shrewd political instincts and entrusted power to solid, talented men, most particularly Cecil, her Secretary, and Walsingham, whom she put in charge of foreign policy. She identified with her country as no previous ruler had and that, in itself, brought on a period of intense nationalism. She was a symbol of Englishness. The defeat of the Spanish armada in 1588 was the direct result of the strong support she had from her own nation.

Drama was the principal form of literature in this age. Religious plays had been a part of the life of England for a long time, particularly the courtly life. But in the Elizabethan age, they became more and more secular and were created primarily for courtly entertainment. By the '60s, Latin drama, particularly the tragedies of Seneca and the comedies of Plautus and Terence began to wield an influence in England. Courtyards of inns became favorite places for the presentation of plays; but in 1576, the Earl of Leicester's Men constructed their own building outside the city and called it The Theatre. Other theatres followed. Each had its own repertory company, and performances were for profit but also for the queen and her court.

It is said that Shakespeare wrote *The Merry Wives of Windsor* at the specific command of the queen, who liked Falstaff and wanted to see him in love. It was also for the courtly audience that poetry was introduced into drama.

Shakespeare and Marlowe dominated the '80s and '90s; and at the turn of the century, only a few years before Elizabeth's death, Ben Jonson began writing his series of satirical comedies.

Court favor was notoriously precarious and depended on the whims of the queen and others. Much of the satire of the period reflects the disappointment of writers like Edmund Spenser and John Lyly and the superficiality and treachery of the court atmosphere. "A thousand hopes, but all nothing," wrote Lyly, "a hundred promises, but yet nothing."

Not all literature was dictated by the court. The middle classes were developing and had their own style. Thomas Heywood and Thomas Deloney catered to bourgeois tastes.

The two universities were also sources for the production of literature. The primary aim of the colleges was to develop ministers since there was a shortage brought on by the break with the Catholic Church. However, most university men couldn't make livings as ministers or academics, so they wrote as a way of earning income. Nashe, Marlowe, Robert Greene, and George Peele all reveal in their writings how difficult this path was. Remuneration came mostly from patrons. Greene had sixteen different patrons from seventeen books whereas Shakespeare had a satisfactory relationship with the Earl of Southampton and didn't need to seek other support. Publishers would also sometimes pay for a manuscript, which they would then own. Unfortunately, if the manuscript did not pass muster with all who could condemn it—the court, the religious leaders, prominent citizens—it was the author who was on the hot seat. Very few became as comfortable as Shakespeare did. His success was not only in writing, however, but also from his business acumen.

Writing was seen more as a craft than as an art in this period. There was not great conflict between art and nature, little distinction between literature, sports of the field, or the arts of the kitchen.

Balance and control were important in the England of this day, and this is reflected in the writing, the poetry in particular. The sestina, a form in which the last words of each line in the first stanza are repeated in a different order in each of the following stanzas, became very popular. Verse forms range from the extremely simple four-line ballad stanza through the rather complicated form of the sonnet to the elaborate and beautiful eighteen-line stanza of Spenser's *Epithalamion*. Sonnets were called "quatorzains." The term "sonnet" was used loosely for any short poem. "Quatorzains" are fourteen-line poems in iambic pentameter with elaborate rhyme schemes.

However, Chaucer's seven-line rhyme royal stanza also survived in the 16th century. Shakespeare used it in *The Rape of Lucrece*, for example. An innovation was Spenser's nine-line stanza, called the Spenserian stanza, as used in *The Faerie Queene*.

As to themes, some of the darkness of the previous period can still be seen in some Elizabethan literature, for example, Shakespeare's Richard II (III.ii152-70). At the same time, a spirit of joy, gaiety, innocence, and lightheartedness can be seen in much of the most popular literature, and pastoral themes became popular. The theme of the burning desire for conquest and achievement was also significant in Elizabethan thought.

Some important writers of the Elizabethan age:
Sir Thomas More (1478-1535)
Sir Thomas Wyatt the Elder (1503-1542)
Sir Philip Sidney (1554-1586)
Edmund Spenser (1552-1599)
Sir Walter Raleigh (1552-1618)
John Lyly (1554-1606)
George Peele (1556-1596)
Christopher Marlowe (1564-1593)
William Shakespeare (1564-1616)

The Industrial Revolution in England began with the development of the steam engine. However, the steam engine was only one component of the major technological, socioeconomic, and cultural innovations of the early 19th century that began in Britain and spread throughout the world. An economy based on manual labor was replaced by one dominated by industry and the manufacture of machinery. The textile industries also underwent very rapid growth and change. Canals were being built, roads were improving, and railways were being constructed.

Steam power (fueled primarily by coal) and powered machinery (primarily in the manufacture of textiles) drove the remarkable amplification of production capacity. All-metal machine tools had entered the picture by 1820 making it possible to produce more machines.

The date of the Industrial Revolution varies according to how it is viewed. Some say that it broke out in the 1780s and wasn't fully perceived until the 1830s or 1840s. Others maintain that the beginning was earlier, about 1760 and began to manifest visible changes by 1830. The effects spread through western Europe and North America throughout the 19th century, eventually affecting all major countries of the world. The impact on society has been compared to the period when agriculture began to develop and the nomadic lifestyle was abandoned.

The first Industrial Revolution was followed immediately by the Second Industrial Revolution around 1850 when the progress in technology and world economy gained momentum with the introduction of steam-powered ships and railways and eventually the internal combustion engine and electrical power generation.

In terms of what was going on socially, the most noticeable effect was the development of a middle class of industrialists and businessmen and a decline in the landed class of nobility and gentry. While working people had more opportunities for employment in the new mills and factories, working conditions were often less than desirable. Exploiting children for labor wasn't new—it had always existed—but it was more apparent and perhaps more egregious as the need for cheap labor increased. In England, laws regarding employment of children began to be developed in 1833. Another effect of industrialization was the enormous shift from hand-produced goods to machine-produced ones and the loss of jobs among weavers and others, which resulted in violence against the factories and machinery beginning in about 1811.

Eventually, the British government took measures to protect industry. Another effect was the organization of labor. Because laborers were now working together in factories, mines, and mills, they were better able to organize to gain advantages they felt they deserved. Conditions were bad enough in these workplaces that the energy to bring about change was significant and eventually trade unions emerged. Laborers learned quickly to use the weapon of the strike to get what they wanted. The strikes were often violent and while the managers usually gave in to most of the demands made by strikers, the animosity between management and labor was endemic.

The mass migration of rural families into urban areas also resulted in poor living conditions, long work hours, extensive use of children for labor, and a polluted atmosphere.

Another effect of industrialization of society was the separation of husband and wife. One person stayed at home and looked after the home and family and the other went off to work, a very different configuration from an agriculture-based economy where the entire family was usually involved in making a living. Eventually, gender roles began to be defined by the new configuration of labor in this new world order.

The application of industrial processes to printing brought about a great expansion in newspaper and popular book publishing. This, in turn, was followed by rapid increases in literacy and eventually in demands for mass political participation.

Romanticism, the literary, intellectual, and artistic movement that occurred along with the Industrial Movement was actually a response to the increasing mechanization of society, an artistic hostility to what was taking over the world. Romanticism stressed the importance of nature in art and language in contrast to the monstrous machines and factories. Blake called them the "dark, satanic mills" in his poem, "And Did Those Feet in Ancient Time."

This movement followed on the heels of the Enlightenment period and was, at least in part, a reaction to the aristocratic and political norms of the previous period. Romanticism is sometimes called the Counter-Enlightenment. It stressed strong emotion, made individual imagination the critical authority, and overturned previous social conventions. Nature was important to the Romanticists and it elevated the achievements of misunderstood heroic individuals and artists who participated in altering society.

Some Romantic Writers:
Johann Wolfgang von Goethe
Walter Scott
Ludwig Tieck
E. T. A. Hoffman
William Wordsworth
Samuel Taylor Coleridge
William Blake
Victor Hugo
Alexander Pushkin
Lord Byron
Washington Irving
James Fenimore Cooper
Henry Wadsworth Longfellow
Edgar Allen Poe
Emily Dickinson
John Keats
Percy Bysshe Shelley

World War I, also known as The First World War, the Great War, and The War to End All Wars raged from July 1914 to the final Armistice on November 11, 1918. It was a world conflict between the Allied Powers led by Great Britain, France, Russia, and the United States (after 1917) and The Central Powers, led by the German Empire, the Austro-Hungarian Empire, and the Ottoman Empire. It brought down four great empires: The Austo-Hungarian, German, Ottoman, and Russian. It reconfigured European and Middle Eastern maps.

More than nine million soldiers died on the various battlefields and nearly that many more in the participating countries' home fronts thanks to food shortages and genocide committed under the cover of various civil wars and internal conflicts. However, more people died of the worldwide influenza outbreak at the end of the war and shortly after than died in the hostilities.

The unsanitary conditions engendered by the war, severe overcrowding in barracks, wartime propaganda interfering with public health warnings, and migration of so many soldiers around the world contributed to causing the outbreak to become a pandemic.

The precipitating event of World War I was the June 28, 1914, assassination in Sarajevo of Archduke Franz Ferdinand, heir to the Austrian throne. Gavrilo Princip, a member of a group called Young Bosnia, whose aim included the unification of the South Slavs and independence from Austria, was the assassin. However, the real reasons for the war are still being debated. In the late '20s and early '30s people felt that the war was an accident that precipitated events that simply got out of control. This was used as a major argument for the organization of the League of Nations to prevent such a thing from happening in the future.

At the same time, Germany, France, and Russia were involved in war plans that created an atmosphere where generals and planning staffs were anxious the take the initiatives and make their careers. Once mobilization orders were issued, there was no turning back. Communications problems in 1914 also played a role. Telegraphy and ambassadors were the primary forms of communication, which accounted for disastrous delays from hours to even days.

President Wilson blamed the war on militarism. He felt that aristocrats and military elites had too much control in Germany, Russia, and Austria, and that the war was a consequence of their desire for military power and disdain for democracy. Lenin famously asserted that the worldwide system of imperialism was responsible for the war This argument proved persuasive in the immediate wake of the war and was a precipitating factor in the rise of Marxism and Communism.

A proposal to Mexico to join the war against the Allies was exposed in February, 1917, bringing war closer to America. Further U-boat (German submarines) attacks on American merchant ships led to Wilson's request that Congress declare war on Germany, which it did on April 6, 1917. Following the U.S. declaration of war, countries in the Western Hemisphere, Cuba, Panama, Haiti, Brazil, Guatemala, Nicaragua, Costa Rica, and Honduras declared war on Germany. The Dominican Republic, Peru, Uruguay, and Ecuador contented themselves with the severance of relations. The entry of the United States into the war was the turning point. It's doubtful that the Allies would have won without the infusion of money, supplies, armament, and troops from the Western Hemisphere, primarily from the United States.

The experiences of the war led to a sort of collective national trauma afterwards for all the participating countries. The optimism of the 1900s was entirely gone and those who fought in the war became what is known as "the Lost Generation" because they never fully recovered from their experiences. For the next few years memorials continued to be erected in thousands of European villages and towns.

Certainly a sense of disillusionment and cynicism became pronounced, and nihilism became popular. The world had never before witnessed such devastation, and the depiction in newspapers and on movie screens made the horrors more personal. War has always spawned creative bursts, and this one was no exception. Poetry, stories, and movies proliferated. In fact, it's still a fertile subject for art of all kinds, particularly literature and movies. In 2006, a young director by the name of Paul Gross created, directed, and starred in *Passchendaele* based on the stories told him by his grandfather, who was haunted all his life by his killing of a young German soldier in this War to End All Wars.

Some literature based on World War I:

"The Soldier," poem by Rupert Brooke
Goodbye to All That, autobiography by Robert Graves
"Anthem for Doomed Youth" and "Strange Meeting," poems by Wilfred Owen, published posthumously by Siegfried Sassoon in 1918
"In Flanders Fields," poem by John McCrae
Three Soldiers, novel by John Dos Passos
Journey's End, play by R. C. Sherriff
All Quiet on the Western Front, novel by Erich Maria Remarque
Death of a Hero, novel by Richard Aldington
A Farewell to Arms, novel by Ernest Hemingway
Memoirs of an Infantry Officer, novel by Siegfried Sassoon
Sergeant York, movie directed by Howard Hawks

The dissolution of the British empire, the most extensive empire in world history and for a time the foremost global power, began in 1867 with its transformation into the modern Commonwealth. Dominion status was granted to the self-governing colonies of Canada in 1867, to Australia in 1902, to New Zealand in 1907, to Newfoundland in 1907, and to the newly-created Union of South Africa in 1910. Leaders of the new states joined with British statesmen in periodic Colonial Conferences, the first of which was held in London in 1887.

The foreign relations of the Dominions were conducted through the Foreign Office of the United Kingdom. Although Canada created a Department of External Affairs in 1909, diplomatic relations with other governments continued to be channeled through the Governors-General, Dominion High Commissioners in London, and British legations abroad. Britain's declaration of war in World War I applied to all of the Dominions, for instance. Even so, the Dominions had substantial freedom in their adoption of foreign policy where this did not explicitly conflict with British interests.

The original arrangement of a single imperial military and naval structure became unsustainable as Britain faced new commitments in Europe and the challenge of an emerging German High Seas fleet after 1900, so in 1919 it was decided that the Dominions should have their own navies, reversing a previous agreement that the then Australasian colonies should contribute to the Royal Navy in return for the permanent stationing of a squadron in the region.

The settlement at the end of World War I gave Britain control of Palestine and Iraq after the collapse of the Ottoman Empire in the Middle East. It also ceded control of the former German colonies of Tanganyika, Southwest Africa (now Namibia), and New Guinea. British zones of occupation in Germany after the war were not considered part of the Empire

Although the Allies won the war and Britain's rule expanded into new areas, the heavy costs of the war made it less and less feasible to maintain the vast empire. Economic losses as well as human losses put increasing pressure on the Empire to give up its far-flung imperial posts in Asia and the African colonies. At the same time, nationalist sentiment was growing in both old and new Imperial territories fueled partly by their troops' contributions to the war and the anger of many non-white ex-servicemen at the racial discrimination they had encountered during their service.

Enthusiasm for the Empire coupled with an increase in nationalism in many of the Dominions came together to create resistance to Britain's intention to take military action against Turkey in 1922.

Full Dominion independence was formalized in the 1926 Balfour Declaration and the 1931 State of Westminster. Each Dominion was henceforth to be equal in status to Britain herself, free of British legislative interference, and autonomous in international relations. The Dominions section created with the Colonial Office in 1907 was upgraded in 1925 to a separate Dominions Office and given its own Secretary of State in 1930.

Canada led the way, becoming the first Dominion to conclude an international treaty entirely independently (1923) and obtaining the appointment (1928) of a British High Commissioner in Ottawa, thereby separating the administrative and diplomatic functions of the Governor-General and ending the latter's anomalous role as the representative of the head of state and of the British Government. Canada's first permanent diplomatic mission to a foreign country opened in Washington, D.C. in 1927. Australia followed in 1940.

Egypt, formally independent by 1922 but bound to Britain by treaty until 1936 and under partial occupation until 1956, similarly severed all constitutional links with Britain. Iraq, which became a British Protectorate in 1922, also gained complete independence in 1932.

In 1948, Ireland became a republic, fully independent from the United Kingdom, and withdrew from the Commonwealth. Ireland's constitution claimed the six counties of Northern Ireland as a part of the Republic of Ireland until 1998. The issue over whether Northern Ireland should remain in the United Kingdom or join the Republic of Ireland has divided Northern Ireland's people and led to a long and bloody conflict known as the Troubles. However, the Good Friday Agreement of 1998 brought about a ceasefire between most of the major organizations on both sides, creating hope for a peaceful resolution.

The rise of anti-colonial nationalist movements in the subject territories and the changing economic situation of the world in the first half of the 20th century challenged an imperial power now increasingly preoccupied with issues nearer home. The Empire's end began with the onset of the Second World War when a deal was reached between the British government and the Indian independence movement whereby India would cooperate and remain loyal during the war but after which they would be granted independence. Following India's lead, nearly all of the other colonies would become independent over the next two decades.

In the Caribbean, Africa, Asia, and the Pacific, post-war decolonization was achieved with almost unseemly haste in the face of increasingly powerful nationalist movements, and Britain rarely fought to retain any territory.

Some Representative Literature:
Heart of Darkness, novel by Joseph Conrad
Passage to India novel by E. M. Forster
"Gunga Din," poem by Rudyard Kipling

Ancient Literature

Between 7000 B.C. and 3000 B.C. critical events occurred that not only led to the invention of writing, thus making possible the emergence of literature, but to the development of human civilization, as well. These critical events included the domestication of animals, the development of agriculture, and the establishment of an agricultural surplus.

These three events allowed the small, nomadic groups of hunters and gathers who had up until then existed in pockets all over the world to evolve into larger, stationary communities. The first of these communities to develop was in an area in the Middle East called Mesopotamia, meaning "Land Between two Rivers," with the two rivers being the Tigris and the Euphrates. This ancestor to civilization as we know it was call Sumer, and the people who lived there and who were to create the wheel and the first written language where the Sumerians.

Perhaps the reason the Sumerians were the first to create so much of what is fundamental to civilization goes back to their unsurpassed ability to create an agricultural surplus. With their position between two flowing rivers, the Sumerians developed an extensive irrigation system, which allowed them to create an abundant surplus. This surplus meant greater economic stability, security, and the ability to support a much larger population within the walls of their city.

Hand in hand with a growing population was the need for governance and specialization. Artisans, governors, builders, regulators, and merchants were needed, as well as priests and temples for the flourishing religion. Keeping track of all this activity required the development of some kind of record keeping. At first, pictographs, or images directly representing concrete objects, were etched into soft clay tablets and allowed to dry.

As time went on, the demand on the record keepers grew from recording how many sacks of barley a farmer brought to the temple to describing in great detail and enthusiasm the exploits of the kings. Thus, with the evolution of the city-state and then the nation, pictographs quickly became insufficient to meet the needs of this new societal structure we have called civilization. Eventually the Sumerians developed symbols not only to represent concrete items such as corn and cattle, but such abstract qualities as courage and love.

http://www.crystalinks.com/sumerart.html (for photo)

Competency 6.0   **Recognizing various strategic approaches to and elements of teaching reading and textual interpretation.**

The question to be asked first when approaching a reading task is what is my objective? What do I want to achieve from this reading? How will I use the information I gain from this reading? Do I only need to grasp the gist of the piece? Do I need to know the line of reasoning—not only the thesis but the subpoints? Will I be reporting important and significant details orally or in a written document?

A written document can be expected to have a thesis—either expressed or derived. To discover the thesis, the reader needs to ask what point the writer intended to make? The writing can also be expected to be organized in some logical way and to have subpoints that support or establish that the thesis is valid. It is also reasonable to expect that there will be details or examples that will support the subpoints. Knowing this, the reader can make a decision about reading techniques required for the purpose that has already been established.

If the reader only needs to know the gist of a written document, speed-reading skimming techniques may be sufficient by using the forefinger, moving the eyes down the page, picking up the important statements in each paragraph and deducing mentally that this piece is about such-and-such.

If the reader needs to get a little better grasp of how the writer achieved his/her purpose in the document, a quick and cursory glance—a skimming—of each paragraph will yield what the subpoints are, the topic sentences of the paragraphs, and how the thesis is developed, yielding a greater understanding of the author's purpose and method of development.

In-depth reading requires the scrutiny of each phrase and sentence with care, looking for the thesis first of all and then the topic sentences in the paragraphs that provide the development of the thesis, also looking for connections such as transitional devices that provide clues to the direction the reasoning is taking.

Sometimes rereading is necessary in order to make use of a piece of writing for an oral or written report upon a document. If this is the purpose of reading it, the first reading should provide a map for the rereading or second reading. The second time through should follow this map, and those points that are going to be used in a report or analysis will be focused upon on more carefully. Some new understandings may occur in this rereading, and it may become apparent that the "map" that was derived from the first reading will need to be adjusted. If this rereading is for the purpose of writing an analysis or using material for a report, either highlighting or note-taking is advisable.

To *interpret* means essentially to read with understanding and appreciation. It is not as daunting as it is made out to be. Simple techniques for interpreting literature are as follows:

- **Context:** This includes the author's feelings, beliefs, past experiences, goals, needs, and physical environment. Incorporate an understanding of how these elements may have affected the writing to enrich an interpretation of it.
- **Symbols:** Also referred to as a sign, a symbol designates something which stands for something else. In most cases, it is standing for something that has a deeper meaning than its literal denotation. Symbols can have personal, cultural, or universal associations. Use an understanding of symbols to unearth a meaning the author might have intended but not expressed, or even something the author never intended at all.
- **Questions:** Asking questions, such as "How would I react in this situation?" may shed further light on how you feel about the work.

Reading emphasis in middle school

Reading for comprehension of factual material - content area textbooks, reference books, and newspapers - is closely related to study strategies in the middle/junior high. Organized study models, such as the SQ3R method, a technique that makes it possible and feasible to learn the content of even large amounts of text (Survey, Question, Read, Recite, and Review Studying), teach students to locate main ideas and supporting details, to recognize sequential order, to distinguish fact from opinion, and to determine cause/ effect relationships.

Strategies

1. Teacher-guided activities that require students to organize and to summarize information based on the author's explicit intent are pertinent strategies in middle grades. Evaluation techniques include oral and written responses to standardized or teacher-made worksheets.

2. Reading of fiction introduces and reinforces skills in inferring meaning from narration and description. Teaching-guided activities in the process of reading for meaning should be followed by cooperative planning of the skills to be studied and of the selection of reading resources. Many printed reading for comprehension instruments as well as individualized computer software programs exist to monitor the progress of acquiring comprehension skills.

3. Older middle school students should be given opportunities for more student-centered activities - individual and collaborative selection of reading choices based on student interest, small group discussions of selected works, and greater written expression. Evaluation techniques include teacher monitoring and observation of discussions and written work samples.

4. Certain students may begin some fundamental critical interpretation - recognizing fallacious reasoning in news media, examining the accuracy of news reports and advertising, explaining their reasons for preferring one author's writing to another's. Development of these skills may require a more learning-centered approach in which the teacher identifies a number of objectives and suggested resources from which the student may choose his course of study. Self-evaluation through a reading diary should be stressed. Teacher and peer evaluation of creative projects resulting from such study is encouraged.

5. Reading aloud before the entire class as a formal means of teacher evaluation should be phased out in favor of one-to-one tutoring or peer-assisted reading. Occasional sharing of favored selections by both teacher and willing students is a good oral interpretation basic.

Reading emphasis in high school

Students in high school literature classes should focus on interpretive and critical reading. Teachers should guide the study of the elements of inferential (interpretive) reading - drawing conclusions, predicting outcomes, and recognizing examples of specific genre characteristics, for example - and critical reading to judge the quality of the writer's work against recognized standards. At this level students should understand the skills of language and reading that they are expected to master and be able to evaluate their own progress.

Strategies

1. The teacher becomes more facilitator than instructor - helping the student to make a diagnosis of his own strengths and weaknesses, keeping a record of progress, and interacting with other students and the teacher in practicing skills.

2. Despite the requisites and prerequisites of most literature courses, students should be encouraged to pursue independent study and enrichment reading.

3. Ample opportunities should be provided for oral interpretation of literature, special projects in creative dramatics, writing for publication in school literary magazines or newspapers, and speech/debate activities. A student portfolio provides for teacher and peer evaluation.

Tracing an idea through a passage goes much better if a strategy if developed for doing so. Good readers usually have these strategies even though they might not be aware of them. A good way to start is by looking for words or phrases that appear more than once or even many times. Following those key words and phrases will make it possible to observe a picture of the idea as it appears in the piece of writing.

Also, most published writers avoid repetition. For that reason, key words in a piece of writing will probably have several synonyms or even more. In strategizing for reading materials for comprehension, this device can be very useful. By focusing on the key words and thinking about their meanings, following the idea will be expedited.

Transitional words and phrases are designed to lead the reader forward and through a piece of writing. Such words as therefore, however, even so, although, etc. are clues to connections between one part of the writing and another and the nature of the connection. Phrases sometimes substitute for words. Some examples, as a matter of fact, in the long run, looking back, etc.

Identification of common morphemes, prefixes, and suffixes

This aspect of vocabulary development is to help students look for structural elements within words which they can use independently to help them determine meaning.

The terms listed below are generally recognized as the key structural analysis components.

Root words: A root word is a word from which another word is developed. The second word can be said to have its "root" in the first. This structural component nicely lends itself to a tree with roots illustration which can concretize the meaning for students. Students may also want to literally construct root words using cardboard trees and/or actual roots from plants to create word family models. This is a lovely way to help students own their root words.

Base words: A stand-alone linguistic unit which can not be deconstructed or broken down into smaller words. For example, in the word "re-tell," the base word is "tell."

Contractions: These are shortened forms of two words in which a letter or letters have been deleted. These deleted letter have been replaced by an apostrophe.

Prefixes: These are beginning units of meaning which can be added (the vocabulary word for this type of structural adding is "affixed") to a base word or root word. They can not stand alone. They are also sometimes known as "bound morphemes," meaning that they can not stand alone as a base word.

Suffixes: These are ending units of meaning which can be "affixed" or added on to the ends of root or base words. Suffixes transform the original meanings of base and root words. Like prefixes, they are also known as "bound morphemes," because they can not stand alone as words.

Compound words: Occur when two or more base words are connected to form a new word. The meaning of the new word is in some way connected with that of the base word.

Inflectional endings: Are types are suffixes that impart a new meaning to the base or root word. These endings in particular change the gender, number, tense, or form of the base or root words. Just like other suffixes, these are also termed "bound morphemes."

Learning approach

Early theories of language development were formulated from learning theory research. The assumption was that language development evolved from learning the rules of language structures and applying them through imitation and reinforcement. This approach also assumed that language, cognitive, and social developments were independent of each other. Thus, children were expected to learn language from patterning after adults who spoke and wrote Standard English. No allowance was made for communication through child jargon, idiomatic expressions, or grammatical and mechanical errors resulting from too strict adherence to the rules of inflection (*childs* instead of *children*) or conjugation (*runned* instead of *ran*). No association was made between physical and operational development and language mastery.

Linguistic approach

Studies spearheaded by Noam Chomsky in the 1950s formulated the theory that language ability is innate and develops through natural human maturation as environmental stimuli trigger acquisition of syntactical structures appropriate to each exposure level. The assumption of a hierarchy of syntax downplayed the significance of semantics. Because of the complexity of syntax and the relative speed with which children acquire language, linguists attributed language development to biological rather than cognitive or social influences.

Cognitive approach

Researchers in the 1970s proposed that language knowledge derives from both syntactic and semantic structures. Drawing on the studies of Piaget and other cognitive learning theorists (see Skill 4.7), supporters of the cognitive approach maintained that children acquire knowledge of linguistic structures after they have acquired the cognitive structures necessary to process language. For example, joining words for specific meaning necessitates sensory motor intelligence. The child must be able to coordinate movement and recognize objects before she can identify words to name the objects or word groups to describe the actions performed with those objects.

Adolescents must have developed the mental abilities for <u>organizing concepts as well as concrete operations</u>, <u>predicting outcomes</u>, and <u>theorizing</u> before they can assimilate and verbalize complex sentence structures, choose vocabulary for particular nuances of meaning, and examine semantic structures for tone and manipulative effect.

Sociocognitive approach

Other theorists in the 1970s proposed that language development results from sociolinguistic competence. Language, cognitive, and social knowledge are interactive elements of total human development. Emphasis on verbal communication as the medium for language expression resulted in the inclusion of speech activities in most language arts curricula.

Unlike previous approaches, the sociocognitive allowed that determining the appropriateness of language in given situations for specific listeners is as important as understanding semantic and syntactic structures. By engaging in conversation, children at all stages of development have opportunities to test their language skills, receive feedback, and make modifications. As a social activity, conversation is as structured by social order as grammar is structured by the rules of syntax. Conversation satisfies the learner's need to be heard and understood and to influence others. Thus, his choices of vocabulary, tone, and content are dictated by his ability to assess the language knowledge of his listeners. He is constantly applying his cognitive skills to using language in a social interaction. If the capacity to acquire language is inborn, without an environment in which to practice language, a child would not pass beyond grunts and gestures as did primitive man.

Of course, the varying degrees of environmental stimuli to which children are exposed at all age levels creates a slower or faster development of language. Some children are prepared to articulate concepts and recognize symbolism by the time they enter fifth grade because they have been exposed to challenging reading and conversations with well-spoken adults at home or in their social groups. Others are still trying to master the sight recognition skills and are not yet ready to combine words in complex patterns.

Concerns for the teacher

Because teachers must, by virtue of tradition and the dictates of the curriculum, teach grammar, usage, and writing as well as reading and later literature, the problem becomes when to teach what to whom. The profusion of approaches to teaching grammar alone are mind-boggling. In the universities, we learn about transformational grammar, stratificational grammar, sectoral grammar, etc. But in practice, most teachers, supported by presentations in textbooks and by the methods they learned themselves, keep coming back to the same traditional prescriptive approach - read and imitate - or structural approach - learn the parts of speech, the parts of sentence, punctuation rules, sentence patterns. After enough of the terminology and rules are stored in the brain, then we learn to write and speak. For some educators, the best solution is the worst - don't teach grammar at all.

The same problems occur in teaching usage. How much can we demand students communicate in only Standard English? Different schools of thought suggest that a study of dialect and idiom and recognition of various jargons is a vital part of language development. Social pressures, especially on students in middle and junior high schools, to be accepted within their peer groups and to speak the non-standard language spoken outside the school make adolescents resistant to the corrective, remedial approach. In many communities where the immigrant populations are high, new words are entering English from other languages even as words and expressions that were common when we were children have become rare or obsolete.

Regardless of differences of opinion concerning language development, it is safe to say that a language arts teacher will be most effective using the styles and approaches with which she is most comfortable. And, if she subscribes to a student-centered approach, she may find that the students have a lot to teach her and each other. Moffett and Wagner in the Fourth Edition of *Student-centered Language Arts K-12* stress the three I's: individualization, interaction, and integration. Essentially, they are supporting the socio-cognitive approach to language development. By providing an opportunity for the student to select his own activities and resources, his instruction is individualized. By centering on and teaching each other, students are interactive. Finally, by allowing students to synthesize a variety of knowledge structures, they integrate them. The teacher's role becomes that of a facilitator.

Benefits of the socio-cognitive approach

This approach has tended to guide the whole language movement, currently in fashion. Most basal readers utilize an integrated, cross-curricular approach to successful grammar, language, and usage. Reinforcement becomes an intradepartmental responsibility. Language incorporates diction and terminology across the curriculum. Standard usage is encouraged and supported by both the core classroom textbooks and current software for technology. Teachers need to acquaint themselves with the computer capabilities in their school district and at their individual school sites. Advances in new technologies require the teacher to familiarize herself with programs that would serve her students' needs. Students respond enthusiastically to technology. Several highly effective programs are available in various formats to assist students with initial instruction or remediation. Grammar texts, such as the Warriner's series, employ various methods to reach individual learning styles. The school library media center should become a focal point for individual exploration.

Second Language Learners

Students who are raised in homes where English is not the first language and/or where standard English is not spoken, may have difficulty with hearing the difference between similar sounding words like "send" and "sent."

Any student who is not in an environment where English phonology operates, may have difficulty perceiving and demonstrating the differences between English language phonemes. If students can not hear the difference between words that "sound the same" like "grow" and "glow," they will be confused when these words appear in a print context. This confusion will of course, sadly, impact their comprehension.

Considerations for teaching to English Language Learners include recognition by the teacher that what works for the English language speaking student from an English language speaking family, does not necessarily work in other languages.

Research recommends that ELL students learn to read initially in their first language. It has been found that a priority for ELL should be learning to speak English before being taught to read English. Research supports oral language development, since it lays the foundation for phonological awareness.

Children who learn to read on schedule and who are avid readers have been seen to have superior vocabularies compared to other children their age. The reason for this is that in order to understand what they read, they often must determine the meaning for a word based on its context. Children who constantly turn to a dictionary for the meaning of a word they don't know will not have this advantage.

This is an important clue for providing students the kinds of exercises and helps they need in order to develop their vocabularies. Learning vocabulary lists is useful, of course, but much less efficient than exercises in determining meaning on the basis of context. It requires an entirely different kind of thinking and learning. Poetry is also useful for developing vocabulary exercises for children, especially rhymed poetry, where the pronunciation of a term may be deduced by what the poet intended for it to rhyme with. In some poets of earlier periods, the teacher may need to intervene because some of the words that would have rhymed when the poem was written do not rhyme in today's English. Even so, this is a good opportunity to help children understand some of the important principles about their constantly-changing language.

Another good exercise for developing vocabulary is the crossword puzzle. A child's ability to think in terms of analogy is a step upward toward mature language understanding and use. The teacher may construct crossword puzzles using items from the class such as students' names or the terms from their literature or language lessons.

DOMAIN II. LANGUAGE AND LINGUISTICS

Competency 7.0 Understanding elements of traditional grammar.

Sentence completeness

Avoid fragments and run-on sentences. Recognition of sentence elements necessary to make a complete thought, proper use of independent and dependent clauses (see *Use correct coordination and subordination*), and proper punctuation will correct such errors.

Sentence structure

Recognize simple, compound, complex, and compound-complex sentences. Use dependent (subordinate) and independent clauses correctly to create these sentence structures.

Simple	Joyce wrote a letter.
Compound	Joyce wrote a letter, and Dot drew a picture.
Complex	While Joyce wrote a letter, Dot drew a picture.
Compound/Complex	When Mother asked the girls to demonstrate their new-found skills, Joyce wrote a letter, and Dot drew a picture.

Note: Do **not** confuse compound sentence elements with compound sentences.

   Simple sentence with compound subject
      Joyce and Dot wrote letters.
      The girl in row three and the boy next to her were passing notes across the aisle.

   Simple sentence with compound predicate
      Joyce wrote letters and drew pictures.
      The captain of the high school debate team graduated with honors and studied broadcast journalism in college.

   Simple sentence with compound object of preposition
      Coleen graded the students' essays for style and mechanical accuracy.

Parallelism

Recognize parallel structures using phrases (prepositional, gerund, participial, and infinitive) and omissions from sentences that create the lack of parallelism.

Prepositional phrase/single modifier

Incorrect: Coleen ate the ice cream with enthusiasm and hurriedly.
Correct: Coleen ate the ice cream with enthusiasm and in a hurry.
Correct: Coleen ate the ice cream enthusiastically and hurriedly.

Participial phrase/infinitive phrase

Incorrect: After hiking for hours and to sweat profusely, Joe sat down to rest and drinking water.
Correct: After hiking for hours and sweating profusely, Joe sat down to rest and drink water.

Recognition of dangling modifiers

Dangling phrases are attached to sentence parts in such a way they create ambiguity and incorrectness of meaning.

Participial phrase

Incorrect: Hanging from her skirt, Dot tugged at a loose thread.
Correct: Dot tugged at a loose thread hanging from her skirt.

Incorrect: Relaxing in the bathtub, the telephone rang.
Correct: While I was relaxing in the bathtub, the telephone rang.

Infinitive phrase

Incorrect: To improve his behavior, the dean warned Fred.
Correct: The dean warned Fred to improve his behavior.

Prepositional phrase

Incorrect: On the floor, Father saw the dog eating table scraps.
Correct: Father saw the dog eating table scraps on the floor.

Recognition of syntactical redundancy or omission

These errors occur when superfluous words have been added to a sentence or key words have been omitted from a sentence.

Redundancy
Incorrect: Joyce made sure that when her plane arrived that she retrieved all of her luggage.
Correct: Joyce made sure that when her plane arrived she retrieved all of her luggage.

Incorrect: He was a mere skeleton of his former self.
Correct: He was a skeleton of his former self.

Omission

Incorrect: Dot opened her book, recited her textbook, and answered the teacher's subsequent question.
Correct: Dot opened her book, recited from the textbook, and answered the teacher's subsequent question.

Avoidance of double negatives

This error occurs from positioning two negatives that, in fact, cancel each other in meaning.

Incorrect: Harold couldn't care less whether he passes this class.
Correct: Harold could care less whether he passes this class.

Incorrect: Dot didn't have no double negatives in her paper.
Correct: Dot didn't have any double negatives in her paper.

Types of Clauses

Clauses are connected word groups that are composed of *at least* one subject and one verb. (A subject is the doer of an action or the element that is being joined. A verb conveys either the action or the link.)

Students are waiting for the start of the assembly.
Subject   Verb

At the end of the play, students wait for the curtain to come down.
           Subject Verb

Clauses can be independent or dependent.

Independent clauses can stand alone or can be joined to other clauses.

Independent clause	for	
	and	
	nor	
Independent clause,	but	Independent clause
	or	
	yet	
	so	

Independent clause   ;   Independent clause

Dependent clause   ,   Independent clause

Independent clause   Dependent clause

Dependent clauses, by definition, contain at least one subject and one verb. However, they cannot stand alone as a complete sentence. They are structurally dependent on the main clause.

There are two types of dependent clauses: (1) those with a subordinating conjunction, and (2) those with a relative pronoun

Sample coordinating conjunctions:
Although
When
If
Unless
Because

Unless a cure is discovered, many more people will die of the disease.
      Dependent clause   +   Independent clause

Sample relative pronouns:
Who
Whom
Which
That

The White House has an official website, which contains press releases, news updates, and biographies of the President and Vice-President.
(Independent clause + relative pronoun + relative dependent clause)

Misplaced and Dangling Modifiers

Particular phrases that are not placed near the one word they modify often result in misplaced modifiers. Particular phrases that do not relate to the subject being modified result in dangling modifiers.

Error: Weighing the options carefully, a decision was made regarding the punishment of the convicted murderer.

Problem: Who is weighing the options? No one capable of weighing is named in the sentence; thus, the participle phrase weighing the options carefully dangles. This problem can be corrected by adding a subject of the sentence capable of doing the action.

Correction: Weighing the options carefully, the judge made a decision regarding the punishment of the convicted murderer.

Error: Returning to my favorite watering hole, brought back many fond memories.

Problem: The person who returned is never indicated, and the participle phrase dangles. This problem can be corrected by creating a dependent clause from the modifying phrase.

Correction: When I returned to my favorite watering hole, many fond memories came back to me.

Error: One damaged house stood only to remind townspeople of the hurricane.

Problem: The placement of the misplaced modifier *only* suggests that the sole reason the house remained was to serve as a reminder. The faulty modifier creates ambiguity.

Correction: Only one damaged house stood, reminding townspeople of the hurricane.

Spelling

Concentration in this section will be on spelling plurals and possessives. The multiplicity and complexity of spelling rules based on phonics, letter doubling, and exceptions to rules - not mastered by adulthood - should be replaced by a good dictionary. As spelling mastery is also difficult for adolescents, our recommendation is the same. Learning the use of a dictionary and thesaurus will be a more rewarding use of time.

Most plurals of nouns that end in hard consonants or hard consonant sounds followed by a silent *e* are made by adding *s*. Some words ending in vowels only add *s*.

      fingers, numerals, banks, bugs, riots, homes, gates, radios, bananas

Nouns that end in soft consonant sounds *s, j, x, z, ch,* and *sh*, add *es*. Some nouns ending in *o* add es.

      dresses, waxes, churches, brushes, tomatoes, potatoes

Nouns ending in *y* preceded by a vowel just add *s*.

      boys, alleys

Nouns ending in *y* preceded by a consonant change the *y* to *i* and add *es*.

> babies, corollaries, frugalities, poppies

Some nouns plurals are formed irregularly or remain the same.

> sheep, deer, children, leaves, oxen

Some nouns derived from foreign words, especially Latin, may make their plurals in two different ways - one of them Anglicized. Sometimes, the meanings are the same; other times, the two plurals are used in slightly different contexts. It is always wise to consult the dictionary.

> appendices, appendixes　　criterion, criteria
> indexes, indices　　　　　crisis, crises

Make the plurals of closed (solid) compound words in the usual way except for words ending in *ful* which make their plurals on the root word.

> timelines, hairpins, cupsful

Make the plurals of open or hyphenated compounds by adding the change in inflection to the word that changes in number.

> fathers-in-law, courts-martial, masters of art, doctors of medicine

Make the plurals of letters, numbers, and abbreviations by adding *s*.

fives and tens, IBMs, 1990s, *p*s and *q*s (Note that letters are italicized.)

Capitalization

Capitalize all proper names of persons (including specific organizations or agencies of government); places (countries, states, cities, parks, and specific geographical areas); and things (political parties, structures, historical and cultural terms, and calendar and time designations); and religious terms (any deity, revered person or group, sacred writings).

> Percy Bysshe Shelley, Argentina, Mount Rainier National Park, Grand Canyon, League of Nations, the Sears Tower, Birmingham, Lyric Theater, Americans, Midwesterners, Democrats, Renaissance, Boy Scouts of America, Easter, God, Bible, Dead Sea Scrolls, Koran

Capitalize proper adjectives and titles used with proper names.

California gold rush, President John Adams, French fries, Homeric epic, Romanesque architecture, Senator John Glenn

Note: Some words that represent titles and offices are not capitalized unless used with a proper name.

Capitalized	Not Capitalized
Congressman McKay	the congressman from Florida
Commander Alger	commander of the Pacific Fleet
Queen Elizabeth	the queen of England

Capitalize all main words in titles of works of literature, art, and music. (See "Using Italics" in the Punctuation section.)

The candidate should be cognizant of proper rules and conventions of punctuation, capitalization, and spelling. Competency exams will generally test the ability to apply the more advanced skills; thus, a limited number of more frustrating rules is presented here. Rules should be applied according to the American style of English, i.e. spelling *theater* instead of *theatre* and placing terminal marks of punctuation almost exclusively within other marks of punctuation.

Punctuation

Using terminal punctuation in relation to quotation marks

In a quoted statement that is either declarative or imperative, place the period inside the closing quotation marks.

"The airplane crashed on the runway during takeoff."

If the quotation is followed by other words in the sentence, place a comma inside the closing quotations marks and a period at the end of the sentence.

"The airplane crashed on the runway during takeoff," said the announcer.

In most instances in which a quoted title or expression occurs at the end of a sentence, the period is placed before either the single or double quotation marks.

"The middle school readers were unprepared to understand Bryant's poem 'Thanatopsis.'"

Early book-length adventure stories like *Don Quixote* and *The Three Musketeers* were known as "picaresque novels."

There is an instance in which the final quotation mark would precede the period - if the content of the sentence were about a speech or quote so that the understanding of the meaning would be confused by the placement of the period.

> The first thing out of his mouth was "Hi, I'm home."
> *but*
> The first line of his speech began "I arrived home to an empty house".

In sentences that are interrogatory or exclamatory, the question mark or exclamation point should be positioned outside the closing quotation marks if the quote itself is a statement or command or cited title.

> Who decided to lead us in the recitation of the "Pledge of Allegiance"?
>
> Why was Tillie shaking as she began her recitation, "Once upon a midnight dreary..."?
>
> I was embarrassed when Mrs. White said, "Your slip is showing"!

In sentences that are declarative but the quotation is a question or an exclamation, place the question mark or exclamation point inside the quotation marks.

> The hall monitor yelled, "Fire! Fire!"
>
> "Fire! Fire!" yelled the hall monitor.
>
> Cory shrieked, "Is there a mouse in the room?" (In this instance, the question supersedes the exclamation.)

Using periods with parentheses or brackets

Place the period inside the parentheses or brackets if they enclose a complete sentence, independent of the other sentences around it.

> Stephen Crane was a confirmed alcohol and drug addict. (He admitted as much to other journalists in Cuba.)

If the parenthetical expression is a statement inserted within another statement, the period in the enclosure is omitted.

> Mark Twain used the character Indian Joe (He also appeared in *The Adventures of Tom Sawyer*) as a foil for Jim in *The Adventures of Huckleberry Finn*.

When enclosed matter comes at the end of a sentence requiring quotation marks, place the period outside the parentheses or brackets.

"The secretary of state consulted with the ambassador [Albright]."

Using commas

Separate two or more coordinate adjectives, modifying the same word and three or more nouns, phrases, or clauses in a list.

Maggie's hair was dull, dirty, and lice-ridden.

Dickens portrayed the Artful Dodger as skillful pickpocket, loyal follower of Fagin, and defendant of Oliver Twist.

Ellen daydreamed about getting out of the rain, taking a shower, and eating a hot dinner.

In Elizabethan England, Ben Johnson wrote comedy, Christopher Marlowe wrote tragedies, and William Shakespeare composed both.

Use commas to separate antithetical or complimentary expressions from the rest of the sentence.

The veterinarian, not his assistant, would perform the delicate surgery.

The more he knew about her, the less he wished he had known.

Randy hopes to, and probably will, get an appointment to the Naval Academy.

His thorough, though esoteric, scientific research could not easily be understood by high school students.

Using double quotation marks with other punctuation

Quotations - whether words, phrases, or clauses - should be punctuated according to the rules of the grammatical function they serve in the sentence.

The works of Shakespeare, "the bard of Avon," have been contested as originating with other authors.

"You'll get my money," the old man warned, "when 'Hell freezes over'."

Sheila cited the passage that began "Four score and seven years ago...." (Note the ellipsis followed by an enclosed period.)

"Old Ironsides" inspired the preservation of the U.S.S. Constitution. Use quotation marks to enclose the titles of shorter works: songs, short poems, short stories, essays, and chapters of books. (See "Using Italics" for punctuating longer titles.)

"The Tell-Tale Heart"   "Casey at the Bat"   "America the Beautiful"

Using semicolons

Use semicolons to separate independent clauses when the second clause is introduced by a transitional adverb. (These clauses may also be written as separate sentences, preferably by placing the adverb within the second sentence.)

The Elizabethans modified the rhyme scheme of the sonnet; thus, it was called the English sonnet.

or

The Elizabethans modified the rhyme scheme of the sonnet. It thus was called the English sonnet.

Use semicolons to separate items in a series that are long and complex or have internal punctuation.

The Italian Renaissance produced masters in the fine arts: Dante Alighieri, author of the *Divine Comedy;* Leonardo da Vinci, painter of *The Last Supper;* and Donatello, sculptor of the *Quattro Coronati*, the four saints.

The leading scorers in the WNBA were Haizhaw Zheng, averaging 23.9 points per game; Lisa Leslie, 22; and Cynthia Cooper, 19.5.

Using colons

Place a colon at the beginning of a list of items. (Note its use in the sentence about Renaissance Italians in the paragraph above.)

The teacher directed us to compare Faulkner's three symbolic novels: *Absalom, Absalom; As I Lay Dying;* and *Light in August*.

Do **not** use a comma if the list is preceded by a verb.

Three of Faulkner's symbolic novels are *Absalom, Absalom; As I Lay Dying,* and *Light in August*.

Using dashes

Place dashes to denote sudden breaks in thought.

> Some periods in literature - the Romantic Age, for example - spanned different time periods in different countries.

Use dashes instead of commas if commas are already used elsewhere in the sentence for amplification or explanation.

> The Fireside Poets included three Brahmans - James Russell Lowell, Henry David Wadsworth, Oliver Wendell Holmes - and John Greenleaf Whittier.

Use italics to punctuate the titles of long works of literature, names of periodical publications, musical scores, works of art and motion picture television, and radio programs. (When unable to write in italics, students should be instructed to underline in their own writing where italics would be appropriate.)

> *The Idylls of the King*   *Hiawatha*   *The Sound and the Fury*
> *Mary Poppins*   *Newsweek*   *The Nutcracker Suite*

Competency 8.0   Understanding various semantic elements.

Slang comes about for many reasons: Amelioration is an important one that results often in euphemisms. Examples are "passed away" for dying; "senior citizens" for old people. Some usages have become so embedded in the language that their sources are long-forgotten. For example, "fame" originally meant rumor. Some words that were originally intended as euphemisms such as "mentally retarded" and "moron" to avoid using "idiot" have themselves become pejorative.

Slang is lower in prestige than Standard English; tends to first appear in the language of groups with low status; is often taboo and unlikely to be used by people of high status; tends to displace conventional terms, either as a shorthand or as a defense against perceptions associated with the conventional term.

Informal and formal language is a distinction made on the basis of the occasion as well as the audience. At a "formal" occasion, for example, a meeting of executives or of government officials, even conversational exchanges are likely to be more formal. A cocktail party or a golf game are examples where the language is likely to be informal. Formal language uses fewer or no contractions, less slang, longer sentences, and more organization in longer segments.

Speeches delivered to executives, college professors, government officials, etc., is likely to be formal. Speeches made to fellow employees are likely to be informal. Sermons tend to be formal; Bible lessons will tend to be informal.

Jargon is a specialized vocabulary. It may be the vocabulary peculiar to a particular industry such as computers or of a field such as religion. It may also be the vocabulary of a social group. Black English is a good example. A Hardee's ad has two young men on the streets of Philadelphia discussing the merits of one of their sandwiches, and bylines are required so others may understand what they're saying. A whole vocabulary that has even developed its own dictionaries is the jargon of bloggers. The speaker must be knowledgeable about and sensitive to the jargon peculiar to the particular audience. That may require some research and some vocabulary development on the speaker's part.

Technical language is a form of jargon. It is usually specific to an industry, profession, or field of study. Sensitivity to the language familiar to the particular audience is important.

Regionalisms are those usages that are peculiar to a particular part of the country. A good example is the second person plural pronoun: you. Because the plural is the same as the singular, various parts of the country have developed their own solutions to be sure that they are understood when they are speaking to more than one "you." In the South, "you-all" or "y'all" is common. In the Northeast, one often hears "youse." In some areas of the Middlewest, "you'ns" can be heard.

Vocabulary also varies from region to region. A small stream is a "creek" in some regions but "crick" in some. In Boston, soft drinks are generically called "tonic," but it becomes "soda" in other parts of the northeast. It is "liqueur" in Canada, and "pop" when you get very far west of New York.

Semantics

To effectively teach language, it is necessary to understand that, as human beings acquire language, they realize that words have <u>denotative</u> and <u>connotative</u> meanings. Generally, denotative words point to things and connotative words deal with mental suggestions that the words convey. The word *skunk* has a denotative meaning if the speaker can point to the actual animal as he speaks the word and intends the word to identify the animal. *Skunk* has connotative meaning depending upon the tone of delivery, the socially acceptable attitudes about the animal, and the speaker's personal feelings about the animal.

Informative connotations

Informative connotations are definitions agreed upon by the society in which the learner operates. A *skunk* is "a black and white mammal of the weasel family with a pair of perineal glands which secrete a pungent odor." The *Merriam Webster Collegiate Dictionary* adds "...and offensive" odor. Identification of the color, species, and glandular characteristics are informative. The interpretation of the odor as *offensive* is affective.

Affective connotations

Affective connotations are the personal feelings a word arouses. A child who has no personal experience with a skunk and its odor or has had a pet skunk will feel differently about the word *skunk* than a child who has smelled the spray or been conditioned vicariously to associate offensiveness with the animal denoted *skunk*. The very fact that our society views a skunk as an animal to be avoided will affect the child's interpretation of the word. In fact, it is not necessary for one to have actually seen a skunk (that is, have a denotative understanding) to use the word in either connotative expression. For example, one child might call another child a skunk, connoting an unpleasant reaction (affective use) or, seeing another small black and white animal, call it a skunk based on the definition (informative use).

Using connotations

In everyday language, we attach affective meanings to words unconsciously; we exercise more conscious control of informative connotations. In the process of language development, the leaner must come not only to grasp the definitions of words but also to become more conscious of the affective connotations and how his listeners process these connotations. Gaining this conscious control over language makes it possible to use language appropriately in various situations and to evaluate its uses in literature and other forms of communication.

The manipulation of language for a variety of purposes is the goal of language instruction. Advertisers and satirists are especially conscious of the effect word choice has on their audiences. By evoking the proper responses from readers/listeners, we can prompt them to take action.

Choice of the medium through which the message is delivered to the receiver is a significant factor in controlling language. Spoken language relies as much on the gestures, facial expression, and tone of voice of the speaker as on the words he speaks. Slapstick comics can evoke laughter without speaking a word. Young children use body language overtly and older children more subtly to convey messages. These refinings of body language are paralleled by an ability to recognize and apply the nuances of spoken language. To work strictly with the written work, the writer must use words to imply the body language.

Competency 9.0   **Understanding subjects relating to the analysis and history of English.**

English is an Indo-European language that evolved through several periods. The origin of English dates to the settlement of the British Isles in the fifth and sixth centuries by Germanic tribes called the Angles, Saxons, and Jutes. The original Britons spoke a Celtic tongue while the Angles spoke a Germanic dialect. Modern English derives from the speech of the Anglo-Saxons who imposed not only their language but also their social customs and laws on their new land. From the fifth to the tenth century, Britain's language was the tongue we now refer to as Old English. During the next four centuries, the many French attempts at English conquest introduced many French words to English. However, the grammar and syntax of the language remained Germanic.

Middle English, most evident in the writings of Geoffrey Chaucer, dates loosely from 1066 to 1509. William Caxton brought the printing press to England in 1474 and increased literacy. Old English words required numerous inflections to indicate noun cases and plurals as well as verb conjugations. Middle English continued the use of many inflections and pronunciations that treated these inflections as separately pronounced syllables. English in 1300 would have been written "Olde Anglishe" with the *e*'s at the ends of the words pronounced as our short *a* vowel. Even adjectives had plural inflections: "long dai" became "longe daies" pronounced "long-a day-as." Spelling was phonetic, thus every vowel had multiple pronunciations, a fact that continues to affect the language.

Modern English dates from the introduction of The Great Vowels Shift because it created guidelines for spelling and pronunciation. Before the printing press, books were copied laboriously by hand; the language was subject to the individual interpretation of the scribes. Printers and subsequently lexicographers like Samuel Johnson and America's Noah Webster influenced the guidelines. As reading matter was mass produced, the reading public was forced to adopt the speech and writing habits developed by those who wrote and printed books.

Despite many students' insistence to the contrary, Shakespeare's writings are in Modern English. It is important to stress to students that language, like customs, morals, and other social factors, is constantly subject to change. Immigration, inventions, and cataclysmic events change language as much as any other facet of life affected by these changes. The domination of one race or nation over others can change a language significantly. Beginning with the colonization of the New World, English and Spanish became dominant languages in the Western hemisphere. American English today is somewhat different in pronunciation and sometimes vocabulary from British English. The British call a truck a "lorry;" baby carriages a "pram," short for "perambulator;" and an elevator a "lift." There are very few syntactical differences, and even the tonal qualities that were once so clearly different are converging.

Though Modern English is less complex than Middle English, having lost many unnecessary inflections, it is still considered difficult to learn because of its many exceptions to the rules. It has, however, become the world's dominant language by reason of the great political, military, and social power of England from the fifteenth to the nineteenth century and of America in the twentieth century.

Modern inventions - the telephone, phonograph, radio, television, and motion pictures - have especially affected English pronunciation. Regional dialects, once a hindrance to clear understanding, have fewer distinct characteristics. The speakers from different parts of the United States of America can be identified by their accents, but more and more as educators and media personalities stress uniform pronunciations and proper grammar, the differences are diminishing.

The English language has a more extensive vocabulary than any other language. Ours is a language of synonyms, words borrowed from other languages, and coined words - many of them introduced by the rapid expansion of technology.

It is important for students to understand that language is in constant flux. Emphasis should be placed on learning and using language for specific purposes and audiences. Negative criticism of a student's errors in word choice or sentence structures will inhibit creativity. Positive criticism that suggests ways to enhance communication skills will encourage exploration.

Historical Events that Affected the Development of English

Perhaps the most basic principle about language in understanding its changes and variations is a simple one: language inevitably changes over time. If a community that speaks a homogeneous language and dialect are for some reason separated with no contact between the two resulting communities, over a few generations, they will be speaking different dialects and eventually will have difficulty understanding each other.

Language changes in all its manifestations: At the phonetic level, the sounds of a language will change as will its orthography. The vocabulary level will probably manifest the greatest changes. Changes in syntax are slower and less likely to occur. For example, English has changed in response to the influences of many other languages and cultures as well as internal cultural changes such as the development of the railroad and the computer; however, its syntax still relies on word order—it has not shifted to an inflected system even though many of the cultures that have impacted it do, in fact, have an inflected language, such as Spanish.

The most significant influence on a language is the blending of cultures. The Norman Conquest that brought the English speakers in the British Isles under the rule of French speakers impacted the language, but it's significant that English speakers did not adopt the language of the ruling class—they did not become speakers of French. Even so, many vocabulary items entered the language in that period. The Great Vowel Shift that occurred between the 14th and 16th centuries is somewhat of a mystery although it's generally attributed to the migration to Southeast England following the plague of the black death. The Great Vowel Shift largely accounts for the discrepancy between orthography and speech—the difficult spelling system in modern English.

Colonization of other countries has also brought new vocabulary items into the language. Indian English not only has its own easily recognizable attributes as does Australian and North American, those cultural interactions have added to items in the usages of each other and in the language at large. The fact that English is the most widely spoken and understood language all over the world in the 21st century implies that it is constantly being changed by the globalized world.

Other influences, of course, impact language. The introduction of television and its domination by the United States has had great influence on the English that is spoken and understood all over the world. The same is true of the computerizing of the world (Tom Friedman called it "flattening" in his *The World is Flat: A Brief History of the Twenty-first Century)*. New terms have been added, old terms have changed meaning ("mouse," for instance), and nouns have been verbalized.

Origins of English Words

Just as countries and families have histories, so do words. Knowing and understanding the origin of a word, where it has been used down through the years, and the history of its meaning as it has changed is an important component of the writing and language teacher's tool kit. Never in the history of the English language or any other language for that matter have the forms and meanings of words changed so rapidly. When America was settled originally, immigration from many countries made it a "melting pot."

Immigration accelerated rapidly within the first hundred years, resulting in pockets of language throughout the country. When trains began to make transportation available and affordable, individuals from those various pockets came in contact with each other, shared vocabularies, and attempted to converse. From that time forward, every generation brought the introduction of a technology that made language interchange not only more possible but more important.

Radio began the trend to standardize dialects. A Bostonian might not be understood by a native of Louisiana, who might not be interested in turning the dial to hear the news or a drama or the advertisements of the vendors that had a vested interest in being heard and understood. Soap and soup producers knew a goldmine when they saw it and created a market for radio announcers and actors who spoke without a pronounced dialect. In return, listeners began to hear the English language in a dialect very different from the one they spoke, and as it settled into their thinking processes, it eventually made its way to their tongues, and spoken English began to lose some of its local peculiarities. It has been a slow process, but most Americans can easily understand other Americans, no matter where they come from. They can even converse with a native of Great Britain with little difficulty. The introduction of television carried the evolution further as did the explosion of electronic communicating devices over the past fifty years.

An excellent example of the changes that have occurred in English is a comparison of Shakespeare's original works with modern translations. Without help, twenty-first-century Americans are unable to read the *Folio*. On the other hand, teachers must constantly be mindful of the vocabularies and etymologies of their students, who are on the receiving end of the escalation brought about by technology and increased global influence and contact.

In the past, the Oxford English Dictionary has been the most reliable source for etymologies. Some of the collegiate dictionaries are also useful. *Merriam-Webster's 3rd Unabridged Dictionary* is useful in tracing the sources of words in American English. *Merriam-Webster's Unabridged Dictionary* may be out of date, so a teacher should also have a *Merriam-Webster's Collegiate Dictionary*, which is updated regularly.

However, there are many up-to-date sources for keeping up and keeping track of the changes that have occurred and are occurring constantly. Google "etymology," for instance, or even the word you're unsure of, and you can find a multitude of sources. Don't trust a single one. The information should be validated by at least three sources. Wikipedia is very useful, but it can be changed by anyone who chooses, so any information on it should be backed up by other sources. If you go to http://www.etymonline.com/sources.php, you will find a long list of resources on etymology.

In order to know when to label a usage "jargon" or "colloquial" nowadays, the teacher must be aware of the possibility that it's a word that is now accepted as standard. In order to be on top of this, the teacher must continually keep up with the etymological aids that are available, particularly online.

Spelling in English is complicated by the fact that it is not phonetic—that is, it is not based on the one-sound/one letter formula used by many other languages. The reason for this is that it is based on the Latin alphabet, which originally had twenty letters, consisting of the present English alphabet minus J, K, V, W, Y, and Z. The Romans added K to be used in abbreviations and Y and Z in words that came from the Greek. This 23-letter alphabet was adopted by the English, who developed W as a ligatured doubling of U and later J and V as consonantal variants of I and U. The result was our alphabet of 26 letters with upper case (capital) and lower case forms.

Spelling is based primarily on 15th century English. The problem is that pronunciation has changed drastically since then, especially long vowels and diphthongs. This Great Vowel Shift affected the seven long vowels. For a long time, spelling was erratic—there were no standards. As long as the meaning was clear, spelling was not considered very important. Samuel Johnson tackled this problem, and his *Dictionary of the English Language* (1755) brought standards to spelling, so important once printing presses were invented. There have been some changes, of course, through the years; but spelling is still not strictly phonetic. There have been many attempts to nudge the spelling into a more phonetic representation of the sounds, but for the most part, all have failed. A good example is Noah Webster's *Spelling Book* (1783), which was a precursor to the first edition (1828) of his *American Dictionary of the English Language*. While there are rules for spelling, and it's important that students learn the rules, there are many exceptions; and memorizing exceptions and giving plenty of opportunities for practicing them seems the only solution for the teacher of English.

| DOMAIN III. | COMPOSITION AND RHETORIC |

Competency 10.0 Understanding strategies for teaching writing and theories of how students learn to write.

Prior to writing, you will need to prewrite for ideas and details as well as decide how the essay will be organized. In the hour you have to write you should spend no more than 5-10 minutes prewriting and organizing your ideas. As you prewrite, it might be helpful to remember you should have at least three main points and at least two to three details to support your main ideas. There are several types of graphic organizers that you should practice using as you prepare for the essay portion of the test.

PREWRITE TO EXPLAIN HOW OR WHY

Select a poem and using the visual organizer on the following page, explain how a poet creates tone and mood and uses imagery and word choice. Then complete filling out the organizer by identifying how the poet effectively creates tone and mood. Support with examples from the poem.

TEACHER CERTIFICATION STUDY GUIDE

VISUAL ORGANIZER: GIVING REASONS

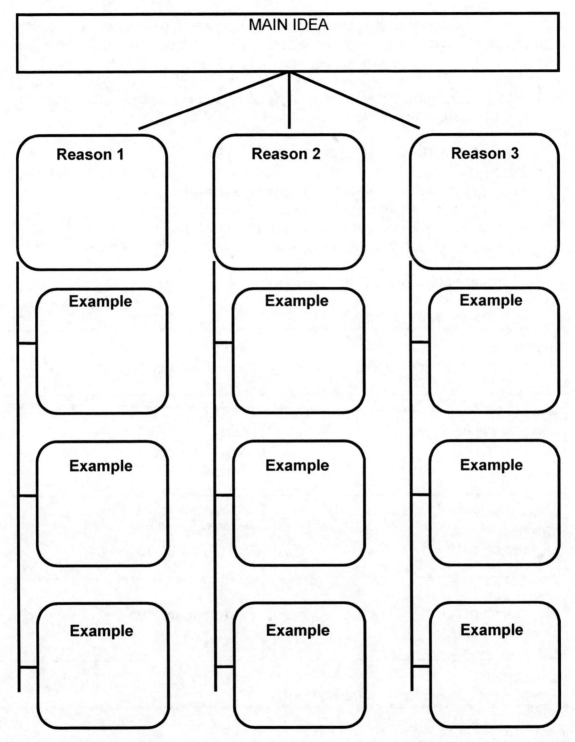

MID. LEVEL HUMANITIES

TEACHER CERTIFICATION STUDY GUIDE

STEP 3: PREWRITE TO ORGANIZE IDEAS

After you have completed a graphic organizer, you need to decide how you will organize your essay. To organize your essay, you might consider one of the following patterns to structure your essay.

1. Examine individual elements such as **plot**, **setting**, **theme**, **character**, **point of view**, **tone**, **mood**, or **style**.

   SINGLE ELEMENT OUTLINE
   Intro - main idea statement
   Main point 1 with at least two supporting details
   Main point 2 with at least two supporting details
   Main point 3 with at least two supporting details
   Conclusion (restates main ideas and summary of main pts)

2. **Compare and contrast two elements**.

POINT-BY-POINT	BLOCK
Introduction Statement of main idea about A and B	Introduction Statement of main idea about A and B
Main Point 1 Discussion of A Discussion of B	Discussion of A Main Point 1 Main Point 2 Main point 3
Main Point 2 Discussion of A Discussion of B	Discussion of B Main Point 1 Main Point 2 Main Point 3
Main Point 3 Discussion of A Discussion of B	Conclusion Restate main idea
Conclusion Restatement or summary of main idea	

PRACTICE:
Using the cluster on the next page, choose an organizing chart and complete for your topic.

MID. LEVEL HUMANITIES

TEACHER CERTIFICATION STUDY GUIDE

VISUAL ORGANIZER: GIVING INFORMATION

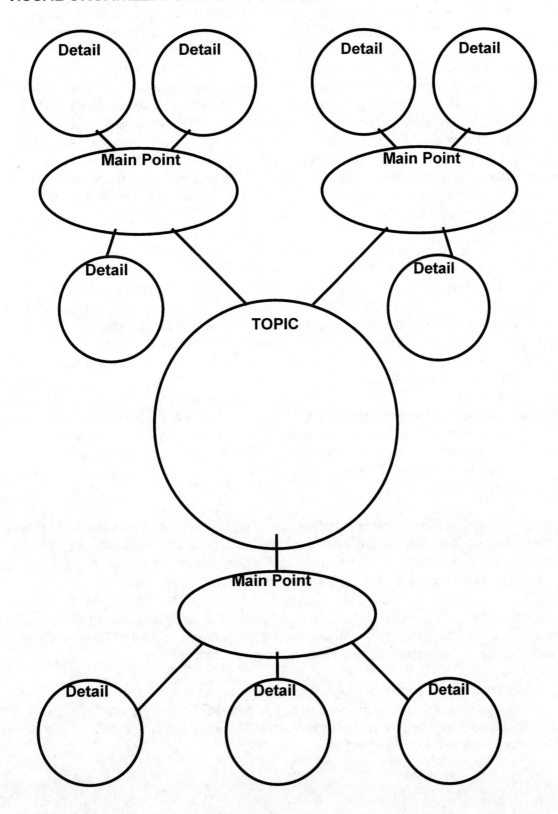

Seeing writing as a process is very helpful in saving preparation time, particularly in the taking of notes and the development of drafts. Once a decision is made about the topic to be developed, some preliminary review of literature is helpful in thinking about the next step, which is to determine what the purpose of the written document will be. For example, if the topic is immigration, a cursory review of the various points of view in the debate going on in the country will help the writer decide what this particular written piece will try to accomplish. The purpose could just be a review of the various points of view, which would be an informative purpose. On the other hand, the writer might want to take a point of view and provide proof and support with the purpose of changing the reader's mind. The writer might even want the reader to take some action as the result of reading. Another possible purpose might be simply to write a description of a family of immigrants.

Once that cursory review has been completed, it's time to begin research in earnest and to prepare to take notes. If the thesis has been clearly defined, and some thought has been given to what will be used to prove or support it, a tentative outline can be developed. A thesis plus three points is typical. Decisions about introduction and conclusion should be deferred until the body of the paper is written. Note-taking is much more effective if the notes are being taken to provide information for an outline. There is much less danger that the writer will go off on time-consuming tangents.

Formal outlines inhibit effective writing. However, a loosely constructed outline can be an effective device for note-taking that will yield the information for a worthwhile statement about a topic. Sentence outlines are better than topic outlines because they require the writer to do some thinking about the direction a subtopic will take.

Once this preliminary note-taking phase is over, the first draft can be developed. The writing at this stage is likely to be highly individualistic. However, successful writers tend to just write, keeping in mind the purpose of the paper, the point that is going to be made in it, and the information that has been turned up in the research. Student writers need to understand that this first draft is just that—the first one. It takes more than one draft to write a worthwhile statement about a topic. This is what successful writers do. It's sometimes helpful to have students read the various drafts of a story by a well-known writer.

Once the draft is on paper, a stage that is sometimes called editing occurs. With word processors, this is much more easily achieved than in the past. Sections can be deleted, words can be changed, and additions can be made without doing the entire project over a second time.

What to look for: mechanics, of course, spelling, punctuation, etc., but it's important that student writers not mistake that for editing. Editing is rereading objectively, testing the effectiveness on a reader of the arrangement and the line of reasoning. The kinds of changes that will need to be made are: rearranging the parts, adding information that is missing and needed, and deleting information that doesn't fit or contribute to the accomplishment of the purpose.

Once the body of the paper has been shaped to the writer's satisfaction, the introduction and conclusion should be fashioned. An introduction should grab the reader's interest and, perhaps, announce the purpose and thesis of the paper unless the reasoning is inductive, in which case, purpose and thesis may come later in the paper. The conclusion is to reaffirm the purpose in some way.

Enhancing Interest:

- Start out with an attention-grabbing introduction. This sets an engaging tone for the entire piece and will be more likely to pull the reader in.
- Use dynamic vocabulary and varied sentence beginnings. Keep the reader on their toes. If they can predict what you are going to say next, switch it up.
- Avoid using clichés (as cold as ice, the best thing since sliced bread, nip it in the bud). These are easy shortcuts, but they are not interesting, memorable, or convincing.

Ensuring Understanding:

- Avoid using the words, "clearly," "obviously," and "undoubtedly." Often, things that are clear or obvious to the author are not as apparent to the reader. Instead of using these words, make your point so strongly that it is clear on its own.
- Use the word that best fits the meaning you intend, even if it is longer or a little less common. Try to find a balance, a go with a familiar yet precise word.
- When in doubt, explain further.

Techniques to Maintain Focus:
- **Focus on a main point.** The point should be clear to readers, and all sentences in the paragraph should relate to it.
- **Start the paragraph with a topic sentence.** This should be a general, one-sentence summary of the paragraph's main point, relating both back towards the thesis and toward the content of the paragraph. (A topic sentence is sometimes unnecessary if the paragraph continues a developing idea clearly introduced in a preceding paragraph, or if the paragraph appears in a narrative of events where generalizations might interrupt the flow of the story.)

- **Stick to the point.** Eliminate sentences that do not support the topic sentence.

Be flexible. If there is not enough evidence to support the claim your topic sentence is making, do not fall into the trap of wandering or introducing new ideas within the paragraph. Either find more evidence, or adjust the topic sentence to collaborate with the evidence that is available.

Stories.

It seems simplistic, yet it's an often-overlooked truism: the first and most important measure of a story is the story itself. *The story's the thing*. However, a good story must have certain characteristics. Without conflict there is no story, so determining what the conflicts are should be a priority for the writer. Once the conflicts are determined, the outcome of the story must be decided. Who wins? Who loses? And what factors go into making one side of the equation win out over the other one? The pattern of the plot is also an important consideration. Where is the climax going to occur? Is denouement necessary? Does the reader need to see the unwinding of all the strands? Many stories fail because a denouement is needed but not supplied.

Characterization, the choice the writer makes about the devices he/she will use to reveal character, requires an understanding of human nature and the artistic skill to convey a personality to the reader. This is usually accomplished subtly through dialogue, interior monologue, description, and the character's actions and behavior. In some successful stories, the writer comes right out and tells the reader what this character is like. However, sometimes there will be discrepancies between what the narrator tells the reader about the character and what is revealed to be actual, in which case the narrator is unreliable, and that unreliability of the voice the reader must depend on becomes an important and significant device for understanding the story.

Point of view is a powerful tool not only for the writer but for the enjoyment and understanding of the reader. The writer must choose among several possibilities: first-person narrator objective, first-person narrator omniscient, third-person objective, third-person omniscient, and third-person limited omniscient. The most successful story-writers use point of view very creatively to accomplish their purposes. If a writer wishes to be successful, he/she must develop point-of-view skills.

Style—the unique way a writer uses language—is often the writer's signature. The reader does not need to be told that William Faulkner wrote a story to know it because his style is so distinctive that it is immediately recognizable. Even the writing of Toni Morrison, which could be said to be Faulknerian, cannot be mistaken for the work of Faulkner, himself.

The writer must be cognizant of his/her own strengths and weaknesses and continually work to hone the way sentences are written, words are chosen, and descriptions are crafted until they are razor-sharp. The best advice to the aspiring writer: read the works of successful writers. If a writer wants to write a best-seller, then that writer needs to be reading best-sellers.

Poetry. Writing poetry in the 21st century is quite a different thing from writing it in earlier periods. There was a time when a poem was required to fit a certain pattern or scheme. Poetry was once defined as a piece of writing that was made up of end-rhymes. No more. The rhymed poem makes up only a small percentage of worthwhile and successful poems nowadays.

The first skill to work on for the budding poet is descriptive writing, defined as language that appeals to one or more of the five senses. A good poem makes it possible for the reader to experience an emotional event—seeing a mountain range as the sun dawns, watching small children on a playground, smelling the fragrance of a rose, hearing a carillon peal a religious tune at sunset, feeling fine silk under one's fingers. Creating language that makes that experience available to the readers is only the first step, however, because the ultimate goal is to evoke an emotional response. Feeling the horror of the battleground, weeping with the mother whose child was drowned, exulting with a winning soccer team. It's not enough to tell the reader what it's like. It's the *showing* that is necessary.

The aspiring poet should know the possibilities as well as the limitations of this genre. A poem can tell a story, for instance, but the emotional response is more important than the story itself. Edgar Allen Poe, in an 1842 review of Hawthorne's *Twice-Told Tales* in *Graham's Magazine* had important advice for the writer of poetry: ". . . the unity of effect or impression is a point of the greatest importance." Even though he considered the tale or short story the best way to achieve this, he wrote several memorable poems and much of his prose writing is considered to be as close to poetry as to prose by most critics. He also wrote in 1847, in an expansion of his critique of Hawthorne's works, that ". . .true originality . . .is that which, in bringing out the half-formed, the reluctant, or the unexpressed fancies of mankind, or in exciting the more delicate pulses of the heart's passion, or in giving birth to some universal sentiment or instinct in embryo, thus combines with the pleasurable effect of *apparent* novelty, a real egoistic delight."

Play writing. Play writing uses many of the same skills that are necessary to successful story writing. However, in addition to those skills, there are many more required of the writer who wishes his/her story to be told on stage or on film. The point of view, of course, is always objective unless the writers uses the Shakespearean device of the soliloquy, where a player steps forward and gives information about what's going on. The audience must figure out the meaning of the play on the basis of the actions and speeches of the actors.

A successful playwright is expert in characterization as described above under **Story**. What a character is like is determined by dialogue, appearance (costume, etc.), behavior, actions. A successful playwright also understands motivation. If a character's behavior cannot be traced to motivating circumstances, the audience will probably find the action incoherent—a major barrier to positive reception of the play.

The writing must be very carefully honed. Absolutely no excess of words can be found in a successful play. It takes very little time to lose an audience; every word counts. The playwright should concentrate on saying the most possible with the fewest words possible.

Setting is an important feature of the play. Most plays have only one because changing settings in the middle is difficult and disrupting. This calls for a very special kind of writing. The entire action of the play must either take place within the setting or be brought forth in that setting by the reporting or recounting of what is going on outside of the setting by one or more of the characters. The writer must determine what the setting will be. The actual building and creation of the set is in the hands of another kind of artist—one who specializes in settings.

The plot of most plays is rising; that is, the conflicts are introduced early in the play and continue to develop and intensify over the life of the play. As a general rule, the climax is the last thing that happens before the final curtain falls, but not necessarily. Plots of plays demonstrate the same breadth of patterns that are true of stories. For example, a play may end with nothing resolved. Denouement is less likely to follow a climax in a play than in a story, but epilogues do sometimes occur.

Writing Voice

There are at least thirteen possible choices for point of view (voice) in literature as demonstrated and explained by Wallace Hildick in his *13 Types of Narrative* (London: MacMillan and Co., 1968). However, for purposes of helping students write essays about literature, three, or possibly four, are adequate. The importance of teaching students to use this aspect of a piece of literature to write about it is not just as an analytic exercise but also should help them think about how a writer's choices impact the overall effect of the work.

Point of view or voice is essentially through whose eyes the reader sees the action. The most common is the third-person objective. If the story is seen from this point of view, the reader watches the action, hears the dialogue, reads descriptions and from all of those must deduce characterization—what sort of person a character is. In this point of view, an unseen narrator tells the reader what is happening, using the third person, he, she, it, they. The effect of this point of view is usually a feeling of distance from the plot.

More responsibility is on the reader to make judgments than in other points of view. However, the author may intrude and evaluate or comment on the characters or the action.

The voice of the first-person narrator is often used also. The reader sees the action through the eyes of an actor in the story who is also telling the story. In writing about a story that uses this voice, the narrator must be analyzed as a character. What sort of person is this? What is this character's position in the story—observer, commentator, actor? Can the narrator be believed, or is he/she biased? The value of this voice is that, while the reader is able to follow the narrator around and see what is happening through that character's eyes, the reader is also able to feel what the narrator feels. For this reason, the writer can involve the reader more intensely in the story itself and move the reader by invoking feelings—pity, sorrow, anger, hate, confusion, disgust, etc. Many of the most memorable novels are written in this point of view.

Another voice often used may best be titled "omniscient" because the reader is able to get into the mind of more than one character or sometimes all the characters. This point of view can also bring greater involvement of the reader in the story. By knowing what a character is thinking and feeling, the reader is able to empathize when a character feels great pain and sorrow, which tends to make a work memorable. On the other hand, knowing what a character is thinking makes it possible to get into the mind of a pathological murderer and may elicit horror or disgust.

"Omniscient" can be broken down into third-person omniscient or first-person omniscient. In third-person omniscient, the narrator is not seen or known or acting in the story but is able to watch and record not only what is happening or being said, but what characters are thinking. In first-person omniscient on the other hand, the narrator plays a role in the story but can also record what other characters are thinking. It is possible, of course, that the narrator is the pathological murderer, which creates an effect quite different than a story where the thoughts of the murderer are known but the narrator is standing back and reporting his behavior, thoughts, and intents.

Point of view or voice is a powerful tool in the hands of a skillful writer. The questions to be answered in writing an essay about a literary work are: What point of view has this author used? What effect does it have on the story? If it had been written in a different voice, how would the story be different?

Most credible literary works are consistent in point of view but not always, so consistency is another aspect that should be analyzed. Does the point of view change? Where does it vary? Does it help or hurt the effect of the story?

Competency 11.0 Recognizing individual and collaborative approaches to teaching writing.

Viewing writing as a process allows teachers and students to see the writing classroom as a cooperative workshop where students and teachers encourage and support each other in each writing endeavor. Listed below are some techniques that help teachers to facilitate and create a supportive classroom environment.

1. Create peer response/support groups that are working on similar writing assignments. The members help each other in all stages of the writing process-from prewriting, writing, revising, editing, and publishing.

2. Provide several prompts to give students the freedom to write on a topic of their own. Writing should be generated out of personal experience and students should be introduced to in-class journals. One effective way to get into writing is to let them write often and freely about their own lives, without having to worry about grades or evaluation.

3. Respond in the form of a question whenever possible. Teacher/facilitator should respond noncritically and use positive, supportive language.

4. Respond to formal writing acknowledging the student's strengths and focusing on the composition skills demonstrated by the writing. A response should encourage the student by offering praise for what the student has done well. Give the student a focus for revision and demonstrate that the process of revision has applications in many other writing situations.

5. Provide students with readers' checklists so that students can write observational critiques of others' drafts, and then they can revise their own papers at home using the checklists as a guide.

6. Pair students so that they can give and receive responses. Pairing students keeps them aware of the role of an audience in the composing process and in evaluating stylistic effects.

7. Focus critical comments on aspects of the writing that can be observed in the writing. Comments like "I noticed you use the word 'is' frequently" will be more helpful than "Your introduction is dull" and will not demoralize the writer.

8. Provide the group with a series of questions to guide them through the group writing sessions.

Multimedia refers to a technology for presenting material in both visual and verbal forms. This format is especially conducive to the classroom, since it reaches both visual and auditory learners.

Knowing how to select effective teaching software is the first step in efficient multi-media education. First, decide what you need the software for (creating spreadsheets, making diagrams, creating slideshows, etc.) Consult magazines such as *Popular Computing, PC World, MacWorld,* and *Multimedia World* to learn about the newest programs available. Go to a local computer store and ask a customer service representative to help you find the exact equipment you need. If possible, test the programs you are interested in. Check reviews in magazines such as *Consumer Reports, PCWorld, Electronic Learning* or *MultiMedia Schools* to ensure the software's quality.

Software programs useful for producing teaching material
- Adobe PageMaker, PhotoShop, and Acrobat
- Aldus Freehand
- CorelDRAW!
- DrawPerfect
- Claris Works
- PC Paintbrush
- Harvard Graphics
- Visio
- Microsoft Word
- Microsoft Power Point

In learning to write and in improving one's writing, the most useful exercise is editing/revising. Extensive revision is the hallmark of most successful writers. In the past, writers, student writers in particular, have been reluctant to revise because it meant beginning over to prepare the document for final presentation. However, that time is long gone. The writing of graduate dissertations took on a whole new dimension after the creation of the word processor and before long, classroom writing teachers were able to use this function to help students improve their writing.

Requiring extensive revision in writing classrooms nowadays is not unreasonable and can be an important stage in the production of papers. Microsoft Word has had a "tracking" capability in its last several upgrades, which carries revision a step further. Now the teacher and student can carry on a dialogue on the paper itself. The teacher's deletions and additions can be tracked, the student can respond, and the tracking will be facilitated by automatically putting the changes in a different color. The "comment" function makes it possible for both teacher and student to write notes at the exactly relevant point in the manuscript.

Competency 12.0 Knowledge of various tools and response strategies for assessing student writing.

When assessing and responding to student writing, there are several guidelines to remember.

Responding to non-graded writing (formative).

1. Avoid using a red pen. Whenever possible use a #2 pencil.
2. Explain the criteria that will be used for assessment in advance.
3. Read the writing once while asking the question, "Is the student's response appropriate for the assignment?"
4. Reread and make note at the end whether the student met the objective of the writing task.
5. Responses should be non-critical and use supportive and encouraging language.
6. Resist writing on or over the student's writing.
7. Highlight the ideas you wish to emphasize, question, or verify.
8. Encourage your students to take risks.

Responding to and evaluating graded writing (summative).

1. Ask students to submit prewriting and rough-draft materials including all revisions with their final draft.
2. For the first reading, use a holistic method, examining the work as a whole.
3. When reading the draft for the second time, assess it using the standards previously established.
4. Responses to the writing should be written in the margin and should use supportive language.
5. Make sure you address the process as well as the product. It is important that students value the learning process as well as the final product.
6. After scanning the piece a third time, write final comments at the end of the draft.

Sometimes this exercise is seen by students as simply catching errors in spelling or word use. Students need to reframe their thinking about revising and editing. Some questions that need to be asked:

- Is the reasoning coherent?
- Is the point established?
- Does the introduction make the reader want to read this discourse?
- What is the thesis? Is it proven?
- What is the purpose? Is it clear? Is it useful, valuable, interesting?

- Is the style of writing so wordy that it exhausts the reader and interferes with engagement?
- Is the writing so spare that it is boring?
- Are the sentences too uniform in structure?
- Are there too many simple sentences?
- Are too many of the complex sentences the same structure?
- Are the compounds truly compounds or are they unbalanced?
- Are parallel structures truly parallel?
- If there are characters, are they believable?
- If there is dialogue, is it natural or stilted?
- Is the title appropriate?
- Does the writing show creativity or is it boring?
- Is the language appropriate? Is it too formal? Too informal? If jargon is used, is it appropriate?

Studies have clearly demonstrated that the most fertile area in teaching writing is this one. If students can learn to revise their own work effectively, they are well on their way to becoming effective, mature writers. Word processing is an important tool for teaching this stage in the writing process. Microsoft Word has tracking features that make the revision exchanges between teachers and students more effective than ever before.

- Have students write a short story, essay or other specified genre of writing
- Assess their ability to write about a given body of knowledge in a logical and critical way
- Observe their ability to use language resources appropriate for the required task.
- Use a rating system. For example, a scale from 1 to 4 (where 1=unsatisfactory and 4=excellent).
- Monitor their use of source material
- Evaluate the structure and development of their writing
- Ensure that their writing style is appropriate for the task assigned
- Check for grammatical correctness
- Provide follow-up support for any weaknesses detected

Competency 13.0   Recognizing, understanding, and evaluating rhetorical features of writing and organizational strategies.

Organizational Structures

Authors use a particular organization to best present the concepts which they are writing about. Teaching students to recognize organizational structures helps them to understand authors' literary intentions, and helps them in deciding which structure to use in their own writing.

Cause and Effect: When writing about *why* things happen, as well as *what* happens, authors commonly use the cause and effect structure. For example, when writing about how he became so successful, a CEO might talk about how he excelled in math in high school, moved to New York after college, and stuck to his goals even after multiple failures. These are all *causes* that lead to the *effect*, or result, of him becoming a wealthy and powerful businessman.

Compare and Contrast: When examining the merits of multiple concepts or products, compare and contrast lends itself easily to organization of ideas. For example, a person writing about foreign policy in different countries will put them against each other to point out differences and similarities, easily highlighting the concepts the author wishes to emphasize.

Problem and Solution: This structure is used in a lot of handbooks and manuals. Anything organized around procedure-oriented tasks, such as a computer repair manual, gravitates toward a problem and solution format, because it offers such clear, sequential text organization.

An easy and effective way of organizing information to be used in a work of nonfiction is by asking specific questions that are geared towards a particular mode of presentation. An example of these questions follows:

Useful research questions:

What is it?

It is the process of thinking up and writing down a set of questions that you want to answer about the research topic you have selected.

Why should I do it?

It will keep you from getting lost or off-track when looking for information. You will try to find the answers to these questions when you do your research.

When do I do it?

After you have written your statement of purpose, and have a focused topic to ask questions about, begin research.

How do I do it?

Make two lists of questions. Label one "factual" questions and one "interpretive" questions. The answers to factual questions will give your reader the basic background information they need to understand your topic. The answers to interpretive questions show your creative thinking in your project and can become the basis for your thesis statement.

Asking factual questions:

Assume your reader knows nothing about your subject. Make an effort to tell them everything they need to know to understand what you will say in your project.

Make a list of specific questions that ask: Who? What? When? Where?

Example: For a report about President Abraham Lincoln's attitude and policies towards slavery, people will have to know; Who was Abraham Lincoln? Where and when was he born? What political party did he belong to? When was he elected president? What were the attitudes and laws about slavery during his lifetime? How did his actions affect slavery?

Asking Interpretive Questions:

These kinds of questions are the result of your own original thinking. They can be based on the preliminary research you have done on your chosen topic. Select one or two to answer in your presentation. They can be the basis of forming a thesis statement.

- **Hypothetical**: How would things be different today if something in the past had been different?

Example: How would our lives be different today if the Confederate (southern) states had won the United States Civil War? What would have happened to the course of World War Two if the Atomic Bomb hadn't been dropped on Hiroshima and Nagasaki?

- **Prediction**: How will something look or be in the future, based on the way it is now?

Example: What will happen to sea levels if global warming due to ozone layer depletion continues and the polar caps melt significantly? If the population of China continues to grow at the current rate for the next fifty years, how will that impact its role in world politics?

- **Solution**: What solutions can be offered to a problem that exists today?

Example: How could global warming be stopped? What can be done to stop the spread of sexually transmitted diseases among teenagers?

- **Comparison or Analogy**: Find the similarities and differences between your main subject and a similar subject, or with another subject in the same time period or place.

Example: In what ways is the Civil War in the former Yugoslavia similar to (or different from) the United States Civil War?
What is the difference in performance between a Porsche and a Lamborghini?

- **Judgment**: Based on the information you find, what can you say as your informed opinion about the subject?

Example: How does tobacco advertising affect teen cigarette smoking? What are the major causes of eating disorders among young women? How does teen parenthood affect the future lives of young women and men?

Introductions:

It's important to remember that in the writing process, the introduction should be written last. Until the body of the paper has been determined—thesis, development—it's difficult to make strategic decisions regarding the introduction. The Greek rhetoricians called this part of a discourse *exordium*, a "leading into." The basic purpose of the introduction, then, is to lead the audience into the discourse. It can let the reader know what the purpose of the discourse is and it can condition the audience to be receptive to what the writer wants to say. It can be very brief or it can take up a large percentage of the total word count. Aristotle said that the introduction could be compared to the flourishes that flute players make before their performance—an overture in which the musicians display what they can play best in order to gain the favor and attention of the audience for the main performance.

In order to do this, we must first of all know what we are going to say; who the readership is likely to be; what the social, political, economic, etc., climate is; what preconceived notions the audience is likely to have regarding the subject; and how long the discourse is going to be.

There are many ways to do this:
- Show that the subject is important.
- Show that although the points we are presenting may seem improbable, they are true.
- Show that the subject has been neglected, misunderstood, or misrepresented.
- Explain an unusual mode of development.
- Forestall any misconception of the purpose.
- Apologize for a deficiency.
- Arouse interest in the subject with an anecdotal lead-in.
- Ingratiate oneself with the readership.
- Establish one's own credibility.

The introduction often ends with the thesis, the point or purpose of the paper. However, this is not set in stone. The thesis may open the body of the discussion, or it may conclude the discourse. The most important thing to remember is that the purpose and structure of the introduction should be deliberate if it is to serve the purpose of "leading the reader into the discussion."

Conclusions:

It's easier to write a conclusion after the decisions regarding the introduction have been made. Aristotle taught that the conclusion should strive to do five things:

1. Inspire the reader with a favorable opinion of the writer.
2. Amplify the force of the points made in the body of the paper.
3. Reinforce the points made in the body.
4. Rouse appropriate emotions in the reader.
5. Restate in a summary way what has been said.

The conclusion may be short or it may be long depending on its purpose in the paper. Recapitulation, a brief restatement of the main points or certainly of the thesis is the most common form of effective conclusions. A good example is the closing argument in a court trial.

Text Organization:

In studies of professional writers and how they produce their successful works, it has been revealed that writing is a process that can be clearly defined although in practice it must have enough flexibility to allow for creativity. The teacher must be able to define the various stages that a successful writer goes through in order to make a statement that has value. There must be a discovery stage when ideas, materials, supporting details, etc., are deliberately collected. These may come from many possible sources: the writer's own experience and observations, deliberate research of written sources, interviews of live persons, television presentations, or the internet.

The next stage is organization where the purpose, thesis, and supporting points are determined. Most writers will put forth more than one possible thesis and in the next stage, the writing of the paper, settle on one as the result of trial and error. Once the paper is written, the editing stage is necessary and is probably the most important stage. This is not just the polishing stage. At this point, decisions must be made regarding whether the reasoning is cohesive—does it hold together? Is the arrangement the best possible one or should the points be rearranged? Are there holes that need to be filled in? What form will the introduction take? Does the conclusion lead the reader out of the discourse or is it inadequate or too abrupt, etc.

It's important to remember that the best writers engage in all of these stages recursively. They may go back to discovery at any point in the process. They may go back and rethink the organization, etc. To help students become effective writers, the teacher needs to give them adequate practice in the various stages and encourage them to engage deliberately in the creative thinking that makes writers successful.

TEACHER CERTIFICATION STUDY GUIDE

Short Essays

DOMAIN IV. LITERARY ANALYSIS

Stimulus

The stimulus for the literary analysis question will consist of a selection of prose (fiction or nonfiction) **OR** poetry (a whole short poem or an excerpt from a longer work).

Competency 14.0 Describe and give examples of the use of one or two specified literary element(s) present in the stimulus.

See Competency 3.0.

Competency 15.0 Discuss how the author's use of the literary element(s) contributes to the overall meaning and/or effectiveness of the text.

Writing about an author's use of plot should begin with determining what the conflicts are. In a naturalist story, the conflicts may be between the protagonist and a hostile or indifferent world. Sometimes, the conflicts are between two characters, the protagonist and the antagonist; and sometimes the conflicts are internal—between two forces within an individual character that have created a dilemma. For example, a Catholic priest may be devoted and committed to his role in the Church that calls for a celibate life yet at the same time be deeply in love with a woman.

Once the conflicts have been determined, the pattern of action will hinge on how the story comes out. Who (or what) wins and who (or what) loses. If the protagonist struggles throughout the story but emerges triumphant in the end, the pattern is said to be rising. On the other hand, if the story is about the downfall of the major character, the story can be said to be falling. If there is no winner in the end, the pattern is flat. This is an important point for a writer to make because it is crucial to all other aspects of an analysis of a work of fiction.

Characters are developed in many ways. Sometimes the writer simply tells the reader what kind of person this is. More often, however, the reader is left to deduce the characteristics from dialogue with others; with what other characters think or say about him/her; with description—what the character looks like, tall, short, thin, plump, dark-haired, gray-haired, etc. The techniques a writer uses to define character are called characterization, and a writer will usually deal with these matters when writing an analysis.

Setting can be a period of time, the 1930s, for example. It can also be a place, either a real place like a particular city or a fictional place like a farm or a mansion.

It can be emotional—some of Truman Capote's stories are set in an atmosphere of fear and danger, and the effectiveness of the story depends on that setting. An analysis should deal with the *function* of the setting in the story. For example, if it is set in a particular period of time as *The Great Gatsby* is, would it be a different story if it were set in a different period of time? A setting can sometimes function as a symbol, so the writer should be looking for that as a possibility.

Theme in a work of fiction is similar to a thesis in an essay. It's the *point* the story makes. In a story, it may possibly be spoken by one of the characters; but more often, it is left to the writer to determine. This requires careful reading and should take into account the other aspects of the story before a firm decision is made with regard to the point of the story. Different analysts will come to different conclusions about what a story means. Very often the thesis of an analytical essay will be the writer's declaration of the theme according to his/her own well-reasoned opinion.

Point of view seems simple on the surface, but it rarely is in a story. In fact, Wallace Hildick wrote *Thirteen Types of Narrative* to explain point of view in literature. The most common ones are first person narrator objective in which the person telling the story only records his/her observations of what is happening. In this point of view, the only clues as to what the characters are like come from the narrator. The attitude of the narrator toward the theme or the characters will be an important part of the story and should be dealt with in an analysis. Sometimes, its' apparent that the narrator's view does not square with reality, in which the narrator becomes unreliable and the reader must make an effort to determine what is real and what is not. If a writer uses this device, it's extremely important that the analyst point it out and point out what it does for the story.

The first person narrator may know what one or more of the characters is thinking and that will be important to the analysis of the story. If the narrator knows this, how did he/she acquire the knowledge? The most logical way is that the story was told to the narrator in the first place by that character or those characters.

Third person objective is another common form of development. In this point of view, there is no narrator. The story is told by an unseen observer. The reader does not know what anyone is thinking, only what is being said and described.

Third person omniscient is also fairly common. In this point of view, the story is being told by an unseen observer, but the observer is able to know what at least one person is thinking, which is sometimes called limited omniscient point of view. The reader may also know what most or all of the characters are thinking, and this point of view is simply called third-person omniscient.

Point of view is extremely powerful in the way a story is perceived and must be dealt with in a written analysis.

DOMAIN V.	RHETORICAL ANALYSIS

Stimulus

The stimulus for the rhetorical analysis question will consist of a selection of fiction or nonfiction prose.

Competency 16.0 Identify and describe and/or give examples of the use of one or more rhetorical elements in the stimulus.

A logical argument consists of three stages. First of all, the propositions which are necessary for the argument to continue are stated. These are called the premises of the argument. They are the evidence or reasons for accepting the argument and its conclusions.

Premises (or assertions) are often indicated by phrases such as "because", "since", "obviously" and so on. (The phrase "obviously" is often viewed with suspicion, as it can be used to intimidate others into accepting suspicious premises. If something doesn't seem obvious to you, don't be afraid to question it. You can always say "Oh, yes, you're right, it is obvious" when you've heard the explanation.)

Next, the premises are used to derive further propositions by a process known as inference. In inference, one proposition is arrived at on the basis of one or more other propositions already accepted. There are various forms of valid inference.

The propositions arrived at by inference may then be used in further inference. Inference is often denoted by phrases such as "implies that" or "therefore".

Finally, we arrive at the conclusion of the argument -- the proposition which is affirmed on the basis of the premises and inference. Conclusions are often indicated by phrases such as "therefore", "it follows that", "we conclude" and so on. The conclusion is often stated as the final stage of inference.

Classical Argument

In its simplest form, the classical argument has five main parts:

The **introduction**, which warms up the audience, establishes goodwill and rapport with the readers, and announces the general theme or thesis of the argument.

The **narration**, which summarizes relevant background material, provides any information the audience needs to know about the environment and circumstances that produce the argument, and set up the stakes—what's at risk in this question.

The **confirmation**, which lays out in a logical order (usually strongest to weakest or most obvious to most subtle) the claims that support the thesis, providing evidence for each claim.

The **refutation and concession**, which looks at opposing viewpoints to the writer's claims, anticipating objections from the audience, and allowing as much of the opposing viewpoints as possible without weakening the thesis.

The **summation**, which provides a strong conclusion, amplifying the force of the argument, and showing the readers that this solution is the best at meeting the circumstances.

Competency 17.0   Discuss the degree to which the use of the rhetorical element(s) is effective in conveying the author's point and contributing to the overall meaning of the text.

In studies of professional writers and how they produce their successful works, it has been revealed that writing is a process that can be clearly defined although in practice it must have enough flexibility to allow for creativity. The teacher must be able to define the various stages that a successful writer goes through in order to make a statement that has value. There must be a discovery stage when ideas, materials, supporting details, etc., are deliberately collected. These may come from many possible sources: the writer's own experience and observations, deliberate research of written sources, interviews of live persons, television presentations, or the internet.

The next stage is organization where the purpose, thesis, and supporting points are determined. Most writers will put forth more than one possible thesis and in the next stage, the writing of the paper, settle on one as the result of trial and error. Once the paper is written, the editing stage is necessary and is probably the most important stage. This is not just the polishing stage. At this point, decisions must be made regarding whether the reasoning is cohesive—does it hold together? Is the arrangement the best possible one or should the points be rearranged? Are there holes that need to be filled in? What form will the introduction take? Does the conclusion lead the reader out of the discourse or is it inadequate or too abrupt, etc.

It's important to remember that the best writers engage in all of these stages recursively. They may go back to discovery at any point in the process. They may go back and rethink the organization, etc. To help students become effective writers, the teacher needs to give them adequate practice in the various stages and encourage them to engage deliberately in the creative thinking that makes writers successful.

TEACHER CERTIFICATION STUDY GUIDE

Sample Test: Middle School Language Arts

Essay Question

Read the passage below from *The Diary of Anne Frank* (1947); then complete the exercise that follows.

Written on July 15, 1944, three weeks before the Frank family was arrested by the Nazis, Anne's diary entry explains her worldview and future hopes.

"It's difficult in times like these: ideals, dreams and cherished hopes rise within us, only to be crushed by grim reality. It's a wonder I haven't abandoned all my ideals, they seem so absurd and impractical. Yet I cling to them because I still believe, in spite of everything, that people are truly good at heart.

"It's utterly impossible for me to build my life on a foundation of chaos, suffering and death. I see the world being slowly transformed into a wilderness, I hear the approaching thunder that, one day, will destroy us too, I feel the suffering of millions, And yet, when I look up at the sky, I somehow feel that everything will change for the better, that this cruelty too shall end, that peace and tranquility will return once more. In the meantime, I must hold on to my ideals. Perhaps the day will come when I will be able to realize them!"

Using your knowledge of literature, write a response in which you:

- Compare and contrast Anne's ideals with her awareness of the conditions in which she lives; and
- Discuss how the structure of Anne's writing—her sentences and paragraphs—emphasize the above contrast.

Sample Weak Response

Anne Frank's ideals in this writing make readers clear on the point that she was strongly against Hitler and the Nazis. You can tell that she knows the Nazis are very dangerous and violent people who cause "the suffering of millions." Otherwise, why would she have written this? This fact of Nazis causing the suffering of millions of people, and killing them, is a large contrast to how much she believes "that people are truly good at heart." Anne Frank is right about her ideals. And that is why her whole book is such a large contrast to the conditions in which she lived in WWII, when everything was going wrong in the world. You can also tell from this passage that she is a lot smarter than Hitler was. That is another big contrast in the book.

Anne's sentences and paragraphs emphasize the above contrast. They are not fiction; they are her own real thoughts, and these thoughts don't cause "a grim reality" of "cruelty" or the "absurd and impractical" things that she talks about as the war's fault. No, Anne's words cause us to see what is true and real in her art and in her heart. She makes us see that love is not the fiction. Hitler and the Nazis are the ones who make the fiction. We can read this in between the lines, which sometimes has to be done.

Back when Anne Frank wrote her words down on paper, everything was going wrong around her but she knew what to do, and she did it. She wrote a world classic story about her life. This story is a big contrast to what the Germans were doing.

Sample Strong Response

This excerpt from *The Diary of Anne Frank* reveals the inner strength of a young girl who refuses, despite the wartime violence and danger surrounding her, to let her idealism be overcome by hatred and mass killing. This idealism is reflected, in part, by her emphases on universal human hopes such as peace, tranquility, and goodwill. But Anne Frank is no dreamy Pollyanna. Reflecting on her idealism in the context of the war raging around her, she matter-of-factly writes: "my dreams, they seem so absurd and impractical."

This indicates Anne Frank's awareness of not only her own predicament but of human miseries that extend beyond the immediate circumstances of her life. For elsewhere she writes in a similar vein, "In times like these… I see the world being slowly transformed into a wilderness"; despite her own suffering she can "feel the suffering of millions."

And yet Anne Frank believes, "in spite of everything, that people are truly good at heart." This statement epitomizes the stark existential contrast of her worldview with the wartime reality that ultimately claimed her life.

The statement also exemplifies how Anne's literary form—her syntax and diction—mirror thematic content and contrasts. "In spite of everything," she still believes in people. She can "hear the approaching thunder…yet, when I look up at the sky, I somehow feel that everything will change for the better." At numerous points in this diary entry, first-hand knowledge of violent tragedy stands side-by-side with belief in humanity and human progress.

"I must hold on to my ideals," Anne concludes. "Perhaps the day will come when I'll be able to realize them!" In her diary she has done so, and more.

TEACHER CERTIFICATION STUDY GUIDE

Sample Questions

Choose the best answer for each of the questions.

1. Which of the following bits of information best describes the structure of English?

   A. Syntax based on word order
   B. Inflected
   C. Romantic
   D. Orthography is phonetic

2. Which of the following sentences contains an error in agreement?

   A. Jennifer is one of the women who writes for the magazine.
   B. Each one of their sons plays a different sport.
   C. This band has performed at the Odeum many times.
   D. The data are available online at the listed website.

3. Which item below is not a research-based strategy that supports reading?

   A. reading more
   B. reading along with a more proficient reader
   C. reading a passage no more than twice
   D. self-monitoring progress

4. Use the table below to answer the question that follows it.

	Math Usage	General Usage
bi (two)	bilinear	bicycle
	bimodal	biplane
	binomial	bifocals
cent (100)	centimeter	century
	centigram	centigrade
	percent	centipede
circum (around)	circumference	circumnavigate
	circumradius	circumstance
	circumcenter	Circumspect

   Which vocabulary strategy does the table above exemplify?

   A. Frayer method
   B. morphemic analysis
   C. semantic mapping
   D. word mapping

5. What type of comprehension do questions beginnings with "who," "what," "where," or "how" assess?

   A. evaluative
   B. inferential
   C. literal
   D. narrative

MID. LEVEL HUMANITIES   102

6. A teacher has taught his students to self-monitor their reading by locating where in the passage they are having difficulty, identifying the specific problem there, and restating the difficult sentence or passage in their own words. These strategies are examples of

   A. graphic and semantic organizers
   B. metacognition
   C. recognizing story structure
   D. summarizing

7. Which of the following is not true about English?
   A. English is the easiest language to learn.
   B. English is the least inflected language.
   C. English has the most extensive vocabulary of any language.
   D. English originated as a Germanic tongue.

8. Regularly requiring students to practice reading short, instructional-level texts at least three times to a peer and to give and receive peer feedback about these readings mainly addresses which reading skill?

   A. Comprehension
   B. fluency
   C. evaluation
   D. word-solving

9. A figure of speech in which someone absent or something inhuman is addressed as though present and able to respond describes

   A. personification.
   B. synechdoche.
   C. metonymy
   D. apostrophe.

10. A conversation between two or more people is called a/an:

    A. parody.
    B. dialogue.
    C. monologue.
    D. analogy.

11. Computer-assisted instruction (CAI) accommodates all of the following factors in reading instruction *except for*

    A. free-form responses to comprehension questions
    B. increased motivation
    C. the addition of speech with computer-presented text
    D. the use of computers for word processing, and the integration of writing instruction with reading

12. This statement, "I'll die if I don't pass this course," exemplifies a/an:

    A. barbarism.
    B. oxymoron.
    C. hyperbole.
    D. antithesis.

13. The substitution of "went to his rest" for "died" exemplifies a/an

    A. bowdlerism.
    B. jargon.
    C. euphemism.
    D. malapropism.

14. The appearance of a Yankee from Connecticut in the Court of King Arthur is an example of a/an

    A. rhetoric.
    B. parody.
    C. paradox.
    D. anachronism.

15. To explain or to inform belongs in the category of

    A. exposition.
    B. narration.
    C. persuasion.
    D. description.

16. Which of the four underlined sections of the following sentence contains an error that a word processing spellchecker probably wouldn't catch?

    He tuc the hors by the rains and pulled it back to the stabel.

    A. tuc
    B. hors
    C. rains
    D. stabel

17. For students with poor vocabularies, the teacher should recommend first that

    A. they enroll in a Latin class.
    B. they read newspapers, magazines and books on a regular basis.
    C. they write the words repetitively after looking them up in the dictionary.
    D. they use a thesaurus to locate and incorporate the synonyms found there into their vocabularies.

18. *Diction* is best defined as

    A. The specific word choices an author makes in order to create a particular mood or feeling in the reader.
    B. Writing that explains something thoroughly.
    C. The background, or exposition, for a short story or drama.
    D. Word choices that help teach a truth or moral.

19. Before reading a passage, a teacher gives her students an anticipation guide with a list of statements related to the topic they are about to cover in the reading material. She asks the students to indicate their agreement or disagreement with each statement on the guide. This activity is intended to

   A. elicit students' prior knowledge of the topic and set a purpose for reading
   B. help students to identify the main ideas and supporting details in the text
   C. help students to synthesize information from the text
   D. help students to visualize the concepts and terms in the text

20. Varying the complexity of a graphic organizer exemplifies differentiating which aspect of a lesson?

   A. its content/topic
   B. its environment
   C. its process
   D. its product

21. All of the following techniques are used to observe student progress (conduct ongoing informal assessment) except for

   A. analyzing the student work product at key stages
   B. collecting data from assessment tests
   C. posing strategic questions
   D. observing students as they work

22. A paper explaining the relationship between food and weight gain contains the signal words "because," "consequently," "this is how," and "due to." These words suggest that the paper has which text structure?

   A. cause and effect structure
   B. compare and contrast structure
   C. descriptive structure
   D. sequential structure

23. A paper written in first person and having characters, a setting, a plot, some dialogue, and events sequenced chronologically with some flashbacks exemplifies which genre?

   A. exposition
   B. narration
   C. persuasion
   D. speculation

24. Which group of words is not a sentence?

    A. In keeping with the graduation tradition, the students, in spite of the rain, standing in the cafeteria tossing their mortarboards.
    B. Rosa Parks, who refused to give up her seat on the bus, will be forever remembered for her courage.
    C. Taking advantage of the goalie's being out of the net, we scored our last and winning goal.
    D. When it began to rain, we gathered our possessions and ran for the pavilion.

25. "Clean as a whistle" and "easy as falling off a log" exemplify

    A. semantics.
    B. parody.
    C. irony.
    D. clichés.

26. If a student uses slang and expletives, what is the best course of action to take in order to Improve the student's formal communication skills?

    A. ask the student to rephrase their writing; that is, translate it into language appropriate for the school principal to read.
    B. refuse to read the student's papers until he conforms to a more literate style.
    C. ask the student to read his work aloud to the class for peer evaluation.
    D. rewrite the flagrant passages to show the student the right form of expression.

27. Which of the following is not a theme of Native American writing?

    A. Emphasis on the hardiness of the human body and soul
    B. The strength of multi-cultural assimilation
    C. Indignation about the genocide of native peoples
    D. Remorse for the loss of the Indian way of life

28. Oral debate is most closely associated with which form of discourse?

    A. Description
    B. Exposition
    C. Narration
    D. Persuasion

29. Read the following passage:

"It would have been hard to find a passer-by more wretched in appearance. He was a man of middle height, stout and hardy, in the strength of maturity; he might have been forty-six or seven. A slouched leather cap hid half his face, bronzed by the sun and wind, and dripping with sweat."

What is its main form of discourse?

A. Description
B. Narration
C. Exposition
D. Persuasion

30. The arrangement and relationship of words in sentences or sentence structures best describes

A. style.
B. discourse.
C. thesis.
D. syntax.

31. Identify the sentence that has an error in parallel structure.

A. In order to help your favorite cause, you should contribute time or money, raise awareness, and write congressmen.
B. Many people envision scientists working alone in a laboratory and discovering scientific breakthroughs.
C. Some students prefer watching videos to textbooks because they are used to visual presentation.
D. Tom Hanks, who has won two Academy Awards, is celebrated as an actor, director, and producer.

32. Consider the following sentence:

Mr. Brown is a school volunteer <u>with a reputation and twenty years service</u>.

Which phrase below best represents the logical intent of the underlined phrase above (Choice E is identical to the underlined phrase).

A. with a reputation for twenty years' service
B. with a reputation for twenty year's service
C. who has served twenty years
D. with a service reputation of twenty years

33. Consider the following sentence:

    Joe *didn't hardly know his cousin Fred*, who'd had a rhinoplasty.

    Which word group below best conveys the intended meaning of the underlined section above.

    A. hardly did know his cousin Fred
    B. didn't know his cousin Fred hardly
    C. hardly knew his cousin Fred
    D. didn't know his cousin Fred

34. The literary device of personification is used in which example below?

    A. "Beg me no beggary by soul or parents, whining dog!"
    B. "Happiness sped through the halls cajoling as it went."
    C. "O wind thy horn, thou proud fellow."
    D. "And that one talent which is death to hide."

35. Among junior-high school students of low-to-average readability levels which work would most likely stir reading interest?

    A. *Elmer Gantry*, Sinclair Lewis
    B. *Smiley's People*, John LeCarre
    C. *The Outsiders*, S. E. Hinton
    D. *And Then There Were None*, Agatha Christie

36. Consider the following poem:

    My name is John Welington Wells,
    I'm a dealer in magic and spells,
    In blessings and curses,
    And ever-fill'd purses,
    In prophecies, witches, and knells.

    A. sonnet
    B. haiku
    C. limerick
    D. cinquain

37. Which of the following terms does *not* denote a figure of speech (figurative language)?

    A. Simile
    B. Euphemism
    C. Onomatopoeia
    D. Allusion

38. The first African American to receive the Pulitzer Prize for Poetry was

    A. Gwendolyn Brooks
    B. Harriet E. Wilson
    C. Richard Wright
    D. James Edwin Campbell

39. The principal writer of *The Declaration of Independence* was

    A. Patrick Henry
    B. Thomas Jefferson
    C. Ben Franklin
    D. George Washington

40. Pearl appears as an important character in

    A. *The Scarlet Letter*
    B. *Moby Dick*
    C. *The House of the Seven Gables*
    D. "The Cask of Amontillado"

41. The Old English period refers to

    A. The Fourth Century
    B. The Third through the Eighth Century
    C. The Fifth through the Tenth Century
    D. The Fifth through the Eighth Century

42. What factor below introduced Modern English?

    A. The Great Vowel Shift
    B. The printing press
    C. The invasion of the Normans
    D. Phonetic spelling

43. Students are fluent readers if they

    A. read texts with expression or prosody.
    B. read word-to-word and haltingly.
    C. must intentionally decode a majority of the words.
    D. write disorganized sentences

44. Reading assessment should take place

    A. At the end of the semester.
    B. At the end of a unit.
    C. Constantly.
    D. All of the above.

45. Effective assessment requires that

    A. Students not be involved in the assessment process.
    B. Testing activities are kept separate from the teaching activities.
    C. It assess what classroom instruction has prepared the student to read.
    D. Tests, in order to be reliable, should never use materials previously studied in the classroom

46. Effective assessment means that

    A. It ignores age and cultural considerations
    B. Students' weaknesses are emphasized.
    C. Only reading skills count.
    D. It is integrated with instruction and is not intrusive.

47. Which of the following approaches is *not* useful in assessing slower or immature readers?

    A. Repeated readings.
    B. Echo reading.
    C. Wide reading.
    D. Reading content that is more difficult than their skill levels in order to "stretch" their abilities.

48. All of the following concerns would require a teacher to refer them to another resource *except for*

    A. Auditory trauma.
    B. Ear infection.
    C. Vision problems.
    D. Underdeveloped vocabulary.

49. Middle-School students bring little, if any, initial experience in

    A. Phonics.
    B. Phonemics.
    C. Textbook reading assignments.
    D. Stories read by the teacher.

50. To enhance reading comprehension, experts recommend all of these techniques *except for*

    A. Read material through only once, but read slowly and carefully.
    B. Read material through more than once according to a plan.
    C. Create a map for the next reading.
    D. Highlight or take notes during reading.

51. In the hierarchy of needs for adolescents who are becoming more team-oriented in their approach to learning, which need do they exhibit most?

    A. Need for competence
    B. Need for love/acceptance
    C. Need to know
    D. Need to belong

MID. LEVEL HUMANITIES

52. **What is the best course of action when a child refuses to complete an assignment on the grounds that it is morally objectionable?**

    A. Speak with the parents and explain the necessity of studying this work.
    B. Encourage the child to sample some of the text before making a judgment.
    C. Place the child in another teacher's class where students are studying an acceptable work.
    D. Provide the student with alternative material that serves the same curricular purpose.

53. **Which of the following responses to literature typically give middle school students the most problems?**

    A. Interpretive
    B. Evaluative
    C. Critical
    D. Emotional

54. **Overcrowded classes prevent the individual attention needed to facilitate language development. This drawback can be best overcome by**

    A. Dividing the class into independent study groups.
    B. Assigning more study time at home.
    C. Using more drill practice in class.
    D. Team teaching.

55. **The most significant drawback to applying learning theory research to classroom practice is that**

    A. today's students do not acquire reading skills with the same alacrity as when greater emphasis was placed on reading classical literature.
    B. development rates are complicated by geographical and cultural differences that are difficult to overcome.
    C. homogeneous grouping has contributed to faster development of some age groups.
    D. social and environmental conditions have contributed to an escalated maturity level than research done twenty or more years ago would seem to indicate.

56. **Modeling is a practice that requires students to**

    A. create a style unique to their own language capabilities.
    B. emulate the writing of professionals.
    C. paraphrase passages from good literature.
    D. peer evaluate the writings of other students.

57. Reading a piece of student writing to assess the overall impression of the product is

   A. holistic evaluation.
   B. portfolio assessment.
   C. analytical evaluation.
   D. using a performance system.

58. A formative evaluation of student writing

   A. requires a thorough marking of mechanical errors with a pencil or pen.
   B. makes comments on the appropriateness of the student's interpretation of the prompt and the degree to which the objective was met.
   C. requires the student to hand in all the materials produced during the process of writing.
   D. involves several careful readings of the text for content, mechanics, spelling, and usage.

50. Writing ideas quickly without interruption of the flow of thoughts or attention to conventions is called

   A. brainstorming.
   B. mapping.
   C. listing.
   D. Free writing.

60. The students in Mrs. Cline's seventh grade language arts class were invited to attend a performance of *Romeo and Juliet* presented by the drama class at the high school. To best prepare, they should

   A. read the play as a homework exercise.
   B. read a synopsis of the plot and a biographical sketch of the author.
   C. examine a few main selections from the play to become familiar with the language and style of the author.
   D. read a condensed version of the story and practice attentive listening skills.

61. Which of the following sentences is unambiguously properly punctuated?

   A. The more you eat; the more you want.
   B. The authors—John Steinbeck, Ernest Hemingway, and William Faulkner—are staples of modern writing in American literature textbooks.
   C. Handling a wild horse, takes a great deal of skill and patience.
   D. The man, who replaced our teacher, is a comedian.

62. In a timed essay test of an hour's duration, how much time should be devoted to prewriting.

    A. five
    B. ten
    C. fifteen
    D. twenty

63. A student informative composition should consist of a minimum of how many paragraphs?

    A. three
    B. four
    C. five
    D. six

64. In 'inverted triangle' introductory paragraphs, the thesis sentence occurs

    A. at the beginning of the paragraph.
    B. in the middle of the paragraph.
    C. at the end of the paragraph.
    D. in the second paragraph.

65. A punctuation mark indicating omission, interrupted thought, or an incomplete statement is a/an

    A. ellipsis.
    B. anachronism.
    C. colloquy.
    D. idiom

66. Which of the following would be the most significant factor in teaching Homer's *Iliad* and *Odyssey* to any particular group of students?

    A. Identifying a translation on the appropriate reading level
    B. Determining the students' interest level
    C. Selecting an appropriate evaluative technique
    D. Determining the scope and delivery methods of background study

67. Which of the following contains an error in possessive punctuation?

    A. Doris's shawl
    B. mother's-in-law frown
    C. children's lunches
    D. ambassador's briefcase

68. Which aspect of language is innate?

    A. Biological capability to articulate sounds understood by other humans
    B. Cognitive ability to create syntactical structures
    C. Capacity for using semantics to convey meaning in a social environment
    D. Ability to vary inflections and accents

69. Written on the sixth grade reading level, most of S. E. Hinton's novels (for instance, *The Outsiders*) have the greatest reader appeal with

    A. sixth graders.
    B. ninth graders.
    C. twelfth graders.
    D. adults.

70. After watching a movie of a train derailment, a child exclaims, "Wow, look how many cars fell off the tracks. There's junk everywhere. The engineer must have really been asleep." Using the facts that the child is impressed by the wreckage and assigns blame to the engineer, a follower of Piaget's theories would estimate the child to be about

    A. ten years old.
    B. twelve years old.
    C. fourteen years old.
    D. sixteen years old.

71. Which of the following should not be included in the opening paragraph of an informative essay?

    A. Thesis sentence
    B. Details and examples supporting the main idea
    C. broad general introduction to the topic
    D. A style and tone that grabs the reader's attention

72. Children's literature became established in the

    A. seventeenth century
    B. eighteenth century
    C. nineteenth century
    D. twentieth century

73. Which of the following is the least effective procedure for promoting consciousness of audience?

    A. Pairing students during the writing process
    B. Reading all rough drafts before the students write the final copies
    C. Having students compose stories or articles for publication in school literary magazines or newspapers
    D. Writing letters to friends or relatives

74. Which of the following is not a technique of prewriting?

    A. Clustering
    B. Listing
    C. Brainstorming
    D. Proofreading

Answer Key: Middle School Language Arts

1. A
2. A
3. C
4. B
5. C
6. C
7. A
8. B
9. D
10. B
11. A
12. C
13. C
14. D
15. A
16. C
17. B
18. A
19. A
20. C
21. B
22. A
23. B
24. A
25. D
26. A
27. B
28. D
29. A
30. D
31. C
32. D
33. C
34. B
35. C
36. C
37. D
38. A
39. B
40. A
41. C
42. A
43. A
44. D
45. C
46. D
47. D
48. D
49. C
50. A
51. B
52. D
53. B
54. A
55. D
56. B
57. A
58. B
59. D
60. D
61. B
62. B
63. C
64. C
65. A
66. A
67. B
68. A
69. B
70. A
71. B
72. A
73. B
74. D

TEACHER CERTIFICATION STUDY GUIDE

Rationales with Sample Questions: Middle School Language Arts

1. Which of the following bits of information best describes the structure of English?

   A. Syntax based on word order.
   B. Inflected.
   C. Romantic.
   D. Orthography is phonetic.

The correct answer is A. The syntax of English, reflective of its Germanic origins, relies on word order rather than inflection. Because of this and the many influences of other languages (particularly with regard to vocabulary), the orthography is not phonetic, which complicates the teaching of standardized spelling.

2. Which of the following sentences contains an error in agreement?

   A. Jennifer is one of the women who writes for the magazine.
   B. Each one of their sons plays a different sport.
   C. This band has performed at the Odeum many times.
   D. The data are available online at the listed website.

The correct answer is A. "Women" is the plural antecedent of the relative pronoun "who," which is functioning as the subject in its clause; so "who" is plural and requires the 3rd person plural form for the verb: "write."

3. Which item below is not a research-based strategy that supports reading?

   A. reading more
   B. reading along with a more proficient reader
   C. reading a passage no more than twice
   D. self-monitoring progress

The correct answer is C. Actually, research shows that reading a passage several times improves fluency, and, depending on the complexity of the material, improves comprehension, too. The more complex the material, the more comprehension value in repeated readings.

TEACHER CERTIFICATION STUDY GUIDE

4. Use the table below to answer the question that follows it.

	Math Usage	General Usage
bi (two)	bilinear	bicycle
	bimodal	biplane
	binomial	bifocals
cent (100)	centimeter	century
	centigram	centigrade
	percent	centipede
circum (around)	circumference	circumnavigate
	circumradius	circumstance
	circumcenter	Circumspect

Which vocabulary strategy does the table above exemplify?

A. Frayer method
B. morphemic analysis
C. semantic mapping
D. word mapping

The answer is B. Morphemes are the smallest units of language that have an associated meaning. The purpose of morphemic analysis is to apply morphemic awareness to the task of learning new words. The Frayer method involves having students use their own words to define new words and to link those definitions to personal experiences. Semantic mapping incorporates graphical clues to concepts and is a subset of graphic organizers. Word mapping is another subset of graphic organizers and consists of displaying such information as the various forms a word may take as it transforms through the parts of speech.

5. What type of comprehension do questions beginnings with "who," "what," "where," or "how" assess?

A. evaluative
B. inferential
C. literal
D. narrative

The correct answer is C. Literal questions ask for facts from the reading. The student can put his finger right on the answer and prove that he is correct. These questions are sometimes referred to as "right there" questions. Evaluative questions require a judgement of some sort. Inferential questions ask students to make an educated guess. Narrative questions involve aspects of a story beyond literal considerations.

MID. LEVEL HUMANITIES

6. A teacher has taught his students to self-monitor their reading by locating where in the passage they are having difficulty, by identifying the specific problem there, and by restating the difficult sentence or passage in their own words. These strategies are examples of

   A. graphic and semantic organizers
   B. metacognition
   C. recognizing story structure
   D. summarizing

The correct answer is C. Good readers use metacognitive strategies (various ways of thinking about thinking) to improve their reading. Before reading, they clarify their purpose for reading and preview the text. During reading, they monitor their understanding, adjusting their reading speed to fit the difficulty of the text and fixing any comprehension problems they have. After reading, they check their understanding of what they read.

7. **Which of the following is not true about English?**

   A. English is the easiest language to learn.
   B. English is the least inflected language.
   C. English has the most extensive vocabulary of any language.
   D. English originated as a Germanic tongue.

The answer is A. English has its own inherent quirks which make it difficult to learn, plus it has incorporated words, ands even structures, from many disparate language groups in its lexicon and syntax. Languages with lexicons limited to words governed by a consistent set of relatively simple rules exist, so English is certainly not the easiest language to learn.

8. Regularly requiring students to practice reading short, instructional-level texts at least three times to a peer and to give and receive peer feedback about these readings mainly addresses which reading skill?

   A. Comprehension
   B. fluency
   C. evaluation
   D. word-solving

The correct answer is B. Fluency is the ability to read text quickly with accuracy, phrasing, and expression. Fluency develops over time and requires substantial reading practice. This activity provides just this sort of practice. The peer feedback portion does address comprehension, evaluation, and some word-solving; but the main thrust is on fluency development.

TEACHER CERTIFICATION STUDY GUIDE

9. A figure of speech in which someone absent or something inhuman is addressed as though present and able to respond describes

   A. personification.
   B. synechdoche.
   C. metonymy
   D. apostrophe.

The answer is D. An apostrophe differs from a personification in the important respect that a "someone" cannot be "personified," plus personifications come in far more varieties than are suggested by the definition in question. A synechdoche is a figure of speech which represents some whole or group by one of its or their parts or members. Metonymy is the substitution of a word for a related word.

10. A conversation between two or more people is called a/an

    A. parody.
    B. dialogue.
    C. monologue.
    D. analogy.

The answer is B. Dialogues are the conversations virtually indispensable to dramatic work, and they often appear in narrative and poetry, as well. A parody is a work that adopts the subject and structure of another work in order to ridicule it. A monologue is a work or part of a work written in the first person. An analogy illustrates an idea by means of a more familiar one that is similar or parallel to it.

11. Computer-assisted instruction (CAI) accommodates all of the following factors in reading instruction *except for*

    A. free-form responses to comprehension questions
    B. increased motivation
    C. the addition of speech with computer-presented text
    D. the use of computers for word processing, and the integration of writing instruction with reading

The correct answer is A. CAI does not accommodate free-form responses to comprehension questions, and relies heavily on drill-and-practice and multiple-choice formats. This is a limitation of CAI.

MID. LEVEL HUMANITIES

12. This statement, "I'll die if I don't pass this course," exemplifies a/an

   A. barbarism.
   B. oxymoron.
   C. hyperbole.
   D. antithesis.

The answer is C. A hyperbole is an exaggeration for the sake of emphasis. It is a figure of speech not meant to be taken literally. A barbarism is the use of incorrect or unacceptable language. An oxymoron is a term comprised of opposite or incongruous elements, such as peace fighter.

13. The substitution of "went to his rest" for "died" exemplifies a/an

   A. bowdlerism.
   B. jargon.
   C. euphemism.
   D. malapropism.

The answer is C. A euphemism alludes to a distasteful topic in a pleasant manner in order to obscure or soften the disturbing impact of the original. A bowdlerism is a prudish version of something. Jargon is language specific to some occupation or activity. A Malapropism is the improper use of a word that sounds like the word that would fit the context. The result is most often ludicrous.

14. The appearance of a Yankee from Connecticut in the Court of King Arthur is an example of a/an

   A. rhetoric.
   B. parody.
   C. paradox.
   D. anachronism.

The answer is D. Anachronism is the placing of characters, persons, events or things into time frames incongruent with their actual dates. Parody is poking fun at something. Paradox is a seeming contradiction. Anachronism is something out of time frame.

TEACHER CERTIFICATION STUDY GUIDE

15. To explain or to inform belongs in the category of

    A. exposition.
    B. narration.
    C. persuasion.
    D. description.

The answer is A. Exposition sets forth a systematic explanation of any subject and informs the audience about various topics. It can also introduce the characters of a story and their situations as the story begins. Narration tells a story. Persuasion seeks to influence an audience so that they will adopt some new point of view or take some action. Description provides sensory details and addresses spatial relationships of objects.

16. Which of the four underlined sections of the following sentence contains an error that a word processing spellchecker probably wouldn't catch?

    He <u>tuc</u> the <u>hors</u> by the <u>rains</u> and pulled it back to the <u>stabel</u>.

    A. tuc
    B. hors
    C. rains
    D. stabel

The correct answer is C. Spellcheckers only catch errors in conventional modern English spelling. They cannot catch errors involving incorrect homophone usage. "Rains" is the only one of the four words to conform to conventional English spelling, but it clearly is not the word called for by the context.

17. For students with poor vocabularies, the teacher should recommend first that

    A. they enroll in a Latin class.
    B. they read newspapers, magazines and books on a regular basis.
    C. they write the words repetitively after looking them up in the dictionary.
    D. they use a thesaurus to locate and incorporate the synonyms found there into their vocabularies.

The answer is B. Regularly reading a wide variety of materials for pleasure and information is the best way to develop a stronger vocabulary. The other suggestions have limited application and do not serve to reinforce an enthusiasm for reading.

18. *Diction* is best defined as

    A. The specific word choices an author makes in order to create a particular mood or feeling in the reader.
    B. Writing that explains something thoroughly.
    C. The background, or exposition, for a short story or drama.
    D. Word choices that help teach a truth or moral.

The answer is A. Diction refers to an author's choice of words, expressions and style to convey his/her meaning. The other choices are only marginally related to this meaning, so the choice is a clear one.

19. Before reading a passage, a teacher gives her students an anticipation guide with a list of statements related to the topic they are about to cover in the reading material. She asks the students to indicate their agreement or disagreement with each statement on the guide. This activity is intended to

    A. elicit students' prior knowledge of the topic and set a purpose for reading
    B. help students to identify the main ideas and supporting details in the text
    C. help students to synthesize information from the text
    D. help students to visualize the concepts and terms in the text

The correct answer is A. Establishing a purpose for reading, the foundation for a reading unit or activity, is intimately connected to activating the students' prior knowledge in strategic ways. When the reason for reading is developed in the context of the students' experiences, they are far better prepared to succeed because they can make connections from a base they thoroughly understand. This influences motivation, and with proper motivation, students are more enthused and put forward more effort to understand the text. The other choices are only indirectly supported by this activity and are more specific in focus.

20. **Varying the complexity of a graphic organizer exemplifies differentiating which aspect of a lesson?**

    A. its content/topic
    B. its environment
    C. its process
    D. its product

The correct answer is C. Differentiating the process means offering a variety of learning activities or strategies to students as they manipulate the ideas embedded within the lesson concept. For example, students may use graphic organizers, maps, diagrams, or charts to display their comprehension of concepts covered. Varying the complexity of a graphic organizer can very effectively accommodate differing levels of cognitive processing so that students of differing ability are appropriately engaged. Lesson topic and content remain the same, the lesson is still taking place in the same environment, and, in most lessons, the graphic organizer is not the product of the lesson.

21. **All of the following techniques are used to conduct ongoing informal assessment of student progress except for**

    A. analyzing the student work product at key stages
    B. collecting data from assessment tests
    C. posing strategic questions
    D. observing students as they work

The answer is B. The key here hinges on the adjective, "informal." Assessment tests employ standardized materials and formats to monitor student progress and to report it in statistical terms. The other choices are relatively informal, teacher-specific techniques addressing more current-lesson-specific products and dynamics.

22. A paper explaining the relationship between food and weight gain contains the signal words "because," "consequently," "this is how," and "due to." These words suggest that the paper has which text structure?

   A. cause and effect structure
   B. compare and contrast structure
   C. descriptive structure
   D. sequential structure

The answer is A. These signal words connect events in a causal chain, creating an explanation of some process or event. Compare and contrast structure presents similarities and differences. Descriptive structure presents a sensory impression of something or someone. Sequential structure references what comes first, next, last, and so on.

23. A paper written in first person and having characters, a setting, a plot, some dialogue, and events sequenced chronologically with some flashbacks exemplifies which genre?

   A. exposition
   B. narration
   C. persuasion
   D. speculation

The correct answer is B. Narrative writing tells a story, and all the listed elements pertain to stories. Expository writing explains or informs. Persuasive writing states an opinion and attempts to persuade an audience to accept the opinion or to take some specified action. Speculative writing explores possible developments from given circumstances.

24. Which group of words is not a sentence?

   A. In keeping with the graduation tradition, the students, in spite of the rain, standing in the cafeteria tossing their mortarboards.
   B. Rosa Parks, who refused to give up her seat on the bus, will be forever remembered for her courage.
   C. Taking advantage of the goalie's being out of the net, we scored our last and winning goal.
   D. When it began to rain, we gathered our possessions and ran for the pavilion.

The correct answer is A. This is a sentence fragment because sentences require a subject and a verb and there is no verb. Changing "the students, in spite of the rain, standing" to "the students, in spite of the rain, were standing" corrects the problem.

25. "Clean as a whistle" and "easy as falling off a log" exemplify

   A. semantics.
   B. parody.
   C. irony.
   D. clichés.

The answer is D. A cliché is a phrase or expression that has become dull due to overuse. Semantics is a field of language study. Parody is poking fun at something. Irony is using language to create an unexpected or opposite meaning of the literal words being used.

26. **If a student uses slang and expletives, what is the best course of action to take in order to improve the student's formal communication skills?**

   A. ask the student to rephrase their writing; that is, translate it into language appropriate for the school principal to read.
   B. refuse to read the student's papers until he conforms to a more literate style.
   C. ask the student to read his work aloud to the class for peer evaluation.
   D. rewrite the flagrant passages to show the student the right form of expression.

The answer is A. Asking the student to write to the principal, a respected authority figure, will alert the student to the need to use formal language. Simply refusing to read the paper is not only negative, it also sets up a power struggle. Asking the student to read slang and expletives aloud to the class for peer evaluation is to risk unproductive classroom chaos and to support the class clowns. Rewriting the flagrant passages for the student to model formal expression does not immerse the student in the writing process.

27. Which of the following is not a theme of Native American writing?

   A. Emphasis on the hardiness of the human body and soul
   B. The strength of multi-cultural assimilation
   C. Indignation about the genocide of native peoples
   D. Remorse for the loss of the Indian way of life

The answer is B. Originating in a vast body of oral traditions from as early as before the fifteenth century, Native American literature themes include "nature as sacred," "the interconnectedness of life," "the hardiness of body and soul," "indignation about the destruction of the Native American way of life," and "the genocide of many tribes by the encroaching settlements of European Americans." These themes are still present in today's Native American literature, such as in the works of Duane Niatum, Gunn Allen, Louise Erdrich and N. Scott Momaday.

28. Oral debate is most closely associated with which form of discourse?

   A. Description
   B. Exposition
   C. Narration
   D. Persuasion

The answer is D. The purpose of a debate is to convince some audience or set of judges about something, which is very much the same as persuading some audience or set of judges about something.

29. Read the following passage:

   "It would have been hard to find a passer-by more wretched in appearance. He was a man of middle height, stout and hardy, in the strength of maturity; he might have been forty-six or seven. A slouched leather cap hid half his face, bronzed by the sun and wind, and dripping with sweat."

   What is its main form of discourse?

   A. Description
   B. Narration
   C. Exposition
   D. Persuasion

The answer is A. The passage describes the appearance of a person in detail. Narration tells a story. Exposition explains or informs. Persuasion promotes a point of view or course of action.

30. **The arrangement and relationship of words in sentences or sentence structures best describes**

    A. style.
    B. discourse.
    C. thesis.
    D. syntax.

The answer is D. Syntax is the grammatical structure of sentences. Style is not limited to considerations of syntax only, but includes vocabulary, voice, genre, and other language features. Discourse refers to investigating some idea. A thesis is a statement of opinion.

31. **Identify the sentence that has an error in parallel structure.**

    A. In order to help your favorite cause, you should contribute time or money, raise awareness, and write congressmen.
    B. Many people envision scientists working alone in a laboratory and discovering scientific breakthroughs.
    C. Some students prefer watching videos to textbooks because they are used to visual presentation.
    D. Tom Hanks, who has won two Academy Awards, is celebrated as an actor, director, and producer.

The answer is C. Parallel structure means that certain sentence structures in key positions match-up grammatically. In choice C, "watching videos" is a gerund phrase functioning as the direct object of the verb, and, because the verb implies a comparison, parallel construction requires that "textbooks" (functioning as the object of a currently-missing gerund) be preceded by an appropriate gerund--in this case, "reading." In order for the structure to be parallel, the sentence should read "Some students prefer watching videos to *reading* textbooks because they are used to visual presentation." They prefer something to something else. The other sentences conform to parallel structure. Recognizing parallel structure requires a sophisticated understanding of grammar.

32. Consider the following sentence:

   Mr. Brown is a school volunteer <u>with a reputation and twenty years service</u>.

   Which phrase below best represents the logical intent of the underlined phrase above? (Choice E is identical to the underlined phrase)

   A. with a reputation for twenty years' service
   B. with a reputation for twenty year's service
   C. who has served twenty years
   D. with a service reputation of twenty years

The correct answer is D. His reputation pertains to his service performance, not its duration. Choice A implies that it was for its duration. Choice B has Choice A's problem plus an incorrectly punctuated possessive. Choice C ignores his service reputation. Choice E is extremely vague.

33. Consider the following sentence:

   Joe <u>didn't hardly know his cousin Fred</u>, who'd had a rhinoplasty.

   Which word group below best conveys the intended meaning of the underlined section above?

   A. hardly did know his cousin Fred
   B. didn't know his cousin Fred hardly
   C. hardly knew his cousin Fred
   D. didn't know his cousin Fred

The correct answer is C. It contains a correctly-phrased negative expressed in the appropriate tense. Choice A has tense and awkwardness problems. Choice B has tense and double-negative problems. Choice D ignores the fact that he knew Fred a little. Choice E has tense and double-negative problems.

34. The literary device of personification is used in which example below?

   A. "Beg me no beggary by soul or parents, whining dog!"
   B. "Happiness sped through the halls cajoling as it went."
   C. "O wind thy horn, thou proud fellow."
   D. "And that one talent which is death to hide."

The correct answer is B. Personification is defined as giving human characteristics to inanimate objects or concepts. It can be thought of as a sub-category of metaphor. Happiness, an abstract concept, is "speeding through the halls" and "cajoling," both of which are human behaviors, so Happiness is being compared to a human being. Choice A is figurative and metaphorical, but not a personification. Choice C is, again, figurative and metaphorical, but not a personification. The speaker is, perhaps, telling someone that they are bragging, or "blowing their own horn." Choice D is also figurative and metaphorical, but not personification. Hiding a particular talent is being compared to risking death.

35. Among junior-high school students of low-to-average readability levels, which work would most likely stir reading interest?

   A. *Elmer Gantry*, Sinclair Lewis
   B. *Smiley's People*, John Le Carre
   C. *The Outsiders*, S.E. Hinton
   D. *And Then There Were None*, Agatha Christie.

The answer is C. The students can easily identify with the characters, the social issues, the vocabulary, and the themes in the book. The book deals with teenage concerns such as fitting-in, cliques, and appearance in ways that have proven very engaging for young readers.

36. Consider the following poem:

   My name is John Welington Wells,
   I'm a dealer in magic and spells,
   In blessings and curses,
   And ever-fill'd purses,
   In prophecies, witches, and knells.

   A. sonnet
   B. haiku
   C. limerick
   D. cinquain

The correct answer is C. A limerick is a five line, humorous verse, often nonsensical. with a rhyme scheme of aabba . Lines 1, 2, and 5 usually have eight syllables each; and lines 3 and 4 have five syllables. Line 5 is often some type of 'zinger.' A sonnet is a 14-line poem in iambic pentameter and having a definite rhyme scheme. Shakespearean and Petrarchan sonnets are the main varieties. A cinquain is a five-line poem with one word in line 1, two words in line 2, and so on through line 5.

37. Which of the following terms does *not* denote a figure of speech (figurative language)?

   A. Simile
   B. Euphemism
   C. Onomatopoeia
   D. Allusion

The answer is D. An allusion is an implied reference to a famous person, event, thing, or a part of another text. A simile is a direct comparison between two things. A euphemism is the substitution of an agreeable or inoffensive term for one that might offend. Onomatopoeia is vocal imitation to convey meaning—"bark" or "meow."

38. The first African American to receive the Pulitzer Prize for Poetry was

   A. Gwendolyn Brooks
   B. Harriet E. Wilson
   C. Richard Wright
   D. James Edwin Campbell

The correct answer is A. Gwendolyn Brooks was the first African American to receive the Pulitzer Prize for Poetry. Harriett E. Wilson, who died in 1900, was the first female African American novelist. Richard Wright was a novelist and black activist. James Edwin Campbell was a 19th century African American poet, editor, writer, and educator.

39. The principal writer of *The Declaration of Independence* was

   A. Patrick Henry
   B. Thomas Jefferson
   C. Ben Franklin
   D. George Washington

The correct answer is B. Thomas Jefferson. Although Benjamin Franklin was responsible for editing it and making it the prime example of neoclassical writing that it is, *The Declaration of Independence* came directly from the mind and pen of Jefferson. Patrick Henry was a great orator, and his speeches played an important role in precipitating the revolution. Although George Washington's *Farewell to the Army of the Potomac* is an important piece of writing from that era, he was not the principal writer of the declaration.

40. Pearl appears as an important character in

   A. *The Scarlet Letter*
   B. *Moby Dick*
   C. *The House of the Seven Gables*
   D. "The Cask of Amontillado"

The correct answer is A. Pearl is the illegitimate daughter of Hester Prynne in Nathaniel Hawthorne's *The Scarlet Letter*. *Moby Dick* is Herman Melville's great opus about the pursuit of a great white whale. *The House of the Seven Gables*, like *The Scarlet Letter,* is about a society that promulgates loneliness and suspicion. "The Cask of Amontillado" is one of Poe's horror stories.

41. The Old English period refers to

A. The Fourth Century
B. The Third through the Eighth Century
C. The Fifth through the Tenth Century
D. The Fifth through the Eighth Century

The correct answer is C. The Old English period begins with the settlement of the British Isles in the fifth and sixth centuries by Germanic tribes and continues until the time of Chaucer.

42. What factor below introduced Modern English?

A. The Great Vowel Shift
B. The printing press
C. The invasion of the Normans
D. Phonetic spelling

The correct answer is A. The Great Vowel Shift created guidelines for spelling and pronunciation in the wake of the invention of the printing press. Other answer choices, though related to the question, do not answer it as specifically.

43. Students are fluent readers if they

A. read texts fast enough and with appropriate expression, or prosody.
B. read word-to-word and haltingly.
C. must intentionally decode a majority of the words.
D. write disorganized sentences

The correct answer is A. A fluent reader reads words accurately, at target speeds, and with appropriate expression. It is a positive term. The other choices describe negative outcomes.

44. Reading assessment should take place

A. At the end of the semester.
B. At the end of a unit.
C. Constantly.
D. All of the above.

The correct answer is D. End-of-unit and end-of-semester measurements yield important information regarding achievement of course objectives and the evaluating of students' growth; however, assessment should be going on all the time so that the teacher can adjust instruction to meet the day-to-day needs of the students.

45. **Effective assessment requires that**

    A. Students not be involved in the assessment process.
    B. Testing activities are kept separate from the teaching activities.
    C. References materials that classroom instruction has prepared the students to read.
    D. Tests, in order to be reliable, should never use materials previously studied in the classroom

The correct answer is C. The only reliable measure of the success of a unit will be based on the reading the instruction has focused on. Choice A makes almost no sense; students will at the very least have to do something that can be assessed. Choice B calls into question the whole reason for schools. Choice D uses different phrases to accomplish the same unworthy end as Choice B.

46. **Effective assessment means that**

    A. It ignores age and cultural considerations
    B. Students' weaknesses are emphasized.
    C. Only reading skills count.
    D. It is integrated with instruction and is not intrusive.

The correct answer is D. Effective assessment informs instruction and practice. It is one phase of an integrated instructional cycle. Choice A ignores reality and distorts rather than informs. Choice B discourages students. Choice C ignores other important ways of demonstrating growth in understanding.

47. **Which of the following approaches is *not* useful in assessing slower or immature readers?**

    A. Repeated readings.
    B. Echo reading.
    C. Wide reading.
    D. Reading content that is more difficult than their skill levels in order to "stretch" their abilities.

The correct answer is D. Reading content for such students should be at a level where they can read and understand the word nuances, not at a level beyond such understanding and competence. Repeated readings of appropriate material builds this foundation. So does echo reading, or listening to a skilled reader and then trying to imitate his or her delivery. Wide reading is an approach intended to motivate students to read for pleasure and information from a variety of sources and involving socially-motivating processing routines.

48. A teacher should refer all of the following concerns to the appropriate expert **except for**

   A. Auditory trauma.
   B. Ear infection.
   C. Vision problems.
   D. Underdeveloped vocabulary.

The answer is D. The teacher is the expert in vocabulary development. The other choices require a medical professional.

49. Middle-School students bring little, if any, initial experience in

   A. Phonics.
   B. Phonemics.
   C. Textbook reading assignments.
   D. Stories read by the teacher.

The correct answer is C. In middle school, probably for the first time, the student will be expected to read textbook assignments and come to class prepared to discuss the content. Students get phonics (the systematic study of decoding) in the early grades, and they normally get phonemics (familiarity with the syllable sounds of English) even earlier. They will have almost certainly had stories read to them by a teacher by the time they get to middle school.

50. To enhance reading comprehension, experts recommend all of these techniques **except for**

   A. Read material through only once, but read slowly and carefully.
   B. Read material through more than once according to a plan.
   C. Create a map for the next reading.
   D. Highlight or take notes during reading.

The correct answer is A. While reading at a rate that assures accuracy is desirable, there is no evidence to support a recommendation to avoid rereading something. Choice B is advisable because it proposes a purpose for the re-readings. Choice C is advisable because it also addresses purpose. Choice D is advisable because it helps students maintain focus as they read.

51. In the hierarchy of needs for adolescents who are becoming more team-oriented in their approach to learning, which need do they exhibit most?

   A. Need for competence
   B. Need for love/acceptance
   C. Need to know
   D. Need to belong

The answer is B. Abraham's Maslow's theory of Humanistic Development that such older children and adolescents exhibit most a need for love/acceptance from peers and potential romantic partners. Their need for competence is in the service of gaining the love/acceptance. Their need to know is developing, but is not their primary issue. Their need to belong does not address their emerging sexual identities.

52. What is the best course of action when a child refuses to complete an assignment on the ground that is morally objectionable?

   A. Speak with the parents and explain the necessity of studying this work.
   B. Encourage the child to sample some of the text before making a judgment.
   C. Place the child in another teacher's class where students are studying an acceptable work.
   D. Provide the student with alternative material that serves the same curricular purpose.

The answer is D. This approach is the most time efficient and flexible. Choice A requires conversations involving value systems that aren't going to change. Choice B risks being open to the charge of exposing children to controversial material despite parental input. Choice C is a disproportionate disruption to the student's schedule and the school routine.

53. **Which of the following responses to literature typically give middle school students the most problems?**

    A. Interpretive
    B. Evaluative
    C. Critical
    D. Emotional

The answer is B. Middle school readers will exhibit both emotional and interpretive responses. In middle/junior high school, organized study models enable students to identify main ideas and supporting details, to recognize sequential order, to distinguish fact from opinion, and to determine cause/effect relationships. Middle school students can provide reasons to support their assertions that a particular book was boring or a particular poem made him or her feel sad, and this is to provide a critical reaction on a fundamental level. Evaluative responses, however, require students to address how the piece represents its genre, how well it reflects the social and ethical mores of a given society, or how well the author has employed a fresh approach to the subject. Evaluative responses are more sophisticated than critical responses, and they are appropriate for advanced high school students.

54. **Overcrowded classes prevent the individual attention needed to facilitate language development. This drawback can be best overcome by**

    A. Dividing the class into independent study groups.
    B. Assigning more study time at home.
    C. Using more drill practice in class.
    D. Team teaching.

The answer is A. Dividing a class into small groups maximizes opportunities for engagement. Assigning more study time at home is passing the buck. Using more drill practice in class is likely to bore most students to tears. Team teaching begs the question; if you can get another teacher, then your class should no longer be overcrowded.

55. The most significant drawback to applying learning theory research to classroom practice is that

   A. today's students do not acquire reading skills with the same alacrity as when greater emphasis was placed on reading classical literature.
   B. development rates are complicated by geographical and cultural differences that are difficult to overcome.
   C. homogeneous grouping has contributed to faster development of some age groups.
   D. social and environmental conditions have contributed to an escalated maturity level than research done twenty or more years ago would seem to indicate.

The answer is D. A mismatch exists between what interests today's students and the learning materials presented to them. Choice A is a significant problem only if the school insists on using classical literature exclusively. Choice B does describe a drawback, but students are more alike in their disengagement from anachronistic learning materials than they are different due to their culture and geographical location. Choice C describes a situation that is not widespread.

56. Modeling is a practice that requires students to

   A. create a style unique to their own language capabilities.
   B. emulate the writing of professionals.
   C. paraphrase passages from good literature.
   D. peer evaluate the writings of other students.

The answer is B. Modeling engages students in analyzing the writing of professional writers and in imitating the syntactical, grammatical and stylistic mastery of that writer. Choice A is an issue of voice. Choice C is a less rigorous form of the correct answer. Choice D is only very indirectly related to modeling.

57. Reading a piece of student writing to assess the overall impression of the product is

A. holistic evaluation.
B. portfolio assessment.
C. analytical evaluation.
D. using a performance system.

The answer is A. In holistic scoring, the teacher reads quickly through a paper once to get a general impression and assigns a rating based on a rubric that includes the criteria for achievement in a few, key dimensions of the assignment. Portfolio assessment involves tracking work over stages or over time. Analytical evaluation involves breaking down the assignment into discrete traits and determining achievement in each of those traits. A performance system refers to engaging students in writing assignments meant to generate products in a given time frame. Often, such products are scored holistically.

58. A formative evaluation of student writing

A. requires a thorough marking of mechanical errors with a pencil or pen.
B. makes comments on the appropriateness of the student's interpretation of the prompt and the degree to which the objective was met.
C. requires the student to hand in all the materials produced during the process of writing.
D. involves several careful readings of the text for content, mechanics, spelling, and usage.

The answer is B. Formative evaluations should support the students' writing process through strategic feedback at key points. Teacher comments and feedback should encourage recursive revision and metacognition. Choice A applies, if anywhere, to a summative evaluation of student writing. Choice C is a neutral management strategy. A teacher can make formative evaluations without collecting all the materials. Choice D, again, is more suited for summative evaluation or for the very last issue in the composition process, namely proofreading.

59. Writing ideas quickly without interruption of the flow of thoughts or attention to conventions is called

   A. brainstorming.
   B. mapping.
   C. listing.
   D. Free writing.

The answer is D. Free writing is a particular type of brainstorming (techniques to generate ideas). Mapping is another type and results in products resembling flow charts. Listing is another brainstorming technique that differs from free writing in that free writing is more open-ended and looks more like sentences.

60. The students in Mrs. Cline's seventh grade language arts class were invited to attend a performance of *Romeo and Juliet* presented by the drama class at the high school. To best prepare, they should

   A. read the play as a homework exercise.
   B. read a synopsis of the plot and a biographical sketch of the author.
   C. examine a few main selections from the play to become familiar with the language and style of the author.
   D. read a condensed version of the story and practice attentive listening skills.

The answer is D. By reading a condensed version of the play, students will know the plot and therefore be better able to follow the play on stage. They will also practice being attentive. Choice A is far less dynamic and few will do it. Choice B is likewise dull. Choice C is not thorough enough.

61. Which of the following sentences is unambiguously properly punctuated?

   A. The more you eat; the more you want.
   B. The authors—John Steinbeck, Ernest Hemingway, and William Faulkner—are staples of modern writing in American literature textbooks.
   C. Handling a wild horse, takes a great deal of skill and patience
   D. The man, who replaced our teacher, is a comedian.

The answer is B. Dashes should be used instead of commas when commas are used elsewhere in the sentence for amplification or explanation—here within the dashes. Choice A has a semicolon where there should be a comma. Choice C has a comma that shouldn't be there at all. Choice D could be correct in a non-restrictive context, and so whether or not it is correct is ambiguous.

62. In a timed essay test of an hour's duration, how much time should be devoted to prewriting.

   A. five
   B. ten
   C. fifteen
   D. twenty

The answer is B. Ten minutes of careful planning still allows sufficient time for the other stages of the writing process. Five minutes would result more dead-ends and backtracking. Fifteen and twenty minutes would result in rushing drafting, revising, and editing.

63. A student informative composition should consist of a minimum of how many paragraphs?

   A. three
   B. four
   C. five
   D. six

The answer is C. This composition would consist of an introductory paragraph, three body paragraphs, and a concluding paragraph. A three or four paragraph composition could include all three types of paragraphs, but would not require the students to elaborate at sufficient length in the body of the paper. A six paragraph minimum is slightly excessive, more or less by tradition.

64. In 'inverted triangle' introductory paragraphs, the thesis sentence occurs

   A. at the beginning of the paragraph.
   B. in the middle of the paragraph.
   C. at the end of the paragraph.
   D. in the second paragraph.

The answer is C. The beginning of the paragraph should establish interest, the middle of the paragraph should establish a general context, and the paragraph should end with the thesis that the rest of the paper will develop. Delaying the thesis until the second paragraph would be 'outside the triangle.'

65. A punctuation mark indicating omission, interrupted thought, or an incomplete statement is a/an

   A. ellipsis.
   B. anachronism.
   C. colloquy.
   D. idiom.

The answer is A. In an ellipsis, a word or words that would clarify the sentence's message are missing, yet it is still possible to understand them from the context. An anachronism is something out of its proper time frame. A colloquy is a formal conversation or dialogue. An idiom is a saying peculiar to some language group.

66. Which of the following would be the most significant factor in teaching Homer's *Iliad* and *Odyssey* to any particular group of students?

   A. Identifying a translation on the appropriate reading level
   B. Determining the student's interest level
   C. Selecting an appropriate evaluative technique
   D. Determining the scope and delivery methods of background study

The answer is A. Students will appreciate these two works if the translation reflects both the vocabulary they know and their reading level. Choice B is moot because most students aren't initially interested in Homer. Choice C skips to later matters. Choice D is tempting and significant, but not as crucial as having an accessible text.

67. Which of the following contains an error in possessive punctuation?

   A. Doris's shawl
   B. mother's-in-law frown
   C. children's lunches
   D. ambassador's briefcase

The answer is B. Mother-in-law is a compound common noun, and the apostrophe should come at the end of the word, according to convention. The other choices are correctly punctuated.

68. **Which aspect of language is innate?**

    A. Biological capability to articulate sounds understood by other humans
    B. Cognitive ability to create syntactical structures
    C. Capacity for using semantics to convey meaning in a social environment
    D. Ability to vary inflections and accents

The answer is A. The biological capability to articulate sounds understood by other humans is innate; and, later, children learn semantics and syntactical structures through trial and error. Linguists agree that language is first a vocal system of word symbols that enable a human to communicate his or her feelings, thoughts, and desires to other human beings.

69. **Written on the sixth grade reading level, most of S. E. Hinton's novels (for instance, *The Outsiders*) have the greatest reader appeal with**

    A. sixth graders.
    B. ninth graders.
    C. twelfth graders.
    D. adults.

The answer is B. Adolescents are concerned with their changing bodies, their relationships with each other and adults, and their place in society. Reading *The Outsiders* helps them confront different problems that they are only now beginning to experience as teenagers, such as gangs and social identity. The book is universal in its appeal to adolescents.

70. **After watching a movie of a train derailment, a child exclaims, "Wow, look how many cars fell off the tracks. There's junk everywhere. The engineer must have really been asleep." Using the facts that the child is impressed by the wreckage and assigns blame to the engineer, a follower of Piaget's theories would estimate the child to be about**

    A. ten years old.
    B. twelve years old.
    C. fourteen years old.
    D. sixteen years old.

The answer is A. According to Piaget's theory, children seven to eleven years old begin to apply logic to concrete things and experiences. They can combine performance and reasoning to solve problems. They have internalized moral values and are willing to confront rules and adult authority.

71. Which of the following should not be included in the opening paragraph of an informative essay?

   A. Thesis sentence
   B. Details and examples supporting the main idea
   C. broad general introduction to the topic
   D. A style and tone that grabs the reader's attention

The answer is B. The introductory paragraph should introduce the topic, capture the reader's interest, state the thesis and prepare the reader for the main points in the essay. Details and examples, however, belong in the second part of the essay, the body paragraphs.

72. Children's literature became established in the

   A. seventeenth century
   B. eighteenth century
   C. nineteenth century
   D. twentieth century

The answer is A. In the seventeenth century, Jean de la Fontaine's *Fables*, Pierre Perreault's *Tales*, Mme. d'Aulnoye's novels based on old folktales, and Mme. de Beaumont's *Beauty and the Beast* created a children's literature genre. In England, Perreault was translated, and a work allegedly written by Oliver Smith, *The Renowned History of Little Goody Two Shoes*, helped to establish children's literature in England, too.

73. Which of the following is the least effective procedure for promoting consciousness of audience?

   A. Pairing students during the writing process
   B. Reading all rough drafts before the students write the final copies
   C. Having students compose stories or articles for publication in school literary magazines or newspapers
   D. Writing letters to friends or relatives

The answer is B. Reading all rough drafts will do the least to promote consciousness of audience; they are very used to turning papers into the teacher, and most don't think much about impressing the teacher. Pairing students will ensure a small, constant audience about whom they care; and having them compose stories for literary magazines will encourage them to put their best efforts forward because their work will be read by an actual audience in an impressive format. Writing letters also engages students in thinking about how best to communicate with a particular audience.

74. Which of the following is not a technique of prewriting?

    A. Clustering
    B. Listing
    C. Brainstorming
    D. Proofreading

The answer is D. You cannot proofread something that you have not yet written. While it is true that prewriting involves written techniques, prewriting is not concerned with punctuation, capitalization, and spelling (proofreading). Brainstorming is a general term denoting generating ideas, and clustering and listing are specific methods of brainstorming.

TEACHER CERTIFICATION STUDY GUIDE

DOMAIN VI.   **UNITED STATES HISTORY**

COMPETENCY 18.0   PHYSICAL GEOGRAPHY OF NORTH AMERICA

Skill 18.1   **Demonstrate knowledge of North America's location in the world, and of the continent's rivers, lakes, and important land features**

North America consists of Canada; the United States of America; Mexico; the Caribbean island nations of the West Indies including Cuba, Jamaica, Haiti and the Dominican Republic; and the "land bridge" of Middle America, including Panama, Honduras, El Salvador, Nicaragua, Guatemala, and others.

At its most northern extreme, Alaska and Canada border the Arctic Ocean; and at its most southern extreme, the Isthmus of Panama borders Colombia. The west coast borders the Pacific Ocean, and the east coast borders the Atlantic Ocean, the Caribbean Sea and the Gulf of Mexico, further southeast.

The major freshwater bodies are the Great Lakes—Huron, Ontario, Michigan, Erie and Superior—which lie between Canada and the United States. The Mississippi River is the longest North American river, extending from the U.S.-Canada border to the Gulf of Mexico, draining the Ohio River from the east and the Missouri River to the west. Other significant rivers are the St. Lawrence, which connects Lake Erie to the Atlantic Ocean, and the Rio Grande, forming most of the border between Mexico and the United States.

The three most significant mountain ranges are the Appalachian Mountains, which extend from the Canadian Maritime Provinces south to Georgia in the United States along the eastern seaboard; the Rocky Mountains, which extend from west-central Canada through the United States to Mexico; and the Sierra Nevada cordillera, which extends from Alaska in the United States, through Canada, through the west coast of the United States, and through Mexico and Mesoamerica to South America.

Skill 18.2   Demonstrate knowledge of broad climate patterns and physiographic regions

Climate is average weather or daily weather conditions for a specific region or location over a long or extended period of time. Studying the climate of an area includes information gathered on the area's monthly and yearly temperatures and its monthly and yearly amounts of precipitation. In addition, a characteristic of an area's climate is the length of its growing season. Four reasons for the different climate regions on the earth are differences in:

Latitude,
The amount of moisture,
Temperatures in land and water, and
The earth's land surface.

There are many different climates throughout the earth. It is most unusual if a country contains just one kind of climate. Regions of climates are divided according to latitudes:

0 - 23 1/2 degrees are the "**low latitudes**"
23 1/2 - 66 1/2 degrees are the "**middle latitudes**"
66 1/2 degrees to the Poles are the "**high latitudes**"

The low latitudes are composed of the rainforest, savanna, and desert climates. The tropical rainforest climate is found in equatorial lowlands and is hot and wet. There is sun, extreme heat and rain every day. Although daily temperatures rarely rise above 90 degrees F, the daily humidity is always high, leaving everything sticky and damp. North and south of the tropical rainforests are the tropical grasslands called "savannas," the "lands of two seasons"--a winter dry season and a summer wet season. Further north and south of the tropical grasslands or savannas are the deserts. These areas are the hottest and driest parts of the earth, receiving less than 10 inches of rain a year. These areas have extreme temperatures between night and day. After the sun sets, the land cools quickly dropping the temperature as much as 50 degrees F.

The middle latitudes contain the Mediterranean, humid-subtropical, humid-continental, marine, steppe, and desert climates. Lands containing the Mediterranean climate are considered "sunny" lands found in six areas of the world: lands bordering the Mediterranean Sea, a small portion of southwestern Africa, areas in southern and southwestern Australia, a small part of the Ukraine near the Black Sea, central Chile, and Southern California. Summers are hot and dry with mild winters. The growing season usually lasts all year and what little rain falls are during the winter months. What is rather unusual is that the Mediterranean climate is located between 30 and 40 degrees north and south latitude on the western coasts of countries.

The humid subtropical climate is found north and south of the tropics and is moist indeed. The areas having this type of climate are found on the eastern side of their continents and include Japan, mainland China, Australia, Africa, South America, and the United States--the southeastern coasts of these areas. An interesting feature of their locations is that warm ocean currents are found there. The winds that blow across these currents bring in warm moist air all year round. Long, warm summers; short, mild winters; a long growing season allows for different crops to be grown several times a year. All contribute to the productivity of this climate type which supports more people than any of the other climates.

The marine climate is found in Western Europe, the British Isles, the U.S. Pacific Northwest, the western coast of Canada and southern Chile, along with southern New Zealand and southeastern Australia. A common characteristic of these lands is that they are either near water or surrounded by it. The ocean winds are wet and warm bringing a mild, rainy climate to these areas. In the summer, the daily temperatures average at or below 70 degrees F. During the winter, because of the warming effect of the ocean waters, the temperatures rarely fall below freezing.

In northern and central United States, northern China, south central and southeastern Canada, and the western and southeastern parts of the former Soviet Union is found the "climate of four seasons," the humid continental climate--spring, summer, fall, and winter. Cold winters, hot summers, and enough rainfall to grow a variety of crops are the major characteristics of this climate. In areas where the humid continental climate is found are some of the world's best farmlands as well as important activities such as trading and mining. Differences in temperatures throughout the year are determined by the distance a place is inland, away from the coasts.

The steppe or prairie climate is located in the interiors of the large continents like Asia and North America. These dry flatlands are far from ocean breezes and are called prairies or the Great Plains in Canada and the United States and steppes in Asia. Although the summers are hot and the winters are cold as in the humid continental climate, the big difference is rainfall. In the steppe climate, rainfall is light and uncertain, 10 to 20 inches a year mainly in spring and summer and is considered normal. Where rain is more plentiful, grass grows; in areas of less, the steppes or prairies gradually become deserts. These are found in the Gobi Desert of Asia, central and western Australia, southwestern United States, and in the smaller deserts found in Pakistan, Argentina, and Africa south of the Equator.

The two major climates found in the high latitudes are "tundra" and "taiga." The word *tundra*, meaning "marshy plain," is a Russian word and aptly describes the climatic conditions in the northern areas of Russia, Europe, and Canada. Winters are extremely cold and very long. Most of the year the ground is frozen but becomes rather mushy during the very short summer months. Surprisingly less snow falls in the area of the tundra than in the eastern part of the United States. However, because of the harshness of the extreme cold, very few people live there and no crops can be raised. Despite having a small human population, many plants and animals are found there.

The "taiga" is the northern forest region and is located south of the tundra. In fact, the Russian word *taiga* means "forest." The world's largest forestlands are found here along with vast mineral wealth and forbearing animals. The climate is extreme that very few people live here, not being able to raise crops because of the extremely short growing season. The winter temperatures are colder and the summer temperatures are hotter than those in the tundra are because the taiga climate region is farther from the waters of the Arctic Ocean. The taiga is found in the northern parts of Russia, Sweden, Norway, Finland, Canada, and Alaska with most of their lands covered with marshes and swamps.

In certain areas of the earth there exists a type of climate unique to areas with high mountains, usually different from their surroundings. This type of climate is called a "vertical climate" because the temperatures, crops, vegetation, and human activities change and become different as one ascends the different levels of elevation. At the foot of the mountain, a hot and rainy climate is found with the cultivation of many lowland crops. As one climbs higher, the air becomes cooler, the climate changes sharply and different economic activities change, such as grazing sheep and growing corn. At the top of many mountains, snow is found year-round.

COMPETENCY 19.0 NATIVE AMERICAN PEOPLES

Skill 19.1   Demonstrate knowledge of Native American tribes living in the various regions of North America

There is strong archaeological evidence supporting the contention that the ancestors of today's Native Americans and Latin American Indians crossed the Bering Strait from Asia to Alaska, eventually settling in all parts of the Americas; and there is also some evidence that suggests that some may have arrived from Asia and the Pacific islands via a more southerly transoceanic seafaring route.

Indigenous peoples of North America have been traditionally divided by anthropologists and ethnologists into mutually unintelligible linguistic groups:
Inuit - In the north, from western Arctic Alaska, across Arctic Canada to the Canadian Maritimes
Dineh – From interior Alaska to the Sonoran Desert in Mexico (Athapaskan, Apache, Navajo, etc.)
Anishinabe (Algonquian) – Eastern woodlands United States and Canada (Ojibwe, Mohican, Abenaki)
Siouan – Midwestern and western Great Plains of the United States and Canada (Lakota, Dakota, Nakota)
Iroquoian – Northeastern United States and southeastern Canada woodlands (Seneca, Oneida, Mohawk, Onondaga, Cayuga)
Nahuatl – Central Mexico (Aztec)
Mayan – Southern Mexico and Mesoamerica
Northwest Indian – Southern Alaska Panhandle through Pacific Coastal Canada to the Oregon coast (Tlingit, Haida, Tsimshian, Nitnat)

Skill 19.2   Demonstrate understanding of the political, economic, social, and cultural life of Native American peoples

Native American tribes lived throughout what we now call the United States in varying degrees of togetherness. They adopted different customs, pursued different avenues of agriculture and food gathering, and made slightly different weapons. They fought among themselves and with other peoples. To varying degrees, they had established cultures long before Columbus or any other European explorer arrived on the scene.

Perhaps the most famous of the Native American tribes is the **Algonquians**. We know so much about this tribe because they were one of the first to interact with the newly arrived English settlers in Plymouth, Massachusetts and elsewhere. The Algonquians lived in wigwams and wore clothing made from animal skins. They were proficient hunters, gatherers, and trappers who also knew quite a bit about farming. Beginning with a brave man named Squanto, they shared this agricultural knowledge with the English settlers, including how to plant and cultivate corn, pumpkins, and squash.

Other famous Algonquians included Pocahontas and her father, Powhatan, both of whom are immortalized in English literature, and Tecumseh and Black Hawk, known foremost for their fierce fighting ability. To the overall Native American culture, they contributed wampum and dream catchers.

Another group of tribes who lived in the Northeast were the **Iroquois**, who were fierce fighters but also forward thinkers. They lived in long houses and wore clothes made of buckskin. They, too, were expert farmers, growing the "Three Sisters" (corn, squash, and beans). Five of the Iroquois tribes formed a Confederacy, a shared form of government. The Iroquois also formed the False Face Society, a group of medicine men who shared their medical knowledge with others but kept their identities secret while doing so. These masks are one of the enduring symbols of the Native American era.

Living in the Southeast were the **Seminoles** and **Creeks**, a huge collection of people who lived in chickees (open, bark-covered houses) and wore clothes made from plant fibers. They were expert planters and hunters and were proficient at paddling dugout canoes, which they made. The bead necklaces they created were some of the most beautiful on the continent. They are best known, however, for their struggle against Spanish and English settlers, especially led by the great Osceola.

The **Cherokee** also lived in the Southeast. They were one of the most advanced tribes, living in domed houses and wearing deerskin and rabbit fur. Accomplished hunters, farmers, and fishermen, the Cherokee were known the continent over for their intricate and beautiful basketry and clay pottery. They also played a game called lacrosse, which survives to this day in countries around the world.

In the middle of the continent lived the Plains tribes, such as the **Sioux, Cheyenne, Blackfeet, Comanche, and Pawnee**. These peoples lived in teepees and wore buffalo skins and feather headdresses. (It is this image of the Native American that has made its way into most American movies depicting the period.) They hunted wild animals on the Plains, especially the buffalo. They were well known for their many ceremonies including the Sun Dance and for the peace pipes that they smoked. Famous Plains people include Crazy Horse and Sitting Bull, authors of the Custer Disaster; Sacagawea, leader of the Lewis & Clark expedition; and Chief Joseph, the famous Nez Perce leader.

Dotting the deserts of the Southwest were a handful of tribes, including the famous **Pueblo**, who lived in houses that bear their tribe's name. They wore clothes made of wool and woven cotton, farmed crops in the middle of desert land, created exquisite pottery and Kachina dolls, and had one of the most complex religions of all the tribes. They are perhaps best known for the challenging vista-based villages that they constructed from the sheer faces of cliffs and rocks and for their **adobes**, mud-brick buildings that housed their living and meeting quarters. The Pueblos chose their own chiefs. This was perhaps one of the oldest representative governments in the world.

Another well-known Southwestern tribe was the **Apache**, with their famous leader **Geronimo**. The Apache lived in homes called wickiups, which were made of bark, grass, and branches. They wore cotton clothing and were excellent hunters and gatherers. Adept at basketry, the Apache believed that everything in Nature had special powers and that they were honored just to be part of it all.

The **Navajo**, also residents of the Southwest, lived in hogans (round homes built with forked sticks) and wore clothes of rabbit skin. Their major contribution to the overall culture of the continent was in sand painting, weapon making, silversmithing, and weaving. Navajo hands crafted some of the most beautiful woven rugs.

Living in the Northwest were the **Inuit**, who lived in tents made from animal skins or, in some cases, igloos. They wore clothes made of animal skins, usually seals or caribou. They were excellent fishermen and hunters and crafted efficient kayaks and umiaks to take them through waterways and harpoons with which to hunt animals. The Inuit are perhaps best known for the great carvings that they left behind. Among these are ivory figures and tall totem poles.

COMPETENCY 20.0 EUROPEAN EXPLORATION AND COLONIZATION

Skill 20.1 Identify the major explorers and the reasons for European exploration

A number of individuals and events led to the time of exploration and discoveries. The Vivaldo brothers and Marco Polo wrote of their travels and experiences, which signaled the early beginnings. From the Crusades, the survivors made their way home to different places in Europe, bringing with them fascinating, new information about exotic lands, people, customs, and desired foods and goods such as spices and silks.

The Renaissance ushered in a time of curiosity, learning, and incredible energy sparking the desire for trade to procure these new, exotic products and to find better, faster, cheaper trade routes to get to them. The work of geographers, astronomers and mapmakers made important contributions; and many studied and applied the work of such men as Hipparchus of Greece, Ptolemy of Egypt, Tycho Brahe of Denmark, and Fra Mauro of Italy.

Portugal made the start under the encouragement, support, and financing of Prince Henry the Navigator. The better known explorers who sailed under the flag of Portugal included Cabral, Diaz, and Vasco da Gama, who successfully sailed all the way from Portugal, around the southern tip of Africa, to Calcutta, India.

Christopher Columbus, sailing for Spain, is credited with the discovery of America although he never set foot on its soil. Magellan is credited with the first circumnavigation of the earth. Other Spanish explorers made their marks in parts of what are now the United States, Mexico, and South America.

For France, claims to various parts of North America were the result of the efforts of such men as Verrazano, Champlain, Cartier, LaSalle, Father Marquette and Joliet. Dutch claims were based on the work of one Henry Hudson. John Cabot gave England its stake in North America along with John Hawkins, Sir Francis Drake, and the half-brothers Sir Walter Raleigh and Sir Humphrey Gilbert.

Actually the first Europeans in the New World were Norsemen led by Eric the Red and later, his son Leif the Lucky. However, before any of these, the ancestors of today's Native Americans and Latin American Indians crossed the Bering Strait from Asia to Alaska, eventually settling in all parts of the Americas.

Skill 20.2 Demonstrate understanding of the consequences of early contacts between Europeans and Native Americans

The first documented contact between Europeans and Native Americans that has archaeological evidence to support it was the Viking settlement of eastern Canada in 1000 CE. Under the leadership of Leif Eriksson, the Norse immigrants first encountered hostile Inuit in what is now northeastern Quebec and ventured south to Inland, what is now leans ax Meadows, to establish a permanent settlement. Again, their encounter with the Native Americans was hostile and eventually the incessant warfare between the Viking immigrants and the Native Americans was fought under conditions of relative parity of weapons, compelled the Vikings to abandon the Inland settlement, never to return.

The next recorded contact was in 1492 CE, when Christopher Columbus, a Genoese adventurer commanding a squadron of Spanish ships, landed in what is now believed to be the island of Hispaniola, what is now Haiti or the Dominican Republic. Although the Native American inhabitants were initially curious and welcomed the newcomers, hostilities quickly ensued as the Spaniards raided indigenous villages for gold and slaves. Unlike the Vikings of five centuries earlier, the Spaniards had an advantage in arms, they had firearms, and many of the Native Americans perished as a result of contracting diseases for which they had no immunity from the European and African immigrants, such as smallpox, measles, shingles, cholera, influenza, etc. As successive Spanish expeditions established landfalls in Florida, the Gulf Coast, Mesoamerica and other locations, a similar pattern of the search for gold, the taking of native populations for slaves and the introduction of new diseases spelled disaster for the Native Americans in their early contacts with Europeans.

Skill 20.3   Demonstrate knowledge of colonization by various European powers

The part of North America claimed by France was called New France and consisted of the land west of the Appalachian Mountains. This area of claims and settlement included the St. Lawrence Valley, the Great Lakes, the Mississippi Valley, and the entire region of land westward to the Rocky Mountains. They established the permanent settlements of Montreal and New Orleans, thus giving them control of the two major gateways into the heart of North America, the vast, rich interior. The St. Lawrence River, the Great Lakes, and the Mississippi River along with its tributaries made it possible for the French explorers and traders to roam at will, virtually unhindered in exploring, trapping, trading, and furthering the interests of France.

Most of the French settlements were in Canada along the St. Lawrence River. Only scattered forts and trading posts were found in the upper Mississippi Valley and Great Lakes region. The rulers of France originally intended New France to have vast estates owned by nobles and worked by peasants who would live on the estates in compact farming villages--the New World version of the Old World's medieval system of feudalism. However, it didn't work out that way. Each of the nobles wanted his estate to be on the river for ease of transportation. The peasants working the estates wanted the prime waterfront location, also. The result of all this real estate squabbling was that New France's settled areas wound up mostly as a string of farmhouses stretching from Quebec to Montreal along the St. Lawrence and Richelieu Rivers.

In the non-settled areas in the interior were the French fur traders. They made friends with the friendly tribes of Indians, spending the winters with them getting the furs needed for trade. In the spring, they would return to Montreal in time to take advantage of trading their furs for the products brought by the cargo ships from France, which usually arrived at about the same time. Most of the wealth for New France and its "Mother Country" was from the fur trade, which provided a livelihood for many, many people. Manufacturers and workmen back in France, ship-owners and merchants, as well as the fur traders and their Indian allies all benefited. However, the freedom of roaming and trapping in the interior was a strong enticement for the younger, stronger men and resulted in the French not strengthening the areas settled along the St. Lawrence.

Spanish settlement had its beginnings in the Caribbean with the establishment of colonies on Hispaniola (at Santo Domingo which became the capital of the West Indies), Puerto Rico, and Cuba. There were a number of reasons for Spanish involvement in the Americas, including:

- the spirit of adventure
- the desire for land
- expansion of Spanish power, influence, and empire
- the desire for great wealth
- expansion of Roman Catholic influence and conversion of native peoples.

The first permanent settlement in what is now the United States was in 1565 at St. Augustine, Florida. A later permanent settlement in the southwestern United States was in 1609 at Santa Fe, New Mexico. At the peak of Spanish power, the area in the United States claimed, settled, and controlled by Spain included Florida and all land west of the Mississippi River--quite a piece of choice real estate. Of course, France and England also lay claim to the same areas. Nonetheless, ranches and missions were built and the Indians who came in contact with the Spaniards were introduced to animals, plants, and seeds from the Old World that they had never seen before. Animals brought in included horses, cattle, donkeys, pigs, sheep, goats, and poultry.

Barrels were cut in half and filled with earth to transport and transplant trees bearing:

apples	olives
oranges	lemons
limes	figs
cherries	apricots
pears	almonds
walnuts	

Even sugar cane and flowers made it to America along with bags bringing seeds of wheat, barley, rye, flax, lentils, rice, and peas.

All Spanish colonies belonged to the King of Spain. He was considered an absolute monarch with complete or absolute power and claimed rule by divine right, the belief being God had given him the right to rule and he answered only to God for his actions. His word was final, was the law. The people had no voice in government. The land, the people, the wealth all belonged to him to use as he pleased. He appointed personal representatives, or viceroys, to rule for him in his colonies. They ruled in his name with complete authority. Since the majority of them were friends and advisers, they were richly rewarded with land grants, gold and silver, privileges of trading, and the right to operate the gold and silver mines.

Spain's control over her New World colonies lasted more than 300 years, longer than that of England or France. To this day, Spanish influence remains in names of places, art, architecture, music, literature, law, and cuisine. The Spanish settlements in North America were not commercial enterprises but were for protection and defense of the trading and wealth from their colonies in Mexico and South America. Russians hunting seals came down the Pacific coast, the English moved into Florida and west into and beyond the Appalachians, and the French traders and trappers were making their way from Louisiana and other parts of New France into Spanish territory. The Spanish never realized or understood that self-sustaining economic development and colonial trade was so important. Consequently, the Spanish settlements in the U.S. never really prospered.

Before 1763, when England was rapidly on the way to becoming the most powerful of the three major Western European powers, its thirteen colonies, located between the Atlantic and the Appalachians, physically occupied the least amount of land. Moreover, it is interesting that even before the Spanish Armada was defeated, two Englishmen, Sir Humphrey Gilbert and his half-brother Sir Walter Raleigh, were unsuccessful in their attempts to build successful permanent colonies in the New World. Nonetheless, the thirteen English colonies were successful and, by the time they had gained their independence from Britain, were more than able to govern themselves. They had a rich historical heritage of law, tradition, and documents leading the way to constitutional government conducted according to laws and customs. The settlers in the British colonies highly valued individual freedom, democratic government, and getting ahead through hard work.

The English colonies, with only a few exceptions, were considered commercial ventures to make a profit for the Crown or the Company or whoever financed its beginnings. One was strictly a philanthropic enterprise and three others were primarily for religious reasons, but the other nine were started for economic reasons. Settlers in these unique colonies came for different reasons:

    a) religious freedom
    b) political freedom
    c) economic prosperity
    d) land ownership

Skill 20.4 Demonstrate knowledge of the establishment and growth of the English colonies, including their political, economic, social, and cultural organization and institutions

The colonies were divided generally into the three regions of **New England, Middle Atlantic, and Southern**. The culture of each was distinct and affected attitudes, ideas towards politics, religion, and economic activities. The geography of each region also contributed to its unique characteristics.

The **New England colonies** consisted of Massachusetts, Rhode Island, Connecticut, and New Hampshire. Life in these colonies was centered on the towns. What farming was done was by each family on its own plot of land; but a short summer growing season and limited amount of good soil gave rise to other economic activities such as manufacturing, fishing, shipbuilding, and trade. The vast majority of the settlers shared similar origins, coming from England and Scotland. Towns were carefully planned and laid out the same way. The form of government was the town meeting, where all adult males met to make the laws. The legislative body, the General Court, consisted of an Upper and Lower House.

The **Middle or Middle Atlantic colonies** included New York, New Jersey, Pennsylvania, Delaware, and Maryland. New York and New Jersey were at one time the Dutch colony of New Netherlands, and Delaware at one time was New Sweden. These five colonies from their beginnings were considered "melting pots," with settlers from many different nations and backgrounds. The main economic activity was farming, with settlers scattered over the countryside cultivating rather large farms. The Indians were not as much of a threat as in New England, so the settlers did not have to settle in small farming villages. The soil was very fertile, the land was gently rolling, and a milder climate provided a longer growing season.

These farms produced a large surplus of food, not only for the colonists themselves but also for sale. This colonial region became known as the "breadbasket" of the New World. The New York and Philadelphia seaports were constantly filled with ships being loaded with meat, flour, and other foodstuffs for the West Indies and England. There were other economic activities such as shipbuilding, iron mines, and factories producing paper, glass, and textiles. The legislative body in Pennsylvania was unicameral or consisted of one house. In the other four colonies, the legislative body had two houses. Also, units of local government were in counties and towns.

The **Southern colonies** were Virginia, North and South Carolina, and Georgia. Virginia was the first permanent successful English colony, and Georgia was the last. The year 1619 was a very important year in the history of Virginia and the United States with three very significant events. First, sixty women were sent to Virginia to marry and establish families, Second, twenty Africans, the first of thousands, arrived. Third, most importantly, the Virginia colonists were granted the right to self-government and they began by electing their own representatives to the House of Burgesses, their own legislative body.

The major economic activity in this region was farming. Here the soil was very fertile and the climate was very mild with an even longer growing season. The large plantations eventually requiring large numbers of slaves were found in the coastal or tidewater areas. Although the wealthy slave-owning planters set the pattern of life in this region, most of the people lived inland, away from coastal areas. They were small farmers; and very few, it any, owned slaves.

In the colonies, the daily life of the colonists differed greatly between the coastal settlements and the inland or interior. The Southern planters and the people living in the coastal cities and towns had a way of life similar to that in towns in England. The influence was seen and heard in how people dressed and talked. The architectural styles of houses and public buildings and the social divisions or levels of society mimicked that of England. Both the planters and city dwellers enjoyed an active social life and had strong emotional ties to England.

On the other hand, life inland on the frontier had marked differences. All facets of daily living--clothing, food, housing, economic and social activities--were connected to what was needed to sustain life and survive in the wilderness. Everything was produced practically themselves. They were self-sufficient and extremely individualistic and independent. There were little, if any, levels of society or class distinctions as they considered themselves to be the equal to all others, regardless of station in life. The roots of equality, independence, individual rights and freedoms were extremely strong and well developed. People were not judged by their fancy dress, expensive house, eloquent language, or titles following their names.

COMPETENCY 21.0 ESTABLISHING A NEW NATION (1776–1791)

Skill 21.1 Demonstrate understanding of the American Revolution, including its causes, leaders, events, and results

One historian explained that the British were interested only in raising money to pay war debts, regulate the trade and commerce of the colonies, and look after business and financial interests between the Mother Country and the rest of her empire. The establishment of overseas colonies was first, and foremost, a commercial enterprise, not a political one. The political aspect was secondary and assumed. The British took it for granted that Parliament was supreme, was recognized so by the colonists, and were very resentful of the colonial challenge to Parliament's authority. They were contemptuously indifferent to politics in America and had no wish to exert any control over it. As resistance and disobedience swelled and increased in America, the British increased their efforts to punish the Americans and put them in their place.

The British had been extremely lax and totally inconsistent in enforcement of the mercantile or trade laws passed in the years before 1754. The government itself was not particularly stable, so actions against the colonies occurred in anger and their attitude was one of a moral superiority, that they knew how to manage America better than the Americans did themselves. This, of course, points to a lack of sufficient knowledge of conditions and opinions in America. The colonists had been left on their own for nearly 150 years; and by the time the Revolutionary War began, they were quite adept at self-government and adequately handling the affairs of their daily lives. The Americans equated ownership of land or property with the right to vote. Property was considered the foundation of life and liberty and, in the colonial mind and tradition, these went together.

Therefore, when an indirect tax on tea was made, the British felt that since it wasn't a direct tax, there should be no objection to it. The colonists viewed any tax, direct or indirect, as an attack on their property. They felt that as a representative body, the British Parliament should protect British citizens, including the colonists, from arbitrary taxation. Since they felt they were not represented, Parliament, in their eyes, gave them no protection. So, war began. On August 23, 1775, George III declared that the colonies were in rebellion and warned them to stop or else.

By 1776, the colonists and their representatives in the Second Continental Congress realized that things were past the point of no return. The Declaration of Independence was drafted and then declared to be in effect on July 4, 1776. George Washington labored against tremendous odds to wage a victorious war. The turning point in the Americans' favor occurred in 1777 with the American victory at Saratoga. This victory decided for the French to align themselves with the Americans against the British. With the aid of French warships blocking the entrance to Chesapeake Bay, British General Cornwallis trapped at Yorktown, Virginia, surrendered in 1781 and the war was over. The Treaty of Paris, officially ending the war, was signed in 1783.

During the war, and after independence was declared, the former colonies now found themselves independent states. The Second Continental Congress was conducting a war with representation by delegates from thirteen separate states. The Congress had no power to act for the states or to require them to accept and follow its wishes. A permanent united government was desperately needed. On November 15, 1777, the Articles of Confederation were adopted, creating a league of free and independent states.

Skill 21.2 Demonstrate knowledge of the Declaration of Independence and other revolutionary documents

The Declaration of independence was the founding document of the United States of America. The Articles of Confederation were the first attempt of the newly independent states to reach a new understanding amongst themselves. The Declaration was intended to demonstrate the reasons that the colonies were seeking separation from Great Britain. Conceived by and written for the most part by Thomas Jefferson, the Declaration is not only important for what it says, but also for how it says it. The Declaration is in many respects a poetic document. Instead of a simple recitation of the colonists' grievances, it set out clearly the reasons for the colonists' seeking their freedom from Great Britain. They had tried all means to resolve the dispute peacefully. It was the right of a people, when all other methods of addressing their grievances have been tried and failed, to separate themselves from that power that was keeping them from fully expressing their rights to "**life, liberty, and the pursuit of happiness.**"

By 1776, the colonists and their representatives in the Second Continental Congress realized that things were past the point of no return. The Declaration of Independence was drafted and declared July 4, 1776. Jefferson authored the Declaration of Independence with assistance from Benjamin Franklin and John Adams. After a long string of inequities imposed by the British government without the consent of the American Colonists, taxation by Parliament, and impositions such as the quartering of British troops without recompense to the hosts, the Continental Congress resolved to address these grievances by a unanimous declaration to break away from the Crown.

American colonists in the English colonies had always considered themselves to be citizens of Great Britain and loyal subjects of the British Crown, with all the traditional rights and privileges pursuant to that status. They had lived their lives as free men and developed their own town governments and colonial legislatures based on beliefs and principles that threaded back through English history to the time of Magna Carta. They had always been vocal participants in their own social, cultural and political development—unique, but considered by them to be British in its essence.

These colonists also had their own tradition of publishing the views and sentiments of individuals regarding issues of parochial interest and matters of concern which crossed colonial boundaries. In print—via newspapers and pamphlets—dialogue and debate over matters quite trivial or quite significant became common public practice in the American colonies. As strains with the mother country began to develop and increase—especially after the French and Indian War—the resulting issues became increasingly focused in print throughout the colonies. No doubt the discussions and debates published carried their sentiments over to the homes, taverns and other places where the people met to discuss events of the day. An important result of this was a growing "Americanism" in the sentiments of those writers published, and a sense of connection among American people that transcended colonial boundaries.

From the initial Stamp Act in 1765, through the "Boston Massacre" in 1770, to the time of the Tea Act in 1773 (which resulted in the "Boston Tea Party") and beyond, colonial presses were rife with discussion and debate about what they considered to be an unacceptable situation. Parliament intended to assert its right to tax and legislatively control the colonies of Great Britain in whatever manner it saw as prudent and appropriate. Most American colonists, believing themselves to be full British subjects, would deny Parliament's assertions so long as they were not provided with full and equal representation within Parliament.

One of the most notable spokesmen for the American cause was, in fact, an Englishman. Thomas Paine (1737-1809) was born in England and came to America in November 1774. He was immediately taken up by the social issues and politics in the American colonies and insinuated himself into the dialogue of current issues, which was ongoing in the colonies—conducted via newspapers and pamphlets. Within months of his arrival, he published his first article in America. Interestingly, his first address to the American public would presage the elaborate exposition of tyranny versus the natural rights of humans to be and act free, which would color and popularize his writings during the war years. But his topic at the time—his bold statement and unusual public stand—was about African slavery.

He is best remembered for "*Common Sense.*" In a series of publications, spanning the war years (from 1776 through 1783), Thomas Paine wrote a series of addresses, inspiring the American people and reprimanding British authorities.

One of his most famous publications, produced at a time of ill fortune for the American cause and disenchantment for many members of the fledgling American Army, began, "THESE are the times that try men's souls. The summer soldier and the sunshine patriot will, in this crisis, shrink from the service of their country; but he that stands it now, deserves the love and thanks of man and woman. Tyranny, like hell, is not easily conquered; yet we have this consolation with us, that the harder the conflict, the more glorious the triumph."

The writings of Thomas Paine, the impact of the publication of *Common Sense,* were credited with influencing the Congress and the populace at large to declare independence.

Other authors, other printers and publishers, and other factions, were also quite active in promoting the new American attitude toward independence. Of significant note was the **Virginia Declaration of Rights**, drafted by George Mason in May 1776 and amended by Thomas Ludwell Lee and the Virginia Convention. Thomas Jefferson was influenced by it when he drafted the Declaration of Independence only a month later. This document would also influence James Madison when drawing up the Bill of Rights (1789) and also the Marquis de Lafayette when drafting the French Declaration of the Rights of Man and Citizen (1789).

The Declaration's text can be divided into three main parts:

1. Statements of the general state of humanity and the natural rights inherent in all civil societies. Jefferson talks about "self-evident" truths, unalienable rights of people to "Life, Liberty and the pursuit of Happiness" which show considerable influence from primarily French thinkers of the Enlightenment during the 17th and 18th Centuries. He also clearly states that a government that no longer respects these inherent rights, loses its legitimacy and has become despotic, and the governed have the right to throw off such a government, a call for insurrection against the sovereign.

2. An enumeration of specific and detailed grievances, which point out why the current sovereign has lost the right to govern. It also lists how the king even subverted English Common Law and legal traditions dating back to antiquity.

3. The last part of the text states that the colonists had exhausted all civil and legal means of having their grievances addressed by British government, and now had the right and duty to break with the crown and be a free and independent nation.

The final section of the Declaration contains the signatures of the representatives of the colonies to the Continental Congress in Philadelphia. Realizing that they had committed an act of treason, punishable by death by hanging, Benjamin Franklin counseled unity, lest they all hang separately. It should also be noted that at that moment, open hostilities between British and Colonists had already been under way for over a year. George Washington had taken command of the Continental Army, organized on June 14, 1775 at Harvard Yard, and in the same year, the Continental Navy and the Marine Corps had been organized.

Skill 21.3 **Demonstrate knowledge of the first government of the United States under the Articles of Confederation**

Articles of Confederation - This was the first political system under which the newly independent colonies tried to organize themselves. It was drafted after the Declaration of Independence, in 1776, was passed by the Continental Congress on November 15, 1777, ratified by the thirteen states, and took effect on March 1, 1781. (See http://www.usconstitution.net/articles.html)

The newly independent states were unwilling to give too much power to a national government. They were already fighting Great Britain. They did not want to replace one harsh ruler with another. After many debates, the form of the thirteen Articles was accepted. Each state agreed to send delegates to the Congress. Each state had one vote in the Congress. The Articles gave Congress the power to declare war, appoint military officers, and coin money. The Congress was also responsible for foreign affairs. The Articles of Confederation limited the powers of Congress by giving the states final authority. Although Congress could pass laws, at least nine of the thirteen states had to approve a law before it went into effect. Congress could not pass any laws regarding taxes. To get money, Congress had to ask each state for it, no state could be forced to pay.

Thus, the Articles created a loose alliance among the thirteen states. The national government was weak, in part, because it didn't have a strong chief executive to carry out laws passed by the legislature. This weak national government might have worked if the states were able to get along with each other. However, many different disputes arose and there was no way of settling them.

The first order of business was the agreement among all the delegates that the convention would be kept secret. No discussion of the convention outside of the meeting room would be allowed. They wanted to be able to discuss, argue, and agree among themselves before presenting the completed document to the American people.

The delegates were afraid that if the people were aware of what was taking place before it was completed, the entire country would be plunged into argument and dissension. It would be extremely difficult, if not impossible, to settle differences and come to an agreement. Between the official notes kept and the complete notes of future President James Madison, an accurate picture of the events of the Convention is part of the historical record.

The delegates went to Philadelphia representing different areas and different interests. They all agreed on a strong central government but not one with unlimited powers.

They also agreed that no one part of government could control the rest. It would be a republican form of government (sometimes referred to as representative democracy) in which the supreme power was in the hands of the voters who would elect the men who would govern for them.

One of the first serious controversies involved the small states versus the large states over representation in Congress. Virginia's Governor Edmund Randolph proposed that state population determine the number of representatives sent to Congress, also known as the Virginia Plan. New Jersey delegate William Paterson countered with what is known as the New Jersey Plan, each state having equal representation.

After much argument and debate, the **Great Compromise** was devised, known also as the Connecticut Compromise, as proposed by Roger Sherman. It was agreed that Congress would have two houses. The Senate would have two Senators, giving equal powers in the Senate. The House of Representatives would have its members elected based on each state's population. Both houses could draft bills to debate and vote on with the exception of bills pertaining to money, which must originate in the House of Representatives.

Another major controversy involved economic differences between North and South. One concerned the counting of African slaves for determining representation in the House of Representatives. The southern delegates wanted this but didn't want it to apply to determining taxes to be paid. The northern delegates argued the opposite: count the slaves for taxes but not for representation. The resulting agreement was known as the "three-fifths" compromise. Three-fifths of the slaves would be counted for both taxes and determining representation in the House.

The last major compromise, also between North and South, was the Commerce Compromise. The economic interests of the northern part of the country were ones of industry and business whereas the south's economic interests were primarily in farming. The Northern merchants wanted the government to regulate and control commerce with foreign nations and with the states. Of course, Southern planters opposed this idea as they felt that any tariff laws passed would be unfavorable to them. The acceptable compromise to this dispute was that Congress was given the power to regulate commerce with other nations and the states, including levying tariffs on imports. However, Congress did not have the power to levy tariffs on any exports. This increased Southern concern about the effect it would have on the slave trade. The delegates finally agreed that the importation of slaves would continue for 20 more years with no interference from Congress. Any import tax could not exceed 10 dollars per person. After 1808, Congress would be able to decide whether to prohibit or regulate any further importation of slaves.

Of course, when work was completed and the document was presented, nine states needed to approve for it to go into effect. There was no little amount of discussion, arguing, debating, and haranguing. The opposition had three major objections:

> 1) The states seemed as if they were being asked to surrender too much power to the national government.
> 2) The voters did not have enough control and influence over the men who would be elected by them to run the government.
> 3) A lack of a "bill of rights" guaranteeing hard-won individual freedoms and liberties.

Eleven states finally ratified the document and the new national government went into effect. It was no small feat that the delegates were able to produce a workable document that satisfied all opinions, feelings, and viewpoints. The separation of powers of the three branches of government and the built-in system of checks and balances to keep power balanced were a stroke of genius. It provided for the individuals and the states as well as an organized central authority to keep a new inexperienced young nation on track. They created a system of government so flexible that it had continued in its basic form to this day. In 1789, the Electoral College unanimously elected George Washington as the first President and the new nation was on its way.

Skill 21.4   Demonstrate understanding of the process of writing and adopting the Constitution and the Bill of Rights

The central government of the new United States of America consisted of a Congress of two to seven delegates from each state, with each state having just one vote. The government under the Articles solved some of the postwar problems but had serious weaknesses. Some of its powers included: borrowing and coining money, directing foreign affairs, declaring war and making peace, building and equipping a navy, regulating weights and measures, asking the states to supply men and money for an army. The delegates to Congress had no real authority as each state carefully and jealously guarded its own interests and limited powers under the Articles. Also, the delegates to Congress were paid by their states and had to vote as directed by their state legislatures. The serious weaknesses were the lack of power: to regulate finances, over interstate trade, over foreign trade, to enforce treaties, and military power. Something better and more efficient was needed. In May of 1787, delegates from all states except Rhode Island began meeting in Philadelphia. At first, they met to revise the Articles of Confederation as instructed by Congress; but they soon realized that much more was needed. Abandoning the instructions, they set out to write a new Constitution, a new document, the foundation of all government in the United States and a model for representative government throughout the world.

The beginnings of civil liberties and the idea of civil rights in the United States go back to the ideas of the Greeks. The early British struggle for civil rights and the very philosophies that led people to come to the New World in the first place were religious freedom, political freedom, and the right to live one's life as one sees fit are basic to the American ideal. These were embodied in the ideas expressed in the Declaration of Independence and the Constitution.

All these ideas found their final expression in the United States Constitution's first ten amendments, known as the Bill of Rights. In 1789, the first Congress passed these first amendments and by December 1791, three-fourths of the states at that time had ratified them. The Bill of Rights protects certain liberties and basic rights. James Madison, who wrote the amendments, said that the Bill of Rights does not give Americans these rights. People, Madison said, already have these rights. They are natural rights that belong to all human beings. The Bill of Rights simply prevents the governments from taking away these rights.

The first amendment guarantees the basic rights of freedom of religion, freedom of speech, freedom of the press, and freedom of assembly.

Freedom of Religion: Religious freedom has not been seriously threatened in the United States historically. The policy of the government has been guided by the premise that church and state should be separate. When religious practices have been at cross-purposes with attitudes prevailing in the nation at particular times, these practices have been restricted. Some of these restrictions have been against the practice of polygamy that is supported by certain religious groups. The idea of animal sacrifice that is promoted by some religious beliefs is generally prohibited. The use of mind-altering illegal substances that some use in religious rituals has been restricted. In the United States, all recognized religious institutions are tax-exempt in following the idea of separation of church and state, and therefore, there have been many quasi-religious groups that have in the past tried to take advantage of this fact. All of these issues continue, and most likely will continue to occupy both political and legal considerations for some time to come.

Freedom of Speech, Press, and Assembly: These rights historically have been given wide latitude in their practices, though there have been instances when one or the other have been limited for various reasons. The classic limitation, for instance, in regards to freedom of speech has been the famous precept that an individual is prohibited from yelling "Fire!" in a crowded theatre. This prohibition is an example of the state saying that freedom of speech does not extend to speech that might endanger other people. There is also a prohibition against slander, or the knowingly stating of a deliberately falsehood against one party by another. Also there are many regulations regarding freedom of the press, the most common example are the various laws against libel (or the printing of a known falsehood). In times of national emergency, various restrictions have been placed on the rights of press, speech and sometimes assembly.

The next three amendments came out of the colonists' struggle with Great Britain. For example, the third amendment prevents Congress from forcing citizens to keep troops in their homes. Before the Revolution, Great Britain tried to coerce the colonists to house soldiers.

Amendments five through eight protect citizens who are accused of crimes and are brought to trial. Every citizen has the right to due process of law (due process as defined earlier, being that the government must follow the same fair rules for everyone brought to trial.) These rules include the right to a trial by an impartial jury, the right to be defended by a lawyer, and the right to a speedy trial.

The last two amendments limit the powers of the federal government to those that are expressly granted in the Constitution; any rights not expressly mentioned in the Constitution, thus, belong to the states or to the people.

The legal system in recent years has also undergone a number of serious changes, some would say challenges, with the interpretation of some constitutional guarantees.

COMPETENCY 22.0 EARLY YEARS OF THE NEW NATION (1791–1829)

Skill 22.1 Demonstrate understanding of political development, including early presidential administrations, establishment of the federal judiciary, and inception and growth of political parties

The early presidential administrations established much of the form and many of the procedures still present today, including the development of the party system. George Washington, the first U.S. President, established a Cabinet form of government, with individual advisors overseeing the various functions of the executive branch and advising the President, who makes a final decision. Divisions within his cabinet and within Congress during his administration eventually led to the development of political parties, which Washington opposed. Washington was also instrumental in establishing the power of the federal government when he rode at the head of militia forces to put down a rebellion in Pennsylvania. Washington was elected to two terms and served from 1789 to 1797.

Washington's Vice President, John Adams, was elected to succeed him. Adams' administration was marked by the new nation's first entanglement in international affairs. Britain and France were at war, with Adams' Federalist Party supporting the British and Vice President Thomas Jefferson's Republican Party supporting the French. The nation was brought nearly to the brink of war with France, but Adams managed to negotiate a treaty that avoided full conflict. In the process, however, he lost the support of his party and was defeated after one term by Thomas Jefferson.

The two parties that developed through the early 1790s were led by Jefferson as the Secretary of State and Alexander Hamilton as the Secretary of the Treasury. Jefferson and Hamilton were different in many ways—not the least was their views on what should be the proper form of government of the United States. This difference helped to shape the parties that formed around them.

Hamilton wanted the federal government to be stronger than the state governments. Jefferson believed that the state governments should be stronger. Hamilton supported the creation of the first Bank of the United States, Jefferson opposed it because he felt that it gave too much power to wealthy investors who would help run it. Jefferson interpreted the Constitution strictly; he argued that nowhere did the Constitution give the federal government the power to create a national bank. Hamilton interpreted the Constitution much more loosely. He pointed out that the Constitution gave Congress the power to make all laws "necessary and proper" to carry out its duties. He reasoned that since Congress had the right to collect taxes, then Congress had the right to create the bank. Hamilton wanted the government to encourage economic growth. He favored the growth of trade, manufacturing, and the rise of cities as the necessary parts of economic growth. He favored the business leaders and mistrusted the common people.

Jefferson believed that the common people, especially the farmers, were the backbone of the nation. He thought that the rise of big cities and manufacturing would corrupt American life.

Finally, Hamilton and Jefferson had their disagreements only in private. But when Congress began to pass many of Hamilton's ideas and programs, Jefferson and his friend James Madison decided to organize support for their own views. They moved quietly and very cautiously in the beginning. In 1791, they went to New York telling people that they were going to just study its wildlife. Actually, Jefferson was more interested in meeting with several important New York politicians such as its governor, George Clinton, and Aaron Burr, a strong critic of Hamilton. Jefferson asked Clinton and Burr to help defeat Hamilton's program by getting New Yorkers to vote for Jefferson's supporters in the next election. Before long, leaders in other states began to organize support for either Jefferson or Hamilton. Jefferson's supporters called themselves Democratic-Republicans (often this was shortened just to Republicans, though in actuality it was the forerunner of today's Democratic Party, not the Republican). Hamilton and his supporters were known as Federalists, because they favored a strong federal government. The Federalists had the support of the merchants and ship owners in the Northeast and some planters in the South. Small farmers, craft workers, and some of the wealthier landowners supported Jefferson and the Democratic-Republicans.

Article III of the US Constitution created a Supreme Court and authorized Congress to create other federal courts as it deemed necessary. In 1789, Congress passed the **Judiciary Act**, which set the number of Supreme Court justices at six, with one Chief Justice and five associates. The Judiciary Act also created 13 judicial districts, each with one district judge who was authorized to hear maritime cases and other types of cases. Most federal trial cases were heard by circuit courts, which were originally made up of two Supreme Court justices and the local district judge. In 1793, Congress changed the circuit court to one Supreme Court justice and the local district judge.

In 1801, the Federalist majority in Congress sought to place more power in the district courts and removed the requirement that a Supreme Court justice preside over circuit courts. The following year, however, Jeffersonian Republicans took the majority in Congress and reversed this decision. As the demands of the growing nation increased in the following decades, the federal judiciary system was expanded by adding Supreme Court justices and enlarging the district and circuit systems.

Skill 22.2   Demonstrate understanding of foreign policy issues, including the Louisiana Purchase, the War of 1812, and the Monroe Doctrine

The next large territorial gain was under President Thomas Jefferson in 1803. In 1800, Napoleon Bonaparte of France secured the Louisiana Territory from Spain, which had held it since 1792. The vast area stretched westward from the Mississippi River to the Rocky Mountains as well as northward to Canada. An effort was made to keep the transaction a secret, but the news reached the U.S. State Department. The U.S. didn't have any particular problem with Spanish control of the territory since Spain was weak and did not pose a threat. However, it was different with France. Though not the world power that Great Britain was, nonetheless France was still strong and, under Napoleon's leadership, was again acquiring an empire. President Jefferson had three major reasons for concern:

   a. With the French controlling New Orleans at the mouth of the Mississippi River, as well as the Gulf of Mexico, Westerners would lose their "right of deposit," which would greatly affect their ability to trade. This was very important to the Americans who were living in the area between the river and the Appalachians. They were unable to get heavy products to eastern markets but had to float them on rafts down the Ohio and Mississippi Rivers to New Orleans to ships heading to Europe or the Atlantic coast ports. If France prohibited this, it would be a financial disaster.

   b. President Jefferson also worried that if the French possessed the Louisiana Territory, America would be extremely limited in its expansion into its interior.

   c. Under Napoleon Bonaparte, France was becoming more powerful and aggressive. This would be a constant worry and threat to the western border of the U.S. President Jefferson was very interested in the western part of the country and firmly believed that it was both necessary and desirable to strengthen western lands. So Jefferson wrote to the American minister to Paris, Robert R. Livingston, to make an offer to Napoleon for New Orleans and West Florida, as much as $10 million for the two. Napoleon countered the offer with the question of how much the U.S. would be willing to pay for all of Louisiana. After some discussion, it was agreed to pay $15 million and the largest land transaction in history was negotiated in 1803, resulting in the eventual formation of 15 states.

In 1804, the United States engaged in the first of a series of armed conflicts with the Barbary pirates of North Africa. The Moslem rulers of Morocco, Algiers, Tunis, and Tripoli, the Barbary States of North Africa, had long been seizing ships of nations that were Christian and demanding ransoms for the crews. The Christian nations of Europe decided it was cheaper and easier to pay annually a tribute or bribe. The U.S. had been doing this since 1783 with the beginnings of trade between the Mediterranean countries and the newly independent nation. When the rulers in Tripoli demanded a ridiculously high bribe and chopped down the flagpole of the American consulate there, Jefferson had had enough. The first skirmish against Tripoli in 1804 and 1805 was successful. In 1815, the payment of bribes to the rulers ceased. The Americans could trade and sail freely in the Mediterranean.

The United States' unintentional and accidental involvement in what was known as the **War of 1812** came about because of the political and economic struggles between France and Great Britain. Napoleon's goal was complete conquest and control of Europe, including and especially Great Britain. Although British troops were temporarily driven off the mainland of Europe, the navy still controlled the seas, the seas across which France had to bring the products needed. America traded with both nations, especially with France and its colonies. The British decided to destroy the American trade with France, mainly for two reasons: (a) Products and goods from the U.S. gave Napoleon what he needed to keep up his struggle with Britain. He and France were the enemy, and it was felt that the Americans were aiding the Mother Country's enemy. (b) Britain felt threatened by the increasing strength and success of the U.S. merchant fleet. They were becoming major competitors with the ship owners and merchants in Britain.

The British issued the Orders in Council, a series of measures prohibiting American ships from entering any French ports, not only in Europe but also in India and the West Indies. At the same time, Napoleon began efforts for a coastal blockade of the British Isles. He issued a series of Orders prohibiting all nations, including the United States, from trading with the British. And he didn't stop there. He threatened seizure of every ship entering any French ports after they stopped at any British port or British colony, even threatening to seize every ship inspected by British cruisers or that paid any duties to their government. Adding to all of this, the British were stopping American ships and seizing, or impressing, American seamen to service on British ships. Americans were outraged.

In 1807, Congress passed the Embargo Act, forbidding American ships from sailing to foreign ports. It couldn't be completely enforced and it really hurt business and trade in America so, in 1809, it was repealed. Two additional acts passed by Congress after James Madison became president attempted to regulate trade with other nations and to get Britain and France to remove all the restrictions they had put on American shipping. The catch was that whichever nation removed restrictions, the U.S. agreed not to trade with the other one. Clever Napoleon was the first to do this, prompting Madison to issue orders prohibiting trade with Britain, ignoring warnings from the British not to do so. Of course, this didn't work either and although Britain eventually rescinded the Orders in Council, war came in June of 1812 and ended Christmas Eve, 1814, with the signing of the Treaty of Ghent.

During the War of 1812, Americans were divided over not only whether or not it was necessary to even fight but also over what territories should be fought for and taken. The nation was still young and just not prepared for war. The primary American objective was to conquer Canada but it failed. Two naval victories and one military victory stand out for the United States. Oliver Perry gained control of Lake Erie and Thomas MacDonough fought on Lake Champlain. Both of these naval battles successfully prevented the British invasion of the United States from Canada. Nevertheless, the troops did land below Washington on the Potomac, marched into the city, and burned the public buildings, including the White House. Andrew Jackson's victory at New Orleans was a great morale boost to Americans, giving them the impression the U.S. had won the war. The battle actually took place after Britain and the United States had reached an agreement and it had no impact on the war's outcome. The peace treaty did little for the United States other than bringing peace, releasing prisoners of war, restoring all occupied territory, and setting up a commission to settle boundary disputes with Canada. Interestingly, the war proved to be a turning point in American history. European events had profoundly shaped U.S. policies, especially foreign policies.

In President Monroe's message to Congress on December 2, 1823, he delivered the Monroe Doctrine. The United States was informing the powers of the Old World that the American continents were no longer open to European colonization and that any effort to extend European political influence into the New World would be considered by the United States "as dangerous to our peace and safety." The United States would not interfere in European wars or internal affairs and expected Europe to stay out of American affairs.

Skill 22.3 **Demonstrate understanding of economic development, including Hamilton's economic plan, tariffs, and changes in agriculture, commerce, and industry**

In domestic affairs of the new nation, the first problems dealt with finances--paying for the war debts of the Revolutionary War and other financial needs. Secretary of the Treasury Alexander Hamilton wanted the government to increase tariffs and put taxes on certain products made in the U.S., for example, liquor. This money in turn would be used to pay war debts of the federal government as well as those of the states. There would be money available for expenses and needed internal improvements.

To provide for this, Hamilton favored a national bank. Secretary of State Thomas Jefferson, along with southern supporters, opposed many of Hamilton's suggested plans. Later, Jefferson relented and gave support to some proposals in return for Hamilton and his northern supporters agreeing to locate the nation's capital in the South. Jefferson continued to oppose a national bank, but Congress set up the first one in 1791, chartered for the next 20 years.

Hamilton's plans and the creation of the bank had an immediate effect on the economics of the new nation. With the creation of paper securities, finance became more liquid, allowing for the creation of a stock market fueled by speculation. These securities could be used as collateral for loans to provide for expansion in industry and the creation of infrastructure such as roads, canals and bridges, which expanded the market for agricultural products. Foreign investment was also stimulated, and exports increased.

Skill 22.4   Demonstrate understanding of social and cultural development in this period, including immigration and the frontier, family life and the role of women, religious life, and nationalism and regionalism

During the years from 1791 to 1829, the Americans were gradually becoming a new and distinct people. The heritage of European colonialism had provided the colonies with many traditions and social practices that were gradually abandoned. Some of the more common customs and traditions, which blended well with the changing attitudes of the American people, continued to be practiced for several decades to come. This was true of many common business practices and traditional mores regarding proper and appropriate social interactions. Concern over European intrigues and a second war against Great Britain served to help the American people distance themselves more and more from any reliance on—and old connections with—the European nations.

Immigration continued and increased during this period, especially as new territories become opened for exploration and settlement. Most of the new arrivals came from the same Western European countries as the original colonists; but there was soon a greater mix of non-English residents than ever before—and an increasing membership in religious faiths other than the traditional Protestant denominations, including Roman Catholics and Jews. The major exception to the ethnicity of most immigrants to the United States, through much of this period, continued to be African slaves, imported against their will to provide a chattel labor force.

Because of compromises made by the federal government with certain states, Congress was unable to act against the importation trade until January 1, 1808. At that time, a bill was unanimously passed forbidding the importation of slaves. However, since smuggling slaves was lucrative and difficult for the government to control, the illicit trade continued for over a decade more. During this time, tens of thousands of additional African slaves were brought into the United States. Finally, in 1819 Congress declared this practice to be piracy. There is no record that any of the practitioners were ever condemned as pirates, but the effort by the federal government seemed to have the desired effect. Of course, the internal trade and sale of slaves continued to flourish up until the Civil War, becoming far more lucrative when importation ceased.

Abigail Adams was a unique individual, but not necessarily an unusual woman for her time. Women of this period lived lives—and had attitudes about life—which might seem quite alien to American people today. The same could be said about men's lives and attitudes. Most people of the time believed there were definite distinctions regarding what it meant to be a woman and what it meant to be a man. They were aware of these distinctions in the natural world and saw them reinforced in the religious doctrine of their faiths.

Social customs, traditions and the practice of lawmaking institutions adopted these distinctions or were adapted to conform to socially acceptable conventions. These conditions were generally accepted by women and men, alike: there were roles for men and there were roles for women—just as there were garments appropriate to each sex.

While most women were excluded from the franchise (they were not allowed to vote), many men were excluded as well. Slaves of either sex could not vote. Freedmen were often prevented from voting. And in various jurisdictions—federal, state, county, municipal elections, etc., a man could be prohibited from voting because of poverty, lack of property ownership, inability to write or any one of many restrictions intended to limit the franchise.

Some women during this period did have the right to vote and participated in the election process. These women were usually residents of a new territory, which did not adhere to the restrictions of the various states. When these territories eventually became states, however, these women were excluded from the franchise. There was one state in which women enjoyed the right to vote. This right was granted to women in the adoption of the constitution of New Jersey in 1776. And this right to vote was revoked for women in New Jersey in 1807.

There was very little agitation for the extension of the franchise to women during this period. The true struggle would begin several decades later, and women's suffrage would not be finally accomplished for nearly a century. But women did have their spheres of influence. These were in the home and family and in the social rather than political aspects of the community. Women organized for the betterment of their community and the society in which they lived. As individuals and in groups they influenced the development and maintenance of religious and educational institutions and those establishments, which provided for the sick and indigent. Through their families and specifically the male members in their role as voters, they influenced the political life of the community as well. It would be an unwise political candidate who proposed a platform which the women of the community would not support.

But political organization and agitation for women were still far in the future. During this period, women of notable accomplishment tended to act as individuals. For example, the Troy Female Seminary was opened in New York by Emma Willard in 1821 to provide an exemplary curriculum for girls. Frances Wright established her own Utopian community in Nashoba, Tennessee, in 1825.

In this new country—this new land—there was a sense of youthful vigor and a view to new opportunities and new ideas. For many, these ideals held true as much in their spiritual life as in any other aspect of life. Many Americans seemed to be seeking something new and meaningful.

The Second Great Awakening was an evangelical Protestant revival that preached personal responsibility for one's actions both individually and socially. This movement was led by preachers, such as Charles Finney, who traveled the country preaching the gospel of social responsibility. This point of view was taken up by the "mainline Protestant denominations" (Episcopal, Methodist, Presbyterian, Lutheran, Congregational). Part of the social reform movement that led to an end to child labor, to better working conditions, and to other changes in social attitudes, arose from this new recognition that the Christian faith should be expressed for the good of society.

Closely allied to the Second Great Awakening was **the temperance movement**. This movement to end the sale and consumption of alcohol arose from religious beliefs, the violence many women and children experienced from heavy drinkers, and from the effect of alcohol consumption on the work force. The Society for the Promotion of Temperance was organized in Boston in 1826.

Other social issues were also addressed. It was during this period that efforts were made to transform the prison system and its emphasis on punishment into a penitentiary system that attempted rehabilitation. It was also during this period that Dorothea Dix led a struggle in the North and the South to establish hospitals for the insane.

Utopianism is the dream of or the desire to create the perfect society. However by the nineteenth century few believed this was possible. One of the major "causes" of utopianism is the desire for moral clarity. Against the backdrop of the efforts of a young nation to define itself and to ensure the rights and freedoms of its citizens, and within the context of the second great awakening, it becomes quite easy to see how the reform movements, the religious sentiment, and the gathering national storm would lead to the rise of expressions of desire to create the perfect society.

As the new country began to stretch its boundaries physically, new territories and opportunities were opened up to new and old Americans, alike. And new concepts like regionalism and sectionalism began to take on more meaning.

Regionalism can be defined as the political division of an area into partially autonomous regions or to loyalty to the interests of a particular region. **Sectionalism** is generally defined as excessive devotion to local interests and customs.

When the United States declared independence from England, the founding fathers created a political point of view that created a national unity while respecting the uniqueness and individual rights of each of the thirteen colonies or states. The colonies had been populated and governed by England and other countries. Some came to America in search of religious freedom, others for a fresh start and others for economic opportunity. Each colony had a particular culture and identity.

As the young nation grew, territories came to be defined as states. The states began to acquire their own particular cultures and identities. In time, regional interests and cultures also began to take shape. Religious interests, economic life, and geography began to be understood as definitive of particular regions. The northeast tended toward industrial development. The south tended to rely upon agriculture. The west was an area of untamed open spaces where people settled and practiced agriculture and animal husbandry.

Each of these regions came to be defined, at least to some extent, on the basis of the way people made their living and the economic and social institutions that supported them. In the industrialized north, the factory system tended to create a division between the tycoons of business and industry and the poor industrial workers. The conditions in which the labor force worked were far from ideal – the hours were long, the conditions were bad, and the pay was small.

The south was characterized by cities that were centers of social and commercial life. The agriculture that supported the region was practiced on "plantations," which were owned by the wealthy and worked by slaves or indentured servants.

The west was a vast expanse to be explored and tamed. Life on a western ranch was distinctly different from life in either the industrial north or the agricultural south. The challenges of each region were also distinctly different. The role of children in the economy was different; the role of women was different; the importance of trade was different. And religion was called upon to support each unique regional lifestyle.

The regional differences between North and South came to a head over the issue of slavery. The rise of the abolitionist movement in the North, the publication of *Uncle Tom's Cabin*, and issues of trade and efforts by the national government to control trade for the regions coalesced around the issue of slavery in a nation that was founded on the principle of the inalienable right of every person to be free. As the South defended its lifestyle and its economy and the right of the states to be self-determining, the North became stronger in its criticism of slavery. The result was a growing sectionalism.

COMPETENCY 23.0 CONTINUED NATIONAL DEVELOPMENT (1829–1850S)

Skill 23.1 Demonstrate understanding of political development, including Jacksonian democracy, the nullification crisis, Manifest Destiny, the Mexican War and Cession, and the Oregon Territory

The election of Andrew Jackson as President signaled a swing of the political pendulum from government influence of the wealthy, aristocratic Easterners to the interests of the Western farmers and pioneers and the era of the "common man." Jacksonian Democracy was a policy of equal political power for all. After the War of 1812, Henry Clay and supporters favored economic measures that came to be known as the American System. This involved tariffs protecting American farmers and manufacturers from having to compete with foreign products, stimulating industrial growth and employment. With more people working, more farm products would be consumed, prosperous farmers would be able to buy more manufactured goods, and the additional monies from tariffs would make it possible for the government to make the needed internal improvements. To get this going, in 1816, Congress not only passed a high tariff, but also chartered a second Bank of the United States. Upon becoming President, Jackson fought to get rid of the bank.

One of the many duties of the bank was to regulate the supply of money for the nation. The President believed that the bank was a monopoly that favored the wealthy. Congress voted in 1832 to renew the bank's charter but Jackson vetoed the bill, withdrew the government's money, and the bank finally collapsed. Jackson also faced the "null and void," or nullification issue from South Carolina. Congress, in 1828, passed a law placing high tariffs on goods imported into the United States. Southerners, led by South Carolina's then Vice-President of the United States, John C. Calhoun, felt that the tariff favored the manufacturing interests of New England. Calhoun denounced it as an abomination and claimed that any state could nullify any of the federal laws it considered unconstitutional. The tariff was lowered in 1832, but not enough to satisfy South Carolina, which promptly threatened to secede from the Union. Although Jackson agreed with the rights of states, he also believed in preservation of the Union. He held firm in his stance that the federal government was sovereign over states. A year later, the tariffs were lowered and the crisis was averted.

As the nation extended its borders into the lands west of the Mississippi, thousands of settlers streamed into this part of the country bringing with them ideas and concepts adapting them to the development of the unique characteristics of the region. Equality for everyone, as stated in the Declaration of Independence, did not yet apply to minority groups, black Americans or American Indians. Voting rights and the right to hold public office were restricted in varying degrees in each state. All of these factors decidedly affected the political, economic, and social life of the country and all three were focused in the attitudes of the three sections of the country on slavery.

All of this was started on an optimistic and scientific note. After the U.S. purchased the Louisiana Territory, Jefferson appointed Captains Meriwether Lewis and William Clark to explore it, to find out exactly what had been bought. The expedition went all the way to the Pacific Ocean, returning two years later with maps, journals, and artifacts. This led the way for future explorers to make available more knowledge about the territory and resulted in the Westward Movement and the later belief in the doctrine of Manifest Destiny.

It was the belief of many that the United States was destined to control all of the land between the two oceans, or as one newspaper editor termed it, "Manifest Destiny." This mass migration westward put the U.S. government on a collision course with the Indians, Great Britain, Spain, and Mexico. The fur traders and missionaries ran up against the Indians in the northwest and the claims of Great Britain for the Oregon country.

In the American southwest, Spain had claimed this area since the 1540s, had spread northward from Mexico City, and, in the 1700s, had established missions, forts, villages, towns, and very large ranches. After the purchase of the Louisiana Territory in 1803, Americans began moving into Spanish territory. A few hundred American families in what is now Texas were allowed to live there but had to agree to become loyal subjects to Spain. In 1821, Mexico successfully revolted against Spanish rule, won independence, and chose to be more tolerant towards the American settlers and traders. The Mexican government encouraged and allowed extensive trade and settlement, especially in Texas. Many of the new settlers were southerners and brought with them their slaves. Slavery was outlawed in Mexico and technically illegal in Texas, although the Mexican government rather looked the other way.

With the influx of so many Americans and the liberal policies of the Mexican government, there came to be concern over the possible growth and development of an American state within Mexico. Settlement restrictions, cancellation of land grants, the forbidding of slavery and increased military activity brought everything to a head. The order of events included the fight for Texas independence, the brief Republic of Texas, eventual annexation of Texas, statehood, and finally war with Mexico.

The Texas controversy was not the sole reason for war. Since American settlers had begun pouring into the Southwest, the cultural differences played a prominent part. Language, religion, law, customs, and government were totally different and opposite between the two groups. A clash was bound to occur.

Friction increased between land-hungry Americans swarming into western lands and the Mexican government, which controlled these lands. The clash was not only political but also cultural and economic. The Spanish influence permeated all parts of southwestern life: law, language, architecture, and customs. By this time, the doctrine of Manifest Destiny was in the hearts and on the lips of those seeking new areas of settlement and a new life.

The impact of the entire westward movement resulted in the completion of the borders of the present-day conterminous United States. Contributing factors include the bloody war with Mexico, the ever-growing controversy over slave versus free states affecting the balance of power or influence in the U.S. Congress, especially the Senate and finally to the Civil War itself.

Skill 23.2   Demonstrate knowledge of geographic expansion, including the development of the transportation network and the displacement of Native Americans

The conclusion of the Civil War opened the floodgates for migration westward and settlement of new land. The availability of cheap land and the expectation of great opportunity prompted thousands, including immigrants, to travel across the Mississippi River and settle the Great Plains and California. The primary bases of the new western economy were farming, mining, and ranching. Both migration and the economy were facilitated by the expansion of the railroad, which largely replaced canal and riverway travel and transport as the preferred mode, and the completion of the transcontinental railroad in 1869. The increased efficiency of rail transport opened up new markets and enhanced existing ones. Agricultural, ranching and other business concerns in the West boomed and flourished with this improved connection to the markets of the East and, through them, the ports of Europe and beyond. This, of course, led to increased migration of people into all the territories of the West, seeking opportunity.

Migration and settlement were not easy. As the settlers moved west, they encountered Native American tribes who believed they had a natural right to the lands upon which their ancestors had lived for generations. Resentment of the encroachment of new settlers was particularly strong among the tribes that had been ordered to relocate to "Indian Country" prior to 1860. Conflict was intense and frequent until 1867, when the Government established two large tracts of land called "reservations" in Oklahoma and the Dakotas to which all tribes would be confined. With the war over, troops were sent west to enforce the relocation and reservation containment policies. There were frequent wars, particularly as white settlers attempted to move onto Indian lands and as the tribes resisted this confinement.

Continuing conflict led to passage of the Dawes Act of 1887. This was a recognition that confinement to reservations was not working. The law was intended to break up the Indian communities and bring about assimilation into white culture by deeding portions of the reservation lands to individual Indians who were expected to farm their land. The policy continued until 1934.

Armed resistance essentially came to an end by 1890, the same year in which the western frontier was demonstrated by the U.S. Census to be finally closed. The surrender of Geronimo and the massacre at Wounded Knee led to a change of strategy by the Indians. Thereafter, the resistance strategy was to preserve their culture and traditions.

Skill 23.3 **Demonstrate knowledge of industrialization, including technological and agricultural innovations, and the early labor movement**

The Industrial Revolution had spread from Great Britain to the United States. Before 1800, most manufacturing activities were done in small shops or in homes. However, starting in the early 1800s, factories with modern machines were built, making it easier to produce goods faster. The eastern part of the country became a major industrial area, although some developed in the West. At about the same time, improvements began to be made in building roads, railroads, canals, and steamboats. The increased ease of travel facilitated the westward movement as well as boosted the economy with faster and cheaper shipment of goods and products, covering larger and larger areas. Some of the innovations include the Erie Canal, connecting the interior and Great Lakes with the Hudson River and the coastal port of New York. Canals to facilitate travel connected many other natural waterways.

Robert Fulton's "**Clermont**," the first commercially successful steamboat, led the way in the fastest method to ship goods, making it the most important way to do so. Later, steam-powered railroads soon became the biggest rival of the steamboat as a means of shipping, eventually being the most important transportation method opening the West. With expansion into the interior of the country, the United States became the leading agricultural nation in the world. The hardy pioneer farmers produced a vast surplus and emphasis went to producing products with a high-sale value. Such implements as the cotton gin and reaper aided in this. Travel and shipping were greatly assisted in areas not yet touched by railroad or, by improved or new roads, such as the National Road in the East and in the West the Oregon and Santa Fe Trails.

Advances in American agriculture were a direct result of the advances in technological development and the new political awareness about the power of organization, shared information and education.

Eli Whitney was born in Massachusetts during the Colonial period and, as a citizen of the recently formed United States, graduated from Yale College in 1792. Early in 1793, he had designed and constructed the first cotton gin ("gin" for engine). This machine automated the process for separating cottonseed from the short-cotton fiber—previously, a long and laborious process. Whitney may have been a bit ahead of his time. He failed to profit from his invention. However, others soon copied his cotton gin and were more successful in reaching the appropriate markets.

By whatever means provided, once Mr. Whitney's cotton gin was accepted by the planters of the South and established on the plantations, the result was that cotton would become king in Southern agriculture. The "peculiar institution" of slavery would become ever more profitable and remain institutionalized for many years to come. The advent of the cotton gin and the resulting increase in the production of cotton for the world's markets meant vast increases in wealth and political power for the South.

Other agricultural areas of the country that were not part of the plantation system also experienced growth and change during these years. In the 1820s, agricultural periodicals began to become commonplace, providing shared information about agriculture and discussing issues of concern to farmers. During the years from 1825 on, some schools and colleges started offering courses in agriculture or in sciences useful in agriculture.

In 1830, it took approximately 250 to 300 labor hours to produce 100 bushels (5 acres) of wheat using the walking plow, brush harrow, hand broadcast of seed, sickle and flail. This effort would be cut dramatically as new technological advances became available for implementation on the farm. Examples of new technology were the patenting of McCormick's reaper in 1834 and John Lane's manufacture of plows faced with steel blades in the same year. There were many other innovations which greatly changed the means of agriculture and the lives of farmers in the United States, from the manufacturing partnership of John Deere and Leonard Andrus in 1837 to the development of the first grain elevator in Buffalo, New York, in 1842.

Non-agricultural laborers in the cities and towns of the United States during this period organized and struggled to improve their lot and the conditions under which they toiled. Women and children and recent immigrants made up a considerable part of the workforce and often worked for the lowest wages and in the worst conditions. Some have compared the "wage slavery" of the factories and mills of the time to the chattel slavery in the plantation South.

One of the most significant issues for labor, during this period, was the struggle to achieve the ten-hour day. Organizers and activists were able to achieve success in the legislatures of several states. But the laws always contained a loophole that allowed workers to contract for longer hours. The ability to remove any employees who were unwilling to agree to such a contract meant that these loopholes allowed employers to retain the upper hand. Among the more notable events in labor history were the following:

1833 – The Workingmen's Ticket is formed as a political party to promote labor ideology.

1834 - The National Trades Union is formed in New York City. This is the first attempt at a national labor federation. The Factory Girls' Association is formed in Lowell and a strike is called over working conditions and wages. In Dover, New Hampshire, 800 women go out on strike over the right to organize and in opposition to wage reductions.

1836 - The first national union for a specific trade, The National Cooperative Association of Cordwainers, was founded in New York City. The Equal Rights Party is formed in Utica, New York, the result of a convention of mechanics, farmers, and workingmen who wrote a Declaration of Rights in opposition to bank notes, paper money, and arbitrary power of the courts. They called for legislation to guarantee labor the right to organize. The Factory Girls' Association in Lowell goes out on strike again over working conditions and wages.

1837 – The Panic of 1837 means an end to the National Trades Union and most other unions. President Jackson declares the ten-hour day for the Philadelphia Navy Yard to quell discontent caused by Panic of 1837.

1838 - One-third of the nation's workers were unemployed because of the economic situation.

1840 – The ten-hour day, without reduction in pay, is proclaimed by President Van Buren for all federal employees on public works.

1842 - In *Commonwealth* v. *Hunt*, the Massachusetts Supreme Court rules that labor unions, as such, are not illegal conspiracies. Legislation passes in Connecticut and Massachusetts prohibiting children from working over ten hours per day.

1844 - The New England Workingmen's Association is formed, with over 200 delegates to fight for the ten-hour day for non-federal workers.

1845 - Female workers in five cotton mills in Allegheny, Pennsylvania strike for the ten-hour day. They are supported by workers in Lowell, Massachusetts, and Manchester, New Hampshire. The first professional teacher's association is created in Massachusetts. The Female Labor Reform Association is formed as an auxiliary of the New England Workingmen's Association in Lowell, Massachusetts to fight for the ten-hour day.

1847 - New Hampshire is the first state to make the ten-hour day the legal workday.

1848 – A new child labor law in Pennsylvania establishes twelve as the minimum age for workers in commercial occupations. Pennsylvania passes a ten-hour day law. When employers violate it, women mill workers riot and attack the factory gates with axes.

Skill 23.4 Demonstrate understanding of social and cultural developments, such as changes in the role of women in society, and reform movements

People were exposed to works of literature, art, newspapers, drama, live entertainment, and political rallies. With better communication and travel, more information was desired about previously unknown areas of the country, especially the West. The discovery of gold and other mineral wealth resulted in a literal surge of settlers and even more interest.

Public schools were established in many of the states with more and more children being educated. With more literacy and more participation in literature and the arts, the young nation was developing its own unique culture becoming less and less influenced by and dependent on that of Europe.

More industries and factories required more and more labor. Women, children, and, at times, entire families worked the long hours and days, until the 1830s. By that time, the factories were getting even larger and employers began hiring immigrants who were coming to America in huge numbers. Before then, efforts were made to organize a labor movement to improve working conditions and increase wages. It never really caught on until after the Civil War, but the seed had been sown.

Following is just a partial list of well-known Americans who contributed their leadership and talents in various fields and reforms:

Lucretia Mott and **Elizabeth Cady Stanton** for women's rights

Emma Hart Willard, Catharine Esther Beecher, and **Mary Lyon** for education for women

Dr. Elizabeth Blackwell, the first woman doctor

Antoinette Louisa Blackwell, the first female minister

Dorothea Lynde Dix for reforms in prisons and insane asylums

Elihu Burritt and **William Ladd** for peace movements

Robert Owen for a Utopian society

Horace Mann, Henry Barmard, Calvin E. Stowe, Caleb Mills, and **John Swett** for public education

Benjamin Lundy, David Walker, William Lloyd Garrison, Isaac Hooper, Arthur and Lewis Tappan, Theodore Weld, Frederick Douglass, Harriet Tubman, James G. Birney, Henry Highland Garnet, James Forten, Robert Purvis, Harriet Beecher Stowe, Wendell Phillips, and John Brown for abolition of slavery and the **Underground Railroad**

Louisa Mae Alcott, James Fenimore Cooper, Washington Irving, Walt Whitman, Henry David Thoreau, Ralph Waldo Emerson, Herman Melville, Richard Henry Dana, Nathaniel Hawthorne, Henry Wadsworth Longfellow, John Greenleaf Whittier, Edgar Allan Poe, Oliver Wendell Holmes, famous writers

John C. Fremont, Zebulon Pike, Kit Carson, explorers

Henry Clay, Daniel Webster, Stephen Douglas, John C. Calhoun, American statesmen

Robert Fulton, Cyrus McCormick, Eli Whitney, inventors

Noah Webster, American dictionary and spellers

The list could go on and on but the contributions of these and many, many others greatly enhanced the unique American culture.

COMPETENCY 24.0 CIVIL WAR ERA (1850–1870S)

Skill 24.1 Demonstrate knowledge of the growth of sectionalism (North, South, and West), and of attempts at political compromise

The first serious clash between North and South occurred during 1819-1820 when James Monroe was in office as President and it was concerning admitting Missouri as a state. In 1819, the U.S. consisted of 21 states: 11 free states and 10 slave states. The Missouri Territory allowed slavery and if admitted would cause an imbalance in the number of U.S. Senators. Alabama had already been admitted as a slave state, and that had balanced the Senate with the North and South each having 22 senators. The first Missouri Compromise resolved the conflict by approving admission of Maine as a free state along with Missouri as a slave state, thus continuing to keep a balance of power in the Senate with the same number of free and slave states.

An additional provision of this compromise was that with the admission of Missouri, slavery would not be allowed in the rest of the Louisiana Purchase territory north of latitude 36 degrees 30'. This was acceptable to the Southern Congressmen since it was not profitable to grow cotton on land north of this latitude line anyway. It was thought that the crisis had been resolved but in the next year, it was discovered that in its state constitution, Missouri discriminated against free blacks. Anti-slavery supporters in Congress went into an uproar, determined to exclude Missouri from the Union. Henry Clay, known as the Great Compromiser, then proposed a second Missouri Compromise, which was acceptable to everyone. His proposal stated that the Constitution of the United States guaranteed protections and privileges to citizens of states and Missouri's proposed constitution could not deny these to any of its citizens. The acceptance in 1820 of this second compromise opened the way for Missouri's statehood--a temporary reprieve only.

Congress took up consideration of new territories between Missouri and present-day Idaho. Again, heated debate over permitting slavery in these areas flared up. Those opposed to slavery used the Missouri Compromise to prove their point showing that the land being considered for territories was part of the area the Compromise had designated as banned to slavery. On May 25, 1854, Congress passed the infamous Kansas-Nebraska Act, which nullified the provision creating the territories of Kansas and Nebraska. This provided for the people of these two territories to decide for themselves whether or not to permit slavery to exist there. Feelings were so deep and divided that any further attempts to compromise would meet with little, if any, success. Political and social turmoil swirled everywhere. Kansas was called "Bleeding Kansas" because of the extreme violence and bloodshed throughout the territory because two governments existed there, one pro-slavery and the other anti-slavery.

The Supreme Court in 1857 handed down a decision guaranteed to cause explosions throughout the country. Dred Scott was a slave whose owner had taken him from slave state Missouri, then to free state Illinois, into Minnesota Territory, free under the provisions of the Missouri Compromise, then finally back to slave state Missouri. Abolitionists pursued the dilemma by presenting a court case, stating that since Scott had lived in a free state and free territory, he was in actuality a free man. Two lower courts had ruled before the Supreme Court became involved, one ruling in favor and one against. The Supreme Court decided that residing in a free state and free territory did not make Scott a free man because Scott (and all other slaves) were not U.S. citizens or state citizens of Missouri. Therefore, he did not have the right to sue in state or federal courts. The Court went a step further and ruled that the old Missouri Compromise was now unconstitutional because Congress did not have the power to prohibit slavery in the Territories.

Anti-slavery supporters were stunned. They had just recently formed the new Republican Party and one of its platforms was keeping slavery out of the Territories. Now, according to the decision in the Dred Scott case, this basic party principle was unconstitutional. The only way to ban slavery in new areas was by a Constitutional amendment, requiring ratification by three-fourths of all states. At this time, this was out of the question because the supporters would be unable to get a majority because of Southern opposition.

In 1858, Abraham Lincoln and Stephen A. Douglas were running for the office of U.S. Senator from Illinois and participated in a series of debates, which directly affected the outcome of the 1860 Presidential election. Douglas, a Democrat, was up for re-election and knew that if he won this race, he had a good chance of becoming President in 1860. Lincoln, a Republican, was not an abolitionist but he believed that slavery was wrong morally and he firmly believed in and supported the Republican Party principle that slavery must not be allowed to extend any further.

Douglas, on the other hand, originated the doctrine of "popular sovereignty" and was responsible for supporting and getting through Congress the inflammatory Kansas-Nebraska Act. In the course of the debates, Lincoln challenged Douglas to show that popular sovereignty reconciled with the Dred Scott decision. Either way he answered Lincoln, Douglas would lose crucial support from one group or the other. If he supported the Dred Scott decision, Southerners would support him but he would lose Northern support. If he stayed with popular sovereignty, Northern support would be his but Southern support would be lost. His reply to Lincoln, stating that Territorial legislatures could exclude slavery by refusing to pass laws supporting it, gave him enough support and approval to be re-elected to the Senate. But it cost him in the race for President in 1860.

Southerners came to the realization that Douglas supported and was devoted to popular sovereignty but not necessarily to the expansion of slavery.

On the other hand, two years later, Lincoln received the nomination of the Republican Party for President.

Skill 24.2 Demonstrate knowledge of the abolitionist movement, including the roles of African-Americans and women in the movement

While there have always been individuals opposed to slavery and the slave trade, during the colonial period in America the Society of Friends (the Quakers) were the only prominent group to denounce slave holding as incompatible with Christian moral values. Perhaps influenced by humanistic values put forth during the Age of Enlightenment and during the American War for Independence, more American communities became like-minded in disdain for slavery. As new areas were added to the country (like the Northwest Territory, in 1787) prohibition of slavery in these lands became a major issue. Some protesters were assuaged when Congress banned the transatlantic slave trade, in 1808. Others were convinced of the necessity to allow the system to exist in order to keep the Southern economy viable. And distance from the "peculiar institution" gave many Northerners cause to ignore the situation as inconsequential to their own lives. The African Colonization Society, founded in 1816, was the major channel for antislavery activity during this period. The goal of this society was to resettle former slaves back in Africa.

In America, the Second Great Awakening seemed to also reawaken a moral revulsion to slavery among many American people. Revivalist preachings were creating abolitionists out of congregations who were brought to believe that slave holding was the product of personal sin and emancipation of slaves was the only means of redemption. Inactivity in the cause of abolition was tantamount to compliance in the sin in the rhetoric of some activists. In the 1830s, newly founded abolitionist groups—most prominently, the American Antislavery Society, founded in 1833—lobbied to change racially discriminatory practices, recognizing that these existing sanctions, based on race, reinforced the argument for the acceptability and necessity of keeping black people in bondage.

The American Anti-Slavery Society grew very quickly, and claimed a membership of tens of thousands. This alone would have been enough to draw great interest to their cause and curious listeners to their rallies. But they were activists, publishing widely and organizing petition drives to change existing laws and sanctions which supported slavery and reinforced racist attitudes. Through their lecturing agents, they provided the public with brilliant and provocative speakers. And several Northern audiences were moved by the personal testimony of runaway slaves—having had little or no contact with slavery, themselves, and having only the justifications of the planters and the denunciations of white abolitionists by which they might draw their conclusions.

Foremost among these speakers—and a genuine celebrity in his own time—was a man who combined all of these qualities that appealed to audiences of abolitionist meetings and rallies. He was the son of a white planter and a slave mother and, under the laws of that time, he was a Negro born to a slave and therefore the slave of his father. He was a runaway slave. He was a self-made man. He was Frederick Douglass. Douglass would become the most recognized spokesman for abolition and civil rights for Negroes in his time. He would impress, confer with, and influence the thoughts and actions of men like William Lloyd Garrison, the committed, hard-line abolition activist from Boston, and the man who would ultimately do the most to abolish slavery, President Abraham Lincoln.

Women were a large portion of the abolitionist movement from its inception. While it was common and considered acceptable for women to be concerned about, and involved in, issues of morality and humanity, their activism (sometimes extreme) in this cause often brought about more criticism than support from men and women who were neutral about their cause. For whatever reasons, the American Anti-Slavery Society originally banned women from their membership. But activist abolitionist women formed their own organizations, which met in national conventions in 1837, 1838 and 1839. Women became an undeniable asset in their activism and fundraising for the cause underpinning the national effort. However, this caused a rift in the general movement. There were many male abolitionists who opposed female activism as improper and possibly, immoral. And there were many who feared that the direct involvement of women may mean the addition, or redirection, of efforts intended to promote the unpopular cause of gender equality.

Garrison and his followers did have a broader platform than many at the time were willing to support. They also promoted the extension of women's rights, temperance and pacifism. When opponents of the election of a female officer to the American Anti-Slavery Society, in 1840, quit their membership, the Garrisonians gained control of that organization. Thereafter, women became more prominent in the Society. And many, including Lucy Stone, Elizabeth Cady Stanton and the former slave, Sojourner Truth tolerated insult and risked physical harm to spread the doctrine in lecture halls and organize supporters. One of the most famous abolitionists of the period, Harriet Tubman, called the "Moses of Her People," ran away from slavery and spoke and worked as an activist in the movement. She also personally returned to Maryland several times to aid other escaping slaves in their transit through the "Underground Railroad."

The "Underground Railroad" was not a conveyance, but rather an apparatus for the escape of slaves, ultimately to Canada. The railroad consisted of information, resources (money, food, clothing, etc,) guides and "safe" houses to aid the runaways in escaping their masters and eluding the law—which was bound to return them to the slave holders.

Because of the great risks involved, it was impossible to consistently provide for the aid of slaves, in the same manner and through the same channels, but the process know as the "Underground Railroad" was instrumental in helping thousands and thousands of escaped slaves achieve freedom.

In philosophical opposition to the Garrisonians, there were many radical and militant abolitionists. Mostly, they acted as individuals, apparently impatient with the methods of the larger organizations. But certain conditions and events would bring these militants to act as a group. "Bleeding Kansas," a situation which brought bloodshed to the contest of whether the state would be "slave" or "free," was just such an event. Some have described it as a prelude to the Civil War. And the most impatient militant to emerge from that fracas was John Brown.

Skill 24.3 Demonstrate understanding of the failure of political institutions in the 1850s

Faced with two opposite choices, Congress opted to compromise. The state of California was admitted as a "free" state. Texas, a slave state, agreed to alter its border and was compensated for its loss of territory. In the New Mexico Territory, which included the area that is now New Mexico, Arizona and Utah, no specific prohibition on slavery was implemented. In addition, the Fugitive Slave law was passed, which required all citizens to assist in the return of runaway slaves to their owners. This group of acts is called the **Compromise of 1850**. It was aimed at balancing the competing claims of the slave-owning southern states, and the free northern states.

Congress had made a similar compromise in 1820, called the **Missouri Compromise**, which had allowed the new state of Missouri to allow slavery, but restricted slavery in any new territories to below latitude 36°30'. Both of these compromises were to be undone in 1854, however, by the Kansas-Nebraska act. This act divided the western territory that had been purchased from France along the 40th parallel, with the Kansas Territory to the south and the Nebraska Territory to the north of this line. Furthermore, it was decided that each territory would decide for itself whether or not to allow slavery. This had the potential to both tip the formerly equal balance between slave and free states to the side of slavery, and to allow slavery north of 36°30' should the new territories opt for it.

Rather than creating a quiet balance, this series of compromises actually increased political tension. The **Kansas-Nebraska Act** was one of the primary campaign issues in the famous Lincoln-Douglas debates, as Stephen Douglas had been the architect of the Act. Congress' intention to balance the interests of the nation's states only served to accentuate them and draw them into the political arena, contributing directly to the secession of the Confederate States and the Civil War.

In 1859, abolitionist John Brown and his followers seized the federal arsenal at Harper's Ferry in what is now West Virginia. His purpose was to take the guns stored in the arsenal, give them to slaves nearby, and lead them in a widespread rebellion. Colonel Robert E. Lee of the United States Army captured Brown and his men and after a trial with a guilty verdict, Brown was hanged. Most Southerners felt that the majority of Northerners approved of Brown's actions but in actuality, most of them were stunned and shocked. Southern newspapers took great pains to quote a small but well-known minority of abolitionists who applauded and supported Brown's actions. This merely served to widen the gap between the two sections.

The final straw came with the election of Lincoln to the Presidency the next year. Because of a split in the Democratic Party, there were four candidates from four political parties. With Lincoln receiving a minority of the popular vote and a majority of electoral votes, the Southern states, one by one, voted to secede from the Union, as they had promised they would do if Lincoln and the Republicans were victorious. The die was cast.

In the decade leading up to the Civil War, tension between the northern and southern states intensified over the issue of slavery. The United States had acquired new territories in the southwest as a result of the Mexican-American War in the late 1840's. In 1850, as the nation was poised to expand, Congress took up the question of whether slavery would be allowed in the new territories.

Skill 24.4   Demonstrate knowledge of the Civil War (1861–1865), including its causes, leaders, and major events

South Carolina was the first state to secede from the Union and the first shots of the war were fired on Fort Sumter in Charleston Harbor. Both sides quickly prepared for war. The North had more in its favor: a larger population; superiority in finances and transportation facilities; manufacturing, agricultural, and natural resources. The North possessed most of the nation's gold, had about 92% of all industries, and almost all known supplies of copper, coal, iron, and various other minerals. Most of the nation's railroads were in the North and Midwest, men and supplies could be moved wherever needed; food could be transported from the farms of the mid-West to workers in the East and to soldiers on the battlefields. Trade with nations overseas could go on as usual due to control of the navy and the merchant fleet. The Northern states numbered 24 and included western (California and Oregon) and border (Maryland, Delaware, Kentucky, Missouri, and West Virginia) states.

The Southern states numbered eleven and included South Carolina, Georgia, Florida, Alabama, Mississippi, Louisiana, Texas, Virginia, North Carolina, Tennessee, and Arkansas, making up the Confederacy. Although outnumbered in population, the South was completely confident of victory. They knew that all they had to do was fight a defensive war and protect their own territory. The North had to invade and defeat an area almost the size of Western Europe. They figured the North would tire of the struggle and gave up. Another advantage of the South was that a number of its best officers had graduated from the U.S. Military Academy at West Point and had had long years of army experience. Many had exercised varying degrees of command in the Indian wars and the war with Mexico. Men from the South were conditioned to living outdoors and were more familiar with horses and firearms than many men from northeastern cities. Since cotton was such an important crop, Southerners felt that British and French textile mills were so dependent on raw cotton that they would be forced to help the Confederacy in the war.

The South had specific reasons and goals for fighting the war, moreso than the North. The major aim of the Confederacy never wavered: to win independence, the right to govern themselves as they wished, and to preserve slavery. The Northerners were not as clear in their reasons for conducting war. At the beginning, most believed, along with Lincoln, that preservation of the Union was paramount. Only a few extremely fanatical abolitionists looked on the war as a way to end slavery. However, by war's end, more and more northerners had come to believe that freeing the slaves was just as important as restoring the Union.

The war strategies for both sides were relatively clear and simple. The South planned a defensive war, wearing down the North until it agreed to peace on Southern terms. The only exception was to gain control of Washington, D.C., go North through the Shenandoah Valley into Maryland and Pennsylvania in order to drive a wedge between the Northeast and Midwest, interrupt the lines of communication, and end the war quickly. The North had three basic strategies:

1. blockade the Confederate coastline in order to cripple the South;
2. seize control of the Mississippi River and interior railroad lines to split the Confederacy in two;
3. seize the Confederate capital of Richmond, Virginia, driving southward and joining up with Union forces coming east from the Mississippi Valley.

The South won decisively until the Battle of Gettysburg, July 1 - 3, 1863. Until Gettysburg, Lincoln's commanders, McDowell and McClellan, were less than desirable, Burnside and Hooker, not what was needed. Lee, on the other hand, had many able officers, Jackson and Stuart depended on heavily by him. Jackson died at Chancellorsville and was replaced by Longstreet. Lee decided to invade the North and depended on J.E.B. Stuart and his cavalry to keep him informed of the location of Union troops and their strengths. Four things worked against Lee at Gettysburg:

1) The Union troops gained the best positions and the best ground first, making it easier to make a stand there.

2) Lee's move into Northern territory put him and his army a long way from food and supply lines. They were more or less on their own.

3) Lee thought that his Army of Northern Virginia was invincible and could fight and win under any conditions or circumstances.

4) Stuart and his men did not arrive at Gettysburg until the end of the second day of fighting and by then, it was too little too late. He and the men had had to detour around Union soldiers and he was delayed getting the information Lee needed.

Consequently, he made the mistake of failing to listen to Longstreet and following the strategy of regrouping back into Southern territory to the supply lines. Lee felt that regrouping was retreating and almost an admission of defeat.

He was convinced the army would be victorious. Longstreet was concerned about the Union troops occupying the best positions and felt that regrouping to a better position would be an advantage. He was also very concerned about the distance from supply lines.

It was not the intention of either side to fight at Gettysburg, but the fighting began when a Confederate brigade, who were looking for shoes, stumbled into a unit of Union cavalry. Intense fighting occupied most of the next two days, with large numbers of deaths on both sides but not much territory transfer. The third and last day Lee launched the final attempt to break Union lines. General George Pickett sent his division of three brigades under Generals Garnet, Kemper, and Armistead against Union troops on Cemetery Ridge under command of General Winfield Scott Hancock. Union lines held, and Lee and the defeated Army of Northern Virginia made their way back to Virginia. Although Lincoln's commander, George Meade, successfully turned back a Confederate charge, he and the Union troops failed to pursue Lee and the Confederates. This battle was the turning point for the North. After this, Lee never again had the troop strength to launch a major offensive. But the war dragged on, in part because Lee and his troops were able to escape back into their homeland.

The day after Gettysburg, on July 4, Vicksburg, Mississippi surrendered to Union General Ulysses Grant, thus severing the western Confederacy from the eastern part. In September 1863, the Confederacy won its last important victory at Chickamauga. In November, the Union victory at Chattanooga made it possible for Union troops to go into Alabama and Georgia, splitting the eastern Confederacy in two. Lincoln gave Grant command of all Northern armies in March of 1864. Grant led his armies into battles in Virginia while Phil Sheridan and his cavalry did as much damage as possible. In a skirmish at a place called Yellow Tavern, Virginia, Sheridan's and Stuart's forces met, with Stuart being fatally wounded. The Union won the Battle of Mobile Bay and in May 1864, William Tecumseh Sherman began his march to successfully demolish Atlanta, then on to Savannah. He and his troops turned northward through the Carolinas to Grant in Virginia. On April 9, 1865, Lee formally surrendered to Grant at Appomattox Courthouse, Virginia.

The Civil War took more American lives than any other war in history, the South losing one-third of its soldiers in battle compared to about one-sixth for the North. More than half of the total deaths were caused by disease and the horrendous conditions of field hospitals. Both sides paid a tremendous economic price, but the South suffered more severely from direct damages. Destruction was pervasive, with towns, farms, trade, industry, lives and homes of men, women, children all destroyed, and an entire Southern way of life was lost. The deep resentment, bitterness, and hatred that remained for generations gradually lessened as the years went by, but legacies of it surface and remain to this day. The South had no voice in the political, social, and cultural affairs of the nation, lessening to a great degree the influence of the more traditional Southern ideals. The Northern Yankee Protestant ideals of hard work, education, and economic freedom became the standard of the United States and helped influence the development of the nation into a modem, industrial power.

The effects of the Civil War were tremendous. It changed the methods of waging war and has been called the first modern war. It introduced weapons and tactics that, when improved later, were used extensively in wars of the late 1800s and 1900s. Civil War soldiers were the first to fight in trenches, first to fight under a unified command, first to wage a defense called "major cordon defense," a strategy of advance on all fronts. They were also the first to use repeating and breech loading weapons. Observation balloons were first used during the war along with submarines, ironclad ships, and mines. Telegraphy and railroads were put to use first in the Civil War. It was considered a modern war because of the vast destruction and was "total war," involving the use of all resources of the opposing sides.

Skill 24.5 Demonstrate knowledge of the Reconstruction period, including the various plans for Reconstruction, the new amendments to the Constitution, and the Compromise of 1877

Following the Civil War, the nation was faced with repairing the torn Union and readmitting the Confederate states. **Reconstruction** refers to this period between 1865 and 1877 when the federal and state governments debated and implemented plans to provide civil rights to freed slaves and to set the terms under which the former Confederate states might once again join the Union.

Planning for Reconstruction began early in the war, in 1861. Abraham Lincoln's Republican Party in Washington favored the extension of voting rights to black men, but was divided as to how far to extend the right. Moderates, such as Lincoln, wanted only literate blacks and those who had fought for the Union to be allowed to vote. Radical Republicans wanted to extend the vote to all black men. Conservative Democrats did not want to give black men the vote at all. In the case of former Confederate soldiers, moderates wanted to allow all but former leaders to vote, while the radicals wanted to require an oath from all eligible voters that they had never borne arms against the US, which would have excluded all former rebels. On the issue of readmission into the Union, moderates favored a much lower standard, with the radicals demanding nearly impossible conditions for rebel states to return.

Lincoln's moderate plan for Reconstruction was actually part of his effort to win the war. Lincoln and the moderates felt that if it remained easy for states to return to the Union, and if moderate proposals on black suffrage were made, that Confederate states involved in the hostilities might be swayed to re-join the Union rather than continue fighting. The radical plan was to ensure that Reconstruction did not actually start until after the war was over.

Executive proclamation and constitutional amendment officially ended slavery, although there remained deep prejudice and racism, still raising its ugly head today. Also, the Union was preserved and the states were finally truly united. Sectionalism, especially in the area of politics, remained strong for another 100 years but not to the degree and with the violence as existed before 1861. It has been noted that the Civil War may have been American democracy's greatest failure for, from 1861 to 1865, calm reason, basic to democracy, fell to human passion. Yet, democracy did survive. The victory of the North established that no state has the right to end or leave the Union. Because of unity, the U.S. became a major global power. Lincoln never proposed to punish the South. He was most concerned with restoring the South to the Union in a program that was flexible and practical rather than rigid and unbending. In fact he never really felt that the states had succeeded in leaving the Union but that they had left the 'family circle" for a short time. His plans consisted of two major steps:

All Southerners taking an oath of allegiance to the Union promising to accept all federal laws and proclamations dealing with slavery would receive a full pardon. The only ones excluded from this were men who had resigned from civil and military positions in the federal government to serve in the Confederacy, those who were part of the Confederate government, those in the Confederate army above the rank of lieutenant, and Confederates who were guilty of mistreating prisoners of war and blacks.

A state would be able to write a new constitution, elect new officials, and return to the Union fully equal to all other states on certain conditions: a minimum number of persons (at least 10% of those who were qualified voters in their states before secession from the Union who had voted in the 1860 election) must take an oath of allegiance.

After the Civil War the Emancipation Proclamation in 1863 and the 13th Amendment in 1865 ended slavery in the United States, but these measures did not erase the centuries of racial prejudices among whites that held blacks to be inferior in intelligence and morality. These prejudices, along with fear of economic competition from newly freed slaves, led to a series of state laws that permitted or required businesses, landlords, school boards and others to physically segregate blacks and whites in their everyday lives.

In 1865, Abraham Lincoln was assassinated, leaving Vice President Andrew Johnson to oversee the beginning of the actual implementation of Reconstruction. Johnson struck a moderate pose and was willing to allow former confederates to keep control of their state governments. These governments quickly enacted Black Codes that denied the vote to blacks and granted them only limited civil rights.

The economic and social chaos in the South after the war was unbelievable with starvation and disease rampant, especially in the cities. The U.S. Army provided some relief of food and clothing for both white and blacks but the major responsibility fell to the Freedmen's Bureau. Though the bureau agents to a certain extent helped southern whites, their main responsibility was to the freed slaves. They were to assist the freedmen to become self-supporting and protect them from being taken advantage of by others. Northerners looked on it as a real, honest effort to help the South out of the chaos it was in. Most white Southerners charged the bureau with causing racial friction, deliberately encouraging the freedmen to consider former owners as enemies.

In 1866, the radical Republicans won control of Congress and passed the Reconstruction Acts, which placed the governments of the southern states under the control of the federal military. With this backing, the Republicans began to implement their radical policies such as granting all black men the vote, and denying the vote to former confederate soldiers. Congress had passed the 13th, 14th and 15th amendments, granting citizenship and civil rights to blacks, and made ratification of these amendments a condition of readmission into the Union by the rebel states. The Republicans found support in the south among Freedmen, as former slaves were called; white southerners who had not supported the Confederacy, called Scalawags; and northerners who had moved to the south, known as Carpetbaggers.

Military control continued throughout Grant's administration, despite growing conflict both inside and outside the Republican Party. Conservatives in Congress and in the states opposed the liberal policies of the Republicans. Some Republicans became concerned over corruption issues among Grant's appointees and dropped support for him.

Segregation laws were foreshadowed in the Black Codes, strict laws proposed by some southern states during the Reconstruction period that sought to essentially recreate the conditions of pre-war servitude. Under these codes, blacks were to remain subservient to their white employers, and were subject to fines and beatings if they failed to work. Freedmen, as newly freed slaves were called, were afforded some civil rights protection during the Reconstruction period, however beginning around 1876, so called Redeemer governments began to take office in southern states after the removal of Federal troops that had supported Reconstruction goals. The Redeemer-state legislatures began passing segregation laws that came to be known as Jim Crow laws.

The Jim Crow laws varied from state to state, but the most significant of them required separate school systems and libraries for blacks and whites and separate ticket windows, waiting rooms and seating areas on trains and, later, other public transportation. Restaurant owners were permitted or sometimes required to provide separate entrances and tables and counters for blacks and whites, so that the two races not see one another while dining. Public parks and playgrounds were constructed for each race. Landlords were not allowed to mix black and white tenants in apartment houses in some states. The Jim Crow laws were given credibility in 1896 when the Supreme Court handed down its decision in the case *Plessy* v. *Ferguson*. In 1890, Louisiana had passed a law requiring separate train cars for blacks and whites. To challenge this law, in 1892 Homer Plessy, a man who had a black great grandparent and so was considered legally "black" in that state, purchased a ticket in the white section and took his seat. Upon informing the conductor that he was black, he was told to move to the black car. He refused and was arrested. His case was eventually elevated to the Supreme Court.

The Court ruled against Plessy, thereby ensuring that the Jim Crow laws would continue to proliferate and be enforced. The Court held that segregating races was not unconstitutional as long as the facilities for each were identical. This became known as the "separate but equal" principle. In practice, facilities were seldom equal. Black schools were not funded at the same level, for instance. Streets and parks in black neighborhoods were not maintained.

Paralleling the development of segregation legislation in the mid-19th Century was the appearance of organized groups opposed to any integration of blacks into white society. The most notable of these was the Ku Klux Klan.

First organized in the Reconstruction south, the KKK was a loose group made up mainly of former Confederate soldiers who opposed the Reconstruction government and espoused a doctrine of white supremacy. KKK members intimidated and sometimes killed their proclaimed enemies. The first KKK was never completely organized, despite having nominal leadership. In 1871, President Grant took action to use federal troops to halt the activities of the KKK, and actively prosecuted them in federal court. Klan activity waned, and the organization disappeared.

The 13th Amendment abolished slavery and involuntary servitude, except as punishment for crime. The amendment was proposed on January 31, 1865. It was declared ratified by the necessary number of states on December 18, 1865. The Emancipation Proclamation had freed slaves held in states that were considered to be in rebellion. This amendment freed slaves in states and territories controlled by the Union. The Supreme Court has ruled that this amendment does not bar mandatory military service.

The 14th Amendment provides for Due Process and Equal Protection under the Law. It was proposed on June 13, 1866 and ratified on July 28, 1868. The drafters of the Amendment took a broad view of national citizenship. The law requires that states provide equal protection under the law to all persons (not just all citizens). This amendment also came to be interpreted as overturning the Dred Scott case (which said that blacks were not and could not become citizens of the U.S.). The full potential of interpretation of this amendment was not realized until the 1950s and 1960s, when it became the basis of ending segregation in the Supreme Court case *Brown* v. *Board of Education*. This amendment includes the stipulation that all children born on American soil, with very few exceptions, are U.S. citizens. There have been recommendations that this guarantee of citizenship be limited to exclude the children of illegal immigrants and tourists, but this has not yet occurred. There is no provision in this amendment for loss of citizenship.

After the Civil War, many Southern states passed laws that attempted to restrict the movements of blacks and prevent them from bringing lawsuits or testifying in court. In the *Slaughterhouse Cases* (1871) the Supreme Court ruled that the Amendment applies only to rights granted by the federal government. In the *Civil Rights Cases*, the Court held that the guarantee of rights did not outlaw racial discrimination by individuals and organizations. In the next few decades the Court overturned several laws barring blacks from serving on juries or discriminating against the Chinese immigrants in regulating the laundry businesses.

The second section of the amendment establishes the "one man, one vote" apportionment of congressional representation. This ended the counting of blacks as 3/5 of a person. Section 3 prevents the election to Congress or the Electoral College of anyone who has engaged in insurrection, rebellion or treason. Section 4 stipulated that the government would not pay "damages" for the loss of slaves or for debts incurred by the Confederate government (e.g., with English or French banks).

The Fifteenth Amendment grants voting rights regardless of race, color or previous condition of servitude. It was ratified on February 3, 1870.

All three of these Constitutional Amendments were part of the Reconstruction effort to create stability and rule of law to provide, protect, and enforce the rights of former slaves throughout the nation.

COMPETENCY 25.0 EMERGENCE OF THE MODERN UNITED STATES (1877–1900)

Skill 25.1 Demonstrate understanding of United States expansion and imperialism, including the displacement of Native Americans, the development of the West, and international involvement

The post-Reconstruction era represents a period of great transformation and expansion for the United States, both economically and geographically, particularly for the South, recovering from the devastation of the Civil War and migration west of the Mississippi River. Great numbers of former slaves moved west, away from their former masters and lured by the promise of land. White migration was also spurred by similar desires for land and resources, leading to boom economies of cotton, cattle and grain starting in Kansas and spreading westward. Although industrial production grew fastest in the South during this period, it was still predominantly agricultural, which featured land tenancy and sharecropping, which did not really advance the remaining freed slaves economically since most of the land was still owned by the large plantation landowners who retained their holdings from before the Civil War. The economic chasm dividing white landowners and black freedmen only widened as the tenants sank further into debt to their landlords.

Westward movement of significant populations from the eastern United States originated with the discovery of gold in the West in the 1840s and picked up greater momentum after the Civil War. Settlers were lured by what they perceived as unpopulated places with land for the taking. However, when they arrived, they found that the lands were populated by earlier settlers of Spanish descent and Native Americans, who did not particularly welcome the newcomers. These original and earlier inhabitants frequently clashed with those who were moving west. Despite having signed treaties with the United States government years earlier, virtually all were ignored and broken as westward settlement accelerated and the government was called upon to protect settlers who were en route and when they had reached their destinations. This led to a series of wars between the United States and the various Native American Nations that were deemed hostile. Although the bloodshed during these encounters was great, it paled compared to the number of Native Americans who died from epidemics of deadly diseases for which they had no resistance. Eventually, the government sought to relocate inconveniently located peoples to Indian reservations, and to Oklahoma, which was lacked the resources they need and was geographically remote from their home range. The justification for this westward expansion, at the expense of the previous inhabitants was that it was America's "Manifest Destiny" to "tame" and settle the continent from coast-to-coast.

Another major factor affecting the opening of the West to migration of Americans and displacement of native peoples was the expansion of the railroad. The transcontinental railroad was completed in 1869, joining the west coast with the existing rail infrastructure terminating at Omaha, Nebraska, its westernmost point. This not only enabled unprecedented movement of people and goods, it also hastened the near extinction of bison, which the Indians of the Great Plains, in particular, depended on for their survival.

Once the American West was subdued and firmly under United States control did the United States start looking beyond its shores. Overseas markets were becoming important as American industry produced goods more efficiently and manufacturing capacity grew. Out of concern for the protection of shipping, the United States modernized and built up the Navy, which by 1900 ranked third in the world, which gave it the means to become an imperial power. The first overseas possessions were Midway Island and Alaska, purchased back in 1867 as championed by William Henry Seward. By the 1880s, Secretary of State James G. Blaine pushed for expanding U.S. trade and influence to Central and South America and in the 1890s, President Grover Cleveland invoked the Monroe Doctrine to intercede in Latin American affairs when it looked like Great Britain was going to exert its influence and power in the Western Hemisphere. In the Pacific, the United States lent its support to American sugar planters who overthrew the Kingdom of Hawaii and eventually annexed it as U.S. territory.

The event that proved a turning point was the Spanish-American War in 1898, which used the explosion of the USS Maine as a pretext for the United States to invade Cuba, when the underlying reason was the ambition for empire and economic gain. The war with Spain also triggered the dispatch of the fleet under Admiral George Dewey to the Philippines, followed up by sending Army troops. Victory over the Spanish proved fruitful for American territorial ambitions. Although Congress passed legislation renouncing claims to annex Cuba, in a rare moment of idealism, the United States gained control of the island of Puerto Rico, a permanent deep-water naval harbor at Guantanamo Bay, Cuba, the Philippines and various other Pacific islands formerly possessed by Spain. The decision to occupy the Philippines, rather than grant it immediate independence, led to a guerrilla war, the "Philippines Insurrection," which lasted until 1902. U.S. rule over the Philippines lasted until 1942, but unlike the guerrilla war years, American rule was relatively benign.

Skill 25.2 Understand the process of industrialization and the political, economic, and social changes associated with industrialization in this period

There was a marked degree of industrialization before and during the Civil War, but at war's end, industry in America was small. After the war, dramatic changes took place. Machines replaced hand labor, extensive nationwide railroad service made possible the wider distribution of goods, invention of new products made available in large quantities, and large amounts of money from bankers and investors for expansion of business operations. American life was definitely affected by this phenomenal industrial growth. Cities became the centers of this new business activity resulting in mass population movements there and tremendous growth. This new boom in business resulted in huge fortunes for some Americans and extreme poverty for many others. The discontent this caused resulted in a number of new reform movements from which came measures controlling the power and size of big business and helping the poor.

Of course, industry before, during, and after the Civil War was centered mainly in the North, especially the tremendous industrial growth after. The late 1800s and early 1900s saw the increasing buildup of military strength and the U.S. becoming a world power.

The use of machines in industry enabled workers to produce a large quantity of goods much faster than by hand. With the increase in business, hundreds of workers were hired, assigned to perform a certain job in the production process. This was a method of organization called "division of labor" and by its increasing the rate of production, businesses lowered prices for their products making the products affordable for more people. As a result, sales and businesses were increasingly successful and profitable.

A great variety of new products or inventions became available such as: the typewriter, the telephone, barbed wire, the electric light, the phonograph, and the gasoline automobile. From this list, the one that had the greatest effect on America's economy was the automobile.

The increase in business and industry was greatly affected by the many rich natural resources that were found throughout the nation. The industrial machines were powered by the abundant water supply. The construction industry as well as products made from wood depended heavily on lumber from the forests. Coal and iron ore in abundance were needed for the steel industry, which profited and increased from the use of steel in such things as skyscrapers, automobiles, bridges, railroad tracks, and machines. Other minerals such as silver, copper, and petroleum played a large role in industrial growth, especially petroleum, from which gasoline was refined as fuel for the increasingly popular automobile.

Skill 25.3   Understand the causes and consequences of urban development in this period

Between 1870 and 1916, more than 25 million immigrants came into the United States, adding to the phenomenal population growth taking place. This tremendous growth aided business and industry in two ways: (1) The number of consumers increased creating a greater demand for products thus enlarging the markets for the products. (2) With increased production and expanding business, more workers were available for newly created jobs. The completion of the nation's transcontinental railroad in 1868 contributed greatly to the nation's economic and industrial growth. Some examples of the benefits of using the railroads include raw materials were shipped quickly by the mining companies and finished products were sent to all parts of the country. Many wealthy industrialists and railroad owners saw tremendous profits steadily increasing due to this improved method of transportation. Another impact of interstate railroad expansion was the standardization of time zones, in order to maintain the reliability and accuracy of train schedules across vast east-west routes.

Innovations in new industrial processes and technology grew at a pace unmatched at any other time in American history. Thomas Edison was the most prolific inventor of that time, using a systematic and efficient method to invent and improve on current technology in a profitable manner. The abundance of resources, together with growth of industry and the pace of capital investments led to the growth of cities. Populations were shifting from rural agricultural areas to urban industrial areas and by the early 1900s, a third of the nation's population lived in cities. Industry needed workers in its factories, mills and plants and rural workers were being displaced by advances in farm machinery and their increasing use and other forms of automation. The dramatic growth of population in cities was fueled by growing industries, more efficient transportation of goods and resources, and the people who migrated to those new industrial jobs, either from rural areas of the United States or immigrants from foreign lands. Increased urban populations, often packed into dense tenements, often without adequate sanitation or clean water, led to public health challenges that required cities to establish sanitation, water and public health departments to cope with and prevent epidemics. Political organizations also saw the advantage of mobilizing the new industrial working class and created vast patronage programs that sometimes became notorious for corruption in big-city machine politics, like Tammany Hall in New York.

As business grew, methods of sales and promotion were developed. Salespersons went to all parts of the country promoting the various products, opening large department stores in the growing cities, offering the varied products at reasonable affordable prices. People who lived too far from the cities, making it impossible to shop there, had the advantage of using a mail order service, buying what they needed from catalogs furnished by the companies.

The developments in communication, such as the telephone and telegraph, increased the efficiency and prosperity of big business.

Skill 25.4   Understand political, cultural, and social movements

The late 1800s and early 1900s were a period of the efforts of many to make significant reforms and changes in the areas of politics, society, and the economy. There was a need to reduce the levels of poverty and to improve the living conditions of those affected by it. Regulations of big business, ridding governmental corruption and making it more responsive to the needs of the people were also on the list of reforms to be accomplished. Until 1890, there was very little success, but from 1890 on, the reformers gained increased public support and were able to achieve some influence in government. Since some of these individuals referred to themselves as "progressives," the period of 1890 to 1917 is referred to by historians as the **Progressive Era**.

Skilled laborers were organized into a labor union called the **American Federation of Labor**, in an effort to gain better working conditions and wages for its members. Farmers joined organizations such as the National Grange and Farmers Alliances. Farmers were producing more food than people could afford to buy. This was the result of (1) new farmlands rapidly sprouting on the plains and prairies, and (2) development and availability of new farm machinery and newer and better methods of farming. They tried selling their surplus abroad but faced stiff competition from other nations selling the same farm products. Other problems contributed significantly to their situation. Items they needed for daily life were priced exorbitantly high. Having to borrow money to carry on fanning activities kept them constantly in debt. Higher interest rates, shortage of money, falling farm prices, dealing with the so-called middlemen, and the increasingly high charges by the railroads to haul farm products to large markets all contributed to the desperate need for reform to relieve the plight of American farmers.

American women began actively campaigning for the right to vote. Elizabeth Cady Stanton and Susan B. Anthony in 1869 founded the organization called **National Women Suffrage Association**, the same year the Wyoming Territory gave women the right to vote. Soon after, a few states followed by giving women the right to vote, limited to local elections only.

Governmental reform began with the passage of the **Civil Service Act**, also known as the Pendleton Act. It provided for the Civil Service Commission, a federal agency responsible for giving jobs based on merit rather than as political rewards or favors. Another successful reform was the adoption of the secret ballot in voting, as were such measures as the direct primary, referendum, recall, and direct election of U.S. Senators by the people rather than by their state legislatures. Following the success of reforms made at the national level, the progressives were successful in gaining reforms in government at state and local levels.

After 1890, more and more attention was called to needs and problems through the efforts of social workers and clergy and the writings of people such as Lincoln Steffans, Ida M. Tarbell, and Upton Sinclair.

Presidents Theodore Roosevelt, William Howard Taft, and Woodrow Wilson supported many of the reform laws after 1890 and in 1884, President Grover Cleveland did much to see that the Civil Service Act was enforced. After 1880, a number of political or "third" parties were formed and although unsuccessful in getting their Presidential candidates elected, significant reform legislation, including Constitutional amendments, were passed by Congress and became law due to their efforts.

Such legislative acts included the **Sherman Antitrust Act of 1890**, the Clayton Antitrust Act of 1914, the Underwood Tariff of 1913, and the establishment of the Federal Trade Commission in 1914. By the 1890s and early 1900s, the United States had become a world power and began a leading role in international affairs. War loomed on the horizon again and the stage was set for increased activity in world affairs, which had been avoided since the end of the Civil War.

COMPETENCY 26.0 PROGRESSIVE ERA THROUGH THE NEW DEAL (1900–1939)

Skill 26.1 Demonstrate knowledge of political, economic, and social developments

During the period of 1823 to the 1890s, the major interests and efforts of the American people were concentrated on expansion, settlement, and development of the continental United States. The Civil War, 1861-1865, preserved the Union and eliminated the system of slavery. From 1865 onward, the focus was on taming the West and developing industry. During this period, travel and trade between the United States and Europe were continuous. By the 1890s, American interests turned to areas outside the boundaries of the United States. The West was developing into a major industrial area and people in the United States became very interested in selling their factory and farm surplus to overseas markets. In fact, some Americans desired getting and controlling land outside the U.S. boundaries. Before the 1890s, the U.S. had little, if anything to do with foreign affairs, was not a strong nation militarily, and had inconsequential influence on international political affairs. In fact, the Europeans looked on the American diplomats as inept and bungling in their diplomatic efforts and activities. However, all of this changed and the Spanish-American War of 1898 saw the entry of the United States as a world power.

During the 1890s, Spain controlled such overseas possessions as Puerto Rico, the Philippines, and Cuba. Cubans rebelled against Spanish rule and the U.S. government found itself besieged by demands from Americans to assist the Cubans in their revolt. When the U.S. battleship Maine blew up off the coast of Havana, Cuba, Americans blamed the Spaniards for it and demanded American action against Spain. Two months later, Congress declared war on Spain and the U.S. quickly defeated them. The peace treaty gave the U.S. possession of Puerto Rico, the Philippines, Guam and Hawaii, which was annexed during the war. This success enlarged and expanded the U.S. role in foreign affairs.

Skill 26.2 Understand the causes of United States participation in the First World War and the consequences at home and abroad

Causes attributed to the United States' participation in World War I included the surge of nationalism, the increasing strength of military capabilities, massive colonization for raw materials needed for industrialization and manufacturing, and military and diplomatic alliances.

In Europe, Italy and Germany were each totally united into one nation from many smaller states. There were revolutions in Austria and Hungary, the Franco-Prussian War, the dividing of Africa among the strong European nations, interference and intervention of Western nations in Asia, and the breakup of Turkish dominance in the Balkans.

In Africa, France, Great Britain, Italy, Portugal, Spain, Germany, and Belgium controlled the entire continent except Liberia and Ethiopia. In Asia and the Pacific Islands, only China, Japan, and present-day Thailand (Siam) kept their independence. The others were controlled by the strong European nations.

This success enlarged and expanded the U.S. role in foreign affairs. Under the administration of Theodore Roosevelt, the U.S. armed forces were built up, greatly increasing its strength. Roosevelt's foreign policy was summed up in the slogan of "Speak softly and carry a big stick," backing up the efforts in diplomacy with a strong military. During the years before the outbreak of World War I, evidence of U.S. emergence as a world power could be seen in a number of actions. In the spirit of the Monroe Doctrine of non-involvement of Europe in the affairs of the Western Hemisphere, President Roosevelt forced Italy, Germany, and Great Britain to remove their blockade of Venezuela. In addition he gained the rights to construct the Panama Canal by threatening force, assumed the finances of the Dominican Republic to stabilize it and prevent any intervention by Europeans and in 1916 under President Woodrow Wilson, to keep order, U.S. troops were sent to the Dominican Republic.

In Europe, war broke out in 1914, eventually involving nearly 30 nations, and ended in 1918. One of the major causes of the war was the tremendous surge of nationalism during the 1800s and early 1900s. People of the same nationality or ethnic group sharing a common history, language or culture began uniting or demanding the right of unification, especially in the empires of Eastern Europe, such as Russian Ottoman and Austrian-Hungarian Empires. Getting stronger and more intense were the beliefs of these peoples in loyalty to common political, social, and economic goals considered to be before any loyalty to the controlling nation or empire.

Emotions ran high and minor disputes magnified into major ones and sometimes quickly led to threats of war. Especially sensitive to these conditions was the area of the states on the Balkan Peninsula. Along with the imperialistic colonization for industrial raw materials, military build-up (especially by Germany), and diplomatic and military alliances, the conditions for one tiny spark to set off the explosion were in place. In July 1914, a Serbian national assassinated the Austrian heir to the throne and his wife and war began a few weeks later. There were a few attempts to keep war from starting, but these efforts were futile.

At the same time, Great Britain intercepted and decoded a secret message from Germany to Mexico urging Mexico to go to war against the U.S. The publishing of this information along with continued German destruction of American ships resulted in the eventual entry of the U.S. into the conflict, the first time the country prepared to fight in a conflict not on American soil. Though unprepared for war, governmental efforts and activities resulted in massive defense mobilization with America's economy directed to the war effort. Though America made important contributions of war materials, its greatest contribution to the war was manpower, soldiers desperately needed by the Allies.

Some ten months before the war ended, President Wilson had proposed a program called the Fourteen Points as a method of bringing the war to an end with an equitable peace settlement. In these Points he had five points setting out general ideals; there were eight pertaining to immediately working to resolve territorial and political problems; and the fourteenth point counseled establishing an organization of nations to help keep world peace.

When Germany agreed in 1918 to an armistice, it assumed that the peace settlement would be drawn up on the basis of these Fourteen Points. However, the peace conference in Paris ignored these points and Wilson had to be content with efforts at establishing the League of Nations. Italy, France, and Great Britain, having suffered and sacrificed far more in the war than America, wanted retribution. The treaties punished severely the Central Powers, taking away arms and territories and requiring payment of reparations. Germany was punished more than the others and, according to one clause in the treaty, was forced to assume the responsibility for causing the war.

Pre-war empires lost tremendous amounts of territories as well as the wealth of natural resources in them. New, independent nations were formed and some predominately ethnic areas came under control of nations of different cultural backgrounds. Some national boundary changes overlapped and created tensions and hard feelings as well as political and economic confusion. The wishes and desires of every national or cultural group could not possibly be realized and satisfied, resulting in disappointments for both; those who were victorious and those who were defeated. Germany received harsher terms than expected from the treaty which weakened its post-war government.

Along with the worldwide depression of the 1930s, the stage was set for the rise of Adolf Hitler and his Nationalist Socialist Party and World War II.

World War I saw the introduction of such warfare as use tanks, airplanes, machine guns, submarines, poison gas, and flame throwers. Fighting on the Western front was characterized by a series of trenches that were used throughout the war. U.S. involvement in the war did not occur until 1917. When the war began in 1914, President Woodrow Wilson declared that the U.S. was neutral and most Americans were opposed to any involvement anyway. In 1916, Wilson was re-elected to a second term based on the slogan proclaiming his efforts at keeping America out of the war. For a few months after, he put forth most of his efforts to stopping the war but German submarines began unlimited warfare against American merchant shipping.

President Wilson lost in his efforts to get the U.S. Senate to approve the peace treaty. The Senate at the time was a reflection of American public opinion and its rejection of the treaty was a rejection of Wilson. The approval of the treaty would have made the U.S. a member of the League of Nations but Americans had just come off a bloody war to ensure that democracy would exist throughout the world. Americans just did not want to accept any responsibility that resulted from its new position of power and were afraid that membership in the League of Nations would embroil the U.S. in future disputes in Europe.

Skill 26.3   Demonstrate knowledge of political, economic, social, and cultural life in the "Roaring Twenties"

The end of World War I and the decade of the 1920s saw tremendous changes in the United States, signifying the beginning of its development into its modern society today. The shift from farm to city life was occurring in tremendous numbers. Social changes and problems were occurring at such a fast pace that it was extremely difficult and perplexing for many Americans to adjust to them. Politically the 18th Amendment to the Constitution, the so-called Prohibition Amendment, prohibited selling alcoholic beverages throughout the U.S. resulting in problems affecting all aspects of society. The passage of the 19th Amendment gave to women the right to vote in all elections. The decade of the 1920s also showed a marked change in roles and opportunities for women with more and more of them seeking and finding careers outside the home. They began to think of themselves as the equal of men and not as much as housewives and mothers.

The influence of the automobile, the entertainment industry, and the rejection of the morals and values of pre-World War I life, resulted in the fast-paced "**Roaring Twenties.**" There were significant effects on events leading to the Depression-era 1930s and another world war. Many Americans greatly desired the pre-war life and supported political policies and candidates in favor of the return to what was considered normal. It was desired to end government's strong role and adopt a policy of isolating the country from world affairs, a result of the war.

Prohibition of the sale of alcohol had caused the increased activities of bootlegging and the rise of underworld gangs and the illegal speakeasies, the jazz music and dances they promoted. The customers of these clubs were considered "modern," reflected by extremes in clothing, hairstyles, and attitudes towards authority and life. Movies and, to a certain degree, other types of entertainment, along with increased interest in sports figures and the accomplishments of national heroes, such as Lindbergh, influenced Americans to admire, emulate, and support individual accomplishments.

As wild and uninhibited modern behavior became, this decade witnessed an increase in a religious tradition known as "revivalism," emotional preaching. Although law and order were demanded by many Americans, the administration of President Warren G. Harding was marked by widespread corruption and scandal, not unlike the administration of Ulysses S. Grant, except Grant was honest and innocent. The decade of the '20s also saw the resurgence of such racist organizations as the Ku Klux Klan.

The U.S. economy experienced a tremendous period of boom. Restrictions on business because of war no longer existed and the conservatives in control adopted policies that helped and encouraged big business. To keep foreign goods from competing with American goods, tariffs were raised to the highest level.

New products were developed by American manufacturers and many different items became readily available to the people. These included refrigerators, radios, washing machines, and, most importantly, the automobile.

Skill 26.4   Demonstrate knowledge of political, economic, and social developments during the Great Depression and the New Deal

The 1929 Stock Market Crash was the powerful event that is generally interpreted as the beginning of the Great Depression in America. Although the crash of the Stock Market was unexpected, it was not without identifiable causes. The 1920s had been a decade of social and economic growth and hope. But the attitudes and actions of the 1920s regarding wealth, production, and investment created several trends that quietly set the stage for the 1929 disaster.

The legislative and executive branches of the Coolidge administration tended to favor business and the wealthy. The Revenue Act of 1926 significantly reduced income taxes for the wealthy. This bill lowered taxes such that a person with a million-dollar income saw his/her taxes reduced from $600,000 to $200,000. Despite the rise of labor unions, even the Supreme Court ruled in ways that further widened the gap between the rich and the middle class.

The majority of the population did not have enough money to buy what was necessary to meet their needs. The concept of buying on credit caught on very quickly. Buying on credit, however, creates artificial demand for products people cannot ordinarily afford. This has two effects: first, at some point there is less need to purchase products (because they have already been bought), and second, at some point paying for previous purchases makes it impossible to purchase new products. This exacerbated the problem of a surplus of goods.

The economy also relied on investment and luxury spending by the rich in the 1920s. Luxury spending, however, only occurs when people are confident with regard to the economy and the future. Should these people lose confidence, that luxury spending would come to an abrupt halt. This is precisely what happened when the stock market crashed in 1929. Investing in business produces returns for the investor. During the 1920s, investing was very healthy. Investors, however, began to expect greater returns on their investments. This led many to make speculative investments in risky opportunities.

Two industries, automotive and radio, drove the economy in the 1920s. During this decade, the government tended to support new industries rather than agriculture. During WWI, the government had subsidized farms and paid ridiculously high prices for grains. Farmers had been encouraged to buy and farm more land and to use new technology to increase production. The nation was feeding much of Europe during and in the aftermath of the war. But when the war ended, these farm policies were cut off. Prices plummeted, farmers fell into debt, and farm prices declined. The agriculture industry was on the brink of ruin before the stock market crash.

The concentration of production and economic stability in the automotive industry and the production and sale of radios was expected to last forever. But there comes a point when the growth of an industry slows due to market saturation. When these two industries declined, due to decreased demand, they caused the collapse of other industries upon which they were dependent (e.g., rubber tires, glass, fuel, construction, etc.).

The other factor contributing to the Great Depression was the economic condition of Europe. The U.S. was lending money to European nations to rebuild. Many of these countries used this money to purchase U.S. food and manufactured goods. But they were not able to pay off their debts. While the U.S. was providing money, food, and goods to Europe, however, it was not willing to buy European goods. Trade barriers were enacted to maintain a favorable trade balance.

Risky speculative investments in the stock market was the second major factor contributing to the stock market crash of 1929 and the ensuing depression. Stock market speculation was spectacular throughout the 1920s. In 1929, shares traded on the New York Stock Exchange reached 1,124,800,410. In 1928 and 1929 stock prices doubled and tripled (RCA stock prices rose from 85 to 420 within one year). The opportunity to achieve such profits was irresistible. In much the same way that buying goods on credit became popular, buying stock on margin allowed people to invest a very small amount of money in the hope of receiving exceptional profit. This created an investing craze that drove the market higher and higher. But brokers were also charging higher interest rates on their margin loans (nearly 20%). If, however, the price of the stock dropped, the investor owed the broker the amount borrowed plus interest.

Some scholars cite several other factors as contributing to the Great Depression. First, in 1929, the Federal Reserve increased interest rates. Second, some believe that as interest rates rose and the stock market began to decline, people began to hoard money. This was certainly the case after the crash. There is a question that it was a cause of the crash.

In September 1929, stock prices began to slip somewhat, yet people remained optimistic. On Monday, October 21, prices began to fall quickly. The volume traded was so high that the tickers were unable to keep up. Investors were frightened, and they started selling very quickly. This caused further collapse. For the next two days prices stabilized somewhat. On **Black Thursday**, October 24, prices plummeted again. By this time investors had lost confidence. On Friday and Saturday an attempt to stop the crash was made by some leading bankers. But on Monday the 28th, prices began to fall again, declining by 13% in one day. The next day, **Black Tuesday, October 29**, saw 16.4 million shares traded. Stock prices fell so far, that at many times no one was willing to buy at any price.

Unemployment quickly reached 25% nation-wide. People thrown out of their homes created makeshift domiciles of cardboard, scraps of wood and tents. With unmasked reference to President Hoover, who was quite obviously overwhelmed by the situation and incompetent to deal with it, these communities were called "**Hoovervilles.**" Families stood in bread lines, rural workers left the dust bowl of the plains to search for work in California, and banks failed. More than 100,000 businesses failed between 1929 and 1932. The despair that swept the nation left an indelible scar on all who endured the Depression.

When the stock market crashed, businesses collapsed. Without demand for products other businesses and industries collapsed. This set in motion a domino effect, bringing down the businesses and industries that provided raw materials or components to these industries. Hundreds of thousands became jobless. Then the jobless often became homeless. Desperation prevailed. Little has been done to assess the toll hunger, inadequate nutrition, or starvation took on the health of those who were children during this time. Indeed, food was cheap, relatively speaking, but there was little money to buy it.

Everyone who lived through the Great Depression was permanently affected in some way. Many never trusted banks again. Many people of this generation later hoarded cash so they would not risk losing everything again. Some permanently rejected the use of credit. In the immediate aftermath of the stock market crash, many urged President Herbert Hoover to provide government relief. Hoover responded by urging the nation to be patient. By the time he signed relief bills in 1932, it was too late.

In several parts of the country, economic disaster was exacerbated by natural disaster. The Florida Keys were hit by the "**Labor Day Hurricane**" in 1935. This was one of only three hurricanes in history to make landfall as a Category 5 storm. More than 400 died in the storm, including 200 WWI veterans who were building bridges for a public works project. In the Northeast, The **Great Hurricane of 1938** struck Long Island, causing more than 600 fatalities, decimating Long Island, and resulting in millions of dollars in damage to the coast from New York City to Boston.

By far the worst natural disaster of the decade came to be known as the **Dust Bowl.** Because of severe and prolonged drought in the Great Plains and previous reliance on inappropriate farming techniques, a series of devastating dust storms occurred in the 1930s that resulted in destruction, economic ruin for many, and dramatic ecological change.

Plowing the plains for agriculture removed the grass and exposed the soil. When the drought occurred, the soil dried out and became dust. Wind blew away the dust. Between 1934 and 1939 winds blew the soil to the east, all the way to the Atlantic Ocean. The dust storms, called "black blizzards" created huge clouds of dust that were visible all the way to Chicago. Topsoil was stripped from millions of acres. In Texas, Arkansas, Oklahoma, New Mexico, Kansas and Colorado over half a million people were homeless. Many of these people journeyed west in the hope of making a new life in California.

Crops were ruined, the land was destroyed, and people either lost or abandoned homes and farms. Fifteen percent of Oklahoma's population left. Because so many of the migrants were from Oklahoma, the migrants came to be called "**Okies**" no matter where they came from. Estimates of the number of people displaced by this disaster range from 300,000 or 400,000 to 2.5 million.

Hoover's bid for re-election in 1932 failed. The new president, Franklin D. Roosevelt, won the White House on his promise to the American people of a "new deal." Upon assuming the office, Roosevelt and his advisers immediately launched a massive program of innovation and experimentation to try to bring the Depression to an end and get the nation back on track. Congress gave the President unprecedented power to act to save the nation. During the next eight years, the most extensive and broadly based legislation in the nation's history was enacted. The legislation was intended to accomplish three goals: relief, recovery, and reform.

The first step in the "**New Deal**" was to relieve suffering. This was accomplished through a number of job-creation projects. The second step, the recovery aspect, was to stimulate the economy. The third step was to create social and economic change through innovative legislation.

The National Recovery Administration attempted to accomplish several goals:
- Restore employment
- Increase general purchasing power
- Provide character-building activity for unemployed youth
- Encourage decentralization of industry and thus divert population from crowded cities to rural or semi-rural communities
- Develop river resources in the interest of navigation and cheap power and light
- Complete flood control on a permanent basis
- Enlarge the national program of forest protection and to develop forest resources
- Control farm production and improve farm prices
- Assist home builders and home owners
- Restore public faith in banking and trust operations
- Recapture the value of physical assets, whether in real property, securities, or other investments.

These objectives and their accomplishments implied a restoration of public confidence and courage.

Among the "alphabet organizations" set up to work out the details of the recovery plan, the most prominent were:

- **Agricultural Adjustment Administration** (AAA), designed to readjust agricultural production and prices thereby boosting farm income
- **Civilian Conservation Corps** (CCC), designed to give wholesome, useful activity in the forestry service to unemployed young men
- **Civil Works Administration** (CWA) and the **Public Works Administration** (PWA), designed to give employment in the construction and repair of public buildings, parks, and highways
- **Works Progress Administration** (WPA), whose task was to move individuals from relief rolls to work projects or private employment

The **Tennessee Valley Authority** (TVA) was of a more permanent nature. Designed to improve the navigability of the Tennessee River and increase productivity of the timber and farm lands in its valley, this program built 16 dams that provided water control and hydroelectric generation.

The **Public Works Administration** employed Americans on over 34,000 public works projects at a cost of more than $4 billion. Among these projects were the construction of a highway that linked the Florida Keys and Miami, the Boulder Dam (now the Hoover Dam) and numerous highway projects.

To provide economic stability and prevent another crash, Congress passed the **Glass-Steagall Act**, which separated banking and investing. The Securities and Exchange Commission was created to regulate dangerous speculative practices on Wall Street. The Wagner Act guaranteed a number of rights to workers and unions in an effort to improve worker-employer relations. The **Social Security Act of 1935** established pensions for the aged and infirm as well as a system of unemployment insurance.

Much of the recovery program was emergency, but certain permanent national policies emerged. The intention of the public through its government was to supervise and, to an extent, regulate business operations, from corporation activities to labor problems. This included protecting bank depositors and the credit system of the country, employing gold resources and currency adjustments to aid permanent restoration of normal living, and, if possible, establishing a line of subsistence below which no useful citizen would be permitted to sink.

Many of the steps taken by the Roosevelt administration have had far-reaching effects. They alleviated the economic disaster of the Great Depression, they enacted controls that would mitigate the risk of another stock market crash, and they provided greater security for workers. The nation's economy, however, did not fully recover until America entered World War II.

During the first 100 days in office, the Roosevelt Administration responded to this crisis with programs designed to restore the ecological balance. One action was the formation of the **Soil Conservation Service** (now the Natural Resources Conservation Service). The story of this natural disaster and its toll in human suffering is poignantly preserved in the photographs of Dorothea Lange.

To be sure, there were negative reactions to some of the measures taken to pull the country out of the depression. There was a major reaction to the deaths of the WWI veterans in the Labor Day Hurricane, ultimately resulting in a Congressional investigation into possible negligence. The Central Valley Project ruffled feathers of farmers who lost tillable land and some water supply to the construction of the aqueduct and the Hoover Dam. Tennesseans were initially unhappy with the changes in river flow and navigation when the Tennessee Valley Authority began its construction of dams and the directing of water to form reservoirs and to power hydroelectric plants. Some businesses and business leaders were not happy with the introduction of minimum wage laws and restrictions and controls on working conditions and limitations of work hours for laborers. The numerous import/export tariffs of the period were the subject of controversy.

In the long view, however, much that was accomplished under the New Deal had positive long-term effects on economic, ecological, social and political issues for the next several decades. The Tennessee Valley Authority and the Central Valley Project in California provided a reliable source and supply of water to major cities, as well as electrical power to meet the needs of an increasingly electricity-dependent society. For the middle class and the poor, the labor regulations, the establishment of the Social Security Administration, and the separation of investment and banking have served the nation admirably for more than six decades.

The charter of the National Recovery Administration included a statement defending the right of labor unions to exist and to negotiate with employers. This was interpreted by thousands as support for unions. But the Supreme Court declared this unconstitutional.

There were several major events or actions that are particularly important to the history of organized labor during this decade:

- The Supreme Court upheld the Railway Labor Act, including its prohibition of employer interference or coercion in the choice of bargaining representatives (1930).
- The Davis-Bacon Act provided employers of contractors and subcontractors on public construction should be paid the prevailing wages (1931).
- The Anti-Injunction Act prohibited Federal injunctions in most labor disputes (1932).
- Wisconsin created the first unemployment insurance act in the country (1932).
- The Wagner-Peyser Act created the United States Employment Service within the Department of Labor (1933).
- Half a million Southern mill workers walked off the job in the Great Uprising of 1934.
- The Secretary of Labor called the first National Labor Legislation Conference to get better cooperation between the Federal Government and the States in defining a national labor legislation program (1934).
- The U.S. joined the International Labor Organization (1934).
- The Wagner Act (The National Labor Relations Act) established a legal basis for unions, set collective bargaining as a matter of national policy required by the law, provided for secret ballot elections for choosing unions, and protected union members from employer intimidation and coercion. This law was later amended by the Taft-Hartley Act (1947) and by the Landrum Griffin Act (1959).
- The Guffey Act stabilized the coal industry and improved labor conditions (1935). It was later declared unconstitutional (1936).
- The Social Security Act was approved (1935).
- The Committee for Industrial Organization (CIO) was formed within the AFL to carry unionism to the industrial sector. (1935).
- The United Rubber Workers staged the first sit-down strike (1936).
- The United Auto Workers used the sit-down strike against General Motors (1936).
- The Anti-Strikebreaker Act (the Byrnes Act) made it illegal to transport or aid strikebreakers in interstate or foreign trade (1936).
- The Public Contracts Act (the Walsh-Healey Act) of 1936 established labor standards, including minimum wages, overtime pay, child and convict labor provisions and safety standards on federal contracts.
- General Motors recognized the United Auto Workers in 1937.
- US Steel recognized the Steel Workers Organizing Committee in 1937.
- The Wagner Act was upheld by the Supreme Court (1937).

- During a strike of the Steel Workers Organizing Committee against Republic Steel, police attacked a crowd gathered in support of the strike, killing ten and injuring eighty. This came to be called **The Memorial Day Massacre** (1937).
- The CIO was expelled from the AFL over charges of dual unionism or competition (1937).
- The National Apprenticeship Act established the Bureau of Apprenticeship within the Department of Labor (1937).
- The Merchant Marine Act created a Federal Maritime Labor Board (1938).
- The Fair Labor Standards Act created a $0.25 minimum wage, stipulated time-and-a-half pay for hours over 40 per week.
- The CIO becomes the Congress of Industrial Organizations.

COMPETENCY 27.0 THE SECOND WORLD WAR AND THE POSTWAR PERIOD (1939-1963)

Skill 27.1 Understand the causes of United States participation in the Second World War and the consequences at home and abroad

In Asia, the U.S. had opposed Japan's invasion of Southeast Asia, an effort to gain Japanese control of that region's rich resources. Consequently, the U.S. stopped all important exports to Japan, whose industries depended heavily on petroleum, scrap metal, and other raw materials. Later Roosevelt refused the Japanese withdrawal of its funds from American banks. General Tojo became the Japanese premier in October 1941 and quickly realized that the U.S. Navy was powerful enough to block Japanese expansion into Asia. Deciding to cripple the Pacific Fleet, the Japanese aircraft, without warning, bombed the Fleet December 7, 1941, while at anchor in Pearl Harbor in Hawaii. Temporarily it was a success. It destroyed many aircraft and disabled much of the U.S. Pacific Fleet. In the end, it was a costly mistake as it quickly motivated the Americans to prepare for and wage war.

Military strategy in the war as developed by Roosevelt, Churchill, and Stalin was to concentrate on Germany's defeat first, then Japan's. The start was made in North Africa, pushing Germans and Italians off the continent, beginning in the summer of 1942 and ending successfully in May, 1943. Before the war, Hitler and Stalin had signed a non-aggression pact in 1939, which Hitler violated in 1941 by invading the Soviet Union. The German defeat at Stalingrad, marking a turning point in the war, was brought about by a combination of entrapment by Soviet troops and death of German troops by starvation and freezing due to the horrendous winter conditions. All this occurred at the same time the Allies were driving the Germans and Italians out of North Africa.

The liberation of Italy began in July 1943 and ended May 2, 1945. The third part of the strategy was D-Day, June 6, 1944, with the Allied invasion of France at Normandy. At the same time, starting in January 1943, the Soviets began pushing the German troops back into Europe and they were greatly assisted by supplies from Britain and the United States. By April 1945, Allies occupied positions beyond the Rhine and the Soviets moved on to Berlin, surrounding it by April 25. Germany surrendered May 7 and the war in Europe was finally over.

Meanwhile, in the Pacific, in the six months after the attack on Pearl Harbor, Japanese forces moved across Southeast Asia and the western Pacific Ocean. By August 1942, the Japanese Empire was at its largest size and stretched northeast to Alaska's Aleutian Islands, west to Burma, south to what is now Indonesia. Invaded and controlled areas included Hong Kong, Guam, Wake Island, Thailand, part of Malaysia, Singapore, the Philippines, and bombed Darwin on the north coast of Australia.

The raid of General Doolittle's bombers on Japanese cities and the American naval victory at Midway along with the fighting in the Battle of the Coral Sea helped turn the tide against Japan. Island-hopping by U.S. Seabees and Marines and the grueling bloody battles fought resulted in gradually pushing the Japanese back towards Japan.

After victory was attained in Europe, concentrated efforts were made to secure Japan's surrender, but it took dropping two atomic bombs on the cities of Hiroshima and Nagasaki to finally end the war in the Pacific. Japan formally surrendered on September 2, 1945, aboard the U.S. battleship Missouri, anchored in Tokyo Bay. The war was finally ended.

Before war in Europe had ended, the Allies had agreed on a military occupation of Germany. It was divided into four zones each one occupied by one of four powers: Great Britain, France, the Soviet Union, and the United. After the war, the Allies agreed that Germany's armed forces would be abolished, the Nazi Party outlawed, and the territory east of the Oder and Neisse Rivers taken away. Nazi leaders were accused of war crimes and brought to trial. After Japan's defeat, the Allies began a military occupation directed by American General Douglas MacArthur, who introduced a number of reforms, eventually ridding Japan of its military institutions and transforming it into a democracy. A constitution was drawn up in 1947, transferring all political rights from the emperor to the people, granting women the right to vote, and denying Japan the right to declare war. War crimes trials of 25 war leaders and government officials were also conducted. The U.S. did not sign a peace treaty until 1951. The treaty permitted Japan to rearm but took away its overseas empire.

Again, after a major world war came efforts to prevent war from occurring again throughout the world. Preliminary work began in 1943 when the U.S., Great Britain, the Soviet Union, and China sent representatives to Moscow where they agreed to set up an international organization that would work to promote peace around the earth. In 1944, the four Allied powers met again and made the decision to name the organization the United Nations. In 1945, a charter for the U. N. was drawn up and signed, taking effect in October of that year.

Major consequences of the war included horrendous death and destruction, millions of displaced persons, the gaining of strength and spread of Communism, and Cold War tensions as a result of the beginning of the nuclear age. World War II ended more lives and caused more devastation than any other war.

Besides the losses of millions of military personnel, the devastation and destruction directly affected civilians, reducing cities, houses, and factories to ruin and rubble and totally wrecking communication and transportation systems. Millions of civilian deaths, especially in China and the Soviet Union, were the results of famine.

More than 12 million people were uprooted by war's end, having no place to live. Those included were prisoners of war, those that survived Nazi concentration camps and slave labor camps, orphans, and people who escaped war-torn areas and invading armies. Changing national boundary lines also caused the mass movement of displaced persons.

Germany and Japan were completely defeated; Great Britain and France were seriously weakened; and the Soviet Union and the United States became the world's leading powers. Although they were allied during the war, the alliance fell apart as the Soviets pushed Communism and the U.S. strove to combat it in Europe and Asia. In spite of the tremendous destruction it suffered, the Soviet Union was stronger than ever. During the war, it took control of Lithuania, Estonia, and Latvia and by mid-1945 parts of Poland, Czechoslovakia, Finland, and Romania. It helped Communist governments gain power in Bulgaria, Romania, Hungary, Czechoslovakia, Poland, and North Korea. China fell to Mao Zedong's Communist forces in 1949. Until the fall of the Berlin Wall in 1989 and the dissolution of Communist governments in Eastern Europe and the Soviet Union, the United States and the Soviet Union faced off in what was called a Cold War. The possibility of the terrifying destruction by nuclear weapons loomed over both nations.

Skill 27.2   Understand domestic and foreign developments during the Cold War

The major thrust of U.S. foreign policy from the end of World War II to 1990 was the post-war struggle between non-Communist nations, led by the United States, and the Soviet Union and the Communist nations who were its allies. It was referred to as a "Cold War" because its conflicts did not lead to a major war of fighting, or a "hot war." Both the Soviet Union and the United States embarked on an arsenal buildup of atomic and hydrogen bombs as well as other nuclear weapons. Both nations had the capability of destroying each other but because of the continuous threat of nuclear war and accidents, extreme caution was practiced on both sides. The efforts of both sides to serve and protect their political philosophies and to support and assist their allies resulted in a number of events during this 45-year period.

In 1946, Josef Stalin stated publicly that the presence of capitalism and its development of the world's economy made international peace impossible. This resulted in an American diplomat in Moscow named George F. Kennan to propose in response to Stalin, a statement of U.S. foreign policy. The idea and goal of the U.S. was to contain or limit the extension or expansion of Soviet Communist policies and activities. After Soviet efforts to make trouble in Iran, Greece, and Turkey, U.S. President Harry Truman stated what is known as the **Truman Doctrine,** which committed the U.S. to a policy of intervention in order to contain or stop the spread of communism throughout the world.

After 1945, social and economic chaos continued in Western Europe, especially in Germany. Secretary of State George C. Marshall came to realize that the U.S. had serious problems. To assist in the recovery, he proposed a program known as the European Recovery Program, or the **Marshall Plan**. Although the Soviet Union withdrew from any participation, the U.S. continued the work of assisting Europe in regaining economic stability. In Germany, the situation was critical with the American Army shouldering the staggering burden of relieving the serious problems of the German economy. In February 1948, Britain and the U.S. combined their two zones, with France joining in June.

The Soviets were opposed to German unification and in April 1948 took serious action to either stop it or to force the Allies to give up control of West Berlin to the Soviets. The Soviets blocked all road traffic access to West Berlin from West Germany. To avoid any armed conflict, it was decided to airlift into West Berlin the needed food and supplies. From June 1948 to mid-May 1949 Allied air forces flew in all that was needed for the West Berliners, forcing the Soviets to lift the blockade and permit vehicular traffic access to the city.

The first "hot war" in the post-World War II era was the Korean War, begun June 25, 1950 and ending July 27, 1953. Troops from Communist North Korea invaded democratic South Korea in an effort to unite both sections under Communist control. The United Nations organization asked its member nations to furnish troops to help restore peace. Many nations responded and President Truman sent American troops to help the South Koreans. The war dragged on for three years and ended with a truce, not a peace treaty. Like Germany then, Korea remained divided and does so to this day.

In 1954, the French were forced to give up their colonial claims in Indochina, the present-day countries of Vietnam, Laos, and Cambodia. Afterwards, the Communist northern part of Vietnam began battling with the democratic southern part over control of the entire country. In the late 1950s and early 1960s, U.S. Presidents Eisenhower and Kennedy sent to Vietnam a number of military advisers and military aid to assist and support South Vietnam's non-Communist government. During Lyndon Johnson's presidency, the war escalated with thousands of American troops being sent to participate in combat with the South Vietnamese. The war was extremely unpopular in America and caused such serious divisiveness among its citizens that Johnson decided not to seek reelection in 1968. It was in President Richard Nixon's second term in office that the U.S. signed an agreement ending war in Vietnam and restoring peace. This was done January 27, 1973, and by March 29, the last American combat troops and American prisoners of war left Vietnam for home. It was the longest war in U.S. history and to this day carries the perception that it was a "lost war."

In 1962, during the administration of President John F. Kennedy, Premier Khrushchev and the Soviets decided, as a protective measure for Cuba against an American invasion, to install nuclear missiles on the island. In October, American U-2 spy planes photographed over Cuba what were identified as missile bases under construction. The decision in the White House was how to handle the situation without starting a war. The only recourse was removal of the missile sites and preventing more being set up. Kennedy announced that the U.S. had set up a "quarantine" of Soviet ships heading to Cuba. It was in reality a blockade but the word itself could not be used publicly as a blockade was actually considered an act of war.

A week of incredible tension and anxiety gripped the entire world until Khrushchev capitulated. Soviet ships carrying missiles for the Cuban bases turned back and the crisis eased. What precipitated the crisis was Khrushchev's underestimation of Kennedy. The President made no effort to prevent the erection of the Berlin Wall and was reluctant to commit American troops to invade Cuba and overthrow Fidel Castro. The Soviets assumed this was a weakness and decided they could install the missiles without any interference.

The Soviets were concerned about American missiles installed in Turkey aimed at the Soviet Union and about a possible invasion of Cuba. If successful, Khrushchev would demonstrate to the Russian and Chinese critics of his policy of peaceful coexistence that he was tough and not to be intimidated. At the same time, the Americans feared that if Russian missiles were put in place and launched from Cuba to the U.S., the short distance of 90 miles would not allow enough time for adequate warning. Furthermore, it would originate from a direction that radar systems could not detect. It was felt that if America gave in and allowed a Soviet presence practically at the back door that the effect on American security and morale would be devastating.

As tensions eased in the aftermath of the crisis, several agreements were made. The missiles in Turkey were removed, as they were obsolete. A telephone "hot line" was set up between Moscow and Washington to make it possible for the two heads of government to have instant contact with each other. The U.S. agreed to sell its surplus wheat to the Soviets.

Probably the highlight of the foreign policy of President Richard Nixon, after the end of the Vietnam War and withdrawal of troops, was his 1972 trip to China. When the Communists gained control of China in 1949, the policy of the U.S. government was refusal to recognize the Communist government. It regarded as the legitimate government of China to be that of Chiang Kai-shek, exiled on the island of Taiwan.

In 1971, Nixon sent Henry Kissinger on a secret trip to Peking to investigate whether or not it would be possible for America to give recognition to China. In February 1972, President and Mrs. Nixon spent a number of days in the country visiting well-known Chinese landmarks, dining with the two leaders, Mao Tse-tung and Chou En-lai. Agreements were made for cultural and scientific exchanges, eventual resumption of trade, and future unification of the mainland with Taiwan. In 1979, formal diplomatic recognition was achieved. With this one visit, the pattern of the Cold War was essentially shifted.

Under the administration of President Jimmy Carter, Egyptian President Anwar el Sadat and Israeli Prime Minister Menachem Begin met at presidential retreat Camp David and agreed, after a series of meetings, to sign a formal treaty of peace between the two countries. In 1979, the Soviet invasion of Afghanistan was perceived by Carter and his advisers as a threat to the rich oil fields in the Persian Gulf but at the time U.S. military capability to prevent further Soviet aggression in the Middle East was weak. The last year of Carter's presidential term was taken up with the 53 American hostages held in Iran. The shah had been deposed and control of the government and the country was in the hands of Muslim leader Ayatollah Ruhollah Khomeini.

Khomeini's extreme hatred for the U.S. was the result of the 1953 overthrow of Iran's Mossadegh government, sponsored by the CIA. To make matters worse, the CIA proceeded to train the shah's ruthless secret police force. So when the terminally ill exiled shah was allowed into the U.S. for medical treatment, a fanatical mob stormed into the American embassy, taking the 53 Americans as prisoners and supported and encouraged by Khomeini.

President Carter froze all Iranian assets in the U.S., set up trade restrictions, and approved a risky rescue attempt, which failed. He had appealed to the UN for aid in gaining release for the hostages and to European allies to join the trade embargo on Iran. Khomeini ignored U.N. requests for releasing the Americans and Europeans refused to support the embargo so as not to risk losing access to Iran's oil. American prestige was damaged, and Carter's chances for re-election were doomed. The hostages were released on the day of Ronald Reagan's inauguration as President when Carter released Iranian assets as ransom.

The foreign policy of President Ronald Reagan was, in his first term, focused primarily on the Western Hemisphere, particularly in Central America and the West Indies. U.S. involvement in the domestic revolutions of El Salvador and Nicaragua continued into Reagan's second term when Congress held televised hearings on what came to be known as the Iran-Contra Affair. A cover-up was exposed showing that profits from secretly selling military hardware to Iran had been used to give support to rebels, called Contras, who were fighting in Nicaragua. In 1983 in Lebanon, 241 American Marines were killed when an Islamic suicide bomber drove an explosive-laden truck into U.S. Marines headquarters located at the airport in Beirut.

This tragic event came as part of the unrest and violence between the Israelis and the Palestinian Liberation Organization (PLO) forces in southern Lebanon. In October, 1983, 1,900 U.S. Marines landed on the island of Grenada to rescue a small group of American medical students at the medical school and depose the leftist government. Perhaps the most intriguing and far-reaching event towards the end of Reagan's second term was the arms-reduction agreement Reagan reached with Soviet General Secretary Mikhail Gorbachev. Gorbachev began easing East-West tensions by stressing the importance of cooperation with the West and easing the harsh and restrictive life of the people in the Soviet Union. In retrospect, it was clearly a prelude to the events occurring during the administration of President George Bush.

After Bush took office, it appeared for a brief period that democracy would gain a hold and influence in China but the brief movement was quickly and decisively crushed. The biggest surprise was the fall of the Berlin Wall, resulting in the unification of all of Germany. The loss of the Communists' power in other Eastern European countries, and the fall of Communism in the Soviet Union and the breakup of its republics into independent nations were no less surprising. The countries of Poland, Hungary, Romania, Czechoslovakia, Albania, and Bulgaria replaced Communist rule with a democratic system.

The former Yugoslavia broke apart into individual ethnic enclaves, with the republics of Serbia, Croatia, and Bosnia-Herzegovina embarking on wars of ethnic cleansing between Catholics, Orthodox, and Muslims. In Russia, as in the other former republics and satellites, democratic governments were put into operation and the difficult task of changing communist economies into ones of capitalistic free enterprise began. For all practical purposes, it appeared that the tensions and dangers of the post-World War II "Cold War" between the U.S. and Soviet-led Communism were over.

Skill 27.3 Demonstrate knowledge of political, economic, social, and cultural life in the 1950s

President Harry Truman's administration entered the 1950s with a daunting task at hand, faced by a former ally, the Soviet Union under Josef Stalin, now turned rival, for geopolitical influence and the Cold War had been underway with East Germany and eastern Europe well into the Soviet sphere of control. China had recently ended a decades-long civil war that put the Communist Party, under the chairmanship of Mao Zedong and exiled the Guomindang (Nationalist Party) under Chiang Kai-shek to Taiwan. In Indochina (Vietnam, Laos and Cambodia), the Viet Minh, under Ho Chi-Minh and whose forces under Vo Nguyen Giap's command had mounted a resistance to French colonial rule. This was evidence for the "Red Menace" and a conspiracy for international domination by the Communist bloc, in the minds of right-wing American politicians. Truman, Democrat, was confronted at home by a Congress controlled by the Republican Party which carried on a series of hearings and investigation to ferret out "Reds" and communist sympathizers, starting with government agencies and soon spreading out to labor organizations, the arts and entertainment industry, leading to the infamous "Blacklist" of individuals suspected of Communist Party affiliations, and preventing the listed individuals from pursuing their chosen professions.

Economically, the post-World War II economic boom continued into the 1950s. The Korean War era, 1950-1953 did not see the kind of general mobilization that World War II had. Most Americans were not directly affected by the war in Korea and the expansion of the economy continued, along with a growing middle class, which was spurred by the GI Bill of Rights, which gave educational, occupational and mortgage assistance to veterans who could enjoy a middle class lifestyle on an unprecedented scale. There was also a population boom of the babies born to veterans and this led to the beginning of another social and cultural phenomenon, the "Baby Boomers." The election of Dwight D. Eisenhower to the Presidency in 1952 marked a continuation of economic progress and a burgeoning suburban population, fueled by low-interest Veterans Administration mortgage loans and new wealth.

After World War II and the Korean War, efforts began to relieve the problems of millions of African-Americans, including ending discrimination in education, housing, and jobs and the grinding widespread poverty. Although President Truman ordered the Armed Forces to integrate in 1947, the same year Jackie Robinson broke the "color barrier" of Major League Baseball, the military services were slow to integrate until the Korean War when African-American soldiers were assigned to front-line Army units without regard to race. The other services followed suit, but only begrudgingly and out of necessity to replace personnel as casualties reduced their ranks. The efforts of civil rights leaders found success in a number of Supreme Court decisions, the best-known case, *Brown* v. *Board of Education of Topeka* (1954)" ending compulsory segregation in public schools.

COMPETENCY 28.0 RECENT DEVELOPMENTS (1960S–PRESENT)

Skill 28.1 Understand political developments, including the war in Vietnam, the "imperial presidency," and the new conservatism

Poverty remained a serious problem in the central sections of large cities, resulting in riots and soaring crime rates, which ultimately found its way to the suburbs. The American entry into, and the escalation of, the war in Vietnam and the social conflict and upheaval of support versus opposition to U.S. involvement, led to antiwar demonstrations. The escalation of drug abuse, weakening of the family unit, homelessness, poverty, mental illness, along with increasing social, mental, and physical problems experienced by the Vietnam veterans returning to families, marriages, contributed to a country divided and torn apart which ran across generational lines.

The 1960 election of President John F. Kennedy signaled a new era in American politics and culture. Kennedy was the first president to have been born in the 20th Century and the second youngest to hold that office, after Theodore Roosevelt. As president, he called for Americans to serve society and the world, to improve it through voluntary service at home and abroad. The Peace Corps was one of the better-known programs that he created as part of his "New Frontiers" platform during the Presidential campaign. His mettle as a world leader was tested early in his administration; the Bay of Pigs invasion to unseat Fidel Castro from power in Cuba ended in disaster for the United States and gave Cuba a propaganda coup. The Cuban Missile Crisis nearly brought the United States to the brink of nuclear war with the Soviet Union and he ordered military advisors to the Republic of Vietnam to support it against the communist National Liberation Front (Viet Cong) who were South Vietnamese proxies for North Vietnam, thus commencing what later turned out to be a political and military quagmire for the United States. When Kennedy was assassinated in 1963, the country had faced an internal period of grief and lost a considerable amount of prestige among world leaders. Vice President Lyndon B. Johnson assumed the Presidency after Kennedy's death in accordance with constitutional rules of succession. As President, Johnson retained Kennedy's cabinet pretty much intact with few leaving and appointing Senator Hubert H. Humphrey of Minnesota as Vice President.

U.S. involvement was the second phase of three in Vietnam's 20th Century history. The first phase began in 1946 when the Vietnamese fought French troops for control of the country. Vietnam prior to 1946 had been part of the French colony of Indochina (since 1861 along with Laos and Kampuchea or Cambodia). In 1954, the defeated French left and the country became divided into Communist North and Democratic South. United States' aid and influence continued as part of the U.S. "Cold War" foreign policy to help any nation threatened by Communism.

The second phase involved the U.S. commitment. The Communist Vietnamese considered the war one of national liberation, a struggle to avoid continual dominance and influence of a foreign power. A cease-fire was arranged in January 1973 and a few months later U.S. troops left for good. The third and final phase consisted of fighting between the Vietnamese but ended April 30, 1975, with the surrender of South Vietnam, the entire country being united under Communist rule.

Participants were the United States of America, Australia, New Zealand, South and North Vietnam, South Korea, Thailand, and the Philippines. With active U.S. involvement from 1957 to 1973, it was the longest war participated in by the U.S.; it was tremendously destructive and completely divided the American public in their opinions and feelings about the war. Many were frustrated and angered by the fact that it was the first war fought on foreign soil in which U.S. combat forces were totally unable to achieve their goals and objectives.

Returning veterans faced not only readjustment to normal civilian life but also bitterness, anger, rejection, and no heroes' welcomes. Many suffered severe physical and deep psychological problems. The war set a precedent with Congress and the American people actively challenging U.S. military and foreign policy. The conflict, though tempered markedly by time, still exists and still has a definite effect on people.

The Vietnam War also divided the Democratic Party, and the 1968 Democratic National Convention in Chicago turned out to be a highly contentious and bitterly fought, both on the floor of the convention and outside, where thousands had gathered to protest the Vietnam War. Vice President Hubert H. Humphrey became the party's nominee, but he led a divided party. 1968 was a bad year for the United States and especially the Democratic Party. In Vietnam, the forces of the Viet Cong and the North Vietnamese Army (NVA) launched a coordinated and devastating offensive on January 30, on the eve of Tet, the Lunar New Year, disproving the Johnson Administration officials who claimed that the Vietnamese Communists were no longer a viable military force. Although the Tet Offensive was a tactical defeat for the Viet Cong because it no longer could field a large enough military force to match American firepower in a set-piece engagement, it was a strategic defeat for the Americans, in public relations and the political will to continue in a seemingly endless conflict. Also, the Reverend Martin Luther King, Jr., an influential leader of the Civil Rights Movement and its most eloquent spokesman, was assassinated in Memphis, Tennessee, sparking racial riots in many American cities. And, Senator Robert F. Kennedy of New York, the late President John F. Kennedy's younger brother, was assassinated in Los Angeles after winning the California Democratic Primary. Before he died, it looked very possible that he would have won the party's nomination, running on an anti-war platform.

The Presidential Election campaign of 1964 pitted President Johnson against the Republican nominee, Senator Barry Goldwater of Arizona. Goldwater represented the "New Conservative" wing of his party, which advocated scaling back of government from Roosevelt's New Deal and of the liberal social policies of the Kennedy and Johnson administrations. The Goldwater campaign also advocated a strong military to counter the "Red Menace" of the Soviet Union, the People's Republic of China and the Communist bloc nations of the Warsaw Pact. Lyndon Johnson successfully won re-election, based partly on depicting Goldwater as a warmonger who would plunge the United States into a mutually destructive thermonuclear war with the Soviet Union. This left President Johnson with a landslide victory.

Unfortunately for Lyndon B. Johnson, the war in Vietnam overshadowed his domestic programs and indelibly marked his legacy and became known as "Johnson's War." The Gulf of Tonkin Resolution was enacted in late 1964 after an incident off the coast of Vietnam involving U.S. Naval ships and North Vietnamese coastal patrol boats, and effectively gave the President the power to prosecute a war without Congress declaring it, as clearly stated in the Constitution. Soon afterward, Johnson authorized the commitment of conventional military forces to Vietnam in 1965. The war proved to be a drain on the nation's economy and a growing burden for the President, as anti-war sentiment divided the nation as it hadn't seen since the Civil War. Eventually, the Vietnam quagmire became such a hindrance to his administration that Johnson declared, in a nationally televised address, that he would halt the bombing of North Vietnam and not be a candidate for the Democratic Party's nominee for the 1968 Presidential Election.

Former Vice President Richard M. Nixon defeated the current Vice President Hubert Humphrey, who had been closely identified with Johnson's Vietnam policy. One of Nixon's campaign promises included a "secret plan" to end American involvement in Vietnam. Ironically, the war dragged on for the length of his first term and he ordered a widening of the war by ordering troops to invade previously neutral Cambodia in 1970. This action led to even more dissent against the war and the killing of four students at Kent State University in Ohio, during a protest over the invasion of Cambodia.

In other international dealings, with a major role played by his National Security Advisor and later Secretary of State Henry Kissinger, Nixon undertook a bold international policy of détente with the Soviet Union and the unexpected step of opening official relations with the People's Republic of China. This was surprising in that both gave political and material support to North Vietnam given Nixon's political reputation as a staunch anti-Communist.

The Nixon administration was characterized by an "**Imperial Presidency,**" due to his aggrandizement of presidential power, usurping powers that have been the purview of Congress and carrying on activities without the express consent of the Congress. The **Watergate** scandal resulting in the first-ever resignation of a sitting American president. The population of the U.S. had greatly increased and along with it the nation's industries and the resulting harmful pollution of the environment. Factory smoke, automobile exhaust, waste from factories and other sources all combined to create hazardous air, water, and ground pollution which, if not brought under control and significantly diminished, would severely endanger all life on earth. The 1980s was the decade of the horrible Exxon Valdez oil spill off the Alaskan coast and the nuclear accident and melt-down at the Ukrainian nuclear power plant at Chernobyl. The U.S. had a narrow escape with the near disaster at Three Mile Island Nuclear Plant in Pennsylvania.

Skill 28.2   Understand economic developments, including changes in industrial structure, the growth of the budget deficit, the impact of deregulation, and energy and environmental issues

Economic problems emerged in the 1960s as a result of the high costs of waging war in Vietnam, the arms race with the Soviet Union and the increasing costs of growing social programs that quickly outstripped military spending as a share of the federal budget, exacerbated by an aversion for raising federal tax rates. The boom times for the economy of the 1950s slowed down by the mid- and late-60s, but America's appetite for non-renewable petroleum to power cars, utilities and industrial production grew unchecked, making the country more reliant on imports as demand outstripped domestic reserves' capacity to keep up. Persian Gulf nations provided the bulk of the imported oil, mainly from Saudi Arabia and Iran. This made the United States dependent on a critical resource from an increasingly unstable part of the world and further complicated by American support for Israel in the 1967 Six Day War against Egypt, Syria and Jordan, and the 1973 Yom Kippur War against Egypt, pitting the Jewish state against its Arabic and predominantly Muslim neighbors, whom the Saudi government supported.

In order to support the unprecedented levels of spending, President Richard Nixon instituted deficit spending, where government spending exceeded collected revenues. This led to a dramatic increase in the national debt, as measured by the outstanding obligations in U.S. Treasury securities (bills, notes and bonds) that were issued to cover the costs of government. The 1970s witnessed a period of high unemployment, the result of a severe recession. This was also accompanied by out-of-control inflation and wage increases, and the Nixon Administration imposed wage and price controls in August 1971 in order to lift the economy out of recession and offset the effects of "stagflation," a stagnant economy in a period of high inflation.

Angered by the United States support of Israel in the Yom Kippur War, the Arabic leading oil-producing nations of OPEC (Organization of Petroleum Exporting Countries), cut back on oil production and boycotted exports to the United States, thus raising the price of a barrel of oil and creating a fuel shortage. This made it clear that energy and fuel conservation was necessary in the American economy, especially since fuel shortages created two energy crises during the decade of the 1970s. Americans experienced shortages of fuel oil for heating and gasoline for cars and other vehicles.

A great awakening to environmental concerns was evident by the mid- and late-1960s as smog, polluted waterways, effects of poisons on the environment and dwindling nonrenewable resources caught the attention of the public. Major oil spills such as the Torrey Canyon spill into the English Channel in 1967 and the gigantic 1969 oil spill off the coast of Santa Barbara, California signaled alarming trends to come. President Nixon signed bills banning DDT, the Environmental Protection Act of 1969 which established the Environmental Protection Agency (EPA), the Occupational Safety and Health Act of 1970 (OSHA) and supported enactment of Clean Air and Clean Water acts.

By 1980, Ronald Reagan, former Governor of California and former "B"-movie actor, was elected President, defeating President Jimmy Carter, former Governor of Georgia and Annapolis-trained naval nuclear engineer, who had previously unseated President Gerald Ford, who had succeeded President Nixon after his resignation. President Reagan was an advocate of "trickle-down" economics, which espoused cutting social programs to save money and decrease the tax burden on the wealthy and corporations, believing that largesse for the top tier of the population would eventually trickle down to the lower income strata of workers. Ronald Reagan was a strong supporter of de-regulation, insisting that private sector corporations could do oversight and self-policing better, which was contradicted by the high level of corporate abuse for safety, health and environmental concerns. Although the Reagan Era was a period of great wealth and financial boom times, the unprecedented level of military spending increased the national debt to its highest levels to date during peacetime.

Fiscal restraint returned during the two terms that President Bill Clinton served. He managed to balance the federal budget, the first since the Nixon Administration, and left office with a $10 trillion budget surplus and a record of high economic growth. This budget surplus was wiped out and replaced by an even conversely deeper budget deficit soon after his successor, President George W. Bush, took office in 2001 and plunged the nation into another economic recession.

Skill 28.3   Understand major social movements and social policy initiatives in this period

President Lyndon B. Johnson continued many of the programs that John F. Kennedy started, notably passage of the **Civil Rights Act** for African-Americans, the "War on Poverty" and sustained support for the Republic of Vietnam. President Johnson pushed for the enactment of the Voting Rights Act to enfranchise Black voters, particularly in states of the former Confederacy, where they were actively discouraged from voting by multiple obstacles to registering to vote and if registered, from voting, including intimidation and lynching.

In the 1960s, the civil rights movement under the leadership of Dr. Martin Luther King, Jr. really gained momentum. Under President Lyndon B. Johnson the Civil Rights Acts of 1964 and 1968 prohibited discrimination in housing sales and rentals, employment, public accommodations, and voter registration. President Johnson's "Great Society" programs, which exceeded Roosevelt's New Deal. As a former public school teacher, Johnson made education a cornerstone of his policy, creating the Head Start Program. He was also responsible for getting legislation enacted to create Medicare, Job Corps, VISTA (Volunteers in Service To America, a domestic counterpart to the Peace Corps) and other programs to help the historically disadvantaged.

Skill 28.4   Understand the social and cultural effects of changes in the American family and in the ethnic composition of the United States population in this period

The first children of the Baby Boom generation born after World War II grew up to maturity in this period. The Vietnam War and the Selective Service loomed large as young men who were born in 1946 became eligible for the draft in 1964 and 1965, just as the United States started deploying conventional military forces to Vietnam. Unlike in previous wars, draft-age men could be granted deferments or exemptions for educational and family reasons. This meant that the upper class, wealthier and mainly white men could avoid military service, leaving predominantly working class and economically disadvantaged families who couldn't afford college to have their sons serve in combat.

Youth activism in political and social activities started as part of the Civil Rights Movement, in a large way, during the voter registration drives in the South for the 1964 elections that college students participated in. These students became leaders of social reform activism in later years of the decade. Organizations like the Students for a Democratic Society (SDS) and the Youth International Party ("Yippies") sprang up too. There was a growing countercultural trend as youth resisted traditional culture and society, taking up artists, rock stars and other cultural icons of the era as models for emulation, including the use of hallucinogenic drugs like LSD and euphoria-inducing marijuana. In 1971, the Constitution was amended to lower the voting age to eighteen.

During this period, there was a growing trend among the nation's ethnic minorities to exhibit a newfound pride. The African-American community found its voice in the Civil Rights Movement a non-violent coalition led by Rev. Martin Luther King, Jr., the militant Black Panther Party led by Eldridge Cleaver, Huey Newton and others, the Black Muslims led by Elijah Muhammad and Malcolm X (who later broke away from the Nation of Islam), which counted among its converts, Cassius Clay, the charismatic heavyweight boxing champion later known as Muhammad Ali who also resisted the war in Vietnam by refusing induction, and the Latino activism, sparked by Cesar Chavez as he organized Mexican-American farm workers in California, reflecting the importance and numbers of Latino workers in the American economy and society. Cultural awareness among Native Americans was heightened after a takeover of Alcatraz in 1969 and the occupation of Wounded Knee in 1973 by the American Indian Movement (AIM).

Gender politics became an issue as feminism and women's liberation became prominent, advocating equality for women in society and the workplace. Challenging many long-held notions of family led to the organization of the National Organization for Women (NOW) which supported an Equal Rights Amendment (ERA) to the Constitution and applauded the Supreme Court's Roe v. Wade decision of 1973 which struck down restrictions against abortion, strengthening women's reproductive rights. The Gay Rights' movement's defining moment came with the Stonewall incident in 1969 which led to greater prominence of gay, lesbian and transgender issues, including the American Psychiatric Association removing homosexuality as a mental disorder in 1974.

Skill 28.5 **Demonstrate understanding of international relations, including United States relations with the Soviet Union and its successor states and the changing role of the United States in world political and economic affairs**

The decade of the '60s started with foreign policy challenges for the new administration of President John F. Kennedy. Tensions between the U.S. and the U.S.S.R. grew, as both nations used proxies in the global rivalry between East and West. Continuing with the Eisenhower Administration policy of containing communism, Kennedy authorized the Bay of Pigs invasion to unseat Fidel Castro from power in Cuba, which ended in disaster. In 1962, Premier Khrushchev and the Soviets decided, as a protective measure for Cuba against an American invasion, to install nuclear missiles on the island. In October, incredible tension and anxiety gripped the entire world until Khrushchev ordered Soviet ships carrying missiles for the Cuban bases to turn back and the crisis eased. What precipitated the crisis was Khrushchev's underestimation of Kennedy since the President made no effort to prevent the erection of the Berlin Wall and was reluctant to commit American troops to invade Cuba and overthrow Fidel Castro. A telephone "hot line" was set up between Moscow and Washington to make it possible for the two heads of government to have instant contact with each other.

The involvement in the Vietnam War was the other major foreign policy challenge of the 1960s and 1970s. For Lyndon B. Johnson, the war in Vietnam overshadowed nearly all foreign policy concerns and led to widespread international disapproval, including the next President. Nixon promised a "secret plan" to end American involvement in Vietnam. However the war escalated during his first term and he ordered a widening of the war by ordering troops to invade previously neutral Cambodia in 1970. Eventually, the combatant sides agreed to the Paris Peace Talks and the end of U.S. involvement in Vietnam.

One of the highlights of the détente foreign policy of President Richard Nixon was his 1972 trip to China. In 1971, Nixon sent Henry Kissinger on a secret trip to Peking to investigate whether or not it would be possible for America to give recognition to China. In February 1972, Nixon spent a number of days in the country visiting well-known Chinese landmarks, dining with the two leaders, Chairman Mao Zedong and Premier Zhou Enlai. Agreements were made for cultural and scientific exchanges, and the eventual resumption of trade. In 1979, formal diplomatic recognition was achieved.

During the administration of President Jimmy Carter, Egyptian President Anwar el-Sadat and Israeli Prime Minister Menachem Begin met at presidential retreat Camp David and agreed, after a series of meetings, to sign a formal treaty of peace between the two countries. In 1979, the Soviet invasion of Afghanistan was perceived by Carter and his advisers as a threat to the rich oil fields in the Persian Gulf but at the time U.S. military capability to prevent further Soviet aggression in the Middle East was weak.

The last year of Carter's presidential term was taken up with the 53 American hostages held in Iran. The shah had been deposed and control of the government and the country was in the hands of Muslim leader, Ayatollah Ruhollah Khomeini, whose extreme hatred for the U.S. was fueled by the 1953 CIA-orchestrated overthrow of Iran's democratically elected Mossadegh government. Also, the CIA trained the Savak, the ruthless secret police. When the terminally ill exiled shah was allowed into the U.S. for medical treatment, a mob stormed the American embassy taking the 53 Americans as hostages, supported and encouraged by Khomeini.

The foreign policy of President Ronald Reagan was, in his first term, focused primarily on the Western Hemisphere, particularly in Central America and the West Indies. U.S. involvement in the domestic revolutions of El Salvador and Nicaragua continued into Reagan's second term when Congress held televised hearings on what came to be known as the Iran-Contra Affair. A cover-up was exposed showing that profits from secretly selling military hardware to Iran had been used to give support to rebels, called Contras, who were fighting in Nicaragua. In 1983 in Lebanon, 241 American Marines were killed when an Islamic suicide bomber drove an explosive-laden truck into U.S. Marines headquarters located at the airport in Beirut.

Toward the end of Reagan's second term, an arms-reduction agreement was reached with Soviet General Secretary Mikhail Gorbachev. Gorbachev began easing East-West tensions by stressing the importance of cooperation with the West and easing the harsh and restrictive life of the people in the Soviet Union. In retrospect, it was clearly a prelude to the events occurring during the administration of President George H. W. Bush, when the Berlin Wall fell, reuniting Germany and the disintegration of the Union of Soviet Socialist Republics (U.S.S.R.) leading to the independence of the Baltic nations of Estonia, Latvia and Lithuania, other former Soviet republics of Ukraine, Armenia, Azerbaijan, Georgia, and other Central Asian countries. Concurrent was the dissolution of the Warsaw Pact of Eastern European nations, who were considered for eventual membership in the European Union and the North Atlantic Treaty Organization (NATO) which was originally formed to be a defensive alliance against the Soviet Union and the Warsaw Pact nations.

The United States, dependent on a critical resource from an increasingly unstable part of the world and further complicated by American support for Israel in the 1967 Six Day War against Egypt, Syria and Jordan, and the 1973 Yom Kippur War against Egypt, pitting the Jewish state against its Arabic and predominantly Muslim neighbors, whom the Saudi government supported. In retaliation for the United States' support of Israel in the Yom Kippur War, the Arabic leading oil-producing nations of OPEC (Organization of Petroleum Exporting Countries) cut back on oil production and boycott exports to the United States, thus raising the price of a barrel of oil and creating a fuel shortage.

DOMAIN VII. WORLD HISTORY

COMPETENCY 29.0 PREHISTORY TO 1400 CE

Skill 29.1 Demonstrate knowledge of human society before approximately 3000 BCE

Prehistory is defined as the period of man's achievements before the development of writing. In the Stone Age cultures, there were three different periods. The **Lower Paleolithic Period** is illustrated with the use of crude tools. The **Upper Paleolithic Period** exhibited a greater variety of better-made tools and implements, the wearing of clothing, highly organized group life, and skills in art. And the **Neolithic Period** featured domesticated animals, food production, the arts of knitting, spinning and weaving cloth, starting fires through friction, building houses rather than living in caves, the development of institutions including the family, religion, and a form of government or the origin of the state.

Hunting and gathering societies are the earliest and most primitive form of human social groups, dating back to the **Paleolithic Age.** They are small bands composed of closely related individuals who established temporary camps as they roamed the land, subsisting on naturally occurring edibles that they could easily gather and hunting for larger game, and they used simple tools and implements. Their only possessions consisted of what they could carry with them from place to place. Generally, the women, children and the elderly remained in their temporary camps, tending to camp chores and foraging for edible plants, insects, eggs, small mammals and birds. The men and older adolescent males organized into hunting parties that cooperatively stalked or trapped larger game. There is evidence dogs were tamed for use in hunting. Typically, freshly killed game was consumed immediately with the remainder preserved by smoking and drying so it could be carried easily. Some hunting and gathering societies fished if they were close to the sea or a large body of water. When competing bands encountered each other, hostility resulted, unless there are kinship ties to inhibit it. This was due to competition for limited resources in a given area and one band's usual territory may not support another competing band.

The Neolithic Age marked several major changes in how people lived. Herd animals such as goats and sheep were domesticated, as were pigs, which meant that it was no longer necessary to hunt animals for meat and hides. Just as significant was the domestication of cereal crops; wheat and barley in Mesopotamia and rice in Asia. Also, pottery makes its appearance during this period. With food now available from a single location, people no longer had to move around to hunt game and forage for their sustenance, and started to live in permanent settlements. There was also a more clearly delineated division of labor, with people specializing in occupations that were not necessarily directly tied to the acquisition of food. Rudimentary metallurgy, in the form of copper smelting was beginning to lead the societies who had it, away from the Stone Age entirely.

Skill 29.2 Understand the development of city civilizations 3000–1500 BCE

Mesopotamia, part of the "Fertile Crescent", extended from the Persian Gulf at the estuary of the Tigris and Euphrates Rivers and following the rivers in a northwesterly direction, is considered the "Cradle of Western Civilization." The Sumerians had established walled city-states, notably at Lagash, Uruk, and Ur. The Sumerians developed a writing system which used ideographs and phonetic symbols called cuneiform. Much of what is known about Sumer comes from the tens of thousands of clay tablets that the Sumerian scribes left. Most of the information concerned commercial, economic and administrative activities, but there were also thousands uncovered that were purely literary texts, implying that Sumerians engaged in extensive trade and centralized urban planning. They also created an irrigation system of canal and dikes to take advantage of the water from the Tigris and Euphrates Rivers to cultivate large areas of arid desert and to control the unpredictable and devastating flooding of the rivers. In Sumerian cities, the lives of the inhabitants was highly diversified, the division of labor that first appeared in Neolithic settlements became even more specialized and in some cases, codified and imposed on the populace by the ruling and religious elite. The Sumerians were conquered by the Akkadian-speaking Babylonian invaders, under the leadership of Sargon the Great. The Babylonians, awed by the cultural sophistication of the Sumerians, retained Sumerian as the language of government and religion. Hammurabi, another notable Babylonian king, had his code of law set in stone pillars and erected throughout the territory of the empire. The Babylonians were in turn conquered by the Assyrians, who also adopted Sumerian language and culture for the court and religious ritual.

The Nile River gave rise to Egypt, another ancient valley civilization. The annual summer floods of the Nile supported a rich agricultural society that enjoyed surpluses that could be stored for leaner times. Two rival kingdoms emerged on the banks of the Nile. Lower Egypt was the Nile Delta in the north where it joins the Mediterranean Sea, and Upper Egypt occupied the land south of the delta, along the banks of the Nile River approximately 800 miles to the First Cataract. Although both kingdoms were sporadically united into one during the Old Kingdom (3000-2200 BCE) period, they represented two distinct cultural and political entities during that time. The Egyptians were well known for their monumental stone structures, statuary and for a highly centralized bureaucracy. The kings were considered gods and worshipped by their subjects. After over a century of intervening disorder, the Middle Kingdom (2100-1800 BCE) period saw a united kingdom, which established its capital at Thebes in the south and later moved north to Memphis for better central control. The Middle Kingdom period ended in 1800 BCE with the invasion of the Hyksos, who introduced the chariot and bow to Egypt. Eventually, the Egyptians drove out the conquerors in 1550 BCE and the New Kingdom period was ushered in.

In the **Indian subcontinent**, the Indus River Valley was first settled by a Dravidian civilization which built elaborate cities at Mohenjo Daro and Harappa (modern place names) that were centrally planned, with streets and structures arranged in uniform grids, sophisticated water and sewage systems and numerous public buildings and facilities. Archaeological evidence shows that the Indus River cities met a sudden and violent end. Most human skeletal remains that have been found show evidence of sword cuts and severe trauma. The invaders, known as Aryans, swept into the Indian subcontinent from the northwest via what is modern-day Iran and Afghanistan, from the Central Asian steppes.

China is considered by some historians to be the oldest, uninterrupted civilization in the world and was in existence around the same time as the ancient civilizations founded in **Egypt**, **Mesopotamia**, and the **Indus Valley**. Early Chinese civilization originally developed in the Huang He (Yellow River) Valley, and is shrouded in mystery, since accounts of the first era of Sage-Emperors (Di) indicate unnaturally long reigns (in excess of 500 years for one emperor). They are credited with the invention of writing, irrigation, flood control, pottery, spinning and weaving silk, jade working, divination by scapulomancy (reading portents from patterns produced by heating livestock shoulder bones and turtle plastrons), and domestication of pigs, dogs, oxen, sheep, fowl and goats. The Chinese studied nature, astronomy and weather; stressed the importance of family, and a strong monarch who also acted on behalf of populace as a medium to the sky spirit, worshipped spirits that controlled natural and man-made phenomena, including ancestor worship. The Xia Dynasty followed, but its existence has not been proven with physical evidence, it only exists in legends and in the Confucian classics "Classic of Records (History)" and some of the poems contained in the "Classic of Odes (Songs)" are said to date from the Xia Dynasty. It is considered the first Chinese dynasty because it established the pattern of rule being passed from father to eldest son. The Xia Dynasty was overthrown by the next dynasty, the Shang Dynasty, which was also considered legendary and existed only in literature, until archeological evidence was unearthed in the early 20th Century, where the ancient records said it would be. This set the precedent that dynasties rule because they earned that right by the Mandate of Heaven, and had proven that the ruling family was worthy. The notable features of Shang culture are a fully developed writing system (Shang Dynasty writing can still be read by modern readers of Chinese), highly sophisticated and intricate bronze casting and engraving, polished jade pieces of a luster indicating use of micro-abrasives, unmatched until the late 20th Century and a formal system of social hierarchy.

The civilization in **Japan** appeared during this time, having borrowed much of their culture from China and Korea. It was the last of these classical civilizations to develop. The native religion was a form of nature worship, called Shintoism, which worshipped Ame (translation: "The sky above") as its principal deity. The Japanese foundation mythology recounts that the first emperor was a child of the sun goddess and that all Japanese emperors descended from him.

Japan's imperial family has the longest line of continuous rule by the same family of any monarchy still in existence today.

The civilizations in **Africa** south of the Sahara were developing the refining and use of iron, especially for farm implements and later for weapons. Trading was overland using camels and at important seaports. The Arab influence was extremely important, as was their later contact with Indians, Christian Nubians, and Persians. In fact, their trading activities were probably the most important factor in the spread of and assimilation of different ideas and stimulation of cultural growth.

Skill 29.3 Demonstrate knowledge of ancient empires and civilizations 1700 BCE–500 CE

Egypt made numerous significant contributions including construction of the great pyramids; development of hieroglyphic writing; preservation of bodies after death; making paper from papyrus; contributing to developments in arithmetic and geometry; the invention of the method of counting in groups of 1-10 (the decimal system); completion of a solar calendar; and laying the foundation for science and astronomy.

The earliest historical record of **Kush** is in Egyptian sources. They describe a region upstream from the first cataract of the Nile as "wretched." This civilization was characterized by a settled way of life in fortified mud-brick villages. They subsisted on hunting and fishing, herding cattle, and gathering grain. Skeletal remains suggest that the people were a blend of Negroid and Mediterranean peoples. This civilization appears to be the second oldest in Africa (after Egypt).

Either the people were Egyptian or they were heavily influenced by Egyptians at a very early period in the development of the society. They appear to have spoken Nilo-Saharan languages. The area in which they lived is called Nubia. The capital city was Kerma, a major trading center between the northern and southern parts of Africa.

During the period of Egypt's Old Kingdom (ca. 2700-2180 BCE), this civilization was essentially a diffused version of Egyptian culture and religion. When Egypt came under the domination of the Hyksos, Kush reached its greatest power and cultural energy (1700-1500 BCE). When the Hyksos were eventually expelled from Egypt, the New Kingdom brought Kush back under Egyptian colonial control.

The collapse of the New Kingdom in Egypt (ca. 1000 BCE) provided the second opportunity for Kush to develop independently of Egyptian control and to conquer the entire Nubian region. The capital was then moved to Napata.

For the most part, the Kushites apparently considered themselves Egyptian and inheritors of the pharaonic tradition. Their society was organized on the Egyptian model, adopting Egyptian royal titles, etc. Even their art and architecture was based on Egyptian models. But their pyramids were smaller and steeper.

In what has been called "a magnificent irony of history," the Kushites conquered Egypt in the 8th century, creating the 25th dynasty. The dynasty ended in the seventh century when the Assyrians defeated Egypt.

The Kushites were gradually pushed farther south by the Assyrians and later by the Persians. This essentially cut off contact with Egypt, the Middle East and Europe. They moved their capital to Meroe in about 591 BC, when Napata was conquered. Their attention then turned to sub-Saharan Africa. Free of Egyptian dominance, they developed innovations in government and other areas.

In government, the king ruled through a law of custom that was interpreted by priests. The king was elected from the royal family. Descent was determined through the mother's line (as in Egypt). But in *an unparalleled innovation*, the Kushites were ruled by a series of female monarchs.

The Kushite religion was polytheistic, including all of the primary Egyptian gods. There were, however, regional gods that were the principal gods in their regions. Derived from other African cultures, there was also a lion warrior god.

This civilization was vital through the last half of the first millennium BC, but it suffered about 300 years of gradual decline until the Nuba people eventually conquered it.

The ancient civilization of the **Sumerians** invented the wheel; developed irrigation through use of canals, dikes, and devices for raising water; devised the system of cuneiform writing; learned to divide time; and built large boats for trade. The Babylonians devised the famous **Code of Hammurabi**, a code of laws.

The ancient **Assyrians** were warlike and aggressive empire-builders, who possessed a highly organized and disciplined army that featured specialized units of horse drawn chariots, cavalry, elaborate siege engines and other specialized troops to augment well-armed foot soldiers who attacked in massed formations.

The **Hebrews**, also known as the ancient Israelites, instituted "monotheism," which is the worship of one God, Yahweh, and combined the 66 books of the Hebrew and Christian Greek scriptures into the Bible we have today.

The **Minoans** had a system of writing using symbols to represent syllables in words.

They built palaces with multiple levels containing many rooms, water and sewage systems with flush toilets, bathtubs, hot and cold running water, and bright paintings on the walls.

The **Mycenaeans** changed the Minoan writing system to aid their own language and used symbols to represent syllables.

The **Phoenicians** were sea traders well known for their manufacturing skills in glass and metals and the development of their famous purple dye. They became so very proficient in the skill of navigation that they were able to sail by the stars at night. Further, they devised an alphabet using symbols to represent single sounds, which was an improved extension of the Egyptian principle and writing system.

In **India**, the Aryan invaders from the northwest introduced the caste system, which restricted what a person could or could not do as a profession. The principle of zero in mathematics was invented. **Vedic Hinduism,** as practiced by the Aryans, evolved into its now recognizable form, as Dravidian states, south of the Indus River, were conquered and local deities and heroes (such as Krishna, Naga and Hanuman) were incorporated into the Hindu belief system of multiple aspects of a single godhead. Industry and commerce developed along with extensive trading with the Near East. Outstanding advances in the fields of science and medicine were made along with being one of the first to be active in navigation and maritime enterprises during this time.

Buddhism is an offshoot of Brahmanical Hindu thought, which arose during the 5th Century BCE. However, unlike traditional Hinduism, Buddhism was founded by Gautama Siddartha Shakyamuni, a crown prince who renounced the material world after observing suffering in the form of illness, old age and death, much to the dismay of his father, the maharajah, and to seek enlightenment. After years of asceticism and austerities, the prince achieved enlightenment after meditating under a tree for 49 days. He was called the "Buddha" (a Sanskrit word meaning "Awakened One") after his enlightenment and told his followers that life was suffering, suffering was caused by desire, desire was caused by delusion of the mind, which leads to death and rebirth which lead to another cycle of suffering. To avoid suffering, one must get rid of the delusions that cause desire and break the cycle of life, death and rebirth, called "samsara" a concept from Hindu theology. Other concepts adapted from Hindu theology are "karma," which is the balance of action versus later effect, which will trigger samsara and "dharma," which can mean "fate," "destiny," or "unbreakable rules that govern all phenomena," depending on its context. Escape from the cycles of samsara was called "nirvana," or "extinguishment." Buddhism later split off into two main schools: Theravada ("Older Way") or Southern Buddhism and Mahayana ("Great Vehicle").

Theravada Buddhism teaches that individuals can gain enough merit over countless cycles of rebirth and eventually attain enlightenment. This branch of Buddhism is the original one as practiced shortly after the Buddha's death. It is the form that spread south to Sri Lanka and Southeast Asia.

Mahayana Buddhism is a later school that revises the Theravada and teaches that certain individuals, who had achieved enlightenment, but rather than passing into Nirvana, declined and stayed behind to assist other, less enlightened individuals attain enlightenment and all beings pass completely into Nirvana. This is the form that spread to Tibet and eastward to China, Korea and Japan.
China began building the Great Wall; practiced irrigation, flood control, crop rotation and terrace farming; increased the importance of the silk industry, and developed caravan routes across Central Asia for extensive trade. After the fall of the Zhou Dynasty and during the ensuing Warring States period, Confucius edited the Confucian Classics and a collection of his teachings, The Analects was compiled. Daoism emerged as the teachings of Lao Zi were being written down and espoused by Daoist scholars. Also, they increased proficiency in rice cultivation.

During the waning years of the Shang Dynasty, the "Yi Jing" (Classic of Change), the divination manual was first compiled, based on 64 hexagrams, which is still consulted today. Continuing the dynastic cycle, the Shang Dynasty was overthrown by the Zhou Dynasty which in turn earned the Mandate of Heaven to rule. The early Zhou Dynasty was later considered by Confucius, several centuries later, to be the "Golden Age" of rule by enlightened men of ability and moral rectitude. During 5th Century BCE the disintegration of the Zhou Dynasty, and its eventual fall, China split up into several independent kingdoms which were in near constant state of war with each kingdom vying for supremacy over the others in a myriad combination of alliances, which often changed. It was in this period, known as the Warring States period, one of chaos and disarray, that two of the best known figures of the period, Confucius (Kong Zi) and Lao Zi appeared (there are questions regarding whether or not Lao Zi was a real person).

Eventually, after nearly 200 years of fighting, the Qin Dynasty, under Qin Shi Huang Di ("Exalted First Emperor") gained the advantage and conquered the other kingdoms to unite China into a single empire. The Qin emperor commissioned his ministers to standardize weights and measures, and reduced the number of Chinese characters to 3,000 from tens of thousands by eliminating redundant and superfluous characters. The Qin dynasty was known for its harsh authoritarian rule, with an emphasis on severe punishment for even minor infractions. Within twenty years, there was a successful revolt that overthrew the Qin in 206 BCE and replaced it with the Han Dynasty.

The **Han Dynasty** lasted four centuries, longer than any other dynasty in China's history.

Paper and the writing brush, in its present form, were invented during this period and Chinese characters took the form that is familiar to today's readers. The Han, under Emperor Wu Di ("Martial Emperor", reigned 141-87 BCE), expanded China's boundaries to their greatest extent through military conquest, up to that time, including embarking on a campaign to rid the northern borders of the Huns. This set off a chain of events and westward migrations of Huns and other nomadic pastoralists into Europe. In the aftermath of the fall of Qin,

Confucianism became the official political philosophy of the Han. Scholarship and the criterion for appointment to the imperial bureaucracy were based on the Five Classics: Odes, History, Rites (Etiquette), Change (Yi Jing), and the Spring and Autumn Annals (a history of a portion of the Zhou Dynasty edited by Confucius).

Additionally, scholars were expected to have a thorough knowledge of the Analects of Confucius (a collection of his teachings) and Mencius (Meng Zi was a Confucian scholar who expanded on the themes espoused by Confucius and his most esteemed students). The accomplishments of the Han Dynasty were so unprecedented and profound, that later Chinese refer to themselves as "People of the Han" and Chinese characters have been called "Han Words" (literal translation of the two characters that make up the word for "Chinese characters") ever since.

Daoism was one of many schools of thought that sprang up in ancient China, and like **Confucianism**, endured to modern times. Its main tenet is that all phenomena are governed by natural forces that cannot be comprehended by ordinary people's minds and that resisting it or trying to make it act in a contrary manner only leads to frustration and just makes things worse than they already are. The two major literary works that influenced Daoism the most were "Dao De Jing" ("Discourse on the Way and Virtue") and Zhuang Zi's eponymous work "The Zhuang Zi" (most Classical Chinese books were named after their primary contributors or the first words in the body of the text). In order to understand how these cosmic forces work, Lao Zi and Zhuang Zi said that one should not seek anything since the only way to truly know something, one must not think about it and let the Way of nature run its course without interference by not doing anything contrary to the Way.

The ancient **Persians** developed an alphabet; contributed the religions/philosophies of **Zoroastrianism**, **Mithraism**, and **Gnosticism**; and allowed conquered peoples to retain their own customs, laws, and religions.

The classical civilization of **Greece** reached the highest levels in man's achievements based on the foundations already laid by such ancient groups as the Egyptians, Phoenicians, Minoans, and Mycenaeans.

Among the more important contributions of Greece were the Greek alphabet derived from the Phoenician letters which formed the basis for the Roman alphabet and our present-day alphabet. Extensive trading and colonization resulted in the spread of the Greek civilization. The love of sports, with emphasis on a sound body, led to the tradition of the Olympic games. Greece was responsible for the rise of independent, strong city-states. Note the complete contrast between independent, freedom-loving Athens with its practice of pure democracy i.e. direct, personal, active participation in government by qualified citizens and the rigid, totalitarian, militaristic Sparta. Other important areas that the Greeks are credited with influencing include drama, epic and lyric poetry, fables, myths centered on the many gods and goddesses, science, astronomy, medicine, mathematics, philosophy, art, architecture, and recording historical events. The conquests of Alexander the Great spread Greek ideas to the areas he conquered and brought to the Greek world many ideas from Asia. Above all, the value of ideas, wisdom, curiosity, and the desire to learn as much about the world as possible was his objective.

The ancient civilization of **Rome** lasted approximately 1,000 years including the periods of republic and empire, although its lasting influence on Europe and its history was for a much longer period. There was a very sharp contrast between the curious, imaginative, inquisitive Greeks and the practical, simple, down-to-earth, no-nonsense Romans, who spread and preserved the ideas of ancient Greece and other culture groups. The contributions and accomplishments of the Romans are numerous, but their greatest included language, engineering, building, law, government, roads, trade, and the "**Pax Romana,**" the long period of peace enabling free travel and trade and spreading people, cultures, goods, and ideas all over a vast area of the known world.

A most interesting and significant characteristic of the Greek, Hellenic, and Roman civilizations was "secularism," where emphasis shifted away from religion to the state. Men were not absorbed in or dominated by religion as had been the case in Egypt and the nations located in Mesopotamia. Religion and its leaders did not dominate the state and its authority was greatly diminished.

Skill 29.4 Understand the decline of classical civilizations and changes 500–1400 CE

The end of the Western **Roman Empire** came when Germanic tribes migrated to, and controlled most of central and Western Europe. The five major tribes were the Visigoths, Ostrogoths, Vandals, Saxons, and Franks. In later years, the Franks successfully stopped the invasion of southern Europe by Muslims by defeating them under the leadership of Charles Martel at the Battle of Tours in 732 AD. Thirty-six years later in 768 AD, the grandson of Charles Martel became King of the Franks and is known throughout history as Charlemagne. Charlemagne was a man of war but was unique in his respect for and encouragement of learning. He made great efforts to rule fairly and ensure just treatment for his people.

The **Vikings** were Scandinavian Norse seafarers who quickly gained a reputation for ruthlessness and surprise as they raided any settlement or monastery that they could reach on their swift and seaworthy long boats The Vikings had a lot of influence at this time with spreading their ideas and knowledge of trade routes and sailing, accomplished first through their conquests and later through trade. There were two main groups of Vikings, the West Vikings, from Norway and Denmark and the East Vikings, from Sweden. The West Vikings raided and traded with coastal areas of Britain and Ireland, Europe's Atlantic coast and as far as Sicily in the Mediterranean Sea, setting up trading outposts, permanent settlements and in some cases setting themselves up as rulers. They also ventured beyond the North Sea to settle in Iceland, Greenland and North America, although Iceland was the only North Atlantic settlement that was a lasting permanent success. The East Vikings voyaged east and south, through the Baltic nations and via the rivers of eastern Europe to Kiev in what is now Ukraine where they ruled as royalty and were called the "Rus." They further voyaged south to Constantinople, where they also served as mercenaries and functionaries to the Byzantine Roman Emperor.

The **Huns** were a horse-riding pastoral people who originated in Asia, north of the Great Wall of China, and had finally been displaced by the Chinese emperors after centuries of border skirmishes and all-out military campaigns to rid them from the lands bordering China. They were led as far west as the eastern edges of the Roman Empire, by Attila, their leader, attacking swiftly on horseback, spreading terror and havoc among their victims. After Attila suddenly and unexpectedly died after a night of celebrating his marriage to another wife, the Huns stopped their advance on Europe and either returned to Central Asia, or became assimilated into the local populations where they settled.

After the fall of the Han Dynasty, China was once again split into different kingdoms and entered a long period of war and chaos with ever-shifting alliances and counter-alliances, with a brief period of unity and at one point dividing into 17 separate kingdoms.

The Sui (pronounced "Sway") Dynasty, although lasting less than twenty years, heralded the beginning of a long period of national and cultural unity starting in 589 CE, giving way to the Tang Dynasty in 618 CE.

The **Tang Dynasty** consolidated imperial authority and is considered by many historians to be the renaissance and flowering of Chinese culture, helped by the fact that long-term stability had returned to China. The population grew to its historic high during this period and the arts, particularly poetry, found its most creative and aesthetically pleasing levels. The Sui and Tang introduced wide-scale government examinations for recruiting new talent into the imperial bureaucracy from the highest court ministers, all the way to local county and township officials. Also, Buddhism, which was introduced earlier, became the official state religion under the Tang and the emperors endowed monasteries and temples lavishly. Printing was invented during the Ninth Century (several centuries before Gutenberg), spurred by the need to produce and distribute Buddhist literature on a wide scale.

The **Song Dynasty** was a transitional period, which went from late classic China, to early modern China. Buddhism was rejected and a return to Confucianism emerged, and is usually called Neo-Confucianism. Also, aristocratic society, which held sway until the Tang Dynasty, virtually disappeared as a political force, ceding that authority to the landowning class and the blossoming meritocracy that came up through the government examination system, which emphasized Confucian learning. Although mercantile activities were traditionally shunned by the traditional elite of China, there was a commercial revolution and a great expansion of the economy which coincided with an unprecedented rise in population and a similar growth in agricultural production. The Chinese were using the magnetic compass by the Twelfth Century and they made great advances in shipbuilding, which allowed them to trade with people as far away as India and the Persian Gulf. The invention of gunpowder was also a significant development in military technology, although the use of gunpowder for use in pyrotechnic displays also became a more important use as a form of celebration and entertainment. One drawback to the Song Dynasty's developments in commercial and artistic pursuits was the weakening of military power and greater vulnerability along the northern frontier.

The **Mongols** were but one of many "barbarian" pastoral peoples who rode horses, used Bactrian camels for transport of cargo, and herded flocks of sheep and goats. They were a collection of loosely affiliated tribes and clans that competed with each other for pasturage, horses and livestock. They were united by Chinggis (also spelled "Genghis") Khan in the 13th Century CE. As the Mongols under Chinggis conquered other neighboring territories, they gained a reputation as formidable horsemen as their cavalry attacked in swift, disciplined formations that took advantage of maneuver, surprise and skillful and deadly use of archery while riding, overwhelming their foes.

The Mongol Empire was highly adaptable at incorporating absorbed people's expertise, including Chinggis' leading commander, Subotai, who was Tuvan, a distinct Central Asian ethnic group with its own language. Eventually, during Chinggis' lifetime, the empire encompassed nearly all of the north-central Asia and the northwest of China. After his death, his son Ogatei assumed the title "Great Khan." followed by Mongke, one of Chinngis' grandsons.

To the west and south, under the rule of Chinggis' grandsons, the Mongols conquered what is now Russia, South Asia and Southwest Asia, which includes what is now Iraq, Turkey, Iran and Afghanistan, where they acquired a ferocious reputation for wanton destruction and aggression. The most well known of Chinngis' grandsons was Khubilai, who founded the Yuan Dynasty in China and assumed the title of Emperor, whom Marco Polo wrote about when he was a guest of the Mongol court. Khubilai adopted Chinese dress and customs, left government bureaucracy and institutions fairly intact, expanded the empire into Korea, made incursions into what is now Vietnam, and was thwarted in his attempt to invade Japan only by a typhoon (called the "Kamikaze" in Japanese or "Divine Wind"), which demolished the Mongol fleet. After the passing of Chinggis' grandsons, the Mongol Empire quickly lost control over its far-flung domain and was forced to cede political and military power. The Yuan Dynasty in China fell in 1368 CE, succeeded by an ethnically Han-Chinese dynasty.

The **Ming Dynasty** lasted from 1368 to 1644 CE and marked one of the longest eras of order and stability in government and society in world history. It was also a period of great artistic and creative achievements. However, the stability of Chinese government and society was such that it stayed relatively unaltered until the early 20th Century CE, when Imperial China ended with the 1911 Chinese Revolution. As with the Dynastic Cycle, which started with the end of the legendary Xia Dynasty, the Ming came to power as the result of a rebellion that overthrew the Mongols and expelled them from China proper. The Ming revived the purely Chinese mode of rule over China that existed during the Tang and Song Dynasties, with Confucianism and its Classics being put squarely into the forefront as the basis of all knowledge that was important for an enlightened official to possess. Ming scholarship in Confucian studies flourished and produced a myriad of texts on all subjects from commentaries on materialist philosophy to scientific texts to creative prose and poetic literature. Although Chinese elites, including the Ming, were traditionally anti-commercial in their worldview, the Chinese economy and commercial infrastructure expanded dynamically during the Ming Dynasty, including the migration of Chinese merchants to overseas markets. The Ming Dynasty, like all previous ones, in the end, eventually suffered from internal decay and official corruption which led to rebellion, weakening central authority and making it susceptible to external takeover.

The purpose of the **Crusades** was to rid Jerusalem of Muslim control, and this series of violent, bloody conflicts did affect trade and stimulated later explorations seeking the new, exotic products such as silks and spices.

The Crusaders came into contact with other religions and cultures and learned and spread many new ideas.

During this time, the system of **feudalism** became the dominant feature of domestic life. It was a system of loyalty and protection. The strong protected the weak, which returned the service with farm labor, military service, and loyalty. Life was lived out on a vast estate, owned by a nobleman and his family, called a "manor." It was a complete village supporting a few hundred people, mostly peasants. Improved tools and farming methods made life more bearable although most never left the manor or traveled from their village during their lifetime.

Also coming into importance at this time was the era of knighthood and its code of chivalry as well as the tremendous influence of the Church (Roman Catholic). Until the period of the Renaissance, the Church was the only place where people could be educated. The Bible and other books were hand-copied by monks in the monasteries. Cathedrals were built and were decorated with art depicting religious subjects.

With the increase in trade and travel, cities sprang up and began to grow. Craft workers in the cities developed their skills to a high degree, eventually organizing guilds to protect the quality of the work and to regulate the buying and selling of their products. City government developed and flourished centered on strong town councils. Active in city government and the town councils were the wealthy businessmen who made up the rising middle class.

The end of the feudal manorial system was sealed by the outbreak and spread of the infamous **Black Death**, which killed over one-third of the total population of Europe. Those who survived and were skilled in any job or occupation were in demand and many serfs or peasants found freedom and, for that time, a decidedly improved standard of living. Strong nation-states became powerful and people developed a renewed interest in life and learning.

The **Byzantines** (Christians) made important contributions in art and the preservation of Greek and Roman achievements including architecture (especially in eastern Europe and Russia), the Code of Justinian and Roman law. Bordering the east of Europe was the **Byzantine Empire**, which was the Eastern Roman Empire, after it was split into two by Emperor Diocletian. Diocletian's successor, Emperor Constantine, renamed the capital Byzantium to Constantinople, after himself. With the fall of Western Rome in 476 CE, the Byzantine emperors, starting with Justinian, attempted to regain the lost western territories. Because of ineffective rulers between the Seventh and Ninth Centuries CE, any gains were completely lost, reverting the territorial limits to the eastern Balkans of Ancient Greece and Asia Minor. The late Ninth through Eleventh Centuries were considered the Golden Age of Byzantium.

Although Constantine had earlier made Christianity the official state religion of Rome, it left an unresolved conflict between Christian and Classical (Greek and Roman) ideals for the Byzantines. There were points of contention between the Pope in Rome and the Patriarch of Constantinople including celibacy of priests, language of the Liturgy (Latin in the west, Greek in the east), religious doctrine, and other unreconciled issues that led to the Great Schism, which permanently split the church into the Roman Catholic and the Eastern Orthodox Churches.

In secular matters, Emperor Justinian codified Roman law, summarizing a millennia of Roman legal developments into the Justinian Code, which laid the basis for modern western legal systems, still studied and used in European and American legal circles. The Byzantines combined the styles of Greco-Roman and Asia Minor to create monumental domed structures such as the Hagia Sophia church (later converted into a Muslim mosque), elaborate mosaics and a distinctive style of painting, richly embellished icons depicting religious figures. **Islamic** (or Saracenic) civilization, grew out of religious fervor shortly after the founding of Islam (Arabic for "Surrender to God") by Muhammad in the Seventh Century CE. Islam is a monotheistic faith that traces its traditions to the Hebrew Patriarch Abraham and considers the Jewish patriarchs and prophets (especially Moses and King Solomon) and Jesus Christ as earlier "Prophets of God" (the Arabic word "Allah" and its root "'Lh" means "The Almighty" or "God" and is not a name, like "Zeus") and venerates them accordingly. Muhammad preached jihad ("holy war") in two forms; Lesser Jihad was the call to arms to spread Islam by military force and Greater Jihad, the more important of the two, was the battle that an individual undertakes for the salvation of the soul and surrender to the will of God. The Quran was dictated to Muhammad as the Word of God, composed in verse in sections called "sura," each which begin with the invocation, "In the Name of God, the Compassionate, the Merciful."

The Islamic armies spread their faith by conquering the Arabian Peninsula, conquering Mesopotamia, Egypt, Syria and Persia by 650 CE and expanding to North Africa and most of the Iberian Peninsula by 750 CE. During this period of expansion, the Muslim conquerors established great centers of learning, universities, at Baghdad in Mesopotamia, Damascus in Syria, Alexandria in Egypt and Cordoba in Spain. They preserved Classical knowledge of the Greeks and Romans, while Europe was in the depths of the Dark Ages after the fall of the Western Roman Empire. Muslim scholars are credited with great progress in the areas of science and philosophy and were responsible for accomplishments in astronomy, mathematics, physics, chemistry, medicine, literature, art, trade and manufacturing, agriculture, and a marked influence on later European scholarship and intellectual development.

The civilizations in **Africa** south of the Sahara were developing the refining and use of iron, especially for farm implements and later for weapons. Trading was overland using camels and at important seaports. The Arab influence was extremely important, as was their later contact with Indians, Christian Nubians, and Persians. In fact, their trading activities were probably the most important factor in the spread of and assimilation of different ideas and stimulation of cultural growth.

The people who lived in the Americas before Columbus arrived had a thriving, connected society. The civilizations in North America tended to spread out more and were in occasional conflict but maintained their sovereignty, for the most part. The South American civilizations, however, tended to migrate into empires, with the strongest city or tribe assuming control of the lives and resources of the rest of the nearby peoples.

Native Americans in North America had a spiritual and personal relationship with the various Spirits of Nature and a keen appreciation of the ways of woodworking and metalworking. Various tribes dotted the landscape of what is now the U.S. They struggled against one another for control of resources such as food and water but had no concept of ownership of land, since they believed that they were living on the land with the permission of the Spirits. The North Americans mastered the art of growing many crops and, to their credit, were willing to share that knowledge with the various Europeans who eventually showed up. Artwork made of hides, beads, and jewels was popular at this time.

The most well known empires of South America were the **Aztec, Inca, and Maya**. Each of these empires had a central capital where the emperor lived who controlled all aspects of the lives of his subjects. The empires traded with other peoples; and if the relations soured, the results were usually absorption of the trading partners into the empire. These empires, especially the Aztecs, had access to large numbers of metals and jewels, and they created weapons and artwork that continue to impress historians today. The Inca Empire stretched across a vast period of territory down the western coast of South America and was connected by a series of roads. A series of messengers ran along these roads, carrying news and instructions from the capital, Cusco. The Incas, however, did not have the wheel. The Mayas are most well known for their famous pyramids and calendars, as well as their language, which still stumps archaeologists.

COMPETENCY 30.0 WORLD HISTORY: 1400 TO 1914

Skill 30.1 Understand emerging global-wide interactions 1400–1800 CE

At the beginning of this period, most of the economies were based on subsistence agriculture. The farmers produced enough to feed themselves with a little extra to sell to the cities. The slave-based economies eventually gave way to tenant farms in the institution of **feudalism**. Even under feudalism, the tenant farmer was trying to attain greater freedom and rights. The serfs were heavily taxed under feudalism. Many of the owners and lords absented themselves from rural areas and stayed in the cities. This was the later period of feudal society as the medieval society has all but collapsed. These were the last days of the Holy Roman Empire, and the Hapsburg Empire was strong in Europe. The Byzantine Empire was also coming to an end in the 1400s. Russia at this time was ruled by the Golden Horde. In South American the Inca and Aztec Empires were centralized states, with all income going to the state coffers and all trade going through the emperor as well.

The centralized states basically came into being as a result of the feudal lords and the Church. As a result of so much fighting, the stronger of the surviving lords took on the functions of kings and other members of royalty, many due to the support of the Church. Loyalty shifts from the feudal lord to the ruler. As the cities grew, so did commerce as market economies became more developed and trade became more important. The growth of trade resulted in greater reliance on markets. The Renaissance is now taking place in Europe.

The word "Renaissance" literally means "rebirth," and signaled the rekindling of interest in the glory of ancient classical Greek and Roman civilizations. It was the period in human history marking the start of many ideas and innovations leading to our modern age. The Renaissance began in Italy with many of its ideas starting in Florence, controlled by the infamous Medici family. Education, especially for some of the merchants, required reading, writing, math, the study of law, and the writings of classical Greek and Roman writers.

Between the 4th and 9th Centuries, Asia was a story of religions and empires, of kings and wars and of increasing and decreasing contact with the West.

India began this period recovering from the invasion of Alexander the Great. One strong man who met the great Alexander was **Chandragupta Maurya**, who began one of his country's most successful dynasties. Chandragupta conquered most of what we now call India. His grandson, **Asoka**, was more of a peaceful ruler but powerful nonetheless. He was also a great believer in the practices and power of Buddhism, sending missionaries throughout Asia to preach the ways of the Buddha. Succeeding the Mauryas were the Guptas, who ruled India for a longer period of time and brought prosperity and international recognition to their people.

The Guptas were great believers in science and mathematics, especially their uses in production of goods. They invented the decimal system and had a concept of zero, two things that put them ahead of the rest of the world on the mathematics timeline. They were the first to make cotton and calico, and their medical practices were much more advanced than those in Europe and elsewhere in Asia at the time. These inventions and innovations made Indian goods in high demand throughout Asia and Europe.

The idea of a united India continued after the Gupta Dynasty ended. It was especially favorable to the invading Muslims, who took over in the 11th Century, ruling the country for hundreds of years through a series of sultanates. The most famous Muslim leader of India was Tamerlane, who founded the Mogul Dynasty and began a series of conquests that expanded the borders of India. Tamerlane's grandson **Akbar** is considered the greatest Mogul. He believed in freedom of religion and is perhaps most well-known for the series of buildings that he had built, including mosques, palaces, forts and tombs, some of which are still standing today. During the years that Muslims ruled India, Hinduism continued to be respected, although it was a minority religion; Buddhism, however, died out almost entirely from the country that begot its founder.

The imposing mountains to the north of India served as a deterrent to Chinese expansion. India was more vulnerable to invaders who came from the west or by sea from the south. The Indian people were also vulnerable to the powerful monsoons, which came driving up from the south a few times every year, bringing howling winds and devastation in their wake.

The story of **China** during this time is one of dynasties controlling various parts of what are now China and Tibet. The **Tang Dynasty** was one of the most long lasting and the most proficient, inventing the idea of civil service and the practice of block printing. Next up was the Sung Dynasty, which produced some of the world's greatest paintings and porcelain pottery but failed to unify China in a meaningful way. This would prove instrumental in the takeover of China by the Mongols, led by Genghis Khan and his most famous grandson, Kublai. (See Skill 2.1d)

Genghis Khan was known as a conqueror, and Kublai was known as a uniter. They both extended the borders of their empire, however; and at its height, the Mongol Empire was the largest the world has ever seen, encompassing all of China, Russia, Persia, and central Asia. Following the Mongols were the Ming and Manchu Dynasties, both of which focused on isolation. As a result, China at the end of the 18th Century knew very little of the outside world, and vice versa. Ming artists created beautiful porcelain pottery, but not much of it saw its way into the outside world until much later. The Manchus were known for their focus on farming and road building, two practices that were instituted in greater numbers in order to try to keep up with expanding population.

Confucianism, Taoism, and ancestor worship—the staples of Chinese society for hundreds of years—continued to flourish during all this time.

The other major power in Asia was **Japan**, which developed independently and tried to keep itself that way for hundreds of years. Early Japanese society focused on the emperor and the farm, in that order. Japan was early and often influenced by China, from which it borrowed many things, including religion (Buddhism), a system of writing, calendar, and even fashion. The Sea of Japan protected Japan from more than Chinese invasion, including the famous Mongol one that was blown back by the "divine wind." The power of the emperor declined as it was usurped by the era of the Daimyo and his loyal soldiers, the **Samurai**. Japan flourished economically and culturally during many of these years, although the policy of isolation the country developed kept the rest of the world from knowing such things. Buddhism and local religions were joined by Christianity in the 16th Century, but it wasn't until the mid-19th Century that Japan rejoined the world community.

African civilizations during these centuries were few and far between. By this time, Moslem armies had conquered most of northern coastal Africa. The preponderance of deserts and other inhospitable lands restricted African settlements to a few select areas. The city of Zimbabwe became a trading center in south central Africa in the 5th Century but didn't last long. More successful was Ghana, a Muslim-influenced kingdom that arose in the 9th Century and lasted for nearly 300 years. Ghanaians had large farming areas and also raised cattle and elephants. They traded with people from Europe and the Middle East. Eventually overrunning Ghana was Mali, whose trade center Timbuktu survived its own empire's demise and blossomed into one of the world's caravan destinations.

Iron, tin, and leather came out of Mali with a vengeance. The succeeding civilization of the Songhai had relative success in maintaining the success of their predecessors. Religion in all of these places was definitely Muslim; and even after extended contact with other cultures, technological advancements were few and far between.

The word "Renaissance" literally means "rebirth," and signaled the rekindling of interest in the glory of ancient classical Greek and Roman civilizations. It was the period in human history marking the start of many ideas and innovations leading to our modern age. The **Renaissance** began in Italy with many of its ideas starting in Florence, controlled by the famous Medici family. Education, especially for some of the merchants, required reading, writing, math, the study of law, and the writings of classical Greek and Roman writers. A combination of a renewed fascination with the classical world and new infusion of money into the hands of those so fascinated brought on the Renaissance. In the areas of art, literature, music, and science, the world changed for the better.

Most famous are the Renaissance artists, first and foremost the more important artists were **Giotto** and his development of perspective in paintings; **Leonardo da Vinci** was not only an artist but also a scientist and inventor, Michelangelo, and Raphael but also Titian, Donatello, and Rembrandt. All of these men pioneered a new method of painting and sculpture—that of portraying real events and real people as they really looked, not as the artists imagined them to be. One need look no further than Michelangelo's *David* to illustrate this.

Literature was a focus as well during the Renaissance. Humanists Petrarch, Boccaccio, Erasmus, and Sir Thomas More advanced the idea of being interested in life here on earth and the opportunities it can bring, rather than constantly focusing on heaven and its rewards. The monumental works of Shakespeare, Dante, and Cervantes found their origins in these ideas as well as the ones that drove the painters and sculptors. All of these works, of course, owe much of their existence to the invention of the printing press, which occurred during the Renaissance. In the area of political philosophy the writings of **Machiavelli** were considered influential.

The Renaissance changed music as well. No longer just a religious experience, music could be fun and composed for its own sake, to be enjoyed in fuller and more humanistic ways than in the Middle Ages. Musicians worked for themselves, rather than for the churches, as before, and so could command good money for their work, increasing their prestige.

Science advanced considerably during the Renaissance, especially in the area of physics and astronomy. Copernicus, Kepler, and Galileo led a Scientific Revolution in proving that the earth was round and certainly not perfect, an earth-shattering revelation to those who clung to medieval ideals of a geocentric, church-centered existence. In **medicine** the work of Brussels-born **Andrea Vesalius** earned him the title of "father of anatomy" and had a profound influence on the Spaniard **Michael** Servetus and the Englishman **William Harvey.**

In Germany, Gutenberg's invention of the **printing press** with movable type facilitated the rapid spread of Renaissance ideas, writings and innovations, thus ensuring the enlightenment of most of Western Europe. Contributions were also made by Durer and Holbein in art and by Paracelsus in science and medicine.

The effects of the Renaissance in the Low Countries can be seen in the literature and philosophy of Erasmus and the art of van Eyck and Breughel the Elder. Rabelais and de Montaigne in France also contributed to literature and philosophy. In Spain, the art of El Greco and de Morales flourished, as did the writings of Cervantes and De Vega. In England, Sir Thomas More and Sir Francis Bacon wrote and taught philosophy and inspired by Vesalius. William Harvey made important contributions in medicine. The greatest talent was found in literature and drama and given to mankind by Chaucer, Spenser, Marlowe, Johnson, and the incomparable Shakespeare.

The **Reformation** period consisted of two phases: the **Protestant Revolution** and the **Catholic Reformation**. The Protestant Revolution came about because of religious, political, and economic reasons. The religious reasons stemmed from abuses in the Catholic Church including fraudulent clergy with their scandalous immoral lifestyles; the sale of religious offices, indulgences, and dispensations; different theologies within the Church; and frauds involving sacred relics.

The political reasons for the Protestant Revolution involved the increase in the power of rulers who were considered "absolute monarchs," who desired all power and control, especially over the Church. The growth of "nationalism" or patriotic pride in one's own country was another contributing factor.

Economic reasons included the greed of ruling monarchs to possess and control all lands and wealth of the Church, the deep animosity against the burdensome papal taxation, the rise of the affluent middle class and its clash with medieval Church ideals, and the increase of an active system of "intense" capitalism.

The **Protestant Revolution** began in Germany with the revolt of Martin Luther against Church abuses. It spread to Switzerland where Calvin led it. It began in England with the efforts of King Henry VIII to have his marriage to Catherine of Aragon annulled so he could wed another and have a male heir. The results were the increasing support given not only by the people but also by nobles and some rulers, and of course, the attempts of the Church to stop it.

The **Catholic Reformation** was undertaken by the Church to "clean up its act" and to slow or stop the Protestant Revolution. The Council of Trent and the Jesuits supplied the major efforts to this end. Six major results of the Reformation included:
• Religious freedom,
• Religious tolerance,
• More opportunities for education,
• Power and control of rulers limited,
• Increase in religious wars, and
• An increase in fanaticism and persecution.

The Scientific Revolution and the Enlightenment were two of the most important movements in the history of civilization, resulting in a new sense of self-examination and a wider view of the world than ever before. The Scientific Revolution was, above all, a shift in focus from **belief to evidence**. Scientists and philosophers wanted to see the proof, not just believe what other people told them. It was an exciting time, if you were a forward-looking thinker.

A Polish astronomer, **Nicolaus Copernicus**, began the Scientific Revolution.

He crystallized a lifetime of observations into a book that was published about the time of his death; in this book, Copernicus argued that the Sun, not the Earth, was the center of a solar system and that other planets revolved around the Sun, not the Earth. This flew in the face of established (read: Church-mandated) doctrine. The Church still wielded tremendous power at this time, including the power to banish people or sentence them to prison or even death.

The Danish astronomer **Tycho Brahe** was the first to catalog his observations of the night sky, of which he made thousands. Building on Brahe's data, German scientist Johannes Kepler instituted his theory of planetary movement, embodied in his famous Laws of Planetary Movement. Using Brahe's data, Kepler also confirmed Copernicus's observations and argument that the Earth revolved around the Sun.

The most famous defender of this idea was **Galileo Galilei**, an Italian scientist who conducted many famous experiments in the pursuit of science. He is most well known, however, for his defense of the heliocentric (sun-centered) idea. He wrote a book comparing the two theories, but most readers could tell easily that he favored the new one. He was convinced of this mainly because of what he had seen with his own eyes. He had used the relatively new invention of the telescope to see four moons of Jupiter. They certainly did not revolve around the Earth, so why should everything else? His ideas were not at all favored with the Church, which continued to assert its authority in this and many other matters. The Church was still powerful enough at this time, especially in Italy, to order Galileo to be placed under house arrest.

Galileo died under house arrest, but his ideas didn't die with him. Picking up the baton was an English scientist named **Isaac Newton**, who became perhaps the most famous scientist of all. He is known as the discoverer of gravity and a pioneering voice in the study of optics (light), calculus, and physics.

More than any other scientist, Newton argued for (and proved) the idea of a mechanistic view of the world: You can see how the world works and prove how the world works through observation; if you can see these things with your own eyes, they must be so. Up to this time, people believed what other people told them; this is how the Church was able to keep control of people's lives for so long. Newton, following in the footsteps of Copernicus and Galileo, changed all that.

This naturally led to the **Enlightenment**, a period of intense self-study that focused on ethics and logic. More so than at any time before, scientists and philosophers questioned cherished truths, widely held beliefs, and their own sanity in an attempt to discover why the world worked—from within. "I think, therefore I am" was one of the famous sayings of that or any day.

It was uttered by Rene Descartes, a French scientist-philosopher whose dedication to logic and the rigid rules of observation were a blueprint for the thinkers who came after him.

One of the giants of the era was England's **David Hume**. A pioneer of the doctrine of empiricism (believing things only when you've seen the proof for yourself). Hume was also a prime believer in the value of skepticism, in other words, he was naturally suspicious of things that other people told him to be true and constantly set out to discover the truth for himself. These two related ideas influenced many thinkers after Hume, and his writings (of which there are many) continue to inspire philosophers to this day.

The Enlightenment thinker who might be the most famous is **Immanuel Kant** of Germany. He was both a philosopher and a scientist, and he took a definite scientific view of the world. He wrote the movement's most famous essay, "Answering the Question: What Is Enlightenment?" and he answered his famous question with the motto "Dare to Know." For Kant, the human being was a rational being capable of hugely creative thought and intense self-evaluation. He encouraged all to examine themselves and the world around them. He believed that the source of morality lay not in nature of in the grace of God but in the human soul itself. He believed that man believed in God for practical, not religious or mystical, reasons.

Also prevalent during the Enlightenment was the idea of the "**social contract**," the belief that government existed because people wanted it to, that the people had an agreement with the government that they would submit to it as long as it protected them and didn't encroach on their basic human rights. This idea was first made famous by the Frenchman Jean-Jacques Rousseau but was also adopted by England's John Locke and America's Thomas Jefferson. **John Locke** was one of the most influential political writers of the 17th century who put great emphasis on human rights and put forth the belief that when governments violate those rights people should rebel. He wrote the book "Two Treatises of Government" in 1690, which had tremendous influence on political thought in the American colonies and helped shaped the U.S. Constitution and Declaration of Independence

The **Age of Exploration** actually had its beginnings centuries before exploration actually took place. The rise and spread of Islam in the seventh century and its subsequent control over the holy city of Jerusalem led to the European so-called holy wars, **the Crusades**, to free Jerusalem and the Holy Land from this control. Even though the Crusades were not a success, those who survived and returned to their homes and countries in Western Europe brought back with them new products such as silks, spices, perfumes, new and different foods. Luxuries that were unheard of that gave new meaning to colorless, drab, dull lives.

New ideas, new inventions, better maps and charts, newer, more accurate navigational instruments, increased knowledge, great wealth and new methods also went to Western Europe with the returning Crusaders and from these new influences was the intellectual stimulation which led to the period known as the Renaissance. The revival of interest in classical Greek art, architecture, literature, science, astronomy, medicine and increased trade between Europe and Asia and the invention of the printing press helped to push the spread of knowledge and start exploring.

For many centuries, various mapmakers made many maps and charts, which in turn stimulated curiosity and the seeking of more knowledge. At the same time, the Chinese were using the magnetic compass in their ships. Pacific islanders were going from island to island, covering thousands of miles in open canoes navigating by sun and stars. Arab traders were sailing all over the Indian Ocean in their **dhows**. The trade routes between Europe and Asia were slow, difficult, dangerous, and very expensive. Between sea voyages on the Indian Ocean and Mediterranean Sea and the camel caravans in central Asia and the Arabian Desert, the trade was still controlled by the Italian merchants in Genoa and Venice. It would take months and even years for the exotic luxuries of Asia to reach the markets of Western Europe. A faster, cheaper way had to be found. A way had to be found which would bypass traditional routes and end the control of the Italian merchants.

Prince Henry of Portugal (also called the Navigator) encouraged, supported, and financed the Portuguese seamen who led in the search for an all-water route to Asia. A shipyard was built along with a school teaching navigation. New types of sailing ships were built which would carry the seamen safely through the ocean waters. Experiments were conducted in newer maps, newer navigational methods, and newer instruments. These included the astrolabe and the compass enabling sailors to determine direction as well as latitude and longitude for exact location. Although Prince Henry died in 1460, the Portuguese kept on, sailing along and exploring Africa's west coastline. In 1488, Bartholomew Diaz and his men sailed around Africa's southern tip and headed toward Asia. Diaz wanted to push on but turned back because his men were discouraged and weary from the long months at sea, extremely fearful of the unknown, and just refusing to travel any further.

However, the Portuguese were finally successful ten years later in 1498 when **Vasco da Gama** and his men, continuing the route of Diaz, rounded Africa's Cape of Good Hope, sailing across the Indian Ocean, reaching India's port of Calicut (Calcutta). Although, six years earlier, Columbus had reached the New World and an entire hemisphere, da Gama had proved Asia could be reached from Europe by sea.

Of course, everyone knows that **Columbus'** first transatlantic voyage was to try to prove his theory or idea that Asia could be reached by sailing west.

To a certain extent, his idea was true. It could be done but only after figuring how to go around or across or through the landmass in between. Long after Spain dispatched explorers and her famed conquistadors to gather the wealth for the Spanish monarchs and their coffers, the British were searching valiantly for the "Northwest Passage," a land-sea route across North America and open sea to the wealth of Asia. It wasn't until after the Lewis and Clark Expedition when Captains Meriwether Lewis and William Clark proved conclusively that there simply was no Northwest Passage. It did not exist.

However, this did not deter exploration and settlement. Spain, France, and England along with some participation by the Dutch led the way with expanding Western European civilization in the New World. These three nations had strong monarchical governments and were struggling for dominance and power in Europe. With the defeat of Spain's mighty Armada in 1588, England became undisputed mistress of the seas. Spain lost its power and influence in Europe and it was left to France and England to carry on the rivalry, leading to eventual British control in Asia as well.

With the increase in trade and travel, cities sprang up and began to grow. Craft workers in the cities developed their skills to a high degree, eventually organizing guilds to protect the quality of the work and to regulate the buying and selling of their products. City government developed and flourished centered on strong town councils. Active in city government and the town councils were the wealthy businessmen who made up the growing middle class.

In addition, there were a number of individuals and events during the time of exploration and discoveries. The **Vivaldo brothers** and **Marco Polo** wrote of their travels and experiences, which signaled the early beginnings. From the Crusades, the survivors made their way home to different places in Europe bringing with them fascinating, new information about exotic lands, people, customs, and desired foods and goods such as spices and silks.

For France, claims to various parts of North America were the result of the efforts of such men as Verrazano, Champlain, Cartier, LaSalle, Father Marquette and Joliet. Dutch claims were based on the work of one Henry Hudson. John Cabot gave England its stake in North America along with John Hawkins, Sir Francis Drake, and the half-brothers Sir Walter Raleigh and Sir Humphrey Gilbert.

Actually the first Europeans in the New World were Norsemen led by Eric the Red and later, his son Leif the Lucky. However, before any of these, the ancestors of today's Native Americans and Latin American Indians crossed the Bering Strait from Asia to Alaska, eventually settling in all parts of the Americas.

The **North American** and **South American Native Americans** could not have been more different, yet in some ways they were the same as well.

Differences in geography, economic focus, and the preponderance of visitors from overseas produced differing patterns of occupation, survival, and success.

In North America, the landscape was much more hospitable to settlement and exploration. The North American continent, especially in what is now the United States, had a few mountain ranges and a handful of wide rivers but nothing near the dense jungles and staggeringly high mountains that South America did. The area that is now Canada was cold but otherwise conducive to settlement. As a result, the Native Americans in the northern areas of the Americas were more spread out and their cultures more diverse than their South American counterparts.

One of the best known of the North American tribes were the Pueblo, who lived in what is now the American Southwest. They are perhaps best known for the challenging vista-based villages that they constructed from the sheer faces of cliffs and rocks and for their *adobes*, mud-brick buildings that housed their living and meeting quarters. The Pueblos chose their own chiefs. This was perhaps one of the oldest representative governments in the world.

Known also for their organized government were the Iroquoi, who lived in the American Northeast. The famous Five Nations of the Iroquois made treaties among themselves and shared leadership of their peoples.

For the North Americans, life was all about finding and growing food. The people were great farmers and hunters. They grew such famous crops as *maize*, or corn, and potatoes and squash and pumpkins and beans; and they hunted all manner of animals for food, including deer, bears, and buffalo. Despite the preponderance of crop-growing areas, many Native Americans, however, did not domesticate animals except for dogs. They might have killed pigs and chickens for food, but they certainly made it easy on themselves by growing them in pens right outside their houses.

The Native Americans who lived in the wilds of Canada and in the Pacific Northwest lived off the land as well and, in this case, the nearby water. Fishing was a big business in these places. The people used fish to eat and for trade, exchanging the much-needed food for beads and other trinkets from neighboring tribes.

Religion was a personal affair for nearly all of these tribes, with beliefs in higher powers extending to Spirits in the sky and elsewhere in Nature. Native Americans had none of the one-god-only mentality that developed in Europe and the Middle East, nor did they have the wars associated with the conflict that those monotheistic religions had with one another.

Those people who lived in North America had large concentrations of people and houses, but they didn't have the kind of large civilization centers like the cities of elsewhere in the world. These people didn't have an exact system of writing, either. These were two technological advances that were found in many other places in the world, including, to varying degrees, South America.

We know the most about the empires of South America, the **Aztec**, **Inca**, and **Maya**. People lived in South America before the advent of these empires, of course. One of the earliest people of record were the Olmecs, who left behind little to prove their existence except a series of huge carved figures.

The Aztecs dominated Mexico and Central America. They weren't the only people living in these areas, just the most powerful ones. The Aztecs had many enemies, some of who were only too happy to help Hernan Cortes precipitate the downfall of the Aztec society. The Aztecs had access to large numbers of metals and jewels, and they used these metals to make weapons and these jewels to trade for items they didn't already possess. Actually, the Aztecs didn't do a whole lot of trading; rather, they conquered neighboring tribes and demanded tribute from them; this is the source of so much of the Aztec riches. They also believed in a handful of gods and believed that these gods demanded human sacrifice in order to continue to smile on the Aztecs. The center of Aztec society was the great city of Tenochtitlan, which was built on an island so as to be easier to defend and boasted a population of 300,000 at the time of the arrival of the conquistadors. Tenochtitlan was known for its canals and its pyramids, none of which survive today.

The Inca Empire stretched across a vast period of territory down the western coast of South America and was connected by a series of roads. A series of messengers ran along these roads, carrying news and instructions from the capital, Cuzco, another large city along the lines of but not as spectacular as Tenochtitlan. The Incas are known for inventing the *quipu*, a string-based device that provided them with a method of keeping records. The Inca Empire, like the Aztec Empire, was very much a centralized state, with all income going to the state coffers and all trade going through the emperor as well. The Incas worshiped the dead, their ancestors, and nature and often took part in what we could consider strange rituals.

The most advanced Native American civilization were the Maya, who lived primarily in Central America. They were the only Native American civilization to develop writing, which consisted of a series of symbols that has still not been deciphered. The Mayas also built huge pyramids and other stone figures and sculptures, mostly of the gods they worshiped. The Mayas are most famous, however, for their calendars and for their mathematics. The Mayan calendars were the most accurate on the planet until the 16th Century. The Mayas also invented the idea of zero, which might sound like a small thing except that no other culture had thought of such a thing.

Maya worship resembled the practices of the Aztec and Inca, although human sacrifices were rare. The Mayas also traded heavily with their neighbors.

All of these civilizations were destroyed by the invading foreigners. The wealth of resources in these countries was desirable to the Europeans. Slaves were imported from the African countries to work in the Americas. It is estimated that in four centuries of the slave trade, more than 9.5 million slaves were sent to the Americas. The African sellers and leaders used slaves as a form of barter. They traded them for what the Europeans and others offered.

Skill 30.2   Demonstrate knowledge of political and industrial revolutions 1750–1914

The overriding theme of the life in the 18th, 19th, and 20th Centuries was progress. Technological advancements brought great and terrible things in all aspects of life. New theories in economics brought great changes in the way the world does business. New theories in government brought about new nations, uprisings, and wars galore. New theories in art changed the landscape of painting forever.

During the 18th and especially the 19th Centuries, nationalism emerged as a powerful force in Europe and elsewhere in the world. Strictly speaking, nationalism was a belief in one's own nation, or country, people. More so than in previous centuries, the people of the European nations began to think in terms of a nation of people who had similar beliefs, concerns, and needs. This was partly a reaction to a growing discontent with the autocratic governments of the day and also just a general realization that there was more to life than the individual. People could feel a part of something like their nation, making themselves more than just an insignificant soul struggling to survive.

Nationalism precipitated several changes in government, most notably in France; it also brought large groups of people together, as with the unification of Germany and Italy. What it didn't do, however, is provide sufficient outlets for this sudden rise in national fervor. Especially in the 1700s and 1800s, European powers and peoples began looking to Africa and Asia in order to find colonies: rich sources of goods, trade, and cheap labor. Africa, especially, suffered at the hands of European imperialists, bent on expanding their reach outside the borders of Europe. Asia, too, suffered colonial expansion, most notably in India and Southeast Asia.

This colonial expansion would haunt the European imperialists in a very big way, as colonial skirmishes spilled over into alliance that dragged the European powers into World War I. Some of these colonial battles were still being fought as late as the start of World War II as well.

The **Industrial Revolution**, which began in Great Britain and spread elsewhere, was the development of power-driven machinery (fueled by coal and steam) leading to the accelerated growth of industry with large factories replacing homes and small workshops as work centers. The lives of people changed drastically and a largely agricultural society changed to an industrial one. In Western Europe, the period of empire and colonialism began. The industrialized nations seized and claimed parts of Africa and Asia in an effort to control and provide the raw materials needed to feed the industries and machines in the "mother country". Later developments included power based on electricity and internal combustion, replacing coal and steam.

The use of machines in industry enabled workers to produce a large quantity of goods much faster than by hand. With the increase in business, hundreds of workers were hired, assigned to perform a certain job in the production process. This was a method of organization called "**division of labor**" and by its increasing the rate of production, businesses lowered prices for their products making the products affordable for more people. As a result, sales and businesses were increasingly successful and profitable. A great variety of new products or inventions became available such as: the typewriter, the telephone, barbed wire, the electric light, the phonograph, and the gasoline automobile. From this list, the one that had the greatest effect on America's economy was the automobile.

The increase in business and industry was greatly affected by the many rich natural resources that were found throughout the nation. The industrial machines were powered by the abundant water supply. The construction industry as well as products made from wood depended heavily on lumber from the forests. Coal and iron ore in abundance were needed for the steel industry, which profited and increased from the use of steel in such things as skyscrapers, automobiles, bridges, railroad tracks, and machines. Other minerals such as silver, copper, and petroleum played a large role in industrial growth, especially petroleum, from which gasoline was refined as fuel for the increasingly popular automobile.

The late 1800s and early 1900s were a period of the efforts of many to make significant reforms and changes in the areas of politics, society, and the economy. There was a need to reduce the levels of poverty and to improve the living conditions of those affected by it. Regulations of big business, ridding governmental corruption and making it more responsive to the needs of the people were also on the list of reforms to be accomplished. Until 1890, there was very little success, but from 1890 on, the reformers gained increased public support and were able to achieve some influence in government. Since some of these individuals referred to themselves as "**progressives**" the period of 1890 to 1917 is referred to by historians as the Progressive Era.

The **American Revolution** resulted in the successful efforts of the English colonists in America to win their freedom from Great Britain. After more than one hundred years of mostly self-government, the colonists resented the increased British meddling and control, they declared their freedom, won the Revolutionary War with aid from France, and formed a new independent nation.

The **French Revolution** was the revolt of the middle and lower classes against the gross political and economic excesses of the rulers and the supporting nobility. It ended with the establishment of the First in a series of French Republics. Conditions leading to revolt included extreme taxation, inflation, lack of food, and the total disregard for the impossible, degrading, and unacceptable condition of the people on the part of the rulers, nobility, and the Church.

Emboldened by the success of the American and French Revolutions, the Spanish and Portuguese colonies in Central and South America grew dissatisfied with their economic and political dependence on Europe, and in the early decades of the 19th Century, several revolutionary movements gained momentum.

In Europe, France had moved into Spain and captured the Spanish King Ferdinand VII in the Napoleonic Wars, effectively weakening Spain's hold over its colonies in the Americas. The royal family of Portugal fled before Napoleon's armies to Brazil, its South American colony. Efforts by the mother countries to suppress the independence movements were thwarted by junta forces led by such figures as Miguel Hidalgo and Simon Bolivar. They were further discouraged by other countries such as the United States and Great Britain which were eager to gain access to South America's natural resources and lucrative markets.

By 1822, Argentina, Chile, Colombia, Mexico, Paraguay, Venezuela, Peru, Ecuador and Brazil had all succeeded in their battles for independence, and looked to the rest of the world for recognition and assistance. In the United States, President James Monroe announced the Monroe Doctrine, which stated that any designs by European countries to take control of the former colonies in the Western Hemisphere would be interpreted as attacks on the United States.

Socialism – This is a fairly recent political phenomenon though its roots can be traced pretty far back in time in many respects. At the core, both socialism and communism are fundamentally economic philosophies that advocate public rather than private ownership, especially over means of production, yet even here, there are many distinctions. Karl Marx basically concentrated his attention on the industrial worker and on state domination over the means of production.

In practice, this Marxian dogma has largely been followed the most in those countries that profess to be Communist. The emphasis in communism is the massive programs for the development of heavy industry regardless of the wants or comforts of the individual in the given society. Socialism by contrast, usually occurring where industry has already been developed has concerned itself more with the welfare of the individual and the fair distribution of whatever wealth is available.

Communism has a rigid theology, and a bible (*Das Capital*) that sees Communism emerging as a result of almost cosmic laws. Modern socialism is much closer to the ground. It too sees change in human society and hopes for improvement, but there is no unchanging millennium at the end of the road. Communism is sure that it will achieve the perfect state and in this certainty it is willing to use any and all means, however ruthless, to bring it about.

Socialism on the other hand, confident only that the human condition is always changing, makes no easy approximation between ends and means and so cannot justify brutalities. This distinction in philosophy, of course, makes for an immense conflict in methods. Communism, believing that revolution is inevitable, works toward it by emphasizing class antagonisms. Socialism, while seeking change, insists on the use of democratic procedures within the existing social order of a given society. In it, the upper classes and capitalists are not to be violently overthrown but instead won over by logical persuasion.

It is interesting to note that in every perfect, idealized community or society that people have dreamed about throughout history, where human beings are pictured living in a special harmony that transcends their natural instincts, there has been a touch of socialism. This tendency was especially found in the **Utopian-Socialists** of the early 19th century, whose basic aim was the repudiation of the private property system with its economic inefficiency and social injustice. Their criticisms rather than any actual achievements would linger after them.

Like Marx, they envisioned industrial capitalism as becoming more and more inhumane and oppressive. They could not imagine the mass of workers prospering in such a system. Yet the workers soon developed their own powerful organizations and institutions. They began to bend the economic system to their own benefit. Thus a split did occur. First, between those who after the growing success of the labor movement rejected the earlier utopian ideas as being impractical. Second, those who saw in this newfound political awareness of the working class the key to organizing a realistic ability of revolution, who saw this as inevitable based on their previous observations and study of history. Having reached a point where it has managed to jeopardize its very own survival, the inevitable revolution of those opposed to the present capitalist system had to occur, history has proven this so, and history is always right and irrefutable.

These believers in the absolute correctness of this doctrine gathered around Marx in what he called **Scientific Socialism**. In contempt to all other kinds which he considered not to be scientific, and therefore, useless as a realistic political philosophy.

The next split would occur between those who believed in the absolute inevitability of the coming revolution (the **Revolutionary Socialists** or as they came to be known, the **Communists**), and those who accepted the basic idea that the current capitalist system could not last. They saw the growing political awareness of the working class and the beginnings of an ability to effect peaceful and gradual change in the social order. They believed this is better in the long run for everyone concerned as opposed to a cataclysmic, apocalyptic uprising (the **Democratic-Socialists**).

Major strides for the **Democratic-Socialists** were made before the First World War—a war that the Socialists, by philosophy pacifists, initially resisted, giving only reluctant support only once the struggle had begun. During the conflict, public sentiment against pacifism tended generally to weaken the movement, but with peace, reaction set in. The cause of world socialism leaped forward, often overcompensating by adhering to revolutionary communism, which in the Revolution of 1917 had taken hold of in Russia.

The between wars period saw the sudden spurt of socialism, whether their leanings were democratic or not, all socialists were bound together for a time in their resistance to fascism.

In London in 1864, Karl Marx organized the first Socialist International. This radical leftist organization died off after limping along for twelve years, by which time its headquarters had moved to New York. After the passage of about another twelve years, the **Second Socialist International** met in Paris to celebrate the anniversary of the fall of the Bastille in the French Revolution. By this time, serious factions were developing. There were the **Anarchists**, who wanted to tear down everything, **Communists** who wanted to tear down the established order and build another in its place, and the **Democratic-Socialist** majority who favored peaceful political action.

Struggling for internal peace and cohesion right up to the First World War, socialism would remain largely ineffectual at this critical international time. Peace brought them all together again in Bern, Switzerland, but by this time the Soviet Union had been created, and the Russian Communists refused to attend the meeting on the ground that the Second Socialist International opposed the type of dictatorship it saw as necessary in order to achieve revolutions. Thus the **Communist International** was created in direct opposition to the Socialist International. While the socialists went on to advocate the "triumph of democracy, firmly rooted in the principles of liberty". The main objective of this new Socialist International was to maintain the peace, an ironic and very elusive goal in the period between the two world wars.

At the international level, socialism seeks a world of free peoples living together in peace and harmony for the mutual benefit of all. That freedom, at least from colonial rule, has largely been won.   Peace throughout the world, however, is still as far off in most respects as it has ever been. According to the socialist doctrine, putting an end to capitalism will do much to reduce the likelihood of war. Armies and businesses are seen to need each other in a marriage of the weapons-mentality and devotion to private profit through the economic exploitation of weaker countries.

All socialism denies certain freedoms, sometimes hidden in what it considers favorable terms. It deprives the minority of special economic privileges for the benefit of majority. The more left wing, communistic socialism may deny the democratic process entirely. Traditionally defined, democracy holds to the idea that the people, exercising their majority opinion at the polls, will arrive at the common good by electing representative individuals to govern them. Communists would interpret this to mean the tyranny of an uneducated majority obliged to decide between a politically selected group of would-be leaders.

The last important historical economic system to arise was fascism. It has been called a reaction against communism and socialism. It can, at times, cooperate with a monarchy if it has to.

Fascist movements often had socialist origins. For example, in Italy, where fascism first arose in place of socialism, **Benito Mussolini**, sought to impose what he called "*corporativism*". A fascist "*corporate*" state would, in theory, run the economy for the benefit of the whole country like a corporation. It would be centrally controlled and managed by an elite who would see that its benefits would go to everyone.

In general, Fascism is the effort to create, by dictatorial means, a viable national society in which competing interests were to be adjusted to each other by being entirely subordinated to the service of the state. The following features have been characteristic of Fascism in its various manifestations: **(1)** An origin at a time of serious economic disruption and of rapid and bewildering social change. **(2)** A philosophy that rejects democratic and humanitarian ideals and glorifies the absolute sovereignty of the state, the unity and destiny of the people, and their unquestioning loyalty and obedience to the dictator. **(3)** Aggressive nationalism calls for the mobilization and regimentation of every aspect of national life and makes open use of violence and intimidation. **(4)** The simulation of mass popular support, accomplished by outlawing all but a single political party and by using suppression, censorship, and propaganda. **(5)** A program of vigorous action including economic reconstruction, industrialization, pursuit of economic self-sufficiency, territorial expansion and war which is dramatized as bold, adventurous, and promising a glorious future.

Fascism has always declared itself the uncompromising enemy of communism, with which, however, fascist actions have much in common. (In fact, many of the methods of organization and propaganda used by fascists were taken from the experience of the early Russian communists, along with the belief in a single strong political party, secret police, etc.) The propertied interests and the upper classes, fearful of revolution, often gave their support to fascism on the basis of promises by the fascist leaders to maintain the status quo and safeguard property. (In effect, accomplishing a revolution from above with their help as opposed from below against them. However, fascism did consider itself a revolutionary movement of a different type).

Once established, a fascist regime ruthlessly crushes communist and socialist parties as well as all democratic opposition. It regiments the propertied interests to its national goals and wins the potentially revolutionary masses to fascist programs by substituting a rabid nationalism for class conflict. Thus fascism may be regarded as an extreme defensive expedient adopted by a nation faced with the sometimes-illusionary threat of communist subversion or revolution. Under fascism, capital is regulated as much as labor and fascist contempt for legal or constitutional guarantees effectively destroyed whatever security the capitalistic system had enjoyed under pre-fascist governments.

In theory at least, the chief distinction between fascism and communism is that fascism is *nationalist*, exalting the interests of the state and glorifying war between nations, whereas communism is *internationalist,* exalting the interests of a specific economic class (the proletariat) and glorifying worldwide class warfare. In practice, however, this fundamental distinction loses some of its validity. For in its heyday, fascism was also an internationalist movement, a movement dedicated to world conquest (like communism), as evidenced by the events prior to and during the Second World War. At the same time, many elements in communism as it evolved came to be very nationalistic as well.

The time from 1830 to 1914 is characterized by the extraordinary growth and spread of patriotic pride in a nation along with intense, widespread imperialism. Loyalty to one's nation included national pride, extending and maintaining sovereign political boundaries, and unification of smaller states with common language, history, and culture into a more powerful nation. As part of a larger multicultural empire, there were smaller groups who wished to separate into smaller, political, cultural nations. Examples of major events of this time resulting from the insurgence of nationalism include:

In the United States, territorial expansion occurred in the expansion westward under the banner of "Manifest Destiny." In addition, the U.S. was involved in the War with Mexico, the Spanish-American War, and support of the Latin American colonies of Spain in their revolt for independence. In Latin America, the Spanish colonies were successful in their fight for independence and self-government.

Prior to the Industrial Revolution, most urban centers were either ports or centers of government. With the sudden and rapid growth of industry, which started in England, urban centers began growing based on industrial production and proximity to power resources, such as coal and water power. In the 100 years between 1700 and 1800, the population of England went from a majority living in rural areas to a majority living in cities. As industrialization spread to other countries, a similar pattern of urbanization followed. With the advent of the railroad, moving raw materials over land became easier and less expensive, further fueling urban growth.

In Europe, Italy and Germany were each totally united into one nation from many smaller states. There were revolutions in Austria and Hungary, the Franco-Prussian War, the dividing of Africa among the strong European nations, interference and intervention of Western nations in Asia, and the breakup of Turkish dominance in the Balkans.

In Africa, France, Great Britain, Italy, Portugal, Spain, Germany, and Belgium controlled the entire continent except Liberia and Ethiopia. In Asia and the Pacific Islands, only China, Japan, and present-day Thailand (Siam) kept their independence. The others were controlled by the strong European nations.
An additional reason for European imperialism was the harsh, urgent demand for the raw materials needed to fuel and feed the great Industrial Revolution. These resources were not available in the huge quantity so desperately needed which necessitated (and rationalized) the partitioning of the continent of Africa and parts of Asia. In turn, these colonial areas would purchase the finished manufactured goods.

Things changed in the worlds of literature and art as well. The main development in the 19th Century was **Romanticism**, an emphasis on emotion and the imagination that was a direct reaction to the logic and reason so stressed in the preceding Enlightenment. Famous Romantic authors included John Keats, William Wordsworth, Victor Hugo, and Johann Wolfgang von Goethe. The horrors of the Industrial Revolution gave rise to the very famous realists Charles Dickens, Fyodor Dostoevsky, Leo Tolstoy, and Mark Twain, who described life as they saw it, for better or for worse (and it was usually worse).

The most famous movement of the 1800s, however, was **Impressionism**. The idea was to present an impression of a moment in time, one of life's fleeting moments memorialized on canvas. A list of famous impressionists is a who's who of the most famous painters in the world: Monet, Degas, van Gogh, Manet, Cezanne, Renoir, and the list goes on. More than any other time in the history of the arts, Impressionism produced famous faces and famous canvases.
Echoing Dickens's dislike of an industrialized world, 20th Century authors stressed individual action and responsibility. The giants of the 1900s include James Joyce, T.S. Eliot, John Steinbeck, Ernest Hemingway, William Faulkner, and George Orwell, all of whom to varying degrees expressed distrust at the power of machines and weapons and most of modern society.

One of the main places for European imperialist expansion was Africa. Britain, France, Germany, and Belgium took over countries in Africa and claimed them as their own. The resources (including people) were then shipped back to the mainland and claimed as colonial gains. The Europeans made a big deal about "civilizing the savages," reasoning that their technological superiority gave them the right to rule and "educate" the peoples of Africa.

Southeast Asia was another area of European expansion at this time, mainly by France. So, too, was India, colonized by Great Britain. These two nations combined with Spain to occupy countries in Latin America. Spain also seized the rich lands of the Philippines.

COMPETENCY 31.0   1914 TO THE PRESENT

Skill 31.1   Evaluate conflicts, ideologies, and changes in the twentieth century

The **Russian Revolution** occurred first in March (or February on the old calendar) 1917 with the abdication of Tsar Nicholas II and the establishment of a democratic government. Those who were the extreme Marxists and had a majority in Russia's Socialist Party, the Bolsheviks, overcame opposition, and in November (October on the old calendar), did away with the provisional democratic government and set up the world's first Marxist state.

The conditions in Russia in previous centuries led up to this. Russia's harsh climate, tremendous size, and physical isolation from the rest of Europe, along with the brutal despotic rule and control of the Tsars over enslaved peasants, contributed to the final conditions leading to revolution. Despite the tremendous efforts of Peter the Great to bring his country up to the social, cultural, and economic standards of the rest of Europe, Russia always remained a hundred years or more behind. Autocratic rule, the existence of the system of serfdom or slavery of the peasants, lack of money, defeats in wars, lack of enough food and food production, little if any industrialization--all of these contributed to conditions ripe for revolt.

By 1914, Russia's industrial growth was even faster than Germany's and agricultural production was improving, along with better transportation. However, poverty was rampant. The Orthodox Church was steeped in political activities, and the absolute rule of the Tsar was the order of the day. By the time the nation entered World War I, conditions were just right for revolution. Marxist socialism seemed to be the solution or answer to all the problems. Russia had to stop participation in the war, although winning a big battle. Industry could not meet the military's needs.

Transportation by rail was severely disrupted, and it was most difficult to procure supplies from the Allies. The people had had enough of war, injustice, starvation, poverty, slavery, and cruelty. The support for and strength of the Bolsheviks were mainly in the cities. After two or three years of civil war, fighting foreign invasions, and opposing other revolutionary groups, the Bolsheviks were finally successful in making possible a type of "pre-Utopia" for the workers and the people.

As succeeding Marxist or Communist leaders came to power, the effects of this violent revolution were felt all around the earth. From 1989 until 1991, Communism eventually gave way to various forms of democracies and free enterprise societies in Eastern Europe and the former Soviet Union. The foreign policies of all free Western nations were directly and immensely affected by the Marxist-Communist ideology. Its effect on Eastern Europe and the former Soviet Union was felt politically, economically, socially, culturally, and geographically. The people of ancient Russia simply exchanged one autocratic dictatorial system for another, and its impact on all of the people on the earth is still being felt to this day.

World War I 1914 to 1918
In brief, the causes were the surge of nationalism, the increasing strength of military capabilities, massive colonization for raw materials needed for industrialization and manufacturing, and military and diplomatic alliances.
The initial spark that started the conflagration, was the assassination of Austrian Archduke Francis Ferdinand and his wife in Sarajevo.

There were 28 nations involved in the war, not including colonies and territories. It began July 28, 1914 and ended November 11, 1918 with the signing of the Treaty of Versailles. Economically, the war cost a total of $337 billion; increased inflation and huge war debts; and caused a loss of markets, goods, jobs, and factories. Politically, old empires collapsed; many monarchies disappeared; smaller countries gained temporary independence; Communists seized power in Russia; and, in some cases, nationalism increased. Socially, total populations decreased because of war casualties and low birth rates. There were millions of displaced persons, and villages and farms were destroyed. Cities grew while women made significant gains in the work force and the ballot box. There was less social distinction and classes. Attitudes completely changed, and old beliefs and values were questioned. The peace settlement established the League of Nations to ensure peace, but it failed to do so.

Fascism arose following WWI. In general, Fascism is the effort to create, by dictatorial means, a viable national society in which competing interests were to be adjusted to each other by being entirely subordinated to the service of the state. The following features have been characteristic of Fascism in its various manifestations: **(1)** An origin at a time of serious economic disruption and of rapid and bewildering social change. **(2)** A philosophy that rejects democratic and humanitarian ideals and glorifies the absolute sovereignty of the state, the unity and destiny of the people, and their unquestioning loyalty and obedience to the dictator. **(3)** Aggressive nationalism calls for the mobilization and regimentation of every aspect of national life and makes open use of violence and intimidation. **(4)** The simulation of mass popular support, accomplished by outlawing all but a single political party and by using suppression, censorship, and propaganda. **(5)** A program of vigorous action including economic reconstruction, industrialization, pursuit of economic self-sufficiency, territorial expansion and war which is dramatized as bold, adventurous, and promising a glorious future.

Fascist movements often had socialist origins. For example, in Italy, where fascism first arose in place of socialism, **Benito Mussolini**, sought to impose what he called "*corporativism.*" A fascist "*corporate*" state would, in theory, run the economy for the benefit of the whole country like a corporation. It would be centrally controlled and managed by an elite who would see that its benefits would go to everyone.

Fascism has always declared itself the uncompromising enemy of communism, with which, however, fascist actions have much in common. (In fact, many of the methods of organization and propaganda used by fascists were taken from the experience of the early Russian communists, along with the belief in a single strong political party, secret police, etc.) The propertied interests and the upper classes, fearful of revolution, often gave their support to fascism on the basis of promises by the fascist leaders to maintain the status quo and safeguard property. (In effect, this accomplished a revolution from above with their help as opposed from below against them. However, fascism did consider itself a revolutionary movement of a different type).

In addition, fascist or similar regimes are at times anti-Communist, as evidenced by the Soviet-German Treaty of 1939. During the period of alliance created by the treaty, Italy and Germany and their satellite countries ceased their anti-Communist propaganda. They emphasized their own revolutionary and proletarian origins and attacked the so-called plutocratic western democracies.

In theory at least, the chief distinction between fascism and communism is that fascism is *nationalist*, exalting the interests of the state and glorifying war between nations, whereas communism is *internationalist,* exalting the interests of a specific economic class (the proletariat) and glorifying worldwide class warfare. In practice, however, this fundamental distinction loses some of its validity. For in its heyday, fascism was also an internationalist movement, a movement dedicated to world conquest, (like communism), as evidenced by the events prior to and during the Second World War. At the same time, many elements in communism as it evolved came to be very nationalistic as well.

World War II 1939 to 1945

Ironically, the Treaty of Paris, the peace treaty ending World War I, ultimately led to the Second World War. Countries that fought in the first war were either dissatisfied over the "spoils" of war, or were punished so harshly that resentment continued building to an eruption twenty years later.

The economic problems of both winners and losers of the first war were never resolved, and the worldwide Great Depression of the 1930s dealt the final blow to any immediate rapid recovery. Democratic governments in Europe were severely strained and weakened, which in turn gave strength and encouragement to those political movements that were extreme and made promises to end the economic chaos in their countries.

Nationalism, which was a major cause of World War I, grew even stronger and seemed to feed the feelings of discontent, which became increasingly rampant.

Because of unstable economic conditions and political unrest, harsh dictatorships arose in several of the countries, especially where there was no history of experience in democratic government.

Countries such as Germany, Japan, and Italy began to aggressively expand their borders and acquire additional territory.

In all, 59 nations became embroiled in World War II, which began September 1, 1939 and ended September 2, 1945. These dates include both the European and Pacific Theaters of war. The horrible tragic results of this second global conflagration were more deaths and more destruction than in any other armed conflict. It completely uprooted and displaced millions of people. The end of the war brought renewed power struggles, especially in Europe and China, with many Eastern European nations as well as China coming under complete control and domination of the Communists, supported and backed by the Soviet Union. With the development of and two-time deployment of an atomic bomb against two Japanese cities, the world found itself in the nuclear age. The peace settlement established the United Nations Organization, still existing and operating today.

The post WWII years have seen many changes in society. Nations have been involved in a global community since then, partly due to the existence of the United Nations. Governments have been more concerned with the rights of various groups since then, like women and minorities. The role of women has changed throughout the world. Women are now more important to economies. For the most part, they no longer leave the workforce when they have children so they now have a more important role as leaders, consumers and workers. They are also better educated than in the past and have assumed their roles in industry and commerce, as well as politics and government.

Gains have been made in the treatment of minorities and human rights. Much of this is due to the United Nations, which provides a forum for discussion and enforcement by its member nations. International treaties have also come into being to protect the rights of people. The Cold War, of course, also existed during this period.

The Cold War was, more than anything else, an ideological struggle between proponents of democracy and those of communism. The two major players were the United States and the Soviet Union, but other countries were involved as well. It was a "cold" war because no large-scale fighting took place directly between the two big protagonists.

It wasn't just form of government that was driving this war, either. Economics were a main concern as well. A concern in both countries was that the precious resources (such as oil and food) from other like-minded countries wouldn't be allowed to flow to "the other side." These resources didn't much flow between the U.S. and Soviet Union, either.

The Soviet Union kept much more of a tight leash on its supporting countries, including all of Eastern Europe, which made up a military organization called the Warsaw Pact. The Western nations responded with a military organization of their own, NATO. Another prime battleground was Asia, where the Soviet Union had allies in China, North Korea, and North Vietnam and the U.S. had allies in Japan, South Korea, Taiwan, and South Vietnam. The Korean War and Vietnam War were major conflicts in which both big protagonists played big roles but didn't directly fight each other. The main symbol of the Cold War was the arms race, a continual buildup of missiles, tanks, and other weapons that became ever more technologically advanced and increasingly more deadly. The ultimate weapon, which both sides had in abundance, was the nuclear bomb. Spending on weapons and defensive systems eventually occupied great percentages of the budgets of the U.S. and the USSR, and some historians argue that this high level of spending played a large part in the end of the latter.

The war was a cultural struggle as well. Adults brought up their children to hate "the Americans" or "the Communists." Cold War tensions spilled over into many parts of life in countries around the world. The ways of life in countries on either side of the divide were so different that they seemed entirely foreign to outside observers.

The Cold War continued in varying degrees from 1947 to 1991, when the Soviet Union collapsed. Other Eastern European countries had seen their communist governments overthrown by this time as well, marking the shredding of the "Iron Curtain."

The major thrust of U.S. foreign policy from the end of World War II to 1990 was the post-war struggle between non-Communist nations, led by the United States, and the Soviet Union and the Communist nations who were its allies. It was referred to as a "Cold War" because its conflicts did not lead to a major war of fighting, or a "hot war." Both the Soviet Union and the United States embarked on an arsenal buildup of atomic and hydrogen bombs as well as other nuclear weapons. Both nations had the capability of destroying each other but because of the continuous threat of nuclear war and accidents, extreme caution was practiced on both sides. The efforts of both sides to serve and protect their political philosophies and to support and assist their allies resulted in a number of events during this 45-year period.

The problem the world has been dealing with since WWII is population growth, especially in the less developed countries. Economies and the food supply have to expand to accommodate a growing population. This hasn't been the case in many of the less developed countries and as a result they suffer extreme poverty and have a poor quality of life.

Skill 31.2 Understand contemporary trends—1991 to the present

The struggle between the Communist world under Soviet Union leadership and the non-Communist world under Anglo-American leadership resulted in what became known as the Cold War. Communism crept into the Western Hemisphere with Cuban leader Fidel Castro and his regime. Most colonies in Africa, Asia, and the Middle East gained independence from European and Western influence and control. In South Africa in the early 1990s, the system of racial segregation, called "apartheid," was abolished.

The Soviet Union was the first industrialized nation to successfully begin a program of space flight and exploration, launching Sputnik and putting the first man in space. The United States also experienced success in its space program successfully landing space crews on the moon. In the late 1980s and early 1990s, the Berlin Wall was torn down and Communism fell in the Soviet Union and Eastern Europe. The 15 republics of the former USSR became independent nations with varying degrees of freedom and democracy in government and together formed the Commonwealth of Independent States (CIS). The former Communist nations of Eastern Europe also emphasized their independence with democratic forms of government.

Tremendous progress in communication and transportation has tied all parts of the earth and drawn them closer. There are still vast areas of the former Soviet Union that have unproductive land, extreme poverty, food shortages, rampant diseases, violent friction between cultures, the ever-present nuclear threat, environmental pollution, rapid reduction of natural resources, urban overcrowding, acceleration in global terrorism and violent crimes, and a diminishing middle class.

New technologies have changed the way of life for many. This is the computer age and in many places, computers are even in the grade schools. Technology makes the world seem a much smaller place. Even children have cell phones today. The existence of television and modern technology has us watching a war while it is in progress. Outsourcing is now popular because of technological advances. Call centers for European, American and other large countries are now located in India, Pakistan, etc. Multinational corporations located plants in foreign countries to lower costs.

In many places technology has resulted in a mobile population. Popular culture has been shaped by mass production and the mass media. Mass production and technology has made electronic goods affordable to most. This is the day of the cell phone and the PDA. The Internet and email allow people anywhere in the world to be in touch and allows people to learn about world events. In the industrial countries and in many others, the popular culture is oriented towards the electronic era.

DOMAIN VIII. GOVERNMENT/CIVICS

COMPETENCY 32.0 BASIC POLITICAL CONCEPTS

Skill 32.1 Demonstrate understanding of why government is needed

Historically the functions of government, or people's concepts of government and its purpose and function, have varied considerably. In the theory of political science, the function of government is to secure the common welfare of the members of the given society over which it exercises control. In different historical eras, governments have attempted to achieve the common welfare by various means in accordance with the traditions and ideology of the given society. Among *primitive peoples*, systems of control were rudimentary at best. They arose directly from the ideas of right and wrong that had been established in the group and were common in that particular society. Control being exercised most often by means of group pressure, most often in the forms of taboos and superstitions and in many cases by ostracism, or banishment from the group. Thus, in most cases, because of the extreme tribal nature of society in those early times, this led to very unpleasant circumstances for the individual so treated. Without the protection of the group, a lone individual was most often in for a sad and very short fate. (No other group would accept such an individual into their midst, and survival alone was extremely difficult if not impossible).

Among more *civilized peoples*, governments began to assume more institutional forms. They rested on a well-defined legal basis. They imposed penalties on violators of the social order. They used force, which was supported and sanctioned by their people. The government was charged to establish the social order and was supposed to do so in order to be able to discharge its functions.

Eventually the ideas of government, who should govern and how, came to be considered by various thinkers and philosophers. The most influential of these and those who had the most influence on our present society were the ancient Greek philosophers such as Plato and Aristotle.

Aristotle's conception of government was based on a simple idea. The function of government was to provide for the general welfare of its people. A good government, and one that should be supported, was one that did so in the best way possible, with the least pressure on the people. Bad governments were those that subordinated the general welfare to that of the individuals who ruled. At no time should any function of any government be that of personal interest of any one individual, no matter who that individual was. This does not mean that Aristotle had no sympathy for the individual or individual happiness (as at times Plato has been accused by those who read his "**Republic,**" which was the first important philosophical text to explore these issues). Rather, Aristotle believed that a society is greater than the sum of its parts, or that "the good of the many outweighs the good of the few and also of the one."

Yet, a good government and one that is carrying out its functions well, will always weigh the relative merits of what is good for a given individual in society and what is good for the society as a whole.

This basic concept has continued to our own time and has found its fullest expression in the idea of representative democracy and political and personal freedom. In addition, it is a government that maintains good social order, while allowing the greatest possible exercise of autonomy for individuals to achieve.

Skill 32.2   Demonstrate knowledge of political theory

POLITICAL SCIENCE is the study of political life, different forms of government including elections, political parties, and public administration. In addition, political science studies include values such as justice, freedom, power, and equality. There are six main fields of political-study in the United States:

>   1 Political theory and philosophy,
>   2 Comparative governments,
>   3 International relations,
>   4 Political behavior,
>   5 Public administration, and
>   6 American government and politics.

Some contributors to political theory include:

Aristotle and Plato were Greek philosophers who believed that political order was to be the result of political science and that this political order would ensure maximum justice while at the same time remaining totally stable.

Saint Thomas Aquinas elaborated further on Aristotle's theories and adapted them to Christianity, emphasizing certain duties and rights of individuals in the governmental processes. He also laid emphasis on government rule according to those rights and duties. Aquinas helped lay the foundation of the idea of modern constitutionalism by stating that government was limited by law.

Niccolo Machiavelli was the famous politician from Florence who disregarded the ideals of Christianity in favor of realistic power politics.

Thomas Hobbes whose most famous work was "Leviathan" believed that a person's life was a constant unceasing search for power and believed in the state's supremacy to combat this.

John Locke was one of the most influential political writers of the 17th century who put great emphasis on human rights and put forth the belief that when governments violate those rights, people should rebel. He wrote the famous "Two Treatises of Government" in 1690, which had tremendous influence on political thought in the American colonies and helped shaped the U.S. Constitution and Declaration of Independence.

Montesquieu and Rousseau were proponents of "liberalism," the willingness to change ideas, policies, and proposals to solve current problems. They also believed that individual freedom was just as important as any community's welfare. In his work of 1762, "The Social Contract," Rousseau also described the "general will" leading to Socialism.

David Hume and Jeremy Bentham believed that "the greatest happiness of the greatest number was the goal of politics."

John Stuart Mill wrote extensively of the liberal ideas of his time.

Johann Gottlieb Fichte and Friedrich Hegel were well-known German philosophers who contributed significantly in the 18th century. Johann Gottlieb Fichte and Friedrich Hegel supported a liberalism, which included ideas about nationalism and socialism. Immanuel Kant's liberalism included the idea of universal peace through world organization.

Law is the set of established rules or accepted norms of human conduct in their relationship with other individuals, organizations and institutions. The rule of law recognizes that the authority of the government is to be exercised only within the context and boundaries established by laws that are enacted according to established procedure and publicly disclosed. As a Constitutional government and political system, the basis of all laws and all decisions and enforcement of laws is the U.S. Constitution. The Constitution establishes the process by which law can be written and enacted, the basis by which their legitimacy within the context of the principles documented in the Constitution, and the means of interpretation and enforcement of those laws by the police and the courts.

All federal law begins in the Constitution, which grants the Congress of the U.S. the power to enact laws for certain purposes. These statutes are gathered and published in the United States Code. Since ratification of the Constitution, laws have been enacted that give agencies of the executive branch of government the power to create regulations that carry the force of law. The meaning of these laws and regulations when challenged or questioned is determined by the courts, those decisions then assuming the force of law.

The process by which laws and regulations can be enacted is defined by the Constitution, within the protection of the balance of powers of the branches of government. Laws are introduced, debated, and passed by the Congress of the United States, with both houses of Congress passing the same version of the law. The President of the United States then must sign the law. Once signed, the law is considered enacted and is enforced. Challenges to the constitutionality of the law and questions of interpretation of the law are handled by the federal court system. Each state has the authority to make laws covering anything not reserved to the federal government. These laws cannot negate federal laws.

In order to structure and maintain the functionality of a society and the various safeties of the people, the rule of adherence to the law is considered universal for all who live within the jurisdiction to which laws apply. Failure to adhere to the laws of the state or the nation is punishable under the legal code. Civil disobedience, however, is the refusal to obey certain laws, regulations, or requirements of a government because those laws are believed to be detrimental to the freedom or right of the people to exercise government-guaranteed personal and civil liberties. Civil disobedience, in principle, is nonviolent in the steps taken to resist or refuse to obey these laws. Notable examples of the exercise of civil disobedience have included Henry David Thoreau's refusal to pay taxes in protest against slavery and against the Mexican-American War. Dr Martin Luther King, Jr. led the Civil Rights Movement of the 1960s on the principle and within the established techniques of peaceable civil disobedience.

Skill 32.3 Demonstrate understanding of political concepts such as legitimacy, power, authority, and responsibility

The American nation was founded very much with the idea that the people would have a large degree of autonomy and liberty. The famous maxim "no taxation without representation" was a rallying cry for the Revolution, not only because the people didn't want to suffer the increasingly oppressive series of taxes imposed on them by the British Parliament, but also because the people could not in any way influence the lawmakers in Parliament in regard to those taxes. No American colonist had a seat in Parliament, and no American colonist could vote for members of Parliament.

One of the most famous words in the Declaration of Independence is "**liberty**," the pursuit of which all people should be free to attempt. That idea, that a people should be free to pursue their own course, even to the extent of making their own mistakes, has dominated political thought in the 200-plus years of the American republic.

Another key concept in the American ideal is **equality**, the idea that every person has the same rights and responsibilities under the law. The Great Britain that the American colonists knew was one of a stratified society, with social classes firmly in place. Not everyone was equal under the law or in the coffers; and it was clear for all to see that the more money and power a person had, the easier it was for that person to avoid things like serving in the army and being charged with a crime. The goal of the Declaration of Independence and the Constitution was to provide equality for all who read those documents. The reality, though, was vastly different for large sectors of society, including women and non-white Americans.

This feeds into the idea of basic opportunity. The so-called "American Dream" is that every individual has an equal chance to make his or her fortune in a new land and that the country that is the United States will welcome and even encourage that initiative. The history of the country is filled with stories of people who ventured to America and made their fortunes in the Land of Opportunity. Unfortunately for anyone who wasn't a white male, that basic opportunity was sometimes a difficult thing to achieve.

The political concepts of legitimacy, **power, authority and responsibility** are all inter-related. Legitimacy refers to the moral correctness of political system. If the political system is deemed to be morally correct then it will be accepted by its' citizens. The citizen will agree to obey the laws and rules of that system because the citizen accepts its legitimacy. When the citizens no lower accept the legitimacy of a regime, then the political system is overthrown. This is not the same thing as an election. An election is a part of the political system. Capitalism is a political system with legitimacy. Democracy is a political system with legitimacy. A political system's legitimacy is enhanced when it is recognized or acknowledged by another government.

Political authority refers to the people in the various offices within the political system. Their political authority lies in their ability to coerce people to comply with the wishes of the political system. Their political authority stems from the acceptance of the legitimacy of the political system or the citizens wouldn't accept their ability to coerce.

Political power refers to the ability of those with political authority to do or to influence. If a legitimate representative of the political system doesn't have his orders obeyed, there is always the military to enforce those orders.

Political responsibility is the moral obligation of citizens and government to do the morally correct thing. For example in the case of genocide and other atrocities, the political responsibility is to speak out and fight the atrocities.

There is no such thing as political authority and political power with legitimacy.

Skill 32.4 Demonstrate understanding of various political orientations

In regards to the American political system, it is important to realize that political parties are never mentioned in the United States Constitution. In fact, George Washington himself warned against the creation of "factions" in American politics that cause "jealousies and false alarms" and the damage they could cause to the body politic. Thomas Jefferson echoed this warning, yet he would come to lead a party himself.

Americans had good reason to fear the emergence of political parties. They had witnessed how parties worked in Great Britain. Parties, called "factions" in Britain, thus Washington's warning, were made up of a few people who schemed to win favors from the government. They were more interested in their own personal profit and advantage than in the public good. Thus, the new American leaders were very interested in keeping factions from forming. It was, ironically, disagreements between two of Washington's chief advisors, Thomas Jefferson and Alexander Hamilton that spurred the formation of the first political parties in the newly formed United States of America.

The two parties that developed through the early 1790s were led by Jefferson as the Secretary of State and Alexander Hamilton as the Secretary of the Treasury. Jefferson and Hamilton were different in many ways. Not the least was their views on what should be the proper form of government of the United States. This difference helped to shape the parties that formed around them.

Hamilton wanted the federal government to be stronger than the state governments. Jefferson believed that the state governments should be stronger. Hamilton supported the creation of the first Bank of the United States; Jefferson opposed it because he felt that it gave too much power to wealthy investors who would help run it. Jefferson interpreted the Constitution strictly; he argued that nowhere did the Constitution give the federal government the power to create a national bank. Hamilton interpreted the Constitution much more loosely. He pointed out that the Constitution gave Congress the power to make all laws "necessary and proper" to carry out its duties. He reasoned that since Congress had the right to collect taxes, then Congress had the right to create the bank. Hamilton wanted the government to encourage economic growth. He favored the growth of trade, manufacturing, and the rise of cities as the necessary parts of economic growth. He favored the business leaders and mistrusted the common people. Jefferson believed that the common people, especially the farmers, were the backbone of the nation. He thought that the rise of big cities and manufacturing would corrupt American life.

Finally, Hamilton and Jefferson had their disagreements only in private.

But when Congress began to pass many of Hamilton's ideas and programs, Jefferson and his friend, James Madison, decided to organize support for their own views. They moved quietly and very cautiously in the beginning. In 1791, they went to New York telling people that they were going to just study its wildlife. Actually, Jefferson was more interested in meeting with several important New York politicians such as its governor George Clinton and Aaron Burr, a strong critic of Hamilton. Jefferson asked Clinton and Burr to help defeat Hamilton's program by getting New Yorkers to vote for Jefferson's supporters in the next election. Before long, leaders in other states began to organize support for either Jefferson or Hamilton. Jefferson's supporters called themselves Democratic-Republicans (often this was shortened just to Republicans, though in actuality it was the forerunner of today's Democratic Party, not the Republican). Hamilton and his supporters were known as Federalists, because they favored a strong federal government. The Federalists had the support of the merchants and ship owners in the Northeast and some planters in the South. Small farmers, craft workers, and some of the wealthier landowners supported Jefferson and the Democratic-Republicans.

By the time Washington retired from office in 1796, the new political parties would come to play an important role in choosing his successor. Each party would put up its own candidates for office. The election of 1796 was the first one in which political parties played a role, a role that, for better or worse, they have continued to play in various forms for all of American history. By the beginning of the 1800s, the Federalist Party, torn by internal divisions, began suffering a decline. The election in 1800 saw Thomas Jefferson as President, Hamilton's bitter rival, and after its leader Alexander Hamilton was killed in 1804 in a duel with Aaron Burr, the Federalist Party began to collapse. By 1816, after losing a string of important elections, (Jefferson was reelected in 1804, and James Madison, a Democratic-Republican was elected in 1808), the Federalist Party ceased to be an effective political force and soon passed off the national stage.

By the late 1820s, new political parties had grown up. The **Democratic-Republican** Party, or simply the **Republican** Party, had been the major party for many years, but differences within it about the direction the country was headed in caused a split after 1824. Those who favored strong national growth took the name **Whigs** after a similar party in Great Britain and united around then President John Quincy Adams. Many business people in the Northeast as well as some wealthy planters in the South supported it.

Those who favored slower growth and were more worker and small farmer oriented, went on to form the new Democratic Party, with Andrew Jackson being its first leader as well as becoming the first President from it. It is the forerunner of today's present party of the same name.

In the mid-1850s, the slavery issue was beginning to heat up and in 1854, those opposed to slavery, the Whigs, and some Northern Democrats opposed to slavery, united to form the Republican Party. Before the Civil War, the Democratic Party was more heavily represented in the South and was thus pro-slavery for the most part.

Thus, by the time of the Civil War, the present form of the major political parties had been formed. Though there would sometimes be drastic changes in ideology and platforms over the years, no other political parties would manage to gain enough strength to seriously challenge the "Big Two" parties.

In fact, they have shown themselves adaptable to changing times. In many instances, they have managed to shut out other parties by simply adapting their platforms, such as in the 1930s during the Great Depression and in the years immediately preceding. The Democratic Party adapted much of the Socialist Party platform and, under Franklin Roosevelt, put much of it into effect, thus managing to eliminate it as any serious threat. Since the Civil War, no other political party has managed to gain enough support to either elect substantial members to Congress or elect a President. Some have come closer than others, but barring any unforeseen circumstances, the absolute monopoly on national political debate seems very secure in the hands of the Republican and Democratic parties.

Other political parties existed during this period. The Anti-Masonic Party came into being to oppose the Freemasons who they accused of being a secret society trying to take over the country. The Free Soil Party existed for the 1848 and 1852 elections only. They opposed slavery in the lands acquired from Mexico. The Liberty Party of this period was also abolitionist.

In the mid-1850s, the slavery issue was beginning to heat up and in 1854, those opposed to slavery, the Whigs, and some Northern Democrats opposed to slavery, united to form the Republican Party. Before the Civil War, the Democratic Party was more heavily represented in the South and was thus pro-slavery for the most part. The American Party was called the Know Nothings. They lasted from 1854 to 1858 and were opposed to Irish-Catholic immigration. The Constitution Union Party was formed in 1860. It was made up of entities from other extinguished political powers. They claim to support the Constitution above all and thought this would do away with the slavery issue. The National Union Party of 1864 was formed only for the purpose of the Lincoln election. That was the only reason for its existence.

Other political parties came and went in the post-Civil War era. The Liberal Republican Party formed in 1872 to oppose Ulysses S. Grant. They thought that Grant and his administration were corrupt and sought to displace them. The Anti-Monopoly Party of 1789 was more short-lived than the previous one. It billed itself as progressive and supported things like a graduated income tax system, the direct election of senators, etc. The Greenback Party was formed in 1878 and advocated the use of paper money. The Populist Party was a party consisting mostly of farmers who opposed the gold-standard.

The process of political parties with short life spans continued in the twentieth century. Most of this is due to the fact that these parties come into existence in opposition to some policy or politician. Once the "problem" is gone, so is the party that opposed it. The Farmer-Labor Party was a Minnesota based political party. It supported farmers and labor and social security. It had moderate success in electing officials in Minnesota and merged with the Democratic Party in 1944.The Progressive Party was formed in 1912 due to a rift in the Republican Party that occurred when Theodore Roosevelt lost the nomination. This is not the same as the Progressive Party formed in 1924 to back LaFollette of Wisconsin. The Social Democratic Party was an outgrowth of a social movement and didn't have much political success.

There have also been other parties that have had a short termed life in the years following the Great Depression. The American Labor Party was a socialist party that existed in New York for a while. The American Workers Party was another socialist party based on Marxism. They also were short-lived. The Progressive Party came into being in 1948 to run candidates for President and Vice-President. The Dixiecrats, or States Rights Democratic Party also formed in 1948. They were a splinter group from the Democrats who supported Strom Thurmond. They also supported Wallace 1968. There have been various Workers' Parties that have come and gone. Most of these have had left-wing tendencies.

There are other political parties but they are not as strong as the Republicans and the Democrats. The Libertarian Party represents belief in the free rights of individuals to do as they wish without the interference of government. They favor a small government so propose a much lower level of government spending and services. The Libertarians are the third largest political party in America. The Socialist Party is also a political party. They run candidates in the elections. They favor the establishment of a radical democracy in which people control production and communities for all, not for the benefit of a few. The Communist Party is also a political party advocating very radical changes in American society. They are concerned with the revolutionary struggle and moving through Marx's stages of history. There are many other parties. The American First Party is a conservative party as is the American Party. The American Nazi Party is also active in politics. Preaching fascism, they run candidates for elections and occasionally win. The Constitution Party is also representative of conservative views.

The Reform Party was founded by Ross Perot after his bid for President as an independent. The list goes on and on. Many of these parties are regional and small and not on the national scene. Many of them form for a purpose, such as an election, and then dwindle.

Time will tell if the Republicans and Democrats remain the "Big Two." History and political science both teach us that the American people are quite willing to change their support from one area or group to another, especially if it means a better way of doing things or will give them more opportunity and freedoms. As conservative as some might think Americans have become, there has always been and always will be, something of the revolutionary spirit about them.

COMPETENCY 33.0 UNITED STATES POLITICAL SYSTEM

Skill 33.1 Demonstrate understanding of the constitutional foundation of the United States government, including knowledge of the basic content and structure of the United States Constitution, and of the processes of constitutional interpretation and amendment

The Magna Carta - This charter has been considered the basis of English constitution liberties. It was granted to a representative group of English barons and nobles on *June 15, 1215* by the British King John, after they had forced it on him. The English barons and nobles sought to limit what they had come to perceive as the overwhelming power of the Monarchy in public affairs. The Magna Carta is considered to be the first modern document that sought to try to limit the powers of the given state authority. It guaranteed feudal rights, regulated the justice system, and abolished many abuses of the King's power to tax and regulate trade. It said that the king could not raise new taxes without first consulting a Great Council, made up of nobles, barons, and Church people. Significantly, the Magna Carta dealt only with the rights of the upper classes of the nobility, and all of its provisions excluded the rights of the common people. However, gradually the rights won by the nobles were given to other English people.

The Great Council grew into a representative assembly called the Parliament. By the 1600s, Parliament was divided into the House of Lords, made up of nobles and the House of Commons. Members of the House of Commons were elected to office. In the beginning, only a few wealthy men could vote. Still English people firmly believed that the ruler must consult Parliament on money matters and obey the law. Thus, it did set a precedent that there was a limit to the allowed power of the state. A precedent, which would have no small effect on the history of political revolution, is notably the American Revolution.

The Petition of Right - In English history, it was the title of a petition that was addressed to the King of England *Charles I,* by the British parliament in **1628**. The Parliament demanded that the king stop proclaiming new taxes without its consent. Parliament demanded that he cease housing soldiers and sailors in the homes of private citizens, proclaiming martial law in times of peace, and that no subject should be imprisoned without a good cause being shown. After some attempts to circumvent these demands, Charles finally agreed to them. They later had an important effect on the demands of the revolutionary colonists, as these were some of the rights that as Englishmen, they felt were being denied to them. The Petition of Right was also the basis of specific protections that the designers of the Constitution made a point of inserting in the document.

British Bill of Rights - Also known as the **Declaration of Rights**, it spelled out the rights that were considered to belong to Englishmen. It was granted by **King William III** in 1869. It had previously been passed by a convention of the Parliament and it came out of the struggle for power that took place in Great Britain and at that time was known as **The Glorious Revolution**. It was known as a revolution that was accomplished with virtually no bloodshed and led to King William III and Queen Mary II becoming joint sovereigns.

The Declaration itself was very similar in style to the later American Bill of Rights. It protected the rights of individuals and gave anyone accused of a crime the right to trial by jury. It outlawed cruel punishments; also, it stated that a ruler could not raise taxes or an army without the consent of Parliament. The colonists as Englishmen were protected by these provisions. The colonists considered abridgments of these rights that helped to contribute to the revolutionary spirit of the times.

All of these events and the principles that arose from them are of the utmost importance in understanding the process that eventually led to the ideals that are inherent in the Constitution of the United States. In addition, the fact is that all of these ideals are universal in nature and have become the basis for the idea of human freedoms throughout the world.

In the United States, checks and balances refers to the ability of each branch of government (Executive, Legislative, and Judicial) to "check" or limit the actions of the others. Examples of checks and balances would be the Executive branch limits the Legislature by power of veto over bills and appointments in the court system. The Judicial branch limits the power of the Legislature by judicial review and the ability to rule laws unconstitutional and may also determine executive orders unconstitutional. The Legislature checks the Executive by power of impeachment.

Eleven states finally ratified the document, and the new national government went into effect. It was no small feat that the delegates were able to produce a workable document that satisfied all opinions, feelings, and viewpoints. The separation of powers of the three branches of government and the built-in system of checks and balances to keep power balanced were a stroke of genius.

It provided for the individuals and the states as well as an organized central authority to keep a new inexperienced young nation on track. They created a system of government so flexible that it has continued in its basic form to this day. In 1789, the Electoral College unanimously elected George Washington as the first President, and the new nation was on its way.

The Declaration of Independence is an outgrowth of both ancient Greek ideas of democracy and individual rights and the ideas of the European Enlightenment and the Renaissance, especially the ideology of the political thinker **John Locke**. Thomas Jefferson (1743-1826), the principal author of the Declaration, borrowed much from Locke's theories and writings.

Essentially, Jefferson applied Locke's principles to the contemporary American situation. Jefferson argued that the currently reigning King George III had repeatedly violated the rights of the colonists as subjects of the British Crown. Disdaining the colonial petition for redress of grievances (a right guaranteed by the Declaration of Rights of 1689), the King seemed bent on establishing an "absolute tyranny" over the colonies. Such disgraceful behavior itself violated the reasons for which government had been instituted. The American colonists were left with no choice, *"it is their right, it is their duty, to throw off such a government, and to provide new guards for their future security,"* wrote Thomas Jefferson. Yet, though his fundamental principles were derived from Locke's, Jefferson was bolder than his intellectual mentor was. He went farther in that his view of natural rights was much broader than Locke's and less tied to the idea of property rights.

For instance, though both Jefferson and Locke believed very strongly in property rights, especially as a guard for individual liberty, the famous line in the Declaration about people being endowed with the inalienable right to "life, liberty and the pursuit of happiness," was originally Locke's idea. It was "life, liberty, and *private property."* Jefferson didn't want to tie the idea of rights to any one particular circumstance however; thus, he changed Locke's original specific reliance on property and substituted the more general idea of human happiness as being a fundamental right that is the duty of a government to protect.

Locke and Jefferson both stressed that the individual citizen's rights are prior to and more important than any obligation to the state. Government is the servant of the people. The officials of government hold their positions at the sufferance of the people. Their job is to ensure that the rights of the people are preserved and protected by that government. The citizens come first, the government comes second. The Declaration thus produced turned out to be one of the most important and historic documents that expounded the inherent rights of all peoples; it is a document still looked up to as an ideal and an example.

An amendment is a change or addition to the United States Constitution. Two-thirds of both houses of Congress must propose and then pass one. Or two-thirds of the state legislatures must call a convention to propose one and then it must be ratified by three-fourths of the state legislatures.

To date there are only 27 amendments to the Constitution that have passed. An amendment may be used to cancel out a previous one, such as the 18th Amendment (1919) known as Prohibition, canceled by the 21st Amendment (1933). Amending the United States Constitution is an extremely difficult thing to do.

An **amendment** must start in Congress. One or more lawmakers propose it, and then each house votes on it in turn. The Amendment must have the support of two-thirds of each house separately in order to progress on its path into law. (It should be noted here that this two-thirds need be only two-thirds of a quorum, which is just a simple majority.

Thus, it is theoretically possible for an Amendment to be passed and be legal even though it has been approved by less than half of one or both houses.)

The final and most difficult step for an Amendment is the ratification of state legislatures. A total of three-fourths of those must approve the Amendment. Approvals there need be only a simple majority, but the number of states that must approve the Amendment is 38. Hundreds of Amendments have been proposed through the years, but only 27 have become part of the Constitution.

A key element in some of those failures has been the time limit that Congress has the option to put on Amendment proposals. A famous example of an Amendment that got close but didn't reach the threshold before the deadline expired was the Equal Rights Amendment, which was proposed in 1972 but which couldn't muster enough support for passage, even though its deadline was extended from seven to 10 years.

The first ten Amendments are called the Bill of Rights and were approved at the same time, shortly after the Constitution was ratified. The 11th and 12th Amendments were ratified around the turn of the 19th Century and, respectively, voided foreign suits against states and revised the method of presidential election. The 13th, 14th, and 15th Amendments were passed in succession after the end of the Civil War. Slavery was outlawed by the 13th Amendment. The 14th & 15th Amendments provided for equal protection and for voting rights, respectively, without consideration of skin color.

The first 20th Century Amendment was Number 16, which provided for a federal income tax. Providing for direct election to the Senate was the 17th Amendment. (Before this, Senators were appointed by state leaders, not elected by the public at large.)

The 18th Amendment prohibited the use or sale of alcohol across the country. The long battle for voting rights for women ended in success with the passage of the 19th Amendment. The date for the beginning of terms for the President and the Congress was changed from March to January by the 20th Amendment.

With the 21st Amendment came the only instance in which an Amendment was repealed. In this case, it was the 18th Amendment and its prohibition of alcohol consumption or sale.

The 22nd Amendment limited the number of terms that a President could serve to two. Presidents since George Washington had followed Washington's practice of not running for a third term; this changed when Franklin D. Roosevelt ran for re-election a second time, in 1940. He was re-elected that time and a third time, too, four years later. He didn't live out his fourth term, but he did convince Congress and most of the state legislature that some sort of term limit should be in place.

The little-known 23rd Amendment provided for representation of Washington, D.C., in the Electoral College. The 24th Amendment prohibited poll taxes, which people had had to pay in order to vote.

Presidential succession is the focus of the 25th Amendment, which provides a blueprint of what to do if the president is incapacitated or killed. The 26th Amendment lowered the legal voting age for Americans from 21 to 18. The final Amendment, the 27th, prohibits members of Congress from substantially raising their own salaries. This Amendment was one of 12 originally proposed in the late 18th Century. Ten of those 12 became the Bill of Rights, and one has yet to become law.

A host of potential Amendments have made news headlines in recent years. A total of six Amendments have been proposed by Congress and passed muster in both houses but have not been ratified by enough state legislatures. The aforementioned Equal Rights Amendment is one. Another one, which would grant the District of Columbia full voting rights equivalent to states, has not passed; like the Equal Rights Amendment, its deadline has expired. A handful of others remain on the books without expiration dates, including an amendment to regulate child labor.

The Bill of Rights consists of the first ten Amendments to the U.S. Constitution. These amendments were passed almost immediately upon ratification of the Constitution by the states. They reflect the concerns that were raised throughout the country and by the Founding Fathers during the ratification process. These Amendments reflect the fears and concerns of the people that the power and authority of the government be restricted from denying or limiting the rights of the people of the nation. The experiences of the founders of the nation as colonists formed the foundation of the concern to limit the power of government.

The Bill of Rights has been interpreted in different ways at different times by different interpreters. These, and other, Constitutional Amendments may be interpreted very strictly or very loosely. The terms of the amendments may be defined in different ways to enfranchise or to disenfranchise individuals or groups of persons.

1. Freedom of Religion.
2. Right To Bear Arms.
3. Security from the quartering of troops in homes.
4. Right against unreasonable search and seizures.
5. Right against self-incrimination.
6. Right to trial by jury, right to legal council.
7. Right to jury trial for civil actions.
8. No cruel or unusual punishment allowed.
9. These rights shall not deny other rights the people enjoy.
10. Powers not mentioned in the Constitution shall be retained by the states or the people.

Skill 33.2 **Demonstrate knowledge of the functions and powers of the legislative, executive, and judicial branches of government, and of the relationships among them**

In the United States, the three branches of the federal government mentioned earlier, the **Executive**, the **Legislative**, and the **Judicial**, divide up their powers thus:

Legislative – Article 1 of the Constitution established the legislative, or law-making branch of the government called the Congress. It is made up of two houses, the House of Representatives and the Senate. Voters in all states elect the members who serve in each respective House of Congress. The legislative branch is responsible for making laws, raising and printing money, regulating trade, establishing the postal service and federal courts, approving the President's appointments, declaring war and supporting the armed forces. The Congress also has the power to change the Constitution itself, and to *impeach* (bring charges against) the President. Charges for impeachment are brought by the House of Representatives and are then tried in the Senate.

Executive – Article 2 of the Constitution created the Executive branch of the government, headed by the President, who leads the country, recommends new laws, and can veto bills passed by the legislative branch. As the chief of state, the President is responsible for carrying out the laws of the country and the treaties and declarations of war passed by the legislative branch. The President also appoints federal judges and is commander-in-chief of the military when it is called into service. Other members of the Executive branch include the Vice-President, also elected, and various cabinet members as he might appoint: ambassadors, presidential advisors, members of the armed forces, and other appointed and civil servants of government agencies, departments and bureaus. Though the President appoints them, they must be approved by the legislative branch.

Judicial – Article 3 of the Constitution established the judicial branch of government headed by the Supreme Court. The Supreme Court has the power to rule that a law passed by the legislature or an act of the Executive branch is illegal and unconstitutional.

Citizens, businesses, and government officials can, in an appeal capacity, ask the Supreme Court to review a decision made in a lower court if someone believes that the ruling by a judge is unconstitutional. The Judicial branch also includes lower federal courts known as federal district courts that have been established by the Congress. These courts try lawbreakers and review cases referred from other courts.

Skill 33.3 **Demonstrate knowledge of the formation and operation of political institutions not established by the Constitution, such as political parties and interest groups, and of the role of the media and public opinion in American political life**

From the earliest days of political expression in America, efforts were a collaborative affair. One of the first of the democratic movements was the **Sons of Liberty**, an organization that made its actions known but kept the identity of its members a secret. Famous members of this group included John and Samuel Adams. Other patriotic movements sprang up after the success of the Sons of Liberty was assured, and the overall struggle against British oppression was a collaborative effort involving thousands of people throughout the American colonies.

American political discussion built on the example of the British Parliament, which had two houses of its legislative branch of government containing representatives who had great debates on public policy before making laws. Although this process isn't anywhere near as wide open and public and spirited as it is today, the lawmakers nonetheless had their chance to make their views known on the issues of the day. Some laws, like those implementing the infamous taxes following the British and American victory in the French and Indian War, required relatively little debate, since they were so popular and were obviously wanted by the Prime Minister and other heads of the government. Other laws enjoyed spirited debate and took months to pass.

The Assemblies of the American colonies inherited this tradition and enjoyed spirited debate as well, even though they met just one or a few times a year. One of the most famous examples of both collaboration and deliberation was the Stamp Act Congress, a gathering of fed-up Americans who drafted resolutions demanding that Great Britain repeal the unpopular tax on paper and documents. The Americans who met at both of the Continental Congresses and the Constitutional Convention built on this tradition as well.

Thanks to the voluminous notes taken diligently by James Madison, we have a clear record of just how contentious at times the debate over the shape and scope of the American federal government was. Still, every interest was advanced, every argument put forward, and every chance given to repeal the main points of the government document. The result was a blueprint for government approved by the vast majority of the delegates and eventually approved by people in all of the American colonies.

This ratification process has continued throughout the history of the country, through passage by both houses of Congress to ratification by state legislatures and finally to approval by a majority of the people of a majority of states.

With this sometimes spirited and sometimes virulent debate have come countless opportunities to influence that debate. Even in the earliest times, people having special interests were trying to influence political debates in their favor. Plenty of people who favored a strong central government or its opposite, a weak central government, could be found who were not delegates to the Constitutional Convention. No doubt these people were in communication with the delegates.

Also developing at this time were the nation's first political parties, the Federalists and the Democratic-Republicans. It wasn't elected officials who were members of these political parties, although those elected officials were the most famous members. The people who joined these political parties wanted to see their political interests protected and were sometimes very effective in making sure that the people that they voted for did the things that they were elected to do. As the nation grew, so did the number of political parties and so did the number of people who were pursuing the so-called "special interests." Actually, a special interest is nothing more than a subject that a person or people who pursue one issue above all others. As more and more people gained more and more money, they began to pressure their lawmakers more and more to pass laws that favored their interests. Exporters of goods from ports to destinations overseas would not want to see heavy taxes on such exports. People who owned large amounts of land wouldn't want to see a sharp increase in property taxes. The list goes on and on. These special interests can be found today. These days, it's just more money and more ways to influence lawmakers that distinguish special interest pursuits from those made in years past. So, too, can we draw a straight line from the deliberative-collaborative traditions of today to the secret meetings and political conventions of colonial days.

Americans are free and encouraged to join non-business organizations both public and private. America is a land full of groups—religious groups, political groups, social groups, and economic groups. All these groups meet in public and in private, and the people who belong to these groups are free to associate with any groups that they choose, again as long as the practices of those groups are not illegal or harmful to other people.

Social groups are encouraged as well. The First Amendment gives the American people the right to peaceable assembly. This certainly describes the meetings of most social organizations in America, from clubs to interest groups to veterans organizations. Groups, made up of people with similar interests or experiences, may come together on a regular basis to discuss those interests and experiences and to pursue a joint appreciation. So long as those people in those groups assemble peacefully and don't become violent or speak out in the name of fomenting rebellion, they can go on meeting as often as they like.

One very public interest that many people pursue is politics. Theoretically, anyone who is a U.S. citizen can get on a ballot *somewhere* running for *something*. Participation in politics is encouraged in America and more and more people are getting involved—at the local, state, and federal levels—all the time. The federal and state governments, in particular, will provide money and opportunities for candidates who reach certain thresholds of monetary support of their own

If there's one thing that drives American politics more than any other, it's money. Much more often than not, the candidate who has the most money at his or her disposal has the best chance of getting or keeping political office. Money can buy so many things that are necessary to a successful campaign that is entirely indispensable. Money drives the utilization of every other factor in the running of a campaign. First and foremost, money is needed to pay the people who will run a candidate's campaign. A candidate cannot expect people to give up, in some cases, years of their lives without monetary compensation. Volunteers on a political campaign are plentiful, but they are not at the top levels. The faithful lieutenants of a campaign are paid performers. Money is also needed to buy or rent all of the tangible and intangible *things* that are needed to power a political campaign: office supplies, meeting places, transportation vehicles, and many more. The inventory of these items can add up frighteningly quickly, and money can appear to disappear like water down a drain.

Of course, the expense that gets the most exposure these days is **media advertising**, specifically television advertising. This is the most expensive kind of advertising, but it also has the potential to reach the widest audience. TV ad prices can run into the hundreds of thousands of dollars, depending on when they run; but they have the potential to reach perhaps millions of viewers. Here, too, money can disappear quickly. A political campaign is also a fashion show and candidates cannot afford to go without showing their friendly faces to as wide an audience as possible on a regular basis. Other forms of advertising include radio and Web ads, signs and billboards, and good old-fashioned flyers.

The sources of all this money that is needed to run a successful political campaign are varied. A candidate might have a significant amount of money in his or her own personal coffers. In rare cases, the candidate finances the entire campaign. However, the most prevalent source of money is outside donations. A candidate's friends and family might donate funds to the campaign, as well as the campaign workers themselves. State and federal governments will also contribute to most regional or national campaigns, provided that the candidate can prove that he or she can raise a certain amount of money first. The largest source of campaign finance money, however, comes from so-called "special interests." A large company such as an oil company or a manufacturer of electronic goods will want to keep prices or tariffs down and so will want to make sure that laws lifting those prices or tariffs aren't passed.

To this end, the company will contribute money to the campaigns of candidates who are likely to vote to keep those prices or tariffs down. A candidate is not obligated to accept such a donation, of course, and further is not obligated to vote in favor of the interests of the special interest; however, doing the former might create a shortage of money and doing the latter might ensure that no further donations come from that or any other special interest. An oil company wants to protect its interests, and its leaders don't very much care which political candidate is doing that for them as long as it is being done.

Another powerful source of support for a political campaign is **special interest groups** of a political nature. These are not necessarily economic powers but rather groups whose people want to effect political change (or make sure that such change doesn't take place, depending on the status of the laws at the time). A good example of a special interest group is an anti-abortion group or a pro-choice group. The abortion issue is still a divisive one in American politics, and many groups will want to protect or defend or ban—depending on which side they're on—certain rights and practices. An anti-abortion group, for example, might pay big money to candidates who pledge to work against laws that protect the right for women to have abortions. As long as these candidates continue to assure their supporters that they will keep on fighting the fight, the money will continue to flow. This kind of social group usually has a large number of dedicated individuals who do much more than vote: They organize themselves into political action committees, attend meetings and rallies, and work to make sure that their message gets out to a wide audience. Methods of spreading the word often include media advertising on behalf of their chosen candidates. This kind of expenditure is no doubt welcomed by the candidates, who will get the benefit of the exposure but won't have to spend that money because someone else is signing the checks.

A free press is essential to maintaining responsibility and civic-mindedness in government and in the rest of society. The broadcast, print, and electronic media in America serve as societal and governmental watchdogs, showcasing for the rest of America and for the world what kinds of brilliant and terrible things the rich, powerful, and elected are doing.

First and foremost, the media report on the actions taken and encouraged by leaders of the government. In many cases, these actions are common knowledge. Policy debates, discussions on controversial issues, struggles against foreign powers in economic and wartime endeavors—all are fodder for media reports. The First Amendment guarantees media in America the right to report on these things, and the media reporters take full advantage of that right and privilege in striving not only to inform the American public but also to keep the governmental leaders in check.

The most extreme kind of action that needs reporting on is an illegal one. Officials who perform illegal actions will, in most cases, find those actions part of the public record. These officials are expected to be models of society or, at the very least, following the very laws that they were elected to pass or erase. This is largely a trust issue as well: If you can't trust your elected leaders, who can you trust? Many people would answer that question with the skeptical, "No one can be trusted, especially those in government." Others would say, more simply, that greater scrutiny is needed for those in legislative power, since they are more easily able to hide questionable actions. No one is above the law, especially those charged with making those laws. If a lawmaker thinks that he or she is above the law, then in most cases he or she will be sadly mistaken to discover that that assumption is incorrect. In the vast majority of cases, lawmakers who break the law in a big way are caught and informed on, especially because of reporting done by newspapers, radio stations, magazines, and websites.

The flip side of this is that lawmakers often do positive, noteworthy, and newsworthy things that should be reported on as well. The official who spearheads a campaign to get a certain wide-ranging bill passed will want to take the appropriate credit for those efforts, making his actions known to the media so those actions can be reported to his or her constituents. It's the scandals and jail terms that get most of the screaming headlines in mass media today, but praise-worthy actions are no less important in a national understanding of who the lawmakers are and why they take the actions that they do.

Owners of large companies and charities and especially recognizable figures in popular entertainment are continually under scrutiny for signs of questionable actions or behavior. In the same way that lawmakers are responsible for public legislative policy, many company owners are responsible for public economic policy. If a corporation is stealing money from its employees or shareholders, then those employees and shareholders and the American public at large need to know about it. Such reporting is not only informative but also usually leads to indictments, prosecutions, and jail terms for the perpetrators of such economic crimes.

One time when a free press isn't exactly a good idea, however, is when a country is at war. Troop movements and battle plans aren't the sort of thing that need to be broadcast. Such broadcasts have a way of making their way into the hands of the very people that the country's armed forces are attempting to defeat on the battlefield. (An excellent example of this was seen by all in the lead up and prosecution of the Gulf War, when Iraqi leader Saddam Hussein and his allies and followers kept up with Allied actions by watching CNN.) The government, and especially its armed forces, has the right to refuse to provide information that is vital to national security. This right has been validated time and again by the U.S. Supreme Court and is the law of the land.

Of course, the key word in all of this is *free*. American media reporters are *free* to report on such things as lawmakers' actions (good or bad), company owners' practices (good or bad), and goings-on at the local country club or American Legion house because the Constitution—specifically, the First Amendment—guarantees them the right to do so. This freedom of reporting is a right that is enjoyed by reporters in other countries, to varying degrees. In other countries, most notably China these days, reporters are *not* free to report on everything they see, especially things that the government does not want its people to know. If such reporting is banned, then the government can conceivably conduct all sorts of illegal transactions or escapades without fear of those actions being exposed by the mainstream media. If a country's citizens do not have a handle on how badly their government is behaving on the world stage, then they have no basis for demanding that things change.

It was this idea, after all, which was at the heart of the American Revolution—the idea that a people could stand up and say that they had had enough of their government and its leaders and their actions.

Public officials have an overwhelming need to communicate. They want other people to know what they're doing and why. They want to make sure that the voters who elected know what great jobs they're doing pursuing the agendas that are closest to their hearts. Ultimately, they want to do as much as they can to get themselves re-elected or, if terms limit won't allow such re-election, to leave a memorable public legacy.

This is the key thing to remember if you are reading things on Web pages: They might not have undergone the same sort of scrutiny as comparable efforts released by major media outlets to newspapers, radio, and television. Those media processes have built-in safety measures called editors who will verify information before it is released to the wide world; to be a blogger, all you need is access to a Web-enabled computer and time to write a column. Bloggers routinely do not use editors or run their copy by anyone else before publishing it; as such, they have lower standards of professionalism overall and need to be regarded as such. What they write might be totally true; the blog, however, is known as a *log*, a chronicle of thoughts and opinions about the affairs of the day, not so much a blow-by-blow of facts and figures.

Public officials will hire one or more people or perhaps a whole department or an entire business to conduct **public relations**, which are efforts intended to make the lawmakers look good in the eyes of their constituents. A public relations person or firm will have as its overreaching goal the happiness of the lawmaker who hired her or them and will gladly write press releases, arrange media events (like tours of schools or soup kitchens), and basically do everything else to keep their employer's name in the public eye in a good way. This includes making the lawmaker's position on important issues known to the public.

Especially controversial issues will be embraced on the other side by lawmakers, and those lawmakers will want their constituents to know how they intend to vote those issues. It's also a good idea to find out what your constituents think about these issues of the day, since the fastest way to get yourself bad publicity or thrown out at re-election time is to ignore the weight of public opinion.

Another inherent part of the public official-media relationship is the need to appear to be open and above-board. Even if a politician isn't forthcoming with all the details of what he is doing, he or she needs to look like that is what is happening. A lawmaker who communicates with the public is one who appears to be on the level, since an absence of information seems to imply guilt or complicity in the minds of many people. To this end, lawmakers will go out of their way to make their actions, intentions, and political views known to the people who will vote for them and support them by sending them money.

All of these things are true as well for potential lawmakers who are running for office against those already in office. Since incumbents can often call on the "weight of the office" to give them free publicity just for doings thing like voting on bills or attending local ribbon-cutting or other public functions, challengers routinely face an uphill battle to get their names, views, and deeds into the public debate and will work extra hard to do so.

On the other side of the coin, members of the media will want the public to know what their lawmakers are saying and doing. Many reporters and editors consider it in the best interest of the country to report on the dealings and actions of those in government, especially if those dealings or actions are of a questionable legal or moral nature. It works both ways, and the smart politicians understand the nature of that dichotomy and use it to their advantage.

Skill 33.4 Demonstrate understanding of the relationship among federal, state, and local governments

Powers delegated to the federal government	Powers reserved to the states:
1. To tax.	1. To regulate intrastate trade.
2. To borrow and coin money	2. To establish local governments.
3. To establish postal service.	3. To protect general welfare.
4. To grant patents and copyrights.	4. To protect life and property.
5. To regulate interstate & foreign commerce.	5. To ratify amendments.
6. To establish courts.	6. To conduct elections.
7. To declare war.	7. To make state and local laws.
8. To raise and support the armed forces.	
9. To govern territories.	
10. To define and punish felonies and piracy on the high seas.	
11. To fix standards of weights and measures.	
12. To conduct foreign affairs.	

Concurrent powers of the federal government and states.

1. Both Congress and the states may tax.
2. Both may borrow money.
3. Both may charter banks and corporations.
4. Both may establish courts.
5. Both may make and enforce laws.
6. Both may take property for public purposes.
7. Both may spend money to provide for the public welfare.

Implied powers of the federal government.

1. To establish banks or other corporations, implied from delegated powers to tax, borrow, and to regulate commerce.
2. To spend money for roads, schools, health, insurance, etc. implied from powers to establish post roads, to tax to provide for general welfare and defense, and to regulate commerce.
3. To create military academies, implied from powers to raise and support an armed force.
4. To locate and generate sources of power and sell surplus, implied from powers to dispose of government property, commerce, and war powers.
5. To assist and regulate agriculture, implied from power to tax and spend for general welfare and regulate commerce.

Skill 33.5 Demonstrate understanding of political behavior at both the individual and group levels, including elections and other forms of political participation

The most basic way for citizens to participate in the political process is to vote. Since the passing of the 23rd Amendment in 1965, US citizens who are at least 18 years old are eligible to vote. Elections are held at regular intervals at all levels of government, allowing citizens to weigh in on local matters as well as those of national scope.

The sad reality for most Americans is that they don't play a large role in governmental decision-making, except perhaps at the local level. Only there, in the towns and cities in which they live, can they afford the time and money to personally lobby their lawmakers in the name of passage or defeat of laws. At the state and the national level, the country is just too big for one poor person to have much of a difference individually. Where people make a difference at the higher levels is in joining political parties and, more importantly, citizen action groups or political action committees. Only in the larger numbers that make up these groups can individual people make a difference in government. In such cases, however, people tend to lose their individual voices and are more easily swayed by the will of their peers.

Citizens wishing to engage in the political process to a greater degree have several paths open, such as participating in local government. Counties, states, and sometimes neighborhoods are governed by locally elected boards or councils, which meet publicly. Citizens are usually able to address these boards, bringing their concerns and expressing their opinions on matters being considered. Citizens may even wish to stand for local election and join a governing board, or seek support for higher office.

This is not to say that the avenues of lobbying lawmakers are closed to the average American. Letters are still read, phone calls are still taken, and donations are still appreciated. More cutting-edge methods of communication include e-mail, FAX, and SMS. Personal office visits are definitely appreciated as well. If enough people write or call or visit their lawmakers and say the same thing, those lawmakers will listen. That's why it's still important for people to speak out, not only to their neighbors but also their elected officials. And of course, the ultimate way of expressing one's political views is to elect or oust a lawmaker through the power of the ballot.

This kind of open access and potentially direct role in the political decision-making of the country has not always been with us, though. In the early days of the American colonies, the British settlers could disagree all they wanted with the kind of policies, laws, and taxes that were being impressed on them by the Parliament across the Atlantic. The settlers also couldn't very well decide who their colonial governors were. The British Government appointed those officials.

Supporting a political party is another means by which citizens can participate in the political process. Political parties endorse certain platforms that express general social and political goals, and support member candidates in election campaigns. Political parties make use of much volunteer labor, with supporters making telephone calls, distributing printed material and campaigning for the party's causes and candidates. Political parties solicit donations to support their efforts as well. Contributing money to a political party is another form of participation citizens can undertake.

Another form of political activity is to support an issue-related political group. Several political groups work actively to sway public opinion on various issues or on behalf of a segment of American society. These groups may have representatives who meet with state and federal legislators to "lobby" them - to provide them with information on an issue and persuade them to take favorable action.

The colonies weren't totally void of representative government, though. Beginning in 1619, the Virginia colony had such an entity, the House of Burgesses. This was one of the most famous governing bodies in colonial American history. Among its members over time were some of the shining lights of the American Revolution, including George Washington, Thomas Jefferson, James Madison, and Patrick Henry. It was Henry who introduced the resolutions that ultimately resulted in the repeal of the dreaded Stamp Act, the devastating tax on paper goods.

The people of Virginia elected a total of 15 of the 22 members of the House of Burgesses. (The governor, of course, was appointed.) The Burgesses could make laws, and the governor could veto them. The Burgesses also met just once a year. But the elements of representative government were there.

Other lawmaking bodies followed. Generally, each colony had one. They had various names; most were called the Assembly. As with the Virginia House of Burgesses, these Assemblies met just once a year and dealt with financial matters, like taxes and budgets. The governor, however, had the power to dissolve the Assembly, keeping it from meeting even once, which was done relatively frequently during the months leading up to the Revolutionary War.

Representative is a relative term, however. Although it is true that the Assembly had members who were voted in by their peers, those peers were *true* peers in the sense that they all looked exactly like. Serving in government and voting for those who did was limited to white, property-owning males. Women couldn't vote or even own property. African-American men and women certainly could do either of those things, even if they weren't enslaved. It's one thing to say that the members of the Burgesses or Assembly were elected by *the people*; it's another thing entirely to say that *the people* included *everyone in the colonies*.

Still, the cry for representation was a key rallying point of the Revolution and the War to preserve it, and eventually the Colonial Army had its day in the sun. The Constitution was a blueprint of a representative government such that the world had never seen. The reality, though, was still that white, property-owning males were the ones doing the voting and the legislating.

One holdover from the colonial appointing days was that Senators, who made up the upper house of Government, were appointed by the Legislature of each state. This practice lasted until the passage of the Twelfth Amendment, in the early 19th Century. African-American men, however, had to wait to vote and run for office until the Fourteenth Amendment, ratified in 1868, and women of any color had to wait until the 20th Century to vote for nationwide office.

A person who lives in a democratic society theoretically has an entire laundry list guaranteed to him or her by the government. In the United States, this is the Constitution and its Amendments. Among these very important rights are:

- the right to speak out in public;
- the right to pursue any religion;
- the right for a group of people to gather in public for *any* reason that doesn't fall under a national security cloud;
- the right *not* to have soldiers stationed in your home;
- the right *not* to be forced to testify against yourself in a court of law;
- the right to a speedy and public trial by a jury of your peers;
- the right *not* to the victim of cruel and unusual punishment;
- and the right to avoid unreasonable search and seizure of your person, your house, and your vehicle.

The average citizen of an authoritarian country has little if any of these rights and must watch his or her words, actions, and even magazine subscriptions and Internet visits in order to avoid *the appearance* of disobeying one of the many oppressive laws that help the government govern its people.

Both the democratic-society and the authoritarian-society citizens can serve in government. They can even run for election and can be voted in by their peers. One large difference exists, however: In an authoritarian society, the members of government will most likely be of the same political party. A country with this setup, like China, will have a government that includes representatives elected by the Chinese people, but all of those elected representatives will belong to the Communist Party, which runs the government and the country. When the voters vote, they see only Communist Party members on the ballot. in fact, in many cases, only one candidate is on the ballot for each office. China, in fact, chooses its head of government through a meeting of the Party leaders. In effect, the Party is higher in the governmental hierarchy than the leader of the country. Efforts to change this governmental structure and practice are clamped down and discouraged.

On the other side of this spectrum is the citizen of the democratic society, who can vote for whomever he or she wants to and can run for any office he or she wants to. On those ballots will appear names and political parties that run the spectrum, including the Communist Party. Theoretically, *any* political party can get its candidates on ballots locally, statewide, or nationwide; varying degrees of effort have to be put in to do this, of course. Building on the First Amendment freedom to peacefully assembly, American citizens can have political party meetings, fund-raisers, and even conventions without fearing reprisals from the Government.

COMPETENCY 34.0 OTHER FORMS OF GOVERNMENT

Skill 34.1 Demonstrate understanding of the structures of various forms of government

Parliamentary System - A system of government with a legislature, usually involving a multiplicity of political parties and often coalition politics. There is division between the head of state and head of government. Head of government is usually known as a Prime Minister who is also usually the head of the largest party. The head of government and cabinet usually both sit and vote in the parliament. Head of state is most often an elected president (though in the case of a constitutional monarchy, like Great Britain, the sovereign may take the place of a president as head of state). A government may fall when a majority in parliament votes "no confidence" in the government.

Anarchism - Political movement believing in the elimination of all government and its replacement by a cooperative community of individuals. Sometimes it has involved political violence such as assassinations of important political or governmental figures. The historical banner of the movement is a black flag.

Communism - A belief as well as a political system, characterized by the ideology of class conflict and revolution, one party state and dictatorship, repressive police apparatus, and government ownership of the means of production and distribution of goods and services. A revolutionary ideology preaching the eventual overthrow of all other political orders and the establishment of one world Communist government.   Same as Marxism. The historical banner of the movement is a red flag and variation of stars, hammer and sickles, representing the various types of workers.

Dictatorship - The rule by an individual or small group of individuals (Oligarchy) that centralizes all political control in itself and enforces its will with a terrorist police force.

Fascism - A belief as well as a political system, opposed ideologically to Communism, though similar in basic structure, with a one party state, centralized political control and a repressive police system. It however tolerates private ownership of the means of production, though it maintains tight overall control. Central to its belief is the idolization of the Leader, a "Cult of the Personality," and most often an expansionist ideology. Examples have been German Nazism and Italian Fascism. (See: Fascism, Section 5.4)

Monarchy - The rule of a nation by a Monarch, (a non-elected usually hereditary leader), most often a king, or queen. It may or may not be accompanied by some measure of democracy open institutions and elections at various levels. A modern example is Great Britain, where it is called a Constitutional Monarchy.

Socialism - Political belief and system in which the state takes a guiding role in the national economy and provides extensive social services to its population. It may or may not own outright means of production, but even where it does not, it exercises tight control. It usually promotes democracy, (Democratic Socialism), though the heavy state involvement produces excessive bureaucracy and usually inefficiency. Taken to an extreme, it may lead to Communism as government control increases and democratic practices decrease. Ideologically, the two movements are very similar in both belief and practice, as Socialists also preach the superiority of their system to all others and that it will become the eventual natural order. It is also considered for that reason a variant of Marxism. It also has used a red flag as a symbol.

COMPETENCY 35.0 INTERNATIONAL RELATIONS

Skill 35.1 Demonstrate knowledge of the functions and powers of international organizations, such as the United Nations

Individuals and societies have divided the earth's surface through conflict for a number of reasons:

- The domination of peoples or societies, e.g., colonialism
- The control of valuable resources, e.g., oil
- The control of strategic routes, e.g., the Panama Canal

Religion, political ideology, national origin, language, and race can spur conflicts. Conflicts can result from disagreement over how land, ocean or natural resources will be developed, shared, and used. Conflicts have resulted from trade, migration, and settlement rights. Conflicts can occur between small groups of people, between cities, between nations, between religious groups, and between multi-national alliances.

Today, the world is primarily divided by political/administrative interests into state sovereignties. A particular region is recognized to be controlled by a particular government, including its territory, population and natural resources. The only area of the earth's surface that today is not defined by state or national sovereignty is Antarctica.

Alliances are developed among nations on the basis of political philosophy, economic concerns, cultural similarities, religious interests, or for military defense. Some of the most notable alliances today are:
- The United Nations
- The North Atlantic Treaty Organization
- The Caribbean Community
- The Common Market
- The Council of Arab Economic Unity
- The European Union

Large companies and multi-national corporations also compete for control of natural resources for manufacturing, development, and distribution.

Throughout human history there have been conflicts on virtually every scale over the right to divide the Earth according to differing perceptions, needs and values. These conflicts have ranged from tribal conflicts to urban riots, to civil wars, to regional wars, to world wars. While these conflicts have traditionally centered on control of land surfaces, new disputes are beginning to arise over the resources of the oceans and space.

On smaller scales, conflicts have created divisions between rival gangs, use zones in cities, water supply, school districts; economic divisions include franchise areas and trade zones.

DOMAIN IX.   **GEOGRAPHY**

COMPETENCY 36.0 THEMES

Skill 36.1   Identify relative and absolute location and the physical and human characteristics of "place"

Human communities subsisted initially as gatherers – gathering berries, leaves, etc. With the invention of tools it became possible to dig for roots, hunt small animals, and catch fish from rivers and oceans. Humans observed their environments and soon learned to plant seeds and harvest crops. As people migrated to areas in which game and fertile soil were abundant, communities began to develop. When people had the knowledge to grow crops and the skills to hunt game, they began to understand division of labor. Some of the people in the community tended to agricultural needs while others hunted game.

As habitats attracted larger numbers of people, environments became crowded and there was competition. The concept of division of labor and sharing of food soon came, in more heavily populated areas, to be managed. Groups of people focused on growing crops while others concentrated on hunting. Experience led to the development of skills and of knowledge that make the work easier. Farmers began to develop new plant species and hunters began to protect animal species from other predators for their own use. This ability to manage the environment led people to settle down, to guard their resources, and to manage them.

Camps soon became villages. Villages became year-round settlements. Animals were domesticated and gathered into herds that met the needs of the village. With the settled life it was no longer necessary to "travel light." Pottery was developed for storing and cooking food.

By 8000 BCE, culture was beginning to evolve in these villages. Agriculture was developed for the production of grain crops, which led to a decreased reliance on wild plants. Domesticating animals for various purposes decreased the need to hunt wild game. Life became more settled. It was then possible to turn attention to such matters as managing water supplies, producing tools, making cloth, etc. There was both the social interaction and the opportunity to reflect upon existence. Mythologies arose and various kinds of belief systems. Rituals arose that re-enacted the mythologies that gave meaning to life.

As farming and animal husbandry skills increased, the dependence on wild game and food gathering declined. With this change came the realization that a larger number of people could be supported on the produce of farming and animal husbandry.

Two things seem to have come together to produce cultures and civilizations: a society and culture based on agriculture and the development of centers of the community with literate social and religious structures. The members of these hierarchies then managed water supply and irrigation, ritual and religious life, and exerted their own right to use a portion of the goods produced by the community for their own subsistence in return for their management.

Sharpened skills, development of more sophisticated tools, commerce with other communities, and increasing knowledge of their environment, the resources available to them, and responses to the needs to share good, order community life, and protect their possessions from outsiders led to further division of labor and community development.

As trade routes developed and travel between cities became easier, trade led to specialization. Trade enables a people to obtain the goods they desire in exchange for the goods they are able to produce. This, in turn, leads to increased attention to refinements of technique and the sharing of ideas. The knowledge of a new discovery or invention provides knowledge and technology that increases the ability to produce goods for trade.

As each community learns the value of the goods it produces and improves its ability to produce the goods in greater quantity, industry is born.

Skill 36.2   Demonstrate understanding of human-environment interactions

Ecology is the study of how living organisms interact with the physical aspects of their surroundings (their environment), including soil, water, air, and other living things. **Biogeography** is the study of how the surface features of the earth – form, movement, and climate – affect living things.

Three levels of environmental understanding are critical:

1. An **ecosystem** is a community (of any size) consisting of a physical environment and the organisms that live within it.

2. A **biome** is a large area of land with characteristic climate, soil, and mixture of plants and animals. Biomes are made up of groups of ecosystems. Major biomes are: desert, chaparral, savanna, tropical rain forest, temperate grassland, temperate deciduous forest, taiga, and tundra.

3. A **habitat** is the set of surroundings within which members of a species normally live. Elements of the habitat include soil, water, predators, and competitors.

Within habitats interactions between members of the species occur. These interactions occur between members of the same species and between members of different species. Interaction tends to be of three types:

1. **Competition**. Competition occurs between members of the same species or between members of different species for resources required to continue life, to grow, or to reproduce. For example, competition for acorns can occur between squirrels or it can occur between squirrels and woodpeckers. One species can either push out or cause the demise of another species if it is better adapted to obtain the resource. When a new species is introduced into a habitat, the result can be a loss of the native species and/or significant change to the habitat. For example, the introduction of the Asian plant Kudzu into the American South has resulted in the destruction of several species because Kudzu grows and spreads very quickly and smothers everything in its path.

2. **Predation**. Predators are organisms that live by hunting and eating other organisms. The species best suited for hunting other species in the habitat will be the species that survives. Larger species that have better hunting skills reduce the amount of prey available for smaller and/or weaker species. This affects both the amount of available prey and the diversity of species that are able to survive in the habitat.

3. **Symbiosis** is a condition in which two organisms of different species are able to live in the same environment over an extended period of time without harming each other. In some cases, one species may benefit without harming the other. In other cases, both species benefit.

Different organisms are by nature best suited for existence in particular environments. When an organism is displaced to a different environment or when the environment changes for some reason, its ability to survive is determined by its ability to *adapt* to the new environment. Adaptation can take the form of structural change, physiological change, or behavioral modification.

Biodiversity refers to the variety of species and organisms, as well as the variety of habitats available on the earth. Biodiversity provides the life-support system for the various habitats and species. The greater the degree of biodiversity, the more species and habitats will continue to survive.

When human and other population and migration changes, climate changes, or natural disasters disrupt the delicate balance of a habitat or an ecosystem, species either adapt or become extinct.

Natural changes can occur that alter habitats – floods, volcanoes, storms, earthquakes. These changes can affect the species that exist within the habitat, either by causing extinction or by changing the environment in a way that will no longer support the life systems. Climate changes can have similar effects. Inhabiting species, however, can also alter habitats, particularly through migration. Human civilization, population growth, and efforts to control the environment can have many negative effects on various habitats. Humans change their environments to suit their particular needs and interests. This can result in changes that result in the extinction of species or changes to the habitat itself. For example, deforestation damages the stability of mountain surfaces. One particularly devastating example is in the removal of the grasses of the Great Plains for agriculture. Tilling the ground and planting crops left the soil unprotected. Sustained drought dried out the soil into dust. When windstorms occurred, the topsoil was stripped away and blown all the way to the Atlantic Ocean.

Skill 36.3 **Identify significant types of movement such as migration, trade, and the spread of ideas**

The Agricultural Revolution, initiated by the invention of the plow, led to a transformation of human society by making large-scale agricultural production possible and facilitating the development of agrarian societies. During the period during which the plow was invented, the wheel, numbers, and writing were also invented. Coinciding with the shift from hunting wild game to the domestication of animals, this period was one of dramatic social and economic change.

Numerous changes in lifestyle and thinking accompanied the development of stable agricultural communities. Rather than gathering a wide variety of plants as hunter-gatherers, agricultural communities became dependent on a limited number of plants or crops that are harvested. Subsistence becomes vulnerable to the weather and dependent upon planting and harvesting times. Agriculture also required a great deal of physical labor and the development of a sense of discipline. Agricultural communities become sedentary or stable in terms of location. This makes the construction of dwellings appropriate. These tend to be built relatively close together, creating villages or towns. Stable communities also free people from the need to carry everything with them and the move from hunting ground to hunting ground. This facilitates the invention of larger, more complex tools. As new tools are envisioned and developed, it begins to make sense to have some specialization within the society. Skills begin to have greater value, and people begin to do work on behalf of the community that utilizes their particular skills and abilities. Settled community life also gives rise to the notion of wealth. It is now possible to keep possessions.

In the beginning of the transition to agriculture, the tools that were used for hunting and gathering were adequate to the tasks of agriculture. The initial challenge was in adapting to a new way of life. Once that challenge was met, attention turned to the development of more advanced tools and sources of energy. Six thousand years ago, the first plow was invented in Mesopotamia. Animals pulled this plow. Agriculture was now possible on a much larger scale. Soon tools were developed that make such basic tasks as gathering seeds, planting, and cutting grain faster and easier.

It also becomes necessary to maintain social and political stability to ensure that planting and harvesting times are not interrupted by internal discord or a war with a neighboring community. It also becomes necessary to develop ways to store the crop and prevent its destruction by the elements and animals. And then it must be protected from thieves.

Settled communities that produce the necessities of life are self-supporting. Advances in agricultural technology and the ability to produce a surplus of produce create two opportunities: first, the opportunity to trade the surplus goods for other desired goods, and second, the vulnerability to others who steal to take those goods. Protecting domesticated livestock and surplus, as well as stored, crops become an issue for the community. This, in turn, leads to the construction of walls and other fortifications around the community.

The ability to produce surplus crops creates the opportunity to trade or barter with other communities in exchange for desired goods. Traders and trade routes begin to develop between villages and cities. The domestication of animals expands the range of trade and facilitates an exchange of ideas and knowledge.

Competition for control of areas of the earth's surface is a common trait of human interaction throughout history. This competition has resulted in both destructive conflict and peaceful and productive cooperation. Societies and groups have sought control of regions of the earth's surface for a wide variety of reasons including religion, economics, politics and administration. Numerous wars have been fought through the centuries for the control of territory for each of these reasons.

Individuals and societies have divided the earth's surface through conflict for a number of reasons:

- The domination of peoples or societies, e.g., colonialism
- The control of valuable resources, e.g., oil
- The control of strategic routes, e.g., the Panama Canal

Religion, political ideology, national origin, language, and race can spur conflicts. Conflicts can result from disagreement over how land, ocean or natural resources will be developed, shared, and used. Conflicts have resulted from trade, migration, and settlement rights. Conflicts can occur between small groups of people, between cities, between nations, between religious groups, and between multi-national alliances.

Large companies and multi-national corporations also compete for control of natural resources for manufacturing, development, and distribution.

Throughout human history there have been conflicts on virtually every scale over the right to divide the Earth according to differing perceptions, needs and values. These conflicts have ranged from tribal conflicts to urban riots, to civil wars, to regional wars, to world wars. While these conflicts have traditionally centered on control of land surfaces, new disputes are beginning to arise over the resources of the oceans and space.

On smaller scales, conflicts have created divisions between rival gangs, use zones in cities, water supply, school districts; economic divisions include franchise areas and trade zones.

COMPETENCY 37.0 MAP SKILLS

Skill 37.1 Read and interpret various types of maps

We use **illustrations** of various sorts because it is often easier to demonstrate a given idea visually instead of orally. Sometimes it is even easier to do so with an illustration than a description. This is especially true in the areas of education and research because humans are visually stimulated. It is a fact that any idea presented visually in some manner is always easier to understand and to comprehend than simply getting an idea across verbally, by hearing it or reading it. Among the more common illustrations used in political and social sciences are various types of **maps, graphs and charts**.

Photographs and **globes** are useful as well; but because they are limited in what kind of information that they can show, they are rarely used—unless, as in the case of a photograph, it is of a particular political figure or a time that one wishes to visualize.

Although maps have advantages over globes and photographs, they do have a major disadvantage. This problem must be considered as well. The major problem of all maps comes about because most maps are flat and the Earth is a sphere. It is impossible to reproduce exactly on a flat surface an object shaped like a sphere. In order to put the earth's features onto a map they must be stretched in some way. This stretching is called **distortion.**

Distortion does not mean that maps are wrong it simply means that they are not perfect representations of the Earth or its parts. **Cartographers,** or mapmakers, understand the problems of distortion. They try to design their maps so that there is as little distortion as possible.

The process of putting the features of the Earth onto a flat surface is called **projection**. All maps are really map projections. There are many different types. Each one deals in a different way with the problem of distortion. Map projections are made in a number of ways. Some are done using complicated mathematics. However, the basic ideas behind map projections can be understood by looking at the three most common types:

(1) <u>**Cylindrical Projections**</u> - These are done by taking a cylinder of paper and wrapping it around a globe. A light is used to project the globe's features onto the paper. Distortion is least where the paper touches the globe. For example, suppose that the paper was wrapped so that it touched the globe at the equator; the map from this projection would have just a little distortion near the equator. However, in moving north or south of the equator, the distortion would increase as you moved further away from the equator.

The best known and most widely used cylindrical projection is the **Mercator Projection.** Gerardus Mercator, a Flemish mapmaker, first developed it in 1569.

(2). **Conical Projections** - The name for these maps come from the fact that the projection is made onto a cone of paper. The cone is made so that it touches a globe at the base of the cone only. It can also be made so that it cuts through part of the globe in two different places. Again, there is the least distortion where the paper touches the globe. If the cone touches at two different points, there is some distortion at both of them. Conical projections are most often used to map areas in the **middle latitudes**. Maps of the United States are most often conical projections. This is because most of the country lies within these latitudes.

(3). **Flat-Plane Projections** - These are made with a flat piece of paper. It touches the globe at one point only. Areas near this point show little distortion. Flat-plane projections are often used to show the areas of the north and south poles. One such flat projection is called a **Gnomonic Projection**. On this kind of map all meridians appear as straight lines, Gnomonic projections are useful because any straight line drawn between points on it forms a **Great-Circle Route**.

Great-Circle Routes can best be described by thinking of a globe and when using the globe the shortest route between two points on it can be found by simply stretching a string from one point to the other. However, if the string was extended in reality, so that it took into effect the globe's curvature, it would then make a great-circle. A great-circle is any circle that cuts a sphere, such as the globe, into two equal parts. Because of distortion, most maps do not show great-circle routes as straight lines. Gnomonic projections, however, do show the shortest distance between the two places as a straight line; because of this they are valuable for navigation. They are called Great-Circle Sailing Maps.

Maps have four main properties. They are (1) the size of the areas shown on the map. (2) the shapes of the areas, (3) consistent scales, and (4) straight line directions. A map can be drawn so that it is correct in one or more of these properties. No map can be correct in all of them.

Equal areas - One property which maps can have is that of equal areas. In an equal area map, the meridians and parallels are drawn so that the areas shown have the same proportions as they do on the Earth. For example, Greenland is about 118th the size of South America, thus it will be show as 118th the size on an equal area map. The **Mercator projection** is an example of a map that does not have equal areas. In it, Greenland appears to be about the same size of South America. This is because the distortion is very bad at the poles and Greenland lies near the North Pole.

Conformality - A second map property is conformality, or correct shapes. There are no maps that can show very large areas of the earth in their exact shapes. Only globes can really do that; however, Conformal Maps are as close as possible to true shapes. The United States is often shown by a Lambert Conformal Conic Projection Map.

Consistent Scales - Many maps attempt to use the same scale on all parts of the map. Generally, this is easier when maps show a relatively small part of the earth's surface. For example, a map of Florida might be a Consistent Scale Map. Generally, maps showing large areas are not consistent-scale maps. This is so because of distortion. Often, such maps will have two scales noted in the key. One scale, for example, might be accurate to measure distances between points along the Equator. Another might be then used to measure distances between the North Pole and the South Pole.

Maps showing physical features often try to show information about the elevation or **relief** of the land. **Elevation** is the distance above or below the sea level. The elevation is usually shown with colors, for instance, all areas on a map which are at a certain level will be shown in the same color.

Relief Maps - Show the shape of the land surface: flat, rugged, or steep. Relief maps usually give more detail than simply showing the overall elevation of the land's surface. Relief is also sometimes shown with colors, but another way to show relief is by using **contour lines**. These lines connect all points of a land surface which are the same height surrounding the particular area of land.

Thematic Maps - These are used to show more specific information, often on a single **theme**, or topic. Thematic maps show the distribution or amount of something over a certain given area for example, things such as population density, climate, economic information, cultural, political information, etc.

Skill 37.2   Determine distance, direction, latitude, longitude, and the location of physical features

Distance is the measurement between two points of location on a map. Measurement can be in terms of feet, yards, miles, meters, or kilometers. Distance is often correct on equidistant maps only in the direction of latitude.

On a map that has a large scale, 1:125,000 or larger, distance distortion is usually insignificant. An example of a large-scale map is a standard topographic map. On these maps measuring straight line distance is simple. Distance is first measured on the map using a ruler. This measurement is then converted into a real world distance using the map's scale. For example, if we measured a distance of 10 centimeters on a map that had a scale of 1:10,000, we would multiply 10 (distance) by 10,000 (scale). Thus, the actual distance in the real world would be 100,000 centimeters.

Measuring distance along map features that are not straight is a little more difficult. One technique that can be employed for this task is to use a number of straight-line segments. The accuracy of this method is dependent on the number of straight-line segments used. Another method for measuring curvilinear map distances is to use a mechanical device called an **opisometer**. This device uses a small rotating wheel that records the distance traveled. The recorded distance is measured by this device either in centimeters or inches.

Direction is usually measured relative to the location of North or South Pole. Directions determined from these locations are said to be relative to True North or True South. The magnetic poles can also be used to measure direction. However, these points on the Earth are located in spatially different spots from the geographic North and South Pole. The North Magnetic Pole is located at 78.3° North, 104.0° West. In the Southern Hemisphere, the South Magnetic Pole is located in Commonwealth Day, Antarctica, and has a geographical location of 65° South, 139° East. The magnetic poles are also not fixed overtime but shift their spatial position overtime.

There are many different climates throughout the earth. It is most unusual if a country contains just one kind of climate. Regions of climates are divided according to **latitudes**:

0 - 23 1/2 degrees are the "low latitudes"
23 1/2 - 66 1/2 degrees are the "middle latitudes"
66 1/2 degrees to the Poles are the "high latitudes"

The **low latitudes** are composed of the rainforest, savanna, and desert climates. The tropical rainforest climate is found in equatorial lowlands and is hot and wet. There is sun, extreme heat and rain every day. Although daily temperatures rarely rise above 90 degrees F, the daily humidity is always high, leaving everything sticky and damp. North and south of the tropical rainforests are the tropical grasslands called "savannas," the "lands of two seasons"--a winter dry season and a summer wet season. Further north and south of the tropical grasslands or savannas are the deserts. These areas are the hottest and driest parts of the earth, receiving less than 10 inches of rain a year. These areas have extreme temperatures between night and day. After the sun sets, the land cools, quickly dropping the temperature as much as 50 degrees F.

The **middle latitudes** contain the Mediterranean, humid-subtropical, humid-continental, marine, steppe, and desert climates. Lands containing the Mediterranean climate are considered "sunny" lands found in six areas of the world: lands bordering the Mediterranean Sea, a small portion of southwestern Africa, areas in southern and southwestern Australia, a small part of the Ukraine near the Black Sea, central Chile, and Southern California. Summers are hot and dry with mild winters. The growing season usually lasts all year, and what little rain falls are during the winter months. What is rather unusual is that the Mediterranean climate is located between 30 and 40 degrees north and south latitude on the western coasts of countries.

Longitude measures the north-south position of locations on the Earth's surface relative to a point found at the center of the Earth. This central point is also located on the Earth's rotational or **polar axis**. The equator is the starting point for the measurement of latitude. The equator has a value of zero degrees. A line of latitude or **parallel** of 30° North has an angle that is 30° north of the plane represented by the equator. The maximum value that latitude can attain is either 90° North or South. These lines of latitude run parallel to the rotational axis of the Earth. There are 180° of longitude on either side of a starting meridian, which is known the **Prime Meridian**. The Prime Meridian has a designated value of 0°. Measurements of longitude are also defined as being either west or east of the Prime Meridian.

Skill 37.3 Recognize and describe spatial patterns

Maps come in a variety of formats. A thematic map, also known as a statistical or special purpose map, displays the spatial pattern of a theme or series of attributes, for example, population, age and income levels. In contrast to reference maps, which show many geographic features (forests, roads, political boundaries), thematic maps emphasize spatial variation of one or a small number of geographic distributions. These distributions may be physical phenomena such as climate or human characteristics such as population density and health issues. These types of maps are sometimes referred to as graphic essays that portray spatial variations and interrelationships of geographical distributions. Location is important to provide a reference base of where selected phenomena are occurring. While general reference maps show where something is in relation to other points, thematic maps describe attribute(s) about that place.

Skill 37.4 Use a legend or key

To properly analyze a given map, one must be familiar with the various parts and symbols that most modern maps use. For the most part, this is standardized, with different maps using similar parts and symbols, which can include:

The Title - All maps should have a title, just like all books should. The title tells you what information is to be found on the map.

The Legend - Most maps have a legend. A legend tells the reader about the various symbols that are used on that particular map and what the symbols represent (also called a **map key**).

The Grid - A grid is a series of lines that are used to find exact places and locations on the map. There are several different kinds of grid systems in use; however, most maps do use the longitude and latitude system, known as the **Geographic Grid System**.

Directions - Most maps have some directional system to show which way the map is being presented. Often on a map, a small compass will be present, with arrows showing the four basic directions: north, south, east, and west.

The Scale - This is used to show the relationship between a unit of measurement on the map versus the real world measure on the Earth. Maps are drawn to many different scales. Some maps show a lot of detail for a small area. Others show a greater span of distance. Whichever is being used, one should always be aware of just what scale is being used. For instance, the scale might be something like 1 inch = 10 miles for a small area or for a map showing the whole world it might have a scale in which 1 inch = 1,000 miles. The point is that one must look at the map key in order to see what units of measurements the map is using.

COMPETENCY 38.0 PHYSICAL GEOGRAPHY

Skill 38.1 Demonstrate knowledge of landforms and water, climate, and vegetation and natural resources

A landform comprises a geomorphological unit. Landforms are categorized by characteristics such as elevation, slope, orientation, stratification, rock exposure, and soil type. Landforms by name include berms, mounds, hills, cliffs, valleys, and others. Oceans and continents exemplify highest-order landforms. Landform elements are parts of a landform that can be further identified. The generic landform elements are: pits, peaks, channels, ridges, passes, pools, planes, etc., and can be often extracted from a digital elevation model using some automated or semi-automated techniques.

Elementary landforms (segments, facets, relief units) are the smallest homogeneous divisions of the land surface, at the given scale/resolution. A plateau or a hill can be observed at various scales ranging from a few hundred meters to hundreds of kilometers. Hence, the spatial distribution of landforms is often fuzzy and scale-dependent, as is the case for soils and geological strata.

A number of factors, ranging from plate tectonics to erosion and deposition, can generate and affect landforms. Biological factors can also influence landforms—see for example the role of plants in the development of dune systems and salt marshes, and the work of corals and algae in the formation of coral reefs.

Weather is the condition of the air, which surrounds the day-to-day atmospheric conditions including temperature, air pressure, wind and moisture or precipitation which includes rain, snow, hail, or sleet.

Climate is average weather or daily weather conditions for a specific region or location over a long or extended period of time. Studying the climate of an area includes information gathered on the area's monthly and yearly temperatures and its monthly and yearly amounts of precipitation. In addition, a characteristic of an area's climate is the length of its growing season.

In northern and central United States, northern China, south central and southeastern Canada, and the western and southeastern parts of the former Soviet Union is found the "climate of four seasons," the humid continental climate--spring, summer, fall, and winter. Cold winters, hot summers, and enough rainfall to grow a variety of crops are the major characteristics of this climate. In areas where the humid continental climate is found are some of the world's best farmlands as well as important activities such as trading and mining. Differences in temperatures throughout the year are determined by the distance a place is inland, away from the coasts.

The steppe or prairie climate is located in the interiors of the large continents like Asia and North America. These dry flatlands are far from ocean breezes and are called prairies or the Great Plains in Canada and the United States and steppes in Asia. Although the summers are hot and the winters are cold as in the humid continental climate, the big difference is rainfall. In the steppe climate, rainfall is light and uncertain, 10 to 20 inches a year mainly in spring and summer and is considered normal. Where rain is more plentiful, grass grows; in areas of less, the steppes or prairies gradually become deserts. These are found in the Gobi Desert of Asia, central and western Australia, southwestern United States, and in the smaller deserts found in Pakistan, Argentina, and Africa south of the Equator.

The two major climates found in the high latitudes are "**tundra**" and "**taiga**." The word *tundra* meaning "marshy plain" is a Russian word and aptly describes the climatic conditions in the northern areas of Russia, Europe, and Canada. Winters are extremely cold and very long. Most of the year the ground is frozen but becomes rather mushy during the very short summer months. Surprisingly less snow falls in the area of the tundra than in the eastern part of the United States. However, due to the harshness of the extreme cold, very few people live there and no crops can be raised. Despite having a small human population, many plants and animals are found there.

The "taiga" is the northern forest region and is located south of the tundra. In fact, the Russian word *taiga* means "forest." The world's largest forestlands are found here along with vast mineral wealth and forbearing animals. The climate is extreme and very few people live there, not being able to raise crops because of the extremely short growing season. The winter temperatures are colder, and the summer temperatures are hotter than those in the tundra are because the taiga climate region is farther from the waters of the Arctic Ocean. The taiga is found in the northern parts of Russia, Sweden, Norway, Finland, Canada, and Alaska with most of their lands covered with marshes and swamps.

The humid **subtropical climate** is found north and south of the tropics and is moist indeed. The areas having this type of climate are found on the eastern side of their continents and include Japan, mainland China, Australia, Africa, South America, and the United States--the southeastern coasts of these areas. An interesting feature of their locations is that warm ocean currents are found there. The winds that blow across these currents bring in warm moist air all year round. Long, warm summers; short, mild winters; and a long growing season allow for different crops to be grown several times a year. All contribute to the productivity of this climate type that supports more people than any of the other climates.

The **marine climate** is found in Western Europe, the British Isles, the U.S. Pacific Northwest, the western coast of Canada and southern Chile, along with southern New Zealand and southeastern Australia. A common characteristic of these lands is that they are either near water or surrounded by it.

The ocean winds are wet and warm, bringing a mild, rainy climate to these areas. In the summer, the daily temperatures average at or below 70 degrees F. During the winter, because of the warming effect of the ocean waters, the temperatures rarely fall below freezing.

In northern and central United States, northern China, south central and southeastern Canada, and the western and southeastern parts of the former Soviet Union is found the **"climate of four seasons,"** the **humid continental climate**--spring, summer, fall, and winter. Cold winters, hot summers, and enough rainfall to grow a variety of crops are the major characteristics of this climate. In areas where the humid continental climate is found are some of the world's best farmlands as well as important activities such as trading and mining. Differences in temperatures throughout the year are determined by the distance a place is inland.

In certain areas of the earth there exists a type of climate unique to areas with high mountains, usually different from their surroundings. This type of climate is called a "vertical climate" because the temperatures, crops, vegetation, and human activities change and become different as one ascends the different levels of elevation. At the foot of the mountain, a hot and rainy climate is found with the cultivation of many lowland crops. As one climbs higher, the air becomes cooler, the climate changes sharply and different economic activities change, such as grazing sheep and growing corn. At the top of many mountains, snow is found year-round.

Natural resources are naturally occurring substances that are considered valuable in their natural form. A commodity is generally considered a natural resource when the primary activities associated with it are extraction and purification, as opposed to creation. Thus, mining, petroleum extraction, fishing, and forestry are generally considered natural-resource industries, while agriculture is not.

Natural resources are often classified into **renewable** and **non-renewable resources**. Renewable resources are generally living resources (fish, coffee, and forests, for example), which can restock (renew) themselves if they are not over-harvested. Renewable resources can restock themselves and be used indefinitely if they are sustained. Once renewable resources are consumed at a rate that exceeds their natural rate of replacement, the standing stock will diminish and eventually run out. The rate of sustainable use of a renewable resource is determined by the replacement rate and amount of standing stock of that particular resource. Non-living renewable natural resources include soil, as well as water, wind, tides and solar radiation.

Natural resources include soil, timber, oil, minerals, and other goods taken more or less as they are from the Earth.

In recent years, the depletion of natural capital and attempts to move to sustainable development has been a major focus of development agencies. This is of particular concern in rainforest regions, which hold most of the Earth's natural biodiversity - irreplaceable genetic natural capital. Conservation of natural resources is the major focus of Natural Capitalism, environmentalism, the ecology movement, and Green Parties. Some view this depletion as a major source of social unrest and conflicts in developing nations.

Skill 38.2   Demonstrate understanding of human impact on the environment

By nature, people are essentially social creatures. They generally live in communities or settlements of some kind and of some size. Settlements are the cradles of culture, political structure, education, and the management of resources. The relative placement of these settlements or communities are shaped by the proximity to natural resources, the movement of raw materials, the production of finished products, the availability of a work force, and the delivery of finished products. Shared values, language, culture, religion, and subsistence will at least to some extent, determine the composition of communities.

Settlements begin in areas that offer the natural resources to support life – food and water. With the ability to manage the environment one finds a concentration of populations. With the ability to transport raw materials and finished products, comes mobility. With increasing technology and the rise of industrial centers comes a migration of the workforce.

Cities are the major hubs of human settlement. Almost half of the population of the world now lives in cities. These percentages are much higher in developed regions. Established cities continue to grow. The fastest growth, however, is occurring in developing areas. In some regions there are "metropolitan areas" made up of urban and sub-urban areas. In some places cities and urban areas have become interconnected into "megalopoli" (e.g., Tokyo-Kawasaki-Yokohama).

The concentrations of populations and the divisions of these areas among various groups that constitute the cities can differ significantly. North American cities are different from European cities in terms of shape, size, population density, and modes of transportation. While in North America, the wealthiest economic groups tend to live outside the cities, the opposite is true in Latin American cities.

There are significant differences among the cities of the world in terms of connectedness to other cities. While European and North American cities tend to be well linked both by transportation and communication connections, there are other places in the world in which communication between the cities of the country may be inferior to communication with the rest of the world.

Rural areas tend to be less densely populated because of the needs of agriculture. More land is needed to produce crops or for animal husbandry than for manufacturing, especially in a city in which the buildings tend to be taller. Rural areas, however, must be connected via communication and transportation in order to provide food and raw materials to urban areas.

The purpose and aim of social policy is to improve human welfare and to meet basic human needs within the society. Social policy addresses basic human needs for the sustainability of the individual and the society. The concerns of social policy, then, include food, clean water, shelter, clothing, education, health, and social security. Social policy is part of public policy, determined by the city, the state, the nation, or the multi-national organization responsible for human welfare in a particular region.

Environmental policy is concerned with the sustainability of the earth, the region under the administration of the governing group or individual or a local habitat. The concern of environmental policy is the preservation of the region, habitat or ecosystem.

Because humans, both individually and in community, rely upon the environment to sustain human life, social and environmental policy must be mutually supportable. Because humans, both individually and in community, live on the earth, draw on the natural resources of the earth, and affect the environment in many ways, environmental and social policy must be mutually supportive.

If modern societies have no understanding of the limitations on natural resources or how their actions affect the environment, and they act without regard for the sustainability of the earth, it will become impossible for the earth to sustain human existence. At the same time, the resources of the earth are necessary to support the human welfare. Environmental policies must recognize that the planet is the home of humans and other species.

For centuries, social policies, economic policies, and political policies have ignored the impact of human existence and human civilization on the environment. Human civilization has disrupted the ecological balance, contributed to the extinction of animal and plant species, and destroyed ecosystems through uncontrolled harvesting.

In an age of global warming, unprecedented demand on natural resources, and a shrinking planet, social and environmental policies must become increasingly interdependent if the planet is to continue to support life and human civilization.

COMPETENCY 39.0 HUMAN GEOGRAPHY

Skill 39.1 Demonstrate knowledge of human geography, including cultural geography; economic geography; political geography; and population geography

The Industrial Revolution of the eighteenth and nineteenth centuries resulted in even greater changes in human civilization and even greater opportunities for trade, increased production, and the exchange of ideas and knowledge.

The first phase of the Industrial Revolution (1750-1830) saw the mechanization of the textile industry, vast improvements in mining, with the invention of the steam engine, and numerous improvements in transportation, with the development and improvement of turnpikes, canals, and the invention of the railroad.

The second phase (1830-1910) resulted in vast improvements in a number of industries that had already been mechanized through such inventions as the Bessemer steel process and the invention of steam ships. New industries arose as a result of the new technological advances, such as photography, electricity, and chemical processes. New sources of power were harnessed and applied, including petroleum and hydroelectric power. Precision instruments were developed, and engineering was launched. It was during this second phase that the Industrial Revolution spread to other European countries, to Japan, and to the United States.

The direct results of the Industrial Revolution, particularly as they affected industry, commerce, and agriculture, included:

- Enormous increase in productivity
- Huge increase in world trade
- Specialization and division of labor
- Standardization of parts and mass production
- Growth of giant business conglomerates and monopolies
- A new revolution in agriculture facilitated by the steam engine, machinery, chemical fertilizers, processing, canning, and refrigeration

The political results included:

- Growth of complex government by technical experts
- Centralization of government, including regulatory administrative agencies
- Advantages to democratic development, including extension of franchise to the middle class, and later to all elements of the population, mass education to meet the needs of an industrial society, the development of media of public communication, including radio, television, and cheap newspapers
- Dangers to democracy included the risk of manipulation of the media of mass communication, facilitation of dictatorial centralization and totalitarian control, subordination of the legislative function to administrative directives, efforts to achieve uniformity and angles, and social impersonalization.

The economic results were numerous:

- The conflict between free trade and low tariffs and protectionism
- The issue of free enterprise against government regulation
- Struggles between labor and capital, including the trade-union movement
- The rise of socialism
- The rise of the utopian socialists
- The rise of Marxian or scientific socialism

The social results of the Industrial Revolution include:

- Increase of population, especially in industrial centers
- Advances in science applied to agriculture, sanitation and medicine
- Growth of great cities
- Disappearance of the difference between city dwellers and farmers
- Faster tempo of life and increased stress from the monotony of the work routine
- The emancipation of women
- The decline of religion
- Rise of scientific materialism
- Darwin's theory of evolution

Increased mobility produced a rapid diffusion of knowledge and ideas. Increased mobility also resulted in wide-scale immigration to industrialized countries. Cultures clashed and cultures melded.

COMPETENCY 40.0 REGIONAL GEOGRAPHY

Skill 40.1 Demonstrate knowledge of the geography of the major regions of the world

The earth's surface is made up of 70% water and 30% land. Physical features of the land surface include mountains, hills, plateaus, valleys, and plains. Other minor landforms include deserts, deltas, canyons, mesas, basins, foothills, marshes and swamps. Earth's water features include oceans, seas, lakes, rivers, and canals.

Mountains are landforms with rather steep slopes at least 2,000 feet or more above sea level. Mountains are found in groups called mountain chains or mountain ranges. At least one range can be found on six of the earth's seven continents. North America has the Appalachian and Rocky Mountains; South America the Andes; Asia the Himalayas; Australia the Great Dividing Range; Europe the Alps; and Africa the Atlas, Ahaggar, and Drakensburg Mountains.

Hills are elevated landforms rising to an elevation of about 500 to 2000 feet. They are found everywhere on earth including Antarctica, where they are covered by ice.

Plateaus are elevated landforms usually level on top. Depending on location, they range from being an area that is very cold to one that is cool and healthful. Some plateaus are dry because mountains that keep out any moisture surround them. Some examples include the Kenya Plateau in East Africa, which is very cool. The plateau extending north from the Himalayas is extremely dry while those in Antarctica and Greenland are covered with ice and snow.

Plains are described as areas of flat or slightly rolling land, usually lower than the landforms next to them. Sometimes called lowlands (and sometimes located along **seacoasts**)**,** they support the majority of the world's people. Some are found inland, and many have been formed by large rivers. This resulted in extremely fertile soil for successful cultivation of crops and numerous large settlements of people. In North America, the vast plains areas extend from the Gulf of Mexico north to the Arctic Ocean and between the Appalachian and Rocky Mountains. In Europe, rich plains extend east from Great Britain into central Europe on into the Siberian region of Russia. Plains in river valleys are found in China (the Yangtze River valley), India (the Ganges River valley), and Southeast Asia (the Mekong River valley).

Valleys are land areas found between hills and mountains. Some have gentle slopes containing trees and plants; others have steep walls and are referred to as canyons. One example is Arizona's Grand Canyon of the Colorado River.

Deserts are large dry areas of land receiving ten inches or less of rainfall each year.

Among the better known deserts are Africa's large Sahara Desert, the Arabian Desert on the Arabian Peninsula, and the desert Outback covering roughly one third of Australia.

Deltas are areas of lowlands formed by soil and sediment deposited at the mouths of rivers. The soil is generally very fertile and most fertile river deltas are important crop-growing areas. One well-known example is the delta of Egypt's Nile River, known for its production of cotton.

Mesas are the flat tops of hills or mountains usually with steep sides. Sometimes plateaus are also called mesas. Basins are considered to be low areas drained by rivers or low spots in mountains. Foothills are generally considered a low series of hills found between a plain and a mountain range. Marshes and swamps are wet lowlands providing growth of such plants as rushes and reeds.

Oceans are the largest bodies of water on the planet. The four oceans of the earth are the **Atlantic Ocean**, one-half the size of the Pacific and separating North and South America from Africa and Europe; the **Pacific Ocean**, covering almost one-third of the entire surface of the earth and separating North and South America from Asia and Australia; the **Indian Ocean**, touching Africa, Asia, and Australia; and the ice-filled **Arctic Ocean,** extending from North America and Europe to the North Pole. The waters of the Atlantic, Pacific, and Indian Oceans also touch the shores of Antarctica.

Seas are smaller than oceans and are surrounded by land. Some examples include the Mediterranean Sea found between Europe, Asia, and Africa; and the Caribbean Sea, touching the West Indies, South and Central America. A lake is a body of water surrounded by land. The Great Lakes in North America are a good example.

Rivers, considered a nation's lifeblood, usually begin as very small streams, formed by melting snow and rainfall, flowing from higher to lower land, emptying into a larger body of water, usually a sea or an ocean. Examples of important rivers for the people and countries affected by and/or dependent on them include the Nile, Niger, and Zaire Rivers of Africa; the Rhine, Danube, and Thames Rivers of Europe; the Yangtze, Ganges, Mekong, Hwang He, and Irrawaddy Rivers of Asia; the Murray-Darling in Australia; and the Orinoco in South America. River systems are made up of large rivers and numerous smaller rivers or tributaries flowing into them. Examples include the vast Amazon Rivers system in South America and the Mississippi River system in the United States.

Canals are man-made water passages constructed to connect two larger bodies of water. Famous examples include the **Panama Canal** across Panama's isthmus, connecting the Atlantic and Pacific Oceans and the **Suez Canal** in the Middle East between Africa and the Arabian Peninsula, connecting the Red and Mediterranean Seas.

DOMAIN X.   ECONOMICS

COMPETENCY 41.0 MICROECONOMICS I

Skill 41.1   Understand the definition of economics and identify the factors of production and explain how they are used

Economics is a study of how a society allocates its scarce resources to satisfy what are basically unlimited and competing wants. Or economics can be defined as the study of the production, distribution and consumption of goods and resources subject to the constraint of scarce resources. Each of these definitions may look like they are defining different things, but both of them are the same. A resource is an input into the production process. Resources are limited in supply; they are scarce. There are not enough of them to produce all of the goods and services that society wants. Resources are called factors of production, and there are four factors of production: **labor, capital, land, and entrepreneurs**. Labor refers to all kinds of labor used in the production process. It doesn't matter if the labor is skilled or unskilled, part-time or full-time. All laborers are selling their ability to produce goods and services. Capital refers to anything that is made or manufactured to be used in the production process. Included in this definition are plant, equipment, machines, tools, etc. Included in land are not only the land itself, but also all natural resources like lumber, minerals, oil, etc. The entrepreneur is the individual that has the ability to combine the land, labor and capital to produce a good or service. The entrepreneur is the one who bears the risks of failure and loss, and he is the one who will gain from the profits if the product is successful. Each of these four resources is combined in the production of every good and service. Every good and service that is produced uses some combination of each of the four inputs. The combination used is called the production process. The production process refers to the way the four factors are combined to produce the output. If the production technique uses a lot of machinery with very few laborers, then the production process is called capital-intensive. If the production process requires many workers with very little machinery, then it is said to be a labor-intensive production process. Whatever the production technique is, there are not enough resources to produce all of the goods and services that a society wants. The scarcity of resources functions as a constraint on the amounts and kinds of goods and services that the economy can produce and consume. The scarcity of resources then affects the production, distribution and consumption decisions of the society. The available resource supply, both quantity and quality, determines production. For example, if there are not enough workers for a particular productive technique, then the smart owner will find machinery that requires fewer workers if he is going to stay in business in that area. Since the scarcity of resources determines what can be produced, distributed and consumed, than defining economics as a study of how a society allocates its scarce resources to satisfy unlimited and competing desires is saying the same thing. Consumers want more consumer goods, businesses want more investments, and government wants more public goods.

More capital goods mean fewer consumer goods because there are enough resources to produce more of both.

Skill 41.2 Demonstrate understanding of scarcity, choice and opportunity cost

The scarcity of resources is the basis for the existence of economics. Economics is defined as a study of how scarce resources are allocated to satisfy unlimited wants. Resources refer to the four factors of production: labor, capital, land and entrepreneurs. Labor refers to anyone who sells his ability to produce goods and services. Capital is anything that is manufactured to be used in the production process. Land refers to the land itself and everything occurring naturally on it, like oil, minerals, lumber, etc. Entrepreneurship is the ability of an individual to combine the three inputs with his own talents to produce a viable good or service. The entrepreneur takes the risk and experiences the losses or profits.

The fact that the supply of these resources is finite means that society cannot have as much of everything that it wants. There is a constraint on production and consumption and on the kinds of goods and services that can be produced and consumed. **Scarcity** means that choices have to be made. If society decides to produce more of one good, this means that there are fewer resources available for the production of other goods. Assume a society can produce two goods, good X and good Y. The society uses resources in the production of each good. If producing one unit of good X results in an amount of resources used to produce three units of good Y, then producing one more unit of good X results in a decrease in 3 units of good Y. In effect, one unit of good X "costs" three units of good Y. This cost is referred to as **opportunity cost**. Opportunity cost is the value of the sacrificed alternative, the value of what had to be given up in order to have the output of good X. Opportunity cost does not refer just to production. Your opportunity cost of studying with this guide is the value of what you are not doing because you are studying, whether it is watching TV, spending time with family, working, or whatever. Every **choice** has an opportunity cost.

If wants were limited and/or if resources were unlimited, then the concepts of choice and opportunity cost would not exist, and neither would the field of economics. There would be enough resources to satisfy the wants of consumers, businesses, and governments. The allocation of resources wouldn't be a problem. Society could have more of both good X and good Y without having to give up anything. There would be no opportunity cost. But this isn't the situation that societies are faced with.

Because resources are scarce, society doesn't want to waste them. Society wants to obtain the most satisfaction it can from the consumption of the goods and services produced with its scarce resources. The members of the society don't want their scarce resources wasted through inefficiency.

This indicates that producers must choose an efficient production process, which is the lowest cost means of production. High costs mean wasted resources and we then have the situation given above with good X and good Y. Consumers also don't want society's resources wasted by producing goods that they don't want. How do producers know what goods consumers want? Consumers buy the goods they want and vote with their dollar spending. A desirable good, one that consumers want, earns profits. A good that incurs losses is a good that society doesn't want its resources wasted on. This signals the producer that society wants their resources used in another way.

Skill 41.3 Demonstrate knowledge and application of the production possibilities curve to illustrate efficiency, unemployment, and tradeoffs

The scarcity of resources places a constraint on the kinds and amounts of goods and services that a society can produce, distribute, and consume. Because resources are limited in supply, society wants to use them efficiently. They don't want to waste them. They want to obtain the greatest amount of output possible for their available supply of resources. In order to achieve efficiency, two conditions must be fulfilled: full-employment and full-production. **Full-employment** refers to having all resources employed. Idle resources result in lower levels of output. The other condition, **full-production**, means that resources should be employed in their most productive capacity. A resource should be doing what it does best in order to make the greatest contribution to output. Full-production cannot be achieved without allocative and productive efficiency. A society has achieved allocative efficiency when its resources are being used to produce the goods wanted by that society. Productive efficiency means those goods are being produced without waste, that the lowest cost method of production is being used.

All of these concepts come together in the Production Possibilities Curve (PPC). If we assume a two-good economy, capital goods and consumer goods, with fixed resources and fixed technology, the PCC then represents the maximum amounts of output that the society can achieve given efficient production. For example, if the economy uses all of its resources to produce capital goods, it can have 500 units of capital goods and no consumer goods. Its choices are as follows: If it produces 100 consumer goods, then it can have only 450 capital goods; 200 consumer goods and 375 capital goods, 300 consumer goods and 275 capital goods, 400 consumer goods and 150 capital goods, and 500 consumer goods and no capital goods. The opportunity cost is the amount of capital goods given up to produce consumer goods.

The first 100 consumer goods have an opportunity cost of 50 capital goods, the second 100 have an opportunity cost of 75 capital goods, and so on. Plotting the above capital good-consumer good combinations results in a downward sloping curve that is bowed outward. This is the PPC.

Every point on it represents efficient production. Every point on the curve represents a trade-off between capital goods and consumer goods. If society wants more consumer goods, it must give up some capital goods.

Points represent inefficient production to the left of the curve. If society is at a point inside the curve, then there is underemployment or unemployment. If society has unemployed resources, it is producing a lower level of output. Employing those unemployed resources means a higher quantity of output, and society will move from the point inside the curve to the curve itself. Society may have full employment of its resources, but not all the resources are employed in their most productive capacity. If this is the case, society is not obtaining the most output it can with its available supply of resources and is still at a point to the left of the PPC. Employing these resources in the most productive capacity will move them to a point on the curve where they are efficient. Points to the right of or outside the PPC are unattainable. The society must experience economic growth by an increase in the supply of factors and/or technological progress.

Skill 41.4 Demonstrate knowledge of economic systems

Economic systems refer to the arrangements a society has devised to answer what are known as the Three Questions: What goods to produce, How to produce the goods, and For Whom are the goods being produced, or how the allocation of the output is determined. Different economic systems answer these questions in different ways. These are the different "isms" that define the method of resource and output allocation.

A market economy answers these questions in terms of demand and supply and the use of markets. Consumers vote for the products they want with their dollar spending. Goods acquiring enough dollar votes are profitable, signaling to the producers that society wants their scarce resources used in this way. This is how the "What" question is answered. The producer then hires inputs in accordance with the goods consumers want, looking for the most efficient or lowest cost method of production. The lower the firm's costs for any given level of revenue, the higher the firm's profits. This is the way in which the "How" question is answered in a market economy. The "For Whom" question is answered in the marketplace by the determination of the equilibrium price. Price serves to ration the good to those that can and will transact at the market price of better. Those who can't or won't are excluded from the market. The United States has a **market economy**.

The opposite of the market economy is the **centrally planned economy**. This used to be called Communism, even though the term is not correct in a strict Marxian sense. In a planned economy, the means of production are publicly owned with little, if any public ownership. Instead of the Three Questions being solved by markets, they have a planning authority that makes the decisions in place of markets.

The planning authority decides what will be produced and how. Since most planned economies directed resources into the production of capital and military goods, there was little remaining for consumer goods and the result was chronic shortages. Price functioned as an accounting measure and did not reflect scarcity. The former Soviet Union and most of the Eastern Bloc countries were planned economies of this sort.

In between the two extremes is **market socialism**. This is a mixed economic system that uses both markets and planning. Planning is usually used to direct resources at the upper levels of the economy, with markets being used to determine prices of consumer goods and wages. This kind of economic system answers the three questions with planning and markets. The former Yugoslavia was a market socialist economy.

You can put each nation of the world on a continuum in terms of these characteristics and rank them from most capitalistic to the most planned. The United States would probably rank as the most capitalistic, and North Korea would probably rank as the most planned, but this doesn't mean that the United States doesn't engage in planning or that economies like mainland China don't use markets.

Skill 41.5   Demonstrate understanding of the concepts of absolute and comparative advantage, free trade, and the impacts of trade barriers such as tariffs and quotas

Trade theory is based on prices and costs. A nation has an absolute advantage in the production of a good when it can produce that good more efficiently than the other nations can. It is comparative advantage that is the basis for international trade. Trade that takes place on the basis of comparative advantage results in lower output prices and higher resource prices. According to trade theory, nations or regions should specialize in the production of the good, which they can produce at a relatively lower cost than the other country can. In other words, if in country A one unit of X costs one unit of Y, and in country B one unit of X costs three units of Y, good X is cheaper in country A and good Y is cheaper in country B. It takes only one third of a unit of X to produce one unit of Y in country B, whereas it takes one unit of Y in country A. Therefore, country B has the comparative advantage in the production of Y and country A has the comparative advantage in the production of good X. Theory says that each country should specialize in the production of the good in which it has the comparative advantage and trade for the other good. This means country B should use all of its resources to produce good Y and trade for good X. Country A should do the opposite and specialize in the production of good X and trade for good Y. Specialization and trade on this basis result in lower prices in both countries or regions and greater efficiency in the use of resources.

Each country will also experience increased consumption, since it is getting the maximum amount of output from its given inputs by specializing according to comparative advantage. Each country, or region, can consume its own goods and the goods it has traded for.

The introduction of national or international competition into a market can result in greater efficiency if the trade is without restrictions, like tariffs or quotas. Trade barriers cause inefficiencies by resulting in higher prices and lower quantities. A **tariff** is a tax that is added to the price of the import or export. The purpose is to raise the price of the import so people will buy the domestic good. This leads to higher employment levels in the domestic industry and unemployment in the foreign industry. Resources have shifted in the wrong direction because of the tariff. Tariffs are a way of exporting unemployment to the foreign country. **Quotas** are limits set on the physical number of units on imports or exports. An import quota limits the number of units entering a country; an export quota limits the number of units leaving the country. The result of limiting the quantity is to cause a higher price. Whether the trade barrier is a tariff or a quote, the result is to lower the volume of international trade. All of the benefits that were achieved with free trade are being lost. The results of trade barriers are lower levels of production, consumption, employment, and income.

Trade theory says that free trade is best. It results in the highest level of efficiency for the world. It results in the greatest levels of output, production, consumption, income, and employment. Any form of interference with free trade, like tariffs and quotas, deters from the highest level of efficiency. The world has less output from its available inputs. There are lower levels of income and employment. This is why there is a movement on for trade liberalization.

Skill 41.6 Demonstrate understanding of property rights, incentives, and the role of markets

Property rights perform an important function in our economy. The assignment of property rights entitles the owner to a payment for the use of his property. It is when the assignment of property rights is lacking that problems result. Pollution is an example of this situation. Assume a factory is dumping its wastes in a river. If the factory had to dispose of the wastes in another manner, it would have to pay a price for the disposal. It doesn't have to pay to dump its wastes in the river; the river is treated as a **free input**. The pollution is affecting other people in the area. They have dirty water, they can't swim or fish in it, vegetation is dying, there are odors, etc. If property rights for the river were assigned, the owner would charge for its use and the factory would have higher production costs. The pollution results from the river being a free input and the result is overproduction of the factory's product.

Incentives are part of a market economy that are absent in planned economies. All market participants are willing to take a risk for the opportunity of being a financial success. Entrepreneurs are willing to undertake the risk of new business ventures for the purpose of monetary gain. Resources move into higher than normal rate of return industries because they are attracted by the profit potential. Inventors are willing to take the risk of spending time and money trying to come up with new products in the hope of monetary gain. All of these represent the ways financial incentives operate in a market economy. Without a profit incentive, there would be no reason for firms to spend millions and billions on research and development and technological progress would be almost nonexistent. This was a problem in the planned economies in the Soviet era. Since the means of production were owned by the state, there was no incentive to improve technology or to develop new production processes. The individual had no reason to take the risks involved in entrepreneurial activities because there was nothing in it for him but a letter of commendation. The results were slow, inefficient production processes. In a market economy, the entrepreneur is willing to take the risks and knows there is a good probability that his business will fail but there is also a chance that it will succeed.

The existence of economic profits in an industry functions as a market signal to firms to enter the industry. Economic profits means there is an above normal rate of return in this industry. As the number of firms increases, the market supply curve shifts to the right. Assuming that cost curves stay the same, the expansion continues until the economic profits are eliminated and the industry is earning a normal rate of return. Depending on the level of capital intensity, this process might take a few years or it might take many years. The easier it is to shift resources from one industry to another, the faster the process will be. Resources will go where they earn the highest rate of return, especially if they are in a situation earning a lower than normal rate of return.

Profits are the market signal that indicates the proper allocation of resources in accordance with consumer preferences.

Skill 41.7 Demonstrate understanding of the supply and demand model and its application in the determination of equilibrium price in competitive markets

In a market economy, the markets function on the basis of supply and demand and, if markets are free, the result is an efficient allocation of resources. The seller's supply curve represents the different quantities of a good or service the seller is willing and able to bring to the market at different prices during a given period of time. The seller has to have the good and has to be willing to sell it. If either of these isn't true, then he isn't a part of the relevant market supply. The supply curve represents the selling and production decisions of the seller and is based on the costs of production. The costs of production of a product are based on the costs of the resources used in its production. The costs of resources are based on the scarcity of the resource. The scarcer a resource is, relatively speaking, the higher its price. A diamond costs more than paper because diamonds are scarcer than paper is. All of these concepts are embodied in the seller's supply curve.

The same thing is true on the buying side of the market. The buyer's preferences, tastes, income, etc. – all of his buying decisions – are embodied in the demand curve. The demand curve represents the various quantities of a good or a service the buyer is willing and able to buy at different prices during a given period of time. The buyer has to want the good and be willing and able to purchase it. He may want a Ferrari but can't afford one; therefore, he is not a part of the relevant market demand.

The demand side of the market is showing us what buyers are willing and able to purchase, and the supply side of the market is showing us what sellers are willing and able to supply. But we don't know anything about what buyers and sellers actually do buy and sell without putting the two sides together. If we compare the buying decisions of buyers with the selling decisions of sellers, the place where they coincide represents the market equilibrium. This is where the demand and supply curves intersect. At this one point of intersection, the buying decisions of buyers are equal to the selling decisions of sellers. The quantity that buyers want to buy at that particular price is equal to the quantity that sellers want to sell at that particular price. This is the market equilibrium. At this one point, the quantity demanded is equal to the quantity supplied. This price–quantity combination represents an efficient allocation of resources.

Consumers are basically voting for the goods and services that they want with their dollar spending. When a good accumulates enough dollar votes, the producer earns a profit. The existence of profits is the way the market signals the seller that he is using society's resources in a way that society wants them used. Consumers are obtaining the most satisfaction that they can from the way their society's scarce resources are being used. When consumers don't want a good or service, they don't purchase it and the producers don't accumulate enough dollar votes to have profits. **Losses** are the markets' way of signaling that consumers don't want their scarce resources used in the production of that particular good or service and that they want their resources used in some other manner. Firms that incur losses eventually go out of business. They either have a product that consumers don't want or they have an inefficient production process that results in higher costs and, therefore, higher prices. Higher costs than the competitors' means that there is inefficiency in production. All of this occurs naturally in markets in a market economy.

Skill 41.8 Demonstrate understanding of market surpluses and shortages

A market is in equilibrium when there is a price that equates quantity demanded and quantity supplied. The demand curve is based on consumer preferences and represents the different quantities of a good a consumer is willing and able to purchase at different prices during a given period of time. The supply curve is based on costs of production and represents the different quantities of a good that sellers are willing and able to sell at different prices during a given period of time. The point of intersection of demand and supply represents the price that equates quantity demanded and quantity supplied. It is the only price where quantity demanded is equal to quantity supplied. The market is in equilibrium. The equilibrium price is the price that is said to clear the market, and there is no tendency for this price-quantity combination to change. The price that clears the market results in no imbalances between quantities demanded and quantity supplied. The buying decisions of buyers coincide exactly with the selling decisions of sellers.

Market surpluses and shortages exist when the market in not in equilibrium. This occurs when there is an inequality between quantity supplied and quantity demanded. In other words, the market price does not equate quantity demanded with quantity supplied. Let's look at a situation with a price above the market equilibrium price. The higher price results in a larger quantity supplied, as sellers are willing to supply larger quantities at higher prices than they are at lower prices. The higher price also means that buyers don't want as many units of output. Buyers are willing and able to buy larger quantities at lower prices, not at higher prices. So the higher price results in a situation where quantity supplied is greater than quantity demanded, or there is a surplus of the good. The seller begins to offer the surplus goods at a lower price.

As price comes down, more buyers are willing to buy the good. A lower price results in a larger quantity demanded.

So price continues to fall until the surplus is eliminated and the market is back at equilibrium, where quantity demanded is equal to quantity supplied.

Let's consider the effects of a price below the market equilibrium. At the lower price, sellers don't want to sell as much. The lower price results in a smaller quantity supplied by sellers. The lower price means an increase in quantity demanded by buyers, who want to buy larger quantities at lower prices than at higher prices. The result is a situation where quantity demanded exceeds quantity supplied. There is a shortage in the market. Because of the shortage of the good, buyers who want the good begin to bid up the price.

The higher price results in more producers willing to sell the good. As the price rises, there is a decrease in the quantity demanded of consumers, who will buy fewer units of a good at higher prices than at lower prices. This process of bidding up prices continues until the shortage has been eliminated and that market is back in equilibrium, where quantity demanded equals quantity supplied.

Whenever there is a situation of disequilibrium in a market, the market will function to eliminate the inequality. A surplus of goods will cause the price to fall; a shortage of goods will cause the price to rise. A disequilibrium situation will never last for long in a market because the market functions in such a way that it will eliminate the disequilibrium. This is called the rationing function of prices.

Skill 41.9 Demonstrate understanding of the role of government and the impact of price ceilings, price floors, and taxes on market outcomes

Price controls interfere with the market's ability to arrive at an equilibrium price that equates supply and demand. Price controls rob the market of what is called the rationing function of prices—the ability to adjust to equate demand and supply because they are administratively imposed prices above or below the market equilibrium.

A price imposed above the market equilibrium price is called a **price floor**. It represents the highest price that can be charged for the good. The price of the good cannot rise above the price floor. At the imposed floor price, the market cannot equate supply and demand. The higher legally mandated price results in a larger quantity supplied, as sellers are willing to supply larger quantities at higher prices than they are at lower prices. The higher price also means that buyers don't want as many units of output. Buyers are willing and able to buy larger quantities at lower prices than at higher prices.

So the legally imposed floor price results in a situation where quantity supplied is greater than quantity demanded, or there is a surplus of the good and there is no way that the market can function to eliminate the surplus because it can't lower prices to attract more buyers. This has been the situation in agriculture for years.

A **price ceiling** is a legally imposed price below the market equilibrium. Its purpose is to keep prices from rising, as in periods of severe inflation. With a price ceiling, the lower price results in a smaller quantity supplied by sellers. The lower price means an increase in quantity demanded by buyers, who want to buy larger quantities at lower prices than at higher prices. The result is a situation where quantity demanded exceeds quantity supplied, or a shortage. There is no way for the market to eliminate the shortage with buyers bidding up the price for the available quantity. The legally imposed price means that the price can't rise to eliminate the shortage and the shortage will remain as long as the price controls are in effect. When the price ceilings are lifted, prices usually shoot upwards as buyers and sellers try to make up for lost time.

Price controls, whether they are ceilings or floors, are never a good way to deal with economic problems. The market cannot function to remove the distortion in it. They result in misallocations of resources. Price floors, as in agriculture, result in an overallocation of resources to that industry and an overproduction of output that the market cannot eliminate by lowering prices. The resources used in agriculture are not being used elsewhere where they might be more productive. The price ceiling causes the opposite – an underallocation of resources and underproduction of output. Society is not getting enough of the output that it wants and is not having its resources used in the manner it wants them used in. Any interference with the market results in a misallocation.

A tax imposed on goods results in an additional cost to the producer. The higher costs mean the firm produces less output at that level of costs. The result is a decrease, or leftward shift, in the supply curve, causing new market equilibrium with a higher price and smaller quantity. This also results in a misallocation of resources.

Skill 41.10 Demonstrate understanding of the concept of market failure and public policy

Market failure is a situation where the price system doesn't function properly and results in a misallocation of resources. Even though the market is in equilibrium, the market isn't tabulating all of the costs of production and is causing the wrong quantity of a good to be produced. This is where a role for government is defined in the area of public policy.

Pollution is an example of market failure. Pollution is referred to as a negative externality, a situation where the effects of the market are affecting a non-involved third party. Assume a factory is dumping its wastes in a river. If the factory had to dispose of the wastes in another manner, it would have to pay a price for the disposal. It doesn't have to pay to dump its wastes in the river; the river is treated as a free input. The pollution is affecting other people in the area. They have dirty water they can't swim or fish in, vegetation is dying, there are odors, etc.

If property rights for the river were assigned, the owner would charge for its use and the factory would have higher production costs. The pollution results from the river being a free input, and the result is overproduction of the factory's product. Another role for government here is to shift the cost onto the producer with a tax or a fine. This raises the costs to the firm and results in a decrease in supply. This corrects somewhat for the overallocation of resources. The government can also outlaw the pollution.

Another form of market failure concerns public goods. These are goods that the market can't produce or won't produce because it isn't profitable. The best example of a public good is national defense. A public good is indivisible or incapable of being consumed on an individual basis. There is no such thing as buying one unit of national defense. The public good is consumed on a collective basis. No one can be excluded from the public good. The role for government is to provide the public goods that the market can't provide.

Market economies result in some firms acquiring market power. In some cases, called natural monopoly, the cost structure is such that there can be only one firm in the industry, like the electric company. Monopoly results in higher prices and lower levels of output, which is a misallocation of resources. The role for government here is to regulate the natural monopolist so there is more output at an equitable price. In situations where the firm isn't a natural monopolist but has too much market power, government uses anti-trust laws to protect and promote the competitiveness of the marketplace.

Public policy is also required in the areas of income inequality and macro instability. These are also forms of market failure. The market doesn't result in an equal or equitable distribution of income. Government tries to remedy this situation with income redistribution through programs like welfare or food stamps and also through the progressive federal income tax system. Since the business cycle results in periods of inflation and unemployment, government uses monetary and/or fiscal policy to promote stability in the macroeconomy. Whenever the price system doesn't function properly and results in inefficiency, there is a role defined for government and public policy.

COMPETENCY 42.0 MICROECONOMICS II

Skill 42.1 Demonstrate knowledge of types of market structure and the characteristics and behavior of firms in perfect competition, monopoly, oligopoly, and monopolistic competition

Firms sell their outputs in different output market structures. There are four kinds of market structures in the output market: **perfect competition, monopoly, monopolistic competition, and oligopoly**. Each of these market structures differs in terms of competition. Perfect competition is the most competitive of all market structures. For the most part, perfect competition is a theoretical extreme, most closely approximated by agriculture. Products are homogenous in this market structure. The numerous firms sell a product identical to that sold by all other firms in the industry and have no control over the price. There are a large number of buyers and a large number of sellers, and no one buyer or seller is large enough to affect market price. The price is determined by supply and demand, and the price is a given to the firm. This means the individual firm faces a horizontal or perfectly elastic demand curve. Buyers and sellers have full market information, and there are no barriers to entry. A barrier to entry is anything that makes it difficult for firms to enter or leave the industry.

The opposite of perfect competition is a monopoly. **Monopoly** is a market structure in which there is only one seller who is selling a unique product for which there are no substitutes. The firm is the only supplier of the good. The firm can control the price because the firm is equal to the industry. A monopolist becomes a monopolist and remains a monopolist because of barriers to entry, which are very high. These barriers to entry, like a very high fixed cost structure, function to keep new firms from entering the industry. Monopoly in its pure form is rare and is illegal in the U.S. economy.

In between the two extremes are the two market structures that all U.S. firms fall into. **Oligopoly** is a market structure in which there are a few sellers of products that may be either homogeneous, like steel, or heterogeneous, like automobiles. There are high barriers to entry, which is why there are only a few firms in each industry. Each firm has some degree of monopoly power but not as much as a monopolist.

Oligopoly is a market structure in which firms' actions and reactions are dependent on one another. Each firm must consider the actions of its rivals when making any decisions. This is referred to as a mutual interdependence in decision making. If Ford offers rebates, Chrysler will also offer rebates to keep its customers. Monopolistic competition is the market structure you see in shopping centers. There are numerous firms, each selling similar products, but not identical, like brand name shoes or clothing. Products are close substitutes for one another. Each firm has a small market share, since no one firm is large enough to dominate the industry. Barriers to entry are not as high as in oligopoly, which is why there are more firms. It is relatively easy for most firms to enter or leave the industry.

When products are close substitutes for one another, firms engage in advertising, or non-price competition, to try to differentiate their product from their competitors. Advertising and non-price competition occur in monopolistic competition and homogeneous oligopoly.

Skill 42.2 Demonstrate understanding of factor markets and the determination of income distributions and the returns to factors of production

There are input and output markets in the economy. Output markets refer to the market in which goods and services are sold. The input market is the market in which factors of production, or resources, are bought and sold. Factors of production, or inputs, fall into four broad categories: land, labor, capital, and entrepreneurs. Each of these four inputs is used in the production of every good and service. When the consumer goes to the local shoe store to buy a pair of shoes, the shoes are the output and the consumer is taking part in the output market. However, the shoe store is a participant in both the input and output market. The sales clerk and store's workers are hiring out their resource of labor in return for a wage rate. They are participating in the input market. In a market-oriented economy, all of these markets function on the basis of supply and demand, whether they are input or output markets. The equilibrium price is determined where the buying decisions of buyers coincide with the selling decision of sellers. This is true whether the market is an input market with a market rate of wage or an output market with a market price of the output. This results in the most efficient allocation of resources.

A firm's production decisions are based on its costs. Every product is produced using inputs or resources. As said above, these are called factors of production and there are four that are used in the production of every good and service. They are labor, land, capital, and entrepreneurs. The firm hires these factors in the input or resource market. The production process refers to the method in which resources are combined to produce a good or service. Each factor of production earns its factor income in the resource market.

Labor earns the factor income called wages, capital earns interest, land earns rent, and the entrepreneur earns profit. The labor market illustrates the variation in market structure. There can be a competitive market structure, such as the market for unskilled labor. The laborer is the wage-taker with the wage rate more or less given. Labor markets can also be unionized. When there is a union, the wage rate and benefits are negotiated by the employer and the union representatives.

The factor income for capital is the interest rate, which is determined by the intersection of the demand for loanable funds curve and the supply of loanable funds curve. The supply of loanable funds comes from savings. When people save their money, they are delaying consumption. They must receive a payment to induce them to save. This payment is called the **interest rate**. Lenders pay a price for borrowed funds, which is also the interest rate. The interest rate equates the quantity demanded of loanable fund with the quantity supplied of loanable funds and represents the payment to owners of capital.

Land is a factor that is fixed in supply, so it has a perfectly inelastic supply curve. No matter what the price is, it can't result in an increased supply of land. Rent, then, the factor payment to land, is determined solely by demand.

Profit is the factor income for the entrepreneur. Profit is equal to total revenue minus total cost. It is the entrepreneur's reward for the risk he incurs.

COMPETENCY 43.0 MACROECONOMICS I

Skill 43.1 Demonstrate understanding of gross domestic product (GDP) and its components

Macroeconomics refers to the functioning of the economy on the national level and the functioning of the aggregate units that comprise the national economy. It is concerned with a study of the economy's overall economic performance, or what is called the **Gross Domestic Product or GDP.** The GDP is a monetary measure of the economy's output during a specified time period. Tabulating the economy's output can be measured in two ways, both of which give the same result: the expenditures approach and the incomes approach. Basically, what is spent on the national output by each sector of the economy is equal to what is earned producing the national output by each of the factors of production. The two methods have to be equal.

The macro economy consists of four broad sectors: **consumers, businesses, government** and the **foreign sector**. In the expenditures approach, GDP is determined by the amount of spending in each sector. GDP is equal to the consumption expenditures of consumers plus the investment expenditures of businesses plus spending of all three levels of government plus the net export spending in the foreign sector.

$$GDP = C + I + G + (X-M)$$

The above formula is called the GDP identity. The computation of GDP includes only final goods and services, not the value of intermediate goods. An intermediate good is a good that is used in the production of other goods. It is an input, and its value is included in the price of the final good. If the value of intermediate goods is included, there would be double counting and GDP would be overstated.

What is spent buying the national output has to be equal to what is earned in producing the national output. This basically involves computing the incomes of the four factors with several adjustments being made. Labor earns wages, which is called Compensation of Employees. Land earns Rental Income, and capital earns Interest Income. The first three are pretty straightforward. Since entrepreneurial ability can be in the form of individual effort or corporations, there are two different categories here. The return to the individual entrepreneur is called Proprietor's Income. The return to the corporation is called Corporate Profit. Corporations do three things with their profits: they pay the corporate profits tax, they pay dividends and the rest is kept as retained earnings. So these are the three components of corporate profits.

To complete the tabulation of GDP from the incomes approach, we have to adjust for two non-income charges. First are Indirect Business Taxes, like property taxes and sales taxes. Second is depreciation or the amount of capital that is worn out producing the current term's output. Both Indirect Businesses Taxes and depreciation are subtracted, and the figure remaining is GDP. This figure is identical to the figure computed in the expenditures approach.

Skill 43.2   Demonstrate understanding of how unemployment is measured and its causes and consequences

When the economy is functioning smoothly, the amount of national output produced, or the aggregate supply, is just equal to the amount of national output purchased, or **aggregate demand**. Then we have an economy in a period of prosperity without economic instability. But market economies experience the fluctuations of the business cycle, the ups and downs in the level of economic activity. There are four phases: **boom** (period of prosperity), **recession** (a period of declining GDP and rising unemployment), **trough** (the low point of the recession), and **recovery** (a period of lessening unemployment and rising prices). There are no rules pertaining to the duration or severity of any of the phases. The phases result in periods of unemployment and periods of inflation. Inflation results from too much spending in the economy. Buyers want to buy more than sellers can produce and bid up prices for the available output. Unemployment occurs when there is not enough spending in the economy.

Sellers have produced more output than buyers are buying and the result is a surplus situation. Firms faced with surplus merchandise lower their production levels and layoff workers and there is unemployment. These are situations that require government policy actions.

A deficiency in aggregate spending results in **unemployment**. There is not enough aggregate demand in the economy to cause producers to produce enough output that requires the full labor force to be employed. Unemployment is measured by the unemployment rate, which is the percentage of the labor force that is unemployed. The labor force consists of people aged sixteen or older who are working or who want to work and are actively seeking employment. It does not include people who can't work because they are too young or are institutionalized or those who do not want to work, like the retired population or the parent that stays home with the children. There are certain situations that cause these figures to be inaccurate. First of all, the figures don't account for underemployment or for people who are working part-time while looking for full-time employment. They just ask if the person is employed; it doesn't matter if it is full-time employment or part-time employment. This practice tends to understate the unemployment rate. The figures also do not account for the discouraged worker. This is the worker who has given up trying to find employment. The figures treat him as being out of the labor force because he is not actively looking for employment. This practice also understates the published unemployment figures.

The last problem is people who give false information. People may claim to be actively seeking employment when they really aren't, just to collect unemployment compensation. This tends to overstate the published figures.

Unemployment tends to strike certain groups in society harder than other groups. Blue-collar workers are usually more likely to be laid off in a recession than are white-collar workers. Teenagers are more likely to be unemployed than adults are. They have fewer job skills and higher quit rates than do adults. The black population usually has higher unemployment rates than the white population. This is due to discrimination, more blacks in blue-collar jobs, and living in areas where employment opportunities are not that good. Unemployment is not just an individual problem.

Skill 43.3 Demonstrate understanding of inflation and its causes and consequences

The overall macroeconomic instability problems of inflation and unemployment are, for the most part, caused by the inequality of aggregate demand and aggregate supply. They are referred to as the twin evils of capitalism. Inflation results from excess aggregate demand; buyers want to buy a larger quantity of national output at a given price level than sellers can produce and sell.

An economy that is growing too rapidly and has too high a level of spending has inflation, a period of rises in the price level as buyers bid up prices to obtain the given supply of goods and services. Inflation results in a dollar with less purchasing power. When there is, say, five percent inflation, this means the $100 that bought $100 of goods last year buys just $95 of goods this year. Goods and services are more expensive.

The inflation rate is computed from index numbers. The formula is very simple.

$$\text{Price Index} = \frac{\text{Price in any year}}{\text{Price in base year}} \times 100$$

Any year in the series can be selected as the base year, and it is then used to compute the index number for the rest of the years, as given in the above formula.

The index numbers are then used to compute the inflation rate using the formula below:

$$\text{Inflation Rate} = \frac{\text{This year's index \#} - \text{Last year's index \#}}{\text{Last year's index \#}}$$

Inflation affects different people in different ways. Some people are affected more than others are. People on fixed incomes feel the effects of inflation more than people who have flexible incomes. Social security benefits are an example of a fixed income. The recipients can't request a raise like working people can. They lose purchasing power during periods of inflation. The value of tangible assets increases during inflation. If you own assets, like a house, you experience an increase in your net worth because of inflation. On the other hand, the amount of your savings account is fixed and has less purchasing power because of inflation. How inflation affects people depends on the individual position.

Inflation is caused by the economy expanding too quickly. There is excess aggregate demand that is fueling the inflation. This is a situation where the appropriate governmental action is to slow down the economy. The government will implement policies that result in less spending in the economy to end the inflation. These will be **contractionary** monetary and fiscal policy. Contractionary monetary policy will result in the banking system having less money available for loans. Aspects of contractionary monetary policy consist of raising the reserve ratio, raising the discount rate and selling bonds. Contractionary fiscal policy consists of raising taxes and/or decreasing government spending. If there is less money to spend in the economy, it takes the pressure off prices because there is a decrease in aggregate demand, which slows down the economy and stops the rising price level.

COMPETENCY 44.0 MACROECONOMICS II

Skill 44.1 Demonstrate understanding of national income determination using aggregate demand and supply analysis

Macroeconomics is concerned with a study of the economy's overall economic performance, or what is called the Gross Domestic Product or GDP. The GDP is a monetary measure of the economy's output during a specified time period and is used by all nations to measure and compare national production. Tabulating the economy's output can be measured in two ways, both of which give the same result: the expenditures approach and the incomes approach. Basically, what is spent on the national output by each sector of the economy is equal to what is earned producing the national output by each of the factors of production. The two methods have to be equal.

The macro economy consists of four broad sectors: consumers, businesses, government, and the foreign sector. In the expenditures approach, GDP is determined by the amount of spending in each sector. GDP is equal to the consumption expenditures of consumers plus the investment expenditures of businesses plus spending of all three levels of government plus the net export spending in the foreign sector.

$$GDP = C + I + G + (X-M)$$

The above formula is called the GDP identity. The computation of GDP includes only final goods and services, not the value of intermediate goods. An intermediate good is a good that is used in the production of other goods. It is an input, and its value is included in the price of the final good. If the value of intermediate goods is included, there would be double counting and GDP would be overstated.

This can be shown in terms of the aggregate demand-aggregate supply model. The aggregate demand curve represents the different quantities of national output that the people in the economy are willing and able to purchase at different price levels during a given period of time. The aggregate supply curve represents the different quantities of the national output that producers are willing and able to supply at different price levels during a given period of time. Where the aggregate demand and aggregate supply curves intersect determines the price level in the economy and the equilibrium level of output, income, and employment in the economy. The quantity of output is the monetary value of all final goods and services produced by the economy during a given time period, which is the definition of the Gross Domestic Product, shown in the above GDP identity. The intersection of aggregate demand and aggregate supply shows the level of employment because there is a certain level of employment required to produce that dollar amount of output. A lower level of output requires fewer workers; a higher level of output requires more workers.

The figure derived from computing GDP by summing its components in the GDP identity is the same figure that is derived by taking a graphical approach and looking at the intersection of aggregate demand and aggregate supply. Both are giving the monetary value of the output level.

Skill 44.2 Demonstrate understanding of fiscal policy and its instruments

Fiscal policy consists of changing the level of taxes and government spending to influence the level of economic activity. Contractionary fiscal policy consists of decreasing government spending and/or raising taxes and is intended to slow down a rapidly expanding economy and to curb inflation. Expansionary fiscal policy consists of lowering taxes and raising government spending to stimulate a sluggish economy and generate higher levels of employment. Changes take place in government revenues and expenditures when fiscal policy is used.

The **federal budget** is a statement showing government expenditures and revenues for the fiscal year. The government's budget does not have to balance. When government expenditures are equal to revenues, the budget is balanced. When government expenditures are greater than revenues, the government has a budget deficit. When government expenditures are less than revenues, the government has a budget surplus. Whenever there is a budget deficit, whenever government spends more than it receives, the budget deficit has to be financed. The government can finance its deficit by borrowing or by the process of money creation. When government borrows, it sells bonds and uses the funds acquired by the bond sales to finance its deficit. Money creation refers to increasing the reserves in the banking system. Expansionary fiscal policy—lowering taxes and increasing government spending—puts the budget in a deficit position where government is spending more than it is taking in.

If we add all of the deficits that have occurred over time and subtract from it the figures for all of the surpluses, we have the figure for the national debt.

National debt = Total Surpluses – Total Deficits

The figure for the national debt represents the amount of money that government owes to the holders of U.S. government debt obligations. These are basically Treasury bonds, notes, and bills. Every time you buy a U.S. savings bond, you are helping to finance the national debt because you are loaning money to the government. Every year that the federal government has a budget deficit that is financed by borrowing, the size of the national debt increases and so do the interest payments on the debt. Whenever the government implements contractionary fiscal policy to stimulate the economy and this fiscal policy results in a budget deficit, then the size of the national debt increases.

Skill 44.3   Demonstrate understanding of the Federal Reserve System and monetary policy

Nations need a smoothly functioning banking system in order to experience economic growth. The **Federal Reserve System** (Fed) provides the framework for the monetary system in the United States. The Fed implements monetary policy through the banking system, and it is a tool used to promote economic stability at the macro level of the economy. There are three components of monetary policy: the **reserve ratio**, the **discount rate**, and **open market operations**. Changes in any of these three components affect the amount of money in the banking system and, thus, the level of spending in the economy.

The reserve ratio refers to the portion of deposits that banks are required to hold as vault cash or on deposit with the Fed. The purpose of this reserve ratio is to give the Fed a way to control the money supply. These funds can't be used for any other purpose. When the Fed changes the reserve ratio, it changes the money creation and lending ability of the banking system. When the Fed wants to expand the money supply, it lowers the reserve ratio, leaving banks with more money to loan. This is one aspect of expansionary monetary policy. When the reserve ratio is increased, this results in banks having less money to make loans with, which is a form of contractionary monetary policy, which leads to a lower level of spending in the economy.

Another way in which monetary policy is implemented is by changing the discount rate. When banks have temporary cash shortages, they can borrow from the Fed. The interest rate on the funds they borrow is called the discount rate. Raising and lowering the discount rate is a way of controlling the money supply. Lowering the discount rate encourages banks to borrow from the Fed, instead of restricting their lending to deal with the temporary cash shortage. By encouraging banks to borrow, their lending ability is increased and this results in a higher level of spending in the economy. Lowering the discount rate is a form of expansionary monetary policy. Discouraging bank lending by raising the discount rate, then, is a form of contractionary monetary policy.

The final tool of monetary policy is called open market operations. This consists of the Fed buying or selling government securities with the public or with the banking system. When the Fed sells bonds, it is taking money out of the banking system. The public and the banks pay for the bonds, thus resulting in fewer dollars in the economy and a lower level of spending. The Fed selling bonds is a form of contractionary monetary policy that leads to a lower level of spending in the economy. The Fed is expanding the money supply when it buys bonds from the public or the banking system because it is paying for those bonds with dollars that enter the income-expenditures stream. The result of the Fed buying bonds is to increase the level of spending in the economy.

Skill 44.4 Demonstrate understanding of the major concepts in international finance and investment

All nations have records of their international transactions. A nation's international transactions are recorded in the Balance of Payments. The Balance of Payment consists of two major accounts: the Current Account, which gives the figures for the exchange of goods, services and unilateral transfers; and the Capital Account, which provides the figures for capital flows resulting from the exchange of real and financial assets. The Current Account contains the Balance of Trade, which are a nation's merchandise imports minus its merchandise exports. If the nation's exports are greater than its imports, it has a trade surplus. If its imports are greater than its exports, it has a trade deficit. Adding in the category of exports and imports of services gives the Balance on Goods and Services. Adding unilateral transfers, military expenditures and other miscellaneous items yields the Balance on Current Account. The Capital Accounts consists of strictly financial items in various categories. The last category is Statistical Discrepancies, which is a balancing entry so that the overall Balance of Payments always balances. This has to do with floating exchange rate regimes. It is the trade account that is watched closely today.

The exchange rates of most currencies today are determined in a floating exchange rate regime. In a clean float, supply and demand factors for each currency in terms of another are what determine the equilibrium price or the exchange rate. A clean float is a market functioning without any government interference, purely on the basis of demand and supply. Sometimes nations will intervene in the market to affect the value of their currency vis-à-vis the other currency. This situation is referred to as a managed or dirty float. A government is not required to intervene to maintain a currency value, as they were under a regime of fixed exchange rates. A government that intervenes in the currency market now does so because it wants to, not because it is required to intervene to maintain a certain exchange rate value. For example, if the U.S. government thinks the dollar is depreciating too much against the Canadian dollar, the U.S. government will buy U.S. dollars in the open market and pay for them with Canadian dollars. This increases the demand for U.S. dollars and increases the supply of Canadian dollars. The U.S. dollar appreciates, or increases in value, and the Canadian dollar depreciates, or decreases in value, in response to the government intervention. A stronger U.S. dollar means Canadian goods are cheaper for Americans and American goods are more expensive for Canadians.

In the international economy, capital flows where it earns the highest rate of return, regardless of national borders. If the interest rate is higher in London than it is in New York, dollars will be converted into pounds, which results in dollar depreciation and pound appreciation, as capital flows into London in response to the higher interest rate.

The weaker dollar means that U.S. exports are more attractive to foreigners. It also means that U.S. citizens pay a higher price for imports. Markets today are truly international when it comes to capital flows.

Skill 44.5 Demonstrate understanding of the determinants of long run economic growth

Economic growth can be defined as increases in real output over time. The growth rate is computed as the difference between the growth rate in two periods divided by the growth rate in the first period. Obviously, nations want to see their growth rates increase. Nations experience economic growth when there is an increase in the supply of resources or when they use their existing resources more efficiently. In other words, total output will increase whenever there is an increase in labor and a corresponding increase in productivity. There are many factors that enter into this.

Supply factors are factors that affect the physical capabilities of the economy. They involve the quantity and quality of resources. The first factor is natural resources, and this involves the quantity and quality of natural resources that a country has. Human resources are the second factor, and this involves the quantity and quality of the labor force. The quality of the labor force has to do with productivity or how much output they are producing. Factors affecting productivity have to do with education and training, health, nutrition, government policies in health and safety and environment, and the amount and quality of capital like equipment and machinery available for the worker to work with. This last one is determined by the level of investment and is called the Stock of Capital, which is the third factor. Here the capital-labor ratio is important because this shows the amount of capital a worker has to work with. If a nation has a growing labor force, it needs growth in its capital stock in order to experience growth. Higher levels of investment lead to higher growth rates. At the same time, the economy needs public investment in order to improve and expand the infrastructure. The last factor is technological progress. Technological progress results in new and better ways of doing things, new and more productive production processes. These supply factors determine the economy's ability to grow.

The other side of the growth rate has to do with the demand side of the economy. There must be sufficient demand in the economy to generate economic growth. Aggregate demand has to grow steadily to absorb the increased output that comes with growth. The economy must have full employment and full production in order to experience growth. Not only must all factors be employed; they must be employed in their most productive capacity.

The above discussion is illustrated as an outward shift of the Production Possibility Curve. This is the curve that shows the maximum amount of output that an economy can achieve given its supply of resource and its technology.

Technological progress and increases in the quality of labor result in economic growth, or outward shifts of the curve.

Skill 44.6 Demonstrate understanding of current national and international issues and controversies

Current national and international issues and controversies involve employment and trade issues. In today's world, markets are international. Nations are all part of a global economy. No nation exists in isolationism or is totally independent of other nations. **Isolationism** is referred to as autarky or a closed economy. No one nation has all of the resources needed to be totally self-sufficient in everything it produces and consumes. Even a nation with such a well-diversified resource base as the United States has to import items like coffee, tea and other staples. The United States is not as dependent on trade as are other nations, but we still need to trade for goods and items that we either can't produce domestically or that we can't produce as cheaply as other nations can.

Membership in a global economy means that what one nation does affects other nations because economies are linked through international trade, commerce, and finance. They all have open economies. International transactions affect the levels of income, employment and prices in each of the trading economies. The relative importance of trade is based on what percentage of Gross Domestic Product trade constitutes. In a country like the United States, trade represents only a few percent of GDP. In other nations, trade may represent over fifty percent of GDP. For those countries changes in international transactions can cause many economic fluctuations and problems.

Trade barriers are a way in which economic problems are caused in other countries. Suppose the domestic government is confronted with rising unemployment in the domestic industry due to cheaper foreign imports. Consumers are buying the cheaper foreign import instead of the higher priced domestic good. In order to protect domestic labor, government imposes a tariff, thus raising the price of the more efficiently produced foreign good. The result of the tariff is that consumers buy more of the domestic good and less of the foreign good. The problem is that the foreign good is the product of the foreign nation's labor. A decrease in the demand for the foreign good means foreign producers don't need as much labor, so they lay off workers in the foreign country. The result of the trade barrier is that unemployment has been exported from the domestic country to the foreign country. Treaties like NAFTA are a way of lowering or eliminating trade barriers on a regional basis. As trade barriers are lowered or eliminated, this causes changes in labor and output markets. Some grow; some shrink. These adjustments are taking place now for Canada, the United States, and Mexico. Membership in a global economy adds another dimension to economics, in terms of aiding developing countries and in terms of national policies that are implemented.

DOMAIN XI.   **SOCIOLOGY AND ANTHROPOLOGY**

COMPETENCY 45.0 SOCIALIZATION

Skill 45.1   **Demonstrate understanding of the role of socialization in society and of positive and negative sanctions in the socialization process**

Socialization is the process by which humans learn the expectations their society has for their behavior, in order that they might successfully function within that society.

Socialization takes place primarily in children as they learn and are taught the rules and norms of their culture. Children grow up eating the common foods of a culture and develop a "taste" for these foods, for example. By observing adults and older children, they learn about gender roles, and appropriate ways to interact.

Socialization also takes place among adults who change their environment and are expected to adopt new behaviors. Joining the military, for example, requires a different type of dress and behavior than civilian culture. Taking a new job or going to a new school are other examples of situations where adults must re-socialize.

Two primary ways that socialization takes place are through positive and negative sanctions. Positive sanctions are rewards for appropriate or desirable behavior, and negative sanctions are punishments for inappropriate behavior. Recognition from peers and praise from a parent are examples of positive sanctions that reinforce expected social behaviors. Negative sanctions might include teasing by peers for unusual behavior, or punishment by a parent.

Sanctions can be either formal or informal. Public awards and prizes are ways a society formally reinforces positive behaviors. Laws that provide for punishment of specific infractions are formal negative sanctions.

COMPETENCY 46.0 PATTERNS OF SOCIAL ORGANIZATION

Skill 46.1 Demonstrate knowledge of folkways, mores, laws, beliefs, and values

Sociologists have identified three main types of norms, or ways that cultures define behavioral expectations, each associated with different consequences if they are violated. These norms are called folkways, mores, and laws.

Folkways are the informal rules of etiquette and behaviors that a society follows in day-to-day practice. Forming a line at a shop counter or holding a door open for an elderly person are examples of folkways in many societies. Someone who violates a folkway— by pushing to the front of a line, for instance—might be seen as rude, but is not thought to have done anything immoral or illegal.

Mores are stronger than folkways in the consequences they carry for not observing them. Examples of mores might include honesty and integrity. Cheating on a test or lying might violate a social more, and a person who does so may be considered immoral.

Laws are formal adoptions of norms by a society with formal punishment for their violation. Laws are usually based on the mores of a society. The more that it is wrong to kill is codified in a law against murder, for example. Laws are the most formal types of social norm, as their enforcement is specifically provided for. Folkways and mores, on the other hand, are primarily enforced informally by the fellow members of a society.

The folkways, mores, and laws of a society are based on the prevailing beliefs and values of that society. Beliefs and values are similar and interrelated systems.

Beliefs are those things that are thought to be true. Beliefs are often associated with religion, but beliefs can also be based on political or ideological philosophies. "All men are created equal" is an example of an ideological belief.

Values are what a society thinks are right and wrong and are often based on and shaped by beliefs. The value that every member of the society has a right to participate in his government might be considered to be based on the belief that "All mean are created equal," for instance.

Skill 46.2 Demonstrate understanding of social stratification

Social Stratification is the division of a society into different levels based on factors such as race, religion, economic standing or family heritage. Various types of social stratification may be closely related. For instance, stratification by race may result in people of one race being relegated to a certain economic class as well.

The pioneering sociologist Max Weber theorized that there are three components of social stratification: class, status, and political.

Social class, as Weber defined it, is based on economics and a person's relationship to the economic market, e.g. a factory worker is of a different social class than a factory owner. Social status is based on non-economic factors like honor or religion. Political status is based on the relationships and influence one has in the political domain.

The economic revolutionary Karl Marx identified social stratification as the source of exploitation of one level of society by another and based his theory of revolution and economic reform on this belief.

Mobility between social strata may differ between societies. In some societies, a person may move up or down in social class owing to changes in one's personal economic fortunes, for instance. Political status can change when prevailing political thought shifts. Some systems of stratification are quite formal, however, as in the former caste system in India. In these systems, lines between strata are more rigid, with employment, marriage, and other social activities tightly defined by one's position.

COMPETENCY 47.0 SOCIAL INSTITUTIONS

Skill 47.1 Demonstrate understanding of the roles of the following social institutions and of their interactions: the family, education, government, religion, and the economy

Sociologists have identified five different types of institutions around which societies are structured: family, education, government, religion, and economy. These institutions provide a framework for members of a society to learn about and participate in a society and also allow for a society to perpetuate its beliefs and values to succeeding generations.

The **family** is the primary social unit in most societies. It is through the family that children learn the most essential skills for functioning in their society such as language and appropriate forms of interaction. The size of the family unit varies among cultures, with some including grandparents, aunts, uncles, and cousins as part of the basic family, who may all live together. The family is also related to a society's economic institutions, as families often purchase and consume goods as a unit. A family that works to produce its own food and clothing, as was the case historically in many societies, is also a unit of economic production.

Education is an important institution in a society because it allows for the formal passing on of a culture's collected knowledge. The institution of education is connected to the family because that is where a child's earliest education takes place. Educational traditions within a society are also closely associated with economic institutions because some levels of employment require specific academic achievement.

A society's **governmental** institutions often embody its beliefs and values. Laws, for instance, reflect a society's values by enforcing its ideas of right and wrong. The structure of a society's government can reflect a society's ideals about the role of an individual in his society. A democracy may emphasize that an individual's rights are more important than the needs of the larger society, while a socialist governmental institution may place the needs of the whole group first in importance.

Religion is frequently the institution from which spring a society's primary beliefs and values and can be closely related to other social institutions. Many religions have definite teachings on the structure and importance of the family, for instance. In some societies, the head of the government is also the head of the predominant religion, or the government may be operated on religious principles. Historically, formal educational institutions in many societies were primarily religious, and all religions include an educational aspect to teach their beliefs.

A society's **economic** institutions define how an individual can contribute and receive economic reward from his society. Economic institutions are usually closely tied to governmental institutions, each informing and regulating the other. They are linked to family institutions, as workers are often supporting more than one person with their wages. A society's economic institutions might affect its educational goals by creating a demand for certain skills and knowledge.

COMPETENCY 48.0 THE STUDY OF POPULATIONS

Skill 48.1 Demonstrate knowledge of populations, including the impact on society of changes in population growth and distribution, migration, and immigration

A **population** is a group of people living within a certain geographic area. Populations are usually measured on a regular basis by census, which also measures age, economic, ethnic, and other data. Populations change over time because of many factors, and these changes can have significant impact on cultures.

When a population grows in size, it becomes necessary for it to either expand its geographic boundaries to make room for new people or to increase its density. Population density is simply the number of people in a population divided by the geographic area in which they live. Cultures with a high population density are likely to have different ways of interacting with one another than those with low density, as people live in closer proximity to one another.

As a population grows, its economic needs change. More basic needs are required, and more workers are needed to produce them. If a population's production or purchasing power does not keep pace with its growth, its economy can be adversely affected. The age distribution of a population can impact the economy as well, if the number of young and old people who are not working is disproportionate to those who are.

Growth in some areas may spur migration to other parts of a population's geographic region that are less densely populated. This redistribution of population also places demands on the economy, since infrastructure is needed to connect these new areas to older population centers and land is put to new use.

Populations can grow naturally, when the rate of birth is higher than the rate of death, or by adding new people from other populations through immigration. Immigration is often a source of societal change as people from other cultures bring their institutions and language to a new area. Immigration also impacts a population's educational and economic institutions as immigrants enter the workforce and place their children in schools.

Populations can also decline in number, when the death rate exceeds the birth rate or when people migrate to another area. War, famine, disease, and natural disasters can also dramatically reduce a population. The economic problems from population decline can be similar to those from overpopulation because economic demands may be higher than can be met. In extreme cases, a population may decline to the point where it can no longer perpetuate itself and its members and their culture either disappear or are absorbed into another population.

COMPETENCY 49.0 MULTICULTURAL DIVERSITY

Skill 49.1 Define the concepts of ethnocentrism and cultural relativity

Ethnocentrism and **cultural relativity** are terms used by sociologists to describe two ways of thinking about other cultures in relation to one's own culture. These terms have been expanded to describe two general ways that cultures view themselves and other cultures.

Ethnocentrism, as the word suggests, considers one's own culture to be the central and usually superior culture and views all other cultures in terms of how they are different. An ethnocentric view usually considers these different practices in other cultures as inferior, or even "savage."

Psychologists have suggested that ethnocentrism is a naturally occurring attitude. For the large part, people are most comfortable among other people who share their same upbringing, language, and cultural background and are likely to judge other cultural behaviors as alien or foreign.

In the objective study of other cultures, however, ethnocentrism can skew the way the behaviors of other cultures are interpreted. Current thinking is that the study of another culture should not be made in terms of the observer's own culture, but only in relation to that culture's other attributes. This is called cultural relativity. Cultural relativity aims to remove the biases and prejudices inherent in ethnocentrism to produce a clearer and more complete picture of other cultures.

Skill 49.2   Demonstrate knowledge of variation in race, ethnicity, and religion

Race is a term used most generally to describe a population of people from a common geographic area that share certain common physical traits. Skin color and facial features have traditionally been used to categorize individuals by race. The term has generated some controversy among sociologists, anthropologists, and biologists as to what, if race and racial variation mean anything. Biologically speaking, a race of people shares a common genetic lineage. Socially, race can be more complicated to define, with many people identifying themselves as part of a racial group that others might not. This self-perception of race, and the perception of race by others, is perhaps more crucial than any genetic variation when trying to understand the social implications of variations in race.

An **ethnic** group is a group of people who identify themselves as having a common social background and set of behaviors and who perpetuate their culture by traditions of marriage within their own group. Ethnic groups will often share a common language and ancestral background and frequently exist within larger populations with which they interact. Ethnicity and race are sometimes interlinked but differ in that many ethnic groups can exist within a population of people thought to be of the same race. Ethnicity is based more on common cultural behaviors and institutions than common physical traits.

Religion can be closely tied to ethnicity, as it is frequently one of the common social institutions shared by an ethnic group. Like ethnicity, religion varies in practices and beliefs even within the large major religions. Some religions and religious sects link their beliefs closely to their ancestry and so are closely linked to the concept of race.

Variations in race, ethnicity, and religion—both real and perceived—are primary ways in which cultures and cultural groups are defined. They are useful in understanding cultures but can also be the source of cultural biases and prejudices.

Eight common religions are practiced today. Interestingly, all of these religions have divisions or smaller sects within them. Not one of them is totally completely unified.

Judaism: the oldest of the eight and was the first to teach and practice the belief in one God, Yahweh.

Christianity: came from Judaism, grew and spread in the First Century throughout the Roman Empire, despite persecution. A later schism resulted in the Western (Roman Catholic) and Eastern (Orthodox) parts. Protestant sects developed as part of the Protestant Revolution.

The name "Christian" means one who is a follower of Jesus Christ, who started Christianity. Christians follow his teachings and examples, living by the laws and principles of the Bible.

Islam: founded in Arabia by Mohammed, who preached about God, Allah. Islam spread through trade, travel, and conquest. Followers of Islam, called Muslims, live by the teachings of the Koran, their holy book, and of their prophets.

Hinduism: begun by people called Aryans around 1500 BC and spread into India. The Aryans blended their culture with the culture of the Dravidians, natives they conquered. Today, it has many sects, promotes worship of hundreds of gods and goddesses and belief in reincarnation. Though forbidden today by law, a prominent feature of Hinduism in the past was a rigid adherence to and practice of the caste system.

Buddhism: developed in India from the teachings of Prince Gautama and spread to most of Asia. Its beliefs opposed the worship of numerous deities, the Hindu caste system and the supernatural. Worshippers must be free of attachment to all things worldly and devote themselves to finding release from life's suffering.

Confucianism: is a Chinese philosophy based on the teachings of the Chinese philosopher Confucius. There is no clergy and no belief in a deity or in life after death. It emphasizes political and moral ideas with respect for authority and ancestors. Rulers were expected to govern according to high moral standards.

Daoism: a native Chinese belief system with veneration for many deities and natural phenomena. It teaches all followers to make the effort to achieve the two goals of happiness and immortality. Practices and rituals include meditation, prayer, magic, reciting scriptures, special diets, breath control, beliefs in geomancy, fortune telling, astrology, and communicating with the spirits of the dead.

Shinto: the native religion of Japan developed from native folk beliefs worshipping spirits and demons in animals, trees, and mountains. According to its mythology, deities created Japan and its people, which resulted in worshipping the emperor as a god. Shinto never had strong doctrines on salvation or life after death.

Skill 49.3   Demonstrate understanding of the prevalence and consequences of discrimination and prejudice

Prejudice is the act of pre-judging something or someone without firsthand experience. It often involves making judgments based on stereotypes, or the automatic rejection of a behavior or practice that seems unusual or foreign.

Discrimination takes place when a person or group acts out of prejudice to harm or deny privileges to another. Discrimination takes place between all races and ethnic groups and between men and women at all levels. It can occur between individuals or groups.

In some cases, discrimination based on prejudice is official government policy and is reflected in the laws of a society. The United States has a history of official racial discrimination. The enslavement of black people was legal and common until the end of the Civil War in the mid-19th Century. Once blacks were free, however, dominant prejudicial thinking at the time was that they did not possess the intelligence or moral ability to participate equally in society. As a result, various laws were passed that discriminated against blacks' voting rights, property ownership and education. These "Jim Crow" laws also regulated how and where blacks could participate in commerce. Jim Crow laws remained in effect in many areas of the U.S. until the 1960s.

These racial prejudices also led to a two-tiered educational system in many parts of the country, with black children segregated into black schools. While officially, these schools were to receive the same support as other schools, in practice they were often poorly maintained, understaffed, and did not always have current teaching materials.

While official discrimination toward anyone on the basis of race is no longer legal in the U.S., it is still common and widespread. Unofficial discrimination can be equally damaging. In competitive situations such as applying for a job, racial or gender prejudices of the person making the decision of whom to hire may result in one or more candidates being discriminated against. A similar scenario may play out when a landlord is deciding to whom an apartment will be rented. This kind of discrimination, when it occurs systematically has the consequence of relegating groups of people to a lower economic level.

Skill 49.4 Demonstrate understanding of the concept of pluralism

Cultural **pluralism** is the simultaneous existence of several cultures and ethnic groups, with each afforded the protection and ability to observe their cultural institutions. It is also sometimes called multiculturalism.

The concept of cultural pluralism calls for mutual respect between ethnic groups and cultures, allowing them to exist together and perpetuate their cultures. As an ideal, multiculturalism aims to provide equal access and status to all cultures and so is often described in terms of civil rights, especially in reference to minority ethnic groups. Multiculturalism calls for official support of these ideals in the form of legislation and encourages this approach in school curricula.

Proponents of **multiculturalism** believe it also leads to the interchange of ideas, art, music, and other cultural features between groups. This interchange, it is thought, furthers the understanding and acceptance of a culturally pluralistic society, reducing prejudice and discrimination.

Multiculturalism can be controversial in some societies, especially those experiencing high rates of immigration. In some of these societies, there are a significant number of people who feel that newcomers should aim to assimilate into the dominant culture as much as possible and that multiculturalism should not receive official support or endorsement. As a result of this counter-movement, some groups have passed official language laws and other regulations intended to encourage or require a certain amount of assimilation by immigrants.

COMPETENCY 50.0 SOCIAL PROBLEMS

Skill 50.1 Demonstrate understanding of major contemporary social problems, including causes, consequences, and proposed solutions

The list of major social problems facing the world is long, with each culture approaching them based on their own values and beliefs. Four broad areas where social problems are affecting the world are the global economy, the environment, education, and health.

Economic - The world is becoming more global in its economy, requiring societies to adapt their production and economic strategies to suit these changing conditions. As some countries are able to capitalize on the emergence of new markets, the gap between poor countries that cannot participate is widening. Economic forces are also attracting immigrants from poorer countries to those with job opportunities, creating social stresses.

International organizations such as the U.N. and the World Bank have programs to assist developing nations with loans and education so they might join the international economy. Many countries are taking steps to regulate immigration.

Environmental - The impact a growing world population is having on the world environment is a subject of great concern and some controversy. Increased demand for food and fuel are creating environmental stresses that may have worldwide consequences.

The use of fossil fuels such as coal and natural gas, for instance, are widely thought to be contributing to the gradual warming of the planet by creating "greenhouse gases." The effects of this warming may include the rising of world sea levels and adverse changes in climate. Because oil and gas are non-renewable resources, continual exploration must take place to identify new sources. This drilling itself impacts the environment and presents potential pollution danger from pipelines and oil spills.

The international community has attempted to place limits on the production of greenhouse gases, but not all developed countries have agreed to these protocols. Many countries have placed limits on emissions from factories and automobiles in an effort to reduce the amount of pollution that enters the atmosphere. Alternative, "clean" energy resources are being researched.

Education - As the world's economy changes, educational needs change to provide a skilled workforce, and a society's ability to educate its people is crucial to participating in this economy. Likewise, educational institutions contribute to the artistic, cultural, and academic advancement of a nation.

Disparity in educational opportunities within and between nations can contribute to social and economic disparities. Failure to keep pace with international demands for certain fields of education can leave a country at a disadvantage.

Health - In most developed countries, the population is living longer and placing a higher demand on health care systems. This in turn places a burden on the larger society as taxes used to support the healthcare system rise, in the case of socialized medicine, or health insurance costs increase, as in private systems. In the U.S., people who are unemployed or otherwise unable to obtain health insurance are sometimes unable to meet the high costs of health care.

Diseases such as AIDS and other viruses are rampant in some parts of the world. Treatments can be difficult to come by either because of their high costs, or lack of organization to distribute them. International aid organizations exist to provide treatment to disease victims and to assist local governments in developing plans to reduce disease transmission.

COMPETENCY 51.0 HOW CULTURES CHANGE

Skill 51.1 Demonstrate understanding of how cultures change

Innovation is the introduction of new ways of performing work or organizing societies, and can spur drastic changes in a culture. Prior to the innovation of agriculture, for instance, human cultures were largely nomadic and survived by hunting and gathering their food. Agriculture led directly to the development of permanent settlements and a radical change in social organization. Likewise, technological innovations in the Industrial Revolution of the 19th Century changed the way work was performed and transformed the economic institutions of western cultures. Recent innovations in communications are changing the way cultures interact today.

Cultural diffusion is the movement of cultural ideas or materials between populations independent of the movement of those populations. Cultural diffusion can take place when two populations are close to one another, through direct interaction, or across great distances, through mass media and other routes. American movies are popular all over the world, for instance. Within the U.S., hockey, traditionally a Canadian pastime, has become a popular sport. These are both examples of cultural diffusion.

Adaptation is the process that individuals and societies go through in changing their behavior and organization to cope with social, economic and environmental pressures.

Acculturation is an exchange or adoption of cultural features when two cultures come into regular direct contact. An example of acculturation is the adoption of Christianity and western dress by many Native Americans in the United States.

Assimilation is the process of a minority ethnic group largely adopting the culture of the larger group it exists within. These groups are typically immigrants moving to a new country, as with the European immigrants who traveled to the United States at the beginning of the 20th Century who assimilated to American culture.

Extinction is the complete disappearance of a culture. Extinction can occur suddenly, from disease, famine or war when the people of a culture are completely destroyed, or slowly over time as a culture adapt, acculturate or assimilate to the point where their original features are lost.

Bibliography

Adams, James Truslow. (2006). "The March of Democracy," Vol 1. "The Rise of the Union". New York: Charles Scribner's Sons, Publisher.

Barbini, John & Warshaw, Steven. (2006). "The World Past and Present." New York: Harcourt, Brace, Jovanovich, Publishers.

Berthon, Simon & Robinson, Andrew. (2006. "The Shape of the World." Chicago:
Rand McNally, Publisher.

Bice, David A. (2006). "A Panorama of Florida II". (Second Edition). Marceline,
Missouri: Walsworth Publishing Co., Inc.

Bram, Leon (Vice-President and Editorial Director). (2006). "Funk and Wagnalls New Encyclopedia." United States of America.

Burns, Edward McNall & Ralph, Philip Lee. (2006. "World Civilizations Their History and Culture" (5th ed.). New York: W.W. Norton & Company, Inc., Publishers.

Dauben, Joseph W. (2006). "The World Book Encyclopedia." Chicago: World Book, Inc. A Scott Fetzer Company, Publisher.

De Blij, H.J. & Muller, Peter O. (2006). "Geography Regions and Concepts" (Sixth
Edition). New York: John Wiley & Sons, Inc., Publisher.

Encyclopedia Americana. (2006). Danbury, Connecticut: Grolier Incorporated, Publisher.

Heigh, Christopher (Editor). (2006). "The Cambridge Historical Encyclopedia of Great Britain and Ireland." Cambridge: Cambridge University Press, Publisher.

Hunkins, Francis P. & Armstrong, David G. (2006). "World Geography People and Places." Columbus, Ohio: Charles E. Merrill Publishing Co. A Bell & Howell Company, Publishers.

Jarolimek, John; Anderson, J. Hubert & Durand, Loyal, Jr. (2006). "World Neighbors." New York: Macmillan Publishing Company. London: Collier Macmillan Publishers.

McConnell, Campbell R. (2006). "Economics—Principles, Problems, and Policies" (Tenth Edition). New York: McGraw-Hill Book Company, Publisher.

Millard, Dr. Anne & Vanags, Patricia. (2006). "The Usborne Book of World History." London: Usborne Publishing Ltd., Publisher.

Novosad, Charles (Executive Editor). (2006). "The Nystrom Desk Atlas." Chicago: Nystrom Division of Herff Jones, Inc., Publisher.

Patton, Clyde P.; Rengert, Arlene C.; Saveland, Robert N.; Cooper, Kenneth S. & Cam, Patricia T. (2006). "A World View." Morristown, N.J.: Silver Burdette Companion, Publisher.

Schwartz, Melvin & O'Connor, John R. (2006). "Exploring A Changing World." New York: Globe Book Company, Publisher.

"The Annals of America: Selected Readings on Great Issues in American History 1620-1968." (2006). United States of America: William Benton, Publisher.

Tindall, George Brown & Shi, David E. (2006). "America—A Narrative History" (Fourth Edition). New York: W.W. Norton & Company, Publisher.

Todd, Lewis Paul & Curti, Merle. (2006). "Rise of the American Nation" (Third Edition). New York: Harcourt, Brace, Jovanovich, Inc., Publishers.

Tyler, Jenny; Watts, Lisa; Bowyer, Carol; Trundle, Roma & Warrender, Annabelle (2006) "The Usbome Book of World Geography." London: Usbome Publishing Ltd., Publisher.

Willson, David H. (2006). "A History of England." Hinsdale, Illinois: The Dryder Press, Inc. Publisher.

TEACHER CERTIFICATION STUDY GUIDE

Sample Test: Middle School Social Studies

1. Which of the following best describes current thinking on the major purpose of social science?

   A. Social science is designed primarily for students to acquire facts

   B. Social science should not be taught earlier than the middle school years

   C. A primary purpose of social sciences is the development of good citizens

   D. Social science should be taught as an elective

2. Psychology is a social science because:

   A. It focuses on the biological development of individuals

   B. It focuses on the behavior of individual persons and small groups of persons

   C. It bridges the gap between the natural and the social sciences

   D. It studies the behavioral habits of lower animals

3. A historian would be interested in:

   A. The manner in which scientific knowledge is advanced

   B. The effects of the French Revolution on world colonial policy

   C. The viewpoint of persons who have written previous "history"

   D. All of the above

4. The sub-discipline of linguistics is usually studied under:

   A. Geography

   B. History

   C. Anthropology

   D. Economics

5. Which of the following is not generally considered to be a discipline within the social sciences?

   A. Geometry

   B. Anthropology

   C. Geography

   D. Sociology

MID. LEVEL HUMANITIES

6. Economics is best described as:

   A. The study of how money is used in different societies

   B. The study of how different political systems produce goods and services

   C. The study of how human beings use limited resources to supply their necessities and wants

   D. The study of how human beings have developed trading practices through the years

7. Which of the following is most reasonably studied under the social sciences?

   A. Political science

   B. Geometry

   C. Physics

   D. Grammar

8. For the historian studying ancient Egypt, which of the following would be least useful?

   A. The record of an ancient Greek historian on Greek-Egyptian interaction

   B. Letters from an Egyptian ruler to his/her regional governors

   C. Inscriptions on stele of the Fourteenth Egyptian Dynasty

   D. Letters from a nineteenth century Egyptologist to his wife

9. A political scientist might use all of the following except:

   A. An investigation of government documents

   B. A geological timeline

   C. Voting patterns

   D. Polling data

10. A geographer wishes to study the effects of a flood on subsequent settlement patterns. Which might he or she find most useful?

    A. A film clip of the floodwaters

    B. An aerial photograph of the river's source

    C. Census data taken after the flood

    D. A soil map of the A and B horizons beneath the flood area

11. A social scientist observes how individual persons react to the presence or absence of noise. This scientist is most likely a:

    A. Geographer

    B. Political Scientist

    C. Economist

    D. Psychologist

MID. LEVEL HUMANITIES

12. As a sociologist, you would be most likely to observe:

    A. The effects of an earthquake on farmland

    B. The behavior of rats in sensory-deprivation experiments

    C. The change over time in Babylonian obelisk styles

    D. The behavior of human beings in television focus groups

13. An economist investigates the spending patterns of low-income individuals. Which of the following would yield the most pertinent information?

    A. Prime lending rates of neighborhood banks

    B. The federal discount rate

    C. City-wide wholesale distribution figures

    D. Census data and retail sales figures

14. A teacher and a group of students take a field trip to an Indian mound to examine artifacts. This activity most closely fits under which branch of the social sciences?

    A. Anthropology

    B. Sociology

    C. Psychology

    D. Political Science

15. Which of the following is most closely identified as a sociologist?

    A. Herodotus

    B. John Maynard Keynes

    C. Emile Durkheim

    D. Arnold Toynbee

16. We can credit modern geography with which of the following?

    A. Building construction practices designed to withstand earthquakes

    B. Advances in computer cartography

    C. Better methods of linguistic analysis

    D. Making it easier to memorize countries and their capitals

17. Adam Smith is most closely identified with which of the following?

   A. The law of diminishing returns

   B. The law of supply and demand

   C. The principle of motor primacy

   D. The territorial imperative

18. Margaret Mead may be credited with major advances in the study of:

   A. The marginal propensity to consume

   B. The thinking of the Anti-Federalists

   C. The anxiety levels of non-human primates

   D. Interpersonal relationships in non-technical societies

19. The advancement of understanding in dealing with human beings has led to a number of interdisciplinary areas. Which of the following interdisciplinary studies would NOT be considered under the social sciences?

   A. Molecular biophysics

   B. Peace studies

   C. African-American studies

   D. Cartographic information systems

20. Cognitive, developmental, and behavioral are three types of:

   A. Economists

   B. Political Scientists

   C. Psychologists

   D. Historians

21. A physical geographer would be concerned with which of the following groups of terms?

   A. Landform, biome, precipitation

   B. Scarcity, goods, services

   C. Nation, state, administrative subdivision

   D. Cause and effect, innovation, exploration

22. An economist might engage in which of the following activities?

   A. An observation of the historical effects of a nation's banking practices

   B. The application of a statistical test to a series of data

   C. Introduction of an experimental factor into a specified population to measure the effect of the factor

   D. An economist might engage in all of these

MID. LEVEL HUMANITIES

23. Political science is primarily concerned with _____.

   A. Elections

   B. Economic Systems

   C. Boundaries

   D. Public Policy

24. An anthropologist is studying a society's sororate and avunculate. In general, this scientist is studying the society's:

   A. Level of technology

   B. Economy

   C. Kinship practices

   D. Methods of farming

25. Of the following lists, which includes persons who have made major advances in the understanding of psychology?

   A. Herodotus, Thucydides, Ptolemy

   B. Adam Smith, Milton Friedman, John Kenneth Galbraith

   C. Edward Hall, E.L. Thorndike, B.F. Skinner

   D. Thomas Jefferson, Karl Marx, Henry Kissinger

26. The writing of history is called:

   A. Public policy analysis

   B. Historiography

   C. Historical perspective

   D. Historical analysis

27. If geography is the study of how human beings live in relationship to the earth on which they live, why do geographers include physical geography within the discipline?

   A. The physical environment serves as the location for the activities of human beings

   B. No other branch of the natural or social sciences studies the same topics

   C. The physical environment is more important than the activities carried out by human beings

   D. It is important to be able to subdue natural processes for the advancement of humankind

28. A historian might compare the governmental systems of the Roman Empire and the twentieth century United States with regard to which of the following commonalities?

   A. Totalitarianism

   B. Technological development

   C. Constitutional similarities

   D. Federalism

29. Capitalism and communism are alike in that they are both:

   A. Organic systems

   B. Political systems

   C. Centrally planned systems

   D. Economic systems

30. Which of the following demonstrates evidence of the interaction between physical and cultural anthropology?

   A. Tall Nilotic herdsmen are often expert warriors

   B. Until recent years the diet of most Asian peoples caused them to be shorter in stature than most other peoples

   C. Native South American peoples adopted potato production after invasion by Europeans

   D. Polynesians exhibit different skin coloration than Melanesians

31. A social scientist studies the behavior of four persons in a carpool. This is an example of:

   A. Developmental psychology

   B. Experimental psychology

   C. Social psychology

   D. Macroeconomics

MID. LEVEL HUMANITIES

32. Peace studies might include elements of all of the following disciplines except:

   A. Geography

   B. History

   C. Economics

   D. All of these might contribute to peace studies

33. Which of the following sets of terms relates to the Davisian erosion cycle?

   A. Youth, maturity, old age

   B. Atmospheric erosion, subsurface erosion, superficial erosion

   C. Fluvial, alluvial, estuarine

   D. Mississippian, Pennsylvanian, Illinoisian

34. What is a drumlin?

   A. A narrow ridge of sand, gravel, and boulders deposited by a stream flowing on, in, or under a nonmoving glacier

   B. Accumulated earth, pebbles, and stones carried by and then deposited by a glacier

   C. The active front face of a non-stagnant glacier

   D. An elongated or oval hill formed by drift material of glaciers

35. A coral island or series of islands which consists of a reef which surrounds a lagoon describes a(n):

   A. Needle

   B. Key

   C. Atoll

   D. Mauna

36. What type of cloud usually produces rain?

    A. Cirrus

    B. Cumulonimbus

    C. Altostratus

    D. Cirrostratus

37. Which of the following is NOT a type of rainfall?

    A. Convectional

    B. Cyclonic

    C. Adiabatic

    D. Frontal

38. The Mediterranean type climate is characterized by:

    A. Hot, dry summers and mild, relatively wet winters

    B. Cool, relatively wet summers and cold winters

    C. Mild summers and winters, with moisture throughout the year

    D. Hot, wet summers and cool, dry winters

39. The climate of Southern Florida is the _____ type.

    A. Humid subtropical

    B. Marine West Coast

    C. Humid continental

    D. Tropical wet-dry

40. Which of the following is an island nation?

    A. Luxembourg

    B. Finland

    C. Monaco

    D. Nauru

41. Which location may be found in Canada?

    A. 27 N 93 W

    B. 41 N 93 E

    C. 50 N 111 W

    D. 18 N 120 W

42. The highest point on the North American continent is:

    A. Mt. St. Helen's

    B. Denali

    C. Mt. Everest

    D. Pike's Peak

43. Concerning the present political map of Africa, which statement most closely applies?

   A. The modern states reflect an effort to establish political units based on ethnic groupings

   B. The international community allowed for a period of elasticity with regard to boundaries, so that a condition of relative equilibrium could develop

   C. Africans were given the task of delineating the modern states, using whatever criteria they chose

   D. The modern states reflect imposed boundaries, without regard to ethnic groupings or other indigenous considerations

44. Which of the following areas would NOT be a primary area of hog production?

   A. Midland England

   B. The Mekong delta of Vietnam

   C. Central Syria

   D. Northeast Iowa

45. Indo-European languages are native languages to each of the following EXCEPT:

   A. Germany

   B. India

   C. Italy

   D. Finland

46. A cultural geographer is investigating the implications of The Return of the Native by Thomas Hardy. He or she is most likely concentrating on:

   A. The reactions of British city-dwellers to the in-migration of French professionals

   B. The activities of persons in relation to poorly drained, coarse-soiled land with low-lying vegetation

   C. The capacity of riverine lands to sustain a population of edible amphibians

   D. The propagation of new crops introduced by settlers from North America

47. Which of the following is NOT considered to be an economic need:

   A. Food

   B. Transportation

   C. Shelter

   D. Clothing

48. As your income rises, you tend to spend more money on entertainment. This is an expression of the:

   A. Marginal propensity to consume

   B. Allocative efficiency

   C. Compensating differential

   D. Marginal propensity to save

49. A student buys a candy bar at lunch. The decision to buy a second candy bar relates to the concept of:

   A. Equilibrium pricing

   B. Surplus

   C. Utility

   D. Substitutability

50. If the price of Good G increases, what is likely to happen with regard to comparable Good H?

   A. The demand for Good G will stay the same

   B. The demand for Good G will increase

   C. The demand for Good H will increase

   D. The demand for Good H will decrease

51. A teacher has an extra $1,000 which she wishes to invest and wants to minimize the risk. The best choice for investment, from the following, is:

   A. Money market account

   B. Treasury bills

   C. Stock in a new company

   D. Certificate of deposit

52. In a command economy:

   A. The open market determines how much of a good is produced and distributed

   B. The government determines how much of a good is produced and distributed

   C. Individuals produce and consume a specified good as commanded by their needs

   D. The open market determines the demand for a good, and then the government produces and distributes the good

53. In a barter economy, which of the following would not be an economic factor?

   A. Time

   B. Goods

   C. Money

   D. Services

54. Of the following, the best example of an oligopoly in the United States is:

   A. Automobile industry

   B. Electric power provision

   C. Telephone service

   D. Clothing manufacturing

55. Which best describes the economic system of the United States?

   A. Most decisions are the result of open markets, with little or no government modification or regulation

   B. Most decisions are made by the government, but there is some input by open market forces

   C. Most decisions are made by open market factors, with important regulatory functions and other market modifications the result of government activity

   D. There is joint decision making by government and private forces, with final decisions resting with the government

56. An agreement in which a company allows a business to use its name and sell its products, usually for a fee, is called a:

   A. Sole proprietorship

   B. Partnership

   C. Corporation

   D. Franchise

57. What is a major difference between monopolistic competition and perfect competition?

   A. Perfect competition has many consumers and suppliers, while monopolistic competition does not

   B. Perfect competition provides identical products, while monopolistic competition provides similar but not identical products

   C. Entry to perfect competition is difficult, while entry to monopolistic competition is relatively easy

   D. Monopolistic competition has many consumers and suppliers, while perfect competition does not

58. Which concept is not embodied as a right in the First Amendment to the U.S. Constitution?

A. Peaceable assembly

B. Protection again unreasonable search and seizure

C. Freedom of speech

D. Petition for redress of grievances

59. In the Constitutional system of checks and balances, a primary "check" which accrues to the President is the power of:

A. Executive privilege

B. Approval of judges nominated by the Senate

C. Veto of Congressional legislation

D. Approval of judged nominated by the House of Representatives

60. According to the Constitution, any amendment must be ratified by _____ of the states to become a part of the Constitution:

A. Three-fourths

B. Two-thirds

C. Three-fifths

D. Five-sixths

61. Collectively, the first ten Amendments to the Constitution are known as the:

A. Articles of Confederation

B. Mayflower Compact

C. Bill of Rights

D. Declaration of the Rights of Man

62. In the United States, if a person is accused of a crime and cannot afford a lawyer:

A. The person cannot be tried

B. A court will appoint a lawyer, but the person must pay the lawyer back when able to do so

C. The person must be tried without legal representation

D. A court will appoint a lawyer for the person free of charge

63. Which of the following lists elements usually considered to be responsibilities of citizenship under the American system of government?

   A. Serving in public office, voluntary government service, military duty

   B. Paying taxes, jury duty, upholding the Constitution

   C. Maintaining a job, giving to charity, turning in fugitives

   D. Quartering of soldiers, bearing arms, government service

64. Consider the following passage from the Mayflower Compact: "...covenant, & combine ourselves together into a Civil body politick;" This demonstrates what theory of social organization?

   A. Darwinian

   B. Naturalistic

   C. Nonconsensual

   D. Constitutional

65. Why is the system of government in the United States referred to as a federal system?

   A. There are different levels of government

   B. There is one central authority in which all governmental power is vested

   C. The national government cannot operate except with the consent of the governed

   D. Elections are held at stated periodic times, rather than as called by the head of the government

66. Which of the following are NOT local governments in the United States?

   A. Cities

   B. Townships

   C. School boards

   D. All of these are forms of local government

67. The major expenditures of state governments in the United States go toward:

   A. Parks, education, and highways

   B. Law enforcement, libraries and highways

   C. Education, highways, and law enforcement

   D. Recreation, business regulation, and education

68. How does the government of France differ from that of the United States?

   A. France is a direct democracy, while the United States is a representative democracy

   B. France has a unitary form of national government, while the United States has a federal form of government

   C. France is a representative democracy, while the United States is a direct democracy

   D. France does not elect a President, while the United States elects a President

69. In the Presidential Election of 1888, Grover Cleveland lost to Benjamin Harrison, although Cleveland received more popular votes. How is this possible?

   A. The votes of certain states (New York, Indiana) were thrown out because of voting irregularities

   B. Harrison received more electoral votes than Cleveland

   C. None of the party candidates received a majority of votes, and the House of Representatives elected Harrison according to Constitutional procedures

   D. Because of accusations of election law violations, Cleveland withdrew his name and Harrison became President

70. How are major party candidates chosen to run for President in the United States?

   A. Caucuses of major party officeholders meet to select a state's choice for the party, and the candidate selected by the most states becomes the nominee

   B. Potential Presidential nominees seek pledges from each state party's chair and co-chair, and the candidate with the most pledges becomes the nominee

   C. Nationwide primaries are held by each party, to select delegates to a national nominating convention

   D. Each state party decides how to select delegates to a nominating convention; these selection processes may be caucuses, primaries, or any other method chosen by the state party

71. A person who receives more votes than anyone else in an election is said to have a _____ of the votes cast; a person who has over 50% of the votes in an election is said to have a _____ of the votes cast.

   A. Plurality; majority

   B. Majority; minority

   C. Plurality; minority

   D. Majority; plurality

72. Which of the following developments is most closely associated with the Neolithic Age?

   A. Human use of fire

   B. First use of stone chipping instruments

   C. Domestication of plants

   D. Development of metallurgical alloys

73. The Tigris-Euphrates Valley was the site of which two primary ancient civilizations?

   A. Babylonian and Assyrian

   B. Sumerian and Egyptian

   C. Hyksos and Hurrian

   D. Persian and Phoenician

74. The politics of classical Athens is best described by which of the following?

   A. Limited democracy, including both slaves and free men

   B. One man dictatorial rule

   C. Universal democracy among free owners of property

   D. Oligarchy with a few families controlling all decisions

MID. LEVEL HUMANITIES

75. The _____ were fought between the Roman Empire and Carthage.

   A. Civil Wars

   B. Punic wars

   C. Caesarian Wars

   D. Persian Wars

76. What Holy Roman Emperor was forced to do public penance because of his conflict with Pope Gregory VII over lay investiture of the clergy?

   A. Charlemagne

   B. Henry IV

   C. Charles V

   D. Henry VIII

77. The _____ declared monophysitism (the belief that Jesus was completely divine with no admixture of humanity) to be a heresy?

   A. Council of Nicaea

   B. Diet of Worms

   C. Council of Trent

   D. Council of Chalcedon

78. The painter of the Sistine Ceiling was:

   A. Raphael

   B. Michelangelo

   C. Leonardo da Vinci

   D. Titian

79. Luther issued strong objection to all but which of the following practices of the 15th Century Roman Catholic Church?

   A. The sacrament of baptism

   B. Absolution of sins through the intermediation of a priest and through ceremony

   C. The sale of indulgences, whereby the buyer may purchase purgation of sins

   D. Imposed church control over the individual conscience

80. The first explorer to reach India by sailing around the southern tip of Africa was:

   A. Amerigo Vespucci

   B. Vasco da Gama

   C. Ferdinand Magellan

   D. John Cabot

81. Vasco Nunez de Balboa accomplished which of the following?

    A. Sighting of the Pacific Ocean from lands discovered by Europeans in the 1500's

    B. The conquest of the Inca civilization through treachery and deceit

    C. The murder of the ruler of the Aztecs and subsequent subjugation of the Empire

    D. None of the above

82. Great Britain became the center of technological and industrial development during the nineteenth century chiefly on the basis of:

    A. Central location relative to the population centers of Europe

    B. Colonial conquests and military victories over European powers

    C. Reliance on exterior sources of financing

    D. Resources of coal and production of steel

83. The years 1793-94 in France, characterized by numerous trials and executions of supposed enemies of the Revolutionary Convention, were known as the:

    A. Reign of Terror

    B. Dark Ages

    C. French Inquisition

    D. Glorious Revolution

84. In the first aggression of World War II outside the Orient, identify the aggressor nation and the nation which was invaded:

    A. Germany; Sudetenland

    B. Italy; Abyssinia

    C. Germany; Poland

    D. Italy; Yugoslavia

85. In issuing an ultimatum for Soviet ships not to enter Cuban waters in October, 1962, President John F. Kennedy, as part of his decision, used the provisions of the:

    A. Monroe Doctrine

    B. Declaration of the Rights of Man

    C. Geneva Convention

    D. Truman Doctrine

86. In 1990, Alberto Fujimori was elected president of:

   A. Japan

   B. Okinawa

   C. South Korea

   D. Peru

87. Which of the following most closely characterizes the geopolitical events of the USSR in 1991-92:

   A. The USSR established greater military and economic control over the fifteen Soviet republics

   B. The Baltic States (Estonia, Latvia, Lithuania) declared independence, while the remainder of the USSR remained intact.

   C. Fourteen of fifteen Soviet republics declared some degree of autonomy; the USSR was officially dissolved; the Supreme Soviet rescinded the Soviet Treaty of 1922

   D. All fifteen Soviet republics simultaneously declared immediate and full independence from the USSR, with no provisions for a transitional form of government

88. Chinese civilization is generally credited with the original development of which of the following sets of technologies:

   A. Movable type and mass production of goods

   B. Wool processing and domestication of the horse

   C. Paper and gunpowder manufacture

   D. Leather processing and modern timekeeping

89. Extensive exports of gold and copper; elaborate court and constitution; trade links on both the Atlantic and Indian Oceans; use of heavy stone architecture; these most closely characterize the civilization of:

   A. Mwene Mutapa

   B. Chichen Itza

   C. Great Zimbabwe

   D. Muscat and Oman

90. Which of the following is NOT one of the Pillars of Faith of Islam?

   A. Alms-giving (zakah)

   B. Pilgrimage (hajj)

   C. Membership in a school of law (al-madhahib)

   D. Fasting (sawm)

MID. LEVEL HUMANITIES

91. The native metaphysical outlook of Japan, usually characterized as a religion, is:

    A. Tao

    B. Shinto

    C. Nichiren Shoju

    D. Shaolin

92. The Native Americans of the Eastern Woodlands lived on:

    A. Buffalo and crops such as corn, beans, and sunflowers

    B. Chiefly farming of squash, beans, and corn

    C. A variety of game (deer, bear, moose) and crops (squash, pumpkins, corn)

    D. Wolves, foxes, polar bears, walruses, and fish

93. Apartments built out of cliff faces; shared government by adult citizens; absence of aggression toward other groups. These factors characterize the Native American group known as:

    A. Pueblos

    B. Comanches

    C. Seminoles

    D. Sioux

94. Columbus first reached Western Hemisphere lands in what is now:

    A. Florida

    B. Bermuda

    C. Puerto Rico

    D. Bahamas

95. The "Trail of Tears" relates to:

    A. The removal of the Cherokees from their native lands to Oklahoma Territory

    B. The revolt and subsequent migration of the Massachusetts Pilgrims under pressure from the Iroquois

    C. The journey of the Nez Perce under Chief Joseph before their capture by the U.S. Army

    D. The 1973 standoff between federal marshals and Native Americans at Wounded Knee, S.D.

96. Bartholomeu Dias, in seeking a route around the tip of Africa, was forced to turn back. Nevertheless, the cape he discovered near the southern tip of Africa became known as:

    A. Cape Horn

    B. Cabo Bojador

    C. Cape of Good Hope

    D. Cape Hatteras

97. The Middle Colonies of the Americas were:

   A. Maryland, Virginia, North Carolina

   B. New York, New Jersey, Pennsylvania, Delaware

   C. Rhode Island, Connecticut, New York, New Jersey

   D. Vermont and New Hampshire

98. Slavery arose in the Southern Colonies partly as a perceived economical way to:

   A. Increase the owner's wealth through human beings used as a source of exchange

   B. Cultivate large plantations of cotton, tobacco, rice, indigo, and other crops

   C. Provide Africans with humanitarian aid, such as health care, Christianity, and literacy

   D. Keep ships' holds full of cargo on two out of three legs of the "triangular trade" voyage

99. Of the following, which contributed most to penetration of western areas by colonial Americans?

   A. Development of large ships capable of sailing upstream in rivers such as the Hudson, Susquehanna, and Delaware

   B. The invention of the steamboat

   C. Improved relations with Native Americans, who invited colonial Americans to travel west to settle

   D. Improved roads, mail service, and communications

100. A major quarrel between colonial Americans and the British concerned a series of British Acts of Parliament dealing with:

   A. Taxes

   B. Slavery

   C. Native Americans

   D. Shipbuilding

101. The first shots in what was to become the American Revolution were fired in:

    A. Florida

    B. Massachusetts

    C. New York

    D. Virginia

102. The U.S. Constitution, adopted in 1789, provided for:

    A. Direct election of the President by all citizens

    B. Direct election of the President by citizens meeting a standard of wealth

    C. Indirect election of the President by electors

    D. Indirect election of the President by the U.S. Senate

103. The area of the United States was effectively doubled through purchase of the Louisiana Territory under which President?

    A. John Adams

    B. Thomas Jefferson

    C. James Madison

    D. James Monroe

104. What was a major source of contention between American settlers in Texas and the Mexican government in the 1830s and 1840s?

    A. The Americans wished to retain slavery, which had been outlawed in Mexico

    B. The Americans had agreed to learn Spanish and become Roman Catholic, but failed to do so

    C. The Americans retained ties to the United States, and Santa Ana feared the power of the U.S.

    D. All of the above were contentious issues between American settlers and the Mexican government

105. "Fifty-four Forty or Fight" refers to the desire of some nineteenth century Americans to:

    A. Explore the entire Missouri River valley to its source in the Oregon Territory

    B. Insist that Mexico cede all of Texas to the U.S. or face war

    C. Demand that American territory reach to the border of Russian America

    D. Pay only $54,040,000 for all of the Oregon Territory

106. Which President helped postpone a civil war by supporting the Compromise of 1850?

   A. Henry Clay

   B. Franklin Pierce

   C. Millard Fillmore

   D. James Buchanan

107. Which American Secretary of War oversaw the purchase of Present-day southern Arizona (the Gadsden Purchase) for the purpose of building a railroad to connect California to the rest of the United States?

   A. Henry Clay

   B. William Seward

   C. Franklin Pierce

   D. Jefferson Davis

108. A consequence of the Gold Rush of Americans to California in 1848 and 1849 was that:

   A. California spent the minimum amount of time as a territory and was admitted as a slave state

   B. California was denied admission on its first application, since most Americans felt that the settlers were too "uncivilized" to deserve statehood

   C. California was purchased from Mexico for the express purpose of gaining immediate statehood

   D. California did not go through the normal territorial stage but applied directly for statehood as a free state

109. Of the following groups of states, which were slave states?

   A. Delaware, Maryland, Missouri

   B. California, Texas, Florida

   C. Kansas, Missouri, Kentucky

   D. Virginia, West Virginia, Indiana

110. In the American Civil War, who was the first commander of the forces of the United States?

   A. Gen. Ulysses S. Grant

   B. Gen. Robert E. Lee

   C. Gen. Irwin McDowell

   D. Gen. George Meade

111. Abraham Lincoln won re-election in 1864 chiefly through:

   A. His overwhelming force of personality and appeal to all segments of the electorate

   B. His reputation as the Great Emancipator

   C. The fact that people felt sorry for him because of his difficulties

   D. His shrewd political manipulation, clever use of patronage jobs, and wide-appeal selection of cabinet members

112. How many states re-entered the Union before 1868?

State	Date of Readmission
Alabama	1868
Arkansas	1868
Florida	1868
Georgia	1870
Louisiana	1868
Mississippi	1870
North Carolina	1868
South Carolina	1868
Tennessee	1866
Texas	1870
Virginia	1870

   A. 0 states

   B. 1 state

   C. 2 states

   D. 3 states

113. The Interstate Commerce Commission (ICC) was established in reaction to abuses and corruption in what industry?

   A. Textile

   B. Railroad

   C. Steel

   D. Banking

114. Which of the following sets of inventors is correctly matched with the area in which they primarily worked?

   A. Thomas Edison and George Westinghouse: transportation

   B. Cyrus McCormick and George Washington Carver: household appliances

   C. Alexander Graham Bell and Samuel F. B. Morse: communications

   D. Isaac Singer and John Gorrie: agriculture

115. The Teapot Dome scandal related to:

   A. The improper taxing of tea surpluses in Boston

   B. The improper awarding of building contracts in Washington, D.C.

   C. The improper sale of policy decisions by various Harding administration officials

   D. The improper sale of oil reserves in Wyoming

116. Which of the following was NOT a factor in the United States' entry into World War I?

   A. The closeness of the Presidential election of 1916

   B. The German threat to sink all allied ships, including merchant ships

   C. The desire to preserve democracy as practiced in Britain and France as compared to the totalitarianism of Germany

   D. The sinking of the Lusitania and the Sussex

117. What 1924 Act of Congress severely restricted immigration in the United States?

   A. Taft-Hartley Act

   B. Smoot-Hawley Act

   C. Fordney-McCumber Act

   D. Johnson-Reed Act

118. The first territorial governor of Florida after Florida's purchase by the United States was:

   A. Napoleon B. Broward

   B. William P. Duval

   C. Andrew Jackson

   D. Davy Crockett

119. President Truman suspended Gen. Douglas MacArthur from command of Allied forces in Korea because of:

    A. MacArthur's inability to make any progress against North Korea

    B. MacArthur's criticism of Truman, claiming that the President would not allow him to pursue aggressive tactics against the Communists

    C. The harsh treatment MacArthur exhibited toward the Japanese after World War II

    D. The ability of the U.S. Navy to continue the conflict without the presence of MacArthur

120. Which of the following most closely characterizes the Supreme Court's decision in Brown v. Board of Education?

    A. Chief Justice Warren had to cast the deciding vote in a sharply divided Court

    B. The decision was rendered along sectional lines, with northerners voting for integration and southerners voting for continued segregation

    C. The decision was 7-2, with dissenting justices not even preparing a written dissent

    D. Chief Justice Warren was able to persuade the Court to render a unanimous decision

121. The economic practices under President Ronald Reagan ("Reaganomics") were characterized by:

    A. Low inflation, high unemployment, high interest rates, high national debt

    B. High inflation, low unemployment, low interest rates, low national debt

    C. Low inflation, high unemployment, low interest rates, depletion of national debt

    D. High inflation, low unemployment, high interest rates, low national debt

122. The Harlem Renaissance of the 1920s refers to:

   A. The migration of black Americans out of Harlem, and its resettlement by white Americans

   B. A movement whereby the residents of Harlem were urged to "Return to Africa"

   C. A proliferation in the arts among black Americans, centered on Harlem

   D. The discovery of lost 15th century Italian paintings in a Harlem warehouse

123. Which of the following is most descriptive of the conflict between the U.S. government and the Seminoles between 1818 and 1858?

   A. There was constant armed conflict between the Seminoles and the U.S. during these years

   B. Historians discern three separate phases of hostilities (1818, 1835-42, 1855-58), known collectively as the Seminole Wars

   C. On May 7, 1858, the Seminoles admitted defeat, signed a peace treaty with the U.S., and left for Oklahoma, except for fifty-one individuals

   D. The former Seminole chief Osceola helped the U.S. defeat the Seminoles and effect their removal to Oklahoma

124. Match the railroad entrepreneur with the correct area of development:

    A. Henry Plant: Tampa and the West Coast

    B. Cornelius Vanderbilt: Jacksonville and the Northeast

    C. Henry Flagler: Orlando and the Central Highlands

    D. J.P. Morgan: Pensacola and the Northwest

125. Florida's space exploration industry is centered in:

    A. Baker County

    B. Broward County

    C. Brevard County

    D. Bradford County

Answer Key: Middle School Social Studies

1. C	34. D	67. C	100. A
2. B	35. C	68. B	101. B
3. D	36. B	69. B	102. C
4. C	37. C	70. D	103. B
5. A	38. A	71. A	104. D
6. C	39. A	72. C	105. C
7. A	40. D	73. A	106. C
8. D	41. C	74. C	107. D
9. B	42. B	75. B	108. D
10. C	43. B	76. B	109. A
11. D	44. C	77. D	110. C
12. D	45. D	78. B	111. D
13. D	46. B	79. A	112. B
14. A	47. B	80. B	113. B
15. C	48. A	81. A	114. C
16. B	49. C	82. D	115. D
17. B	50. C	83. A	116. A
18. D	51. D	84. B	117. D
19. A	52. B	85. A	118. C
20. C	53. C	86. D	119. B
21. A	54. A	87. C	120. D
22. D	55. C	88. C	121. A
23. D	56. D	89. C	122. C
24. C	57. B	90. C	123. B
25. C	58. B	91. B	124. A
26. B	59. C	92. C	125. C
27. A	60. A	93. A	
28. D	61. C	94. D	
29. D	62. D	95. A	
30. B	63. B	96. C	
31. C	64. D	97. B	
32. D	65. A	98. B	
33. A	66. D	99. D	

TEACHER CERTIFICATION STUDY GUIDE

Rationales with Sample Questions: Middle School Social Studies

1. Which of the following best describes current thinking on the major purpose of social science?

   A. Social science is designed primarily for students to acquire facts

   B. Social science should not be taught earlier than the middle school years

   C. A primary purpose of social sciences is the development of good citizens

   D. Social science should be taught as an elective

Answer: C

C. A primary purpose of social sciences is the development of good citizens.

By making students aware of the importance of their place in society, how their society and others are governed, how societies develop and advance, and how cultural behaviors arise, the social sciences are currently thought to be of primary importance in (C) developing good citizens.

2. Psychology is a social science because:

   A. It focuses on the biological development of individuals

   B. It focuses on the behavior of individual persons and small groups of persons

   C. It bridges the gap between the natural and the social sciences

   D. It studies the behavioral habits of lower animals

Answer: B

B. It focuses on the behavior of individual persons and small groups of persons
While it is true that (C) psychology draws from natural sciences, it is (B) the study of the behavior of individual persons and small groups that defines psychology as a social science. (A) The biological development of human beings and (D) the behavioral habits of lower animals are studied in the developmental and behavioral branches of psychology.

TEACHER CERTIFICATION STUDY GUIDE

3. **A historian would be interested in:**

   A. The manner in which scientific knowledge is advanced

   B. The effects of the French Revolution on world colonial policy

   C. The viewpoint of persons who have written previous "history"

   D. All of the above

Answer: D

D. All of the above

Historians are interested in broad developments through history (A), as well as how individual events affected the time in which they happened (B). Knowing the viewpoint of earlier historians can also help explain the common thinking among historical cultures and groups (C), so all of these answers are correct (D).

4. **The sub-discipline of linguistics is usually studied under:**

   A. Geography

   B. History

   C. Anthropology

   D. Economics

Answer: C

C. Anthropology

The fields of (A) Geography, (B) History and (D) Economics may study language as part of other subjects that affect these fields of study, but taken by itself language is a defining characteristic of a culture. (C) Anthropology studies human culture and the relationships between cultures, so linguistics is included under this social science.

TEACHER CERTIFICATION STUDY GUIDE

5. Which of the following is not generally considered a discipline within the social sciences?

   A. Geometry

   B. Anthropology

   C. Geography

   D. Sociology

Answer: A

A.   Geometry

(B) Anthropology studies the culture of groups of people. (C) Geography examines the relationship between societies and the physical place on earth where they live. (D) Sociology studies the predominant attitudes, beliefs and behaviors of a society. All three of these fields are related to the social interactions of humans, and so are considered social sciences. (A) Geometry is a field of mathematics and does not relate to the social interactions of people, so it is not considered a social science.

6. Economics is best described as:

   A. The study of how money is used in different societies

   B. The study of how different political systems produces goods and services

   C. The study of how human beings use limited resources to supply their necessities and wants

   D. The study of how human beings have developed trading practices through the years

Answer: C

C.   The study of how human beings use limited resources to supply their necessities and wants

(A) How money is used in different societies might be of interest to a sociologist or anthropologist. (B) The study of how different political systems produce goods and services is a topic of study that could be included under the field of political science. (D) The study of historical trading practices could fall under the study of history. Only (C) is the best general description of the social science of economics as a whole.

7. Which of the following is most reasonably studied under the social sciences?

   A. Political science

   B. Geometry

   C. Physics

   D. Grammar

Answer: A

A.   Political science

Social sciences deal with the social interactions of people. (B) Geometry is a branch of mathematics. (C) Physics is a natural science that studies the physical world. Although it may be studied as part of linguistics, (D) grammar is not recognized as a scientific field of study in itself. Only (A) political science is considered a general field of the social sciences.

8. For the historian studying ancient Egypt, which of the following would be least useful?

   A. The record of an ancient Greek historian on Greek-Egyptian interaction

   B. Letters from an Egyptian ruler to his/her regional governors

   C. Inscriptions on stele of the Fourteenth Egyptian Dynasty

   D. Letters from a nineteenth century Egyptologist to his wife

Answer: D

D.   Letters from a nineteenth century Egyptologist to his wife

Historians use primary sources from the actual time they are studying whenever possible. (A) Ancient Greek records of interaction with Egypt, (B) letters from an Egyptian ruler to regional governors, and (C) inscriptions from the Fourteenth Egyptian Dynasty are all primary sources created at or near the actual time being studied. (D) Letters from a nineteenth century Egyptologist would not be considered primary sources, as they were created thousands of years after the fact and may not actually be about the subject being studied.

TEACHER CERTIFICATION STUDY GUIDE

9. A political scientist might use all of the following except:

   A. An investigation of government documents

   B. A geological timeline

   C. Voting patterns

   D. Polling data

Answer: B

B.   A geological timeline

Political science is primarily concerned with the political and governmental activities of societies. (A) Government documents can provide information about the organization and activities of a government. (C) Voting patterns reveal the political behavior of individuals and groups. (D) Polling data can provide insight into the predominant political views of a group of people. (B) A geological timeline describes the changes in the physical features of the earth over time and would not be useful to a political scientist.

10. A geographer wishes to study the effects of a flood on subsequent settlement patterns. Which might he or she find most useful?

   A. A film clip of the floodwaters

   B. An aerial photograph of the river's source

   C. Census data taken after the flood

   D. A soil map of the A and B horizons beneath the flood area

Answer: C

C.   Census data taken after the flood

(A) A film clip of the flood waters may be of most interest to a historian, (B) an aerial photograph of the river's source, and (D) soil maps tell little about the behavior of the individuals affected by the flood. (C) Census surveys record the population for certain areas on a regular basis, allowing a geographer to tell if more or fewer people are living in an area over time. These would be of most use to a geographer undertaking this study.

MID. LEVEL HUMANITIES

TEACHER CERTIFICATION STUDY GUIDE

11. A social scientist observes how individual persons react to the presence or absence of noise. This scientist is most likely a:

A. Geographer

B. Political Scientist

C. Economist

D. Psychologist

Answer: D

D. Psychologist

(D) Psychologists scientifically study the behavior and mental processes of individuals. Studying how individuals react to changes in their environment falls under this social science. (A) Geographers, (B) political scientists and (C) economists are more likely to study the reactions of groups rather than individual reactions.

12. As a sociologist, you would be most likely to observe:

A. The effects of an earthquake on farmland

B. The behavior of rats in sensory deprivation experiments

C. The change over time in Babylonian obelisk styles

D. The behavior of human beings in television focus groups

Answer: D

D. The behavior of human beings in television focus groups.

Predominant beliefs and attitudes within human society are studied in the field of sociology. (A) The effects of an earthquake on farmland might be studied by a geographer. (B) The behavior of rats in an experiment falls under the field of behavioral psychology. (C) Changes in Babylonian obelisk styles might interest a historian. None of these answers fits easily within the definition of sociology. (D) A focus group, where people are asked to discuss their reactions to a certain product or topic, would be the most likely method for a sociologist of observing and discovering attitudes among a selected group.

TEACHER CERTIFICATION STUDY GUIDE

13. **An economist investigates the spending patterns of low-income individuals. Which of the following would yield the most pertinent information?**

    A. Prime lending rates of neighborhood banks

    B. The federal discount rate

    C. Citywide wholesale distribution figures

    D. Census data and retail sales figures

Answer: D

D.   Census data and retail sales figures

(A) Local lending rates and (B) the federal discount rate might provide information on borrowing habits, but not necessarily spending habits, and give no information on income levels. (C) Citywide wholesale distribution figures would provide information on the business activity of a city, but tell nothing about consumer activities. (D) Census data records the income levels of households within a certain area, and retail sales figures for that area would give an economist data on spending, which can be compared to income levels, making this the most pertinent source.

14. **A teacher and a group of students take a field trip to an Indian mound to examine artifacts. This activity most closely fits under which branch of the social sciences?**

    A. Anthropology

    B. Sociology

    C. Psychology

    D. Political Science

Answer: A

A.   Anthropology

(A) Anthropology is the study of human culture and the way in which people of different cultures live. The artifacts created by people of a certain culture can provide information about the behaviors and beliefs of that culture, making anthropology the best-fitting field of study for this field trip. (B) Sociology, (C) psychology and (D) political science are more likely to study behaviors and institutions directly than through individual artifacts created by a specific culture.

15. Which of the following is most closely identified as a sociologist?

    A. Herodotus

    B. John Maynard Keynes

    C. Emile Durkheim

    D. Arnold Toynbee

Answer: C

C.   Emile Durkheim

(C) Durkheim (1858-1917) was the founder of the first sociological journal in France and the first to apply scientific methods of research to the study of human society. (A) Herodotus (ca. 484-425 BC) was an early Greek historian. (B) John Maynard Keynes (1883-1946) was a British economist who developed the field of modern theoretical macroeconomics. (D) Arnold Toynbee (1882-1853) was also a British economist who took a historical approach to the field.

16. We can credit modern geography with which of the following?

    A. Building construction practices designed to withstand earthquakes

    B. Advances in computer cartography

    C. Better methods of linguistic analysis

    D. Making it easier to memorize countries and their capitals

Answer: B

B.   Advances in computer cartography.

(B) Cartography is concerned with the study and creation of maps and geographical information and falls under the social science of geography.

TEACHER CERTIFICATION STUDY GUIDE

17. Adam Smith is most closely identified with which of the following?

    A. The law of diminishing returns

    B. The law of supply and demand

    C. The principle of motor primacy

    D. The territorial imperative

Answer: B

B.   The law of supply and demand

Adam Smith was an economist who developed the theory that value was linked to the supply of a good or service compared to the demand for it. Something in low supply but high demand will have a high value. Something in great supply but low demand is worth less. This has become known as (B) the law of supply and demand. (A) The law of diminishing returns is an economic principle described by Thomas Malthus in 1798. (C) The principle of motor primacy refers to a stage in developmental psychology. (D) The territorial imperative is a theory of the origin of property outlined by anthropologist Robert Ardrey in 1966.

18. Margaret Mead may be credited with major advances in the study of:

    A. The marginal propensity to consume

    B. The thinking of the Anti-Federalists

    C. The anxiety levels of non-human primates

    D. Interpersonal relationships in non-technical societies

Answer: D

D.   Interpersonal relationships in non-technical societies

Margaret Mead (1901-1978) was a pioneer in the field of anthropology, living among the people of Samoa, observing and writing about their culture in the book <u>Coming of Age in Samoa</u> in 1928. (A) The marginal propensity to consume is an economic subject. (B) The thinking of the Anti-Federalists is a topic in American history. (C) The anxiety levels of non-human primates are a subject studied in behavioral psychology.

MID. LEVEL HUMANITIES

TEACHER CERTIFICATION STUDY GUIDE

19. **The advancement of understanding in dealing with human beings has led to a number of interdisciplinary areas. Which of the following interdisciplinary studies would NOT be considered under the social sciences?**

    A. Molecular biophysics

    B. Peace studies

    C. African-American studies

    D. Cartographic information systems

Answer: A

A. Molecular biophysics

(A) Molecular biophysics is an interdisciplinary field combining the fields of biology, chemistry, and physics. These are all natural sciences and not social sciences

20. **Cognitive, developmental, and behavioral are three types of:**

    A. Economist

    B. Political Scientist

    C. Psychologist

    D. Historian

Answer: C

C. Psychologists

(C) Psychologists study mental processes (cognitive psychology), the mental development of children (developmental psychology), and observe human and animal behavior in controlled circumstances (behavioral psychology.)

TEACHER CERTIFICATION STUDY GUIDE

21. A physical geographer would be concerned with which of the following groups of terms?

    A. Landform, biome, precipitation

    B. Scarcity, goods, services

    C. Nation, state, administrative subdivision

    D. Cause and effect, innovation, exploration

Answer: A

A.   Landform, biome, precipitation.

(A) Landform, biome, and precipitation are all terms used in the study of geography. A landform is a physical feature of the earth, such as a hill or valley. A biome is a large community of plants or animals, such as a forest. Precipitation is the moisture that falls to earth as rain or snow. (B) Scarcity, goods, and services are terms encountered in economics. (C) Nation, state, and administrative subdivision are terms used in political science. (D) Cause and effect, innovation, and exploration are terms in developmental psychology.

22. An economist might engage in which of the following activities?

    A. An observation of the historical effects of a nation's banking practices

    B. The application of a statistical test to a series of data

    C. Introduction of an experimental factor into a specified population to measure the effect of the factor

    D. An economist might engage in all of these

Answer: D

D.   An economist might engage in all of these

Economists use statistical analysis of economic data, controlled experimentation as well as historical research in their field of social science.

TEACHER CERTIFICATION STUDY GUIDE

23. Political science is primarily concerned with _____.

    A. Elections

    B. Economic Systems

    C. Boundaries

    D. Public Policy

Answer: D

D.   Public policy

Political science studies the actions and policies of the government of a society. (D) Public policy is the official stance of a government on an issue and is a primary source for studying a society's dominant political beliefs. (A) Elections are also an interest of political scientists but are not a primary field of study. (B) Economic systems are of interest to an economist and (C) boundaries to a geographer.

24. An anthropologist is studying a society's sororate and avunculate. In general, this scientist is studying the society's:

    A. Level of technology

    B. Economy

    C. Kinship practices

    D. Methods of farming

Answer: C

C.   Kinship practices

Sororate and avunculate are anthropological terms referring to interfamily relationships between sisters and between men and their sisters' sons. These are terms used to describe (C) kinship practices.

TEACHER CERTIFICATION STUDY GUIDE

25. Of the following lists, which includes persons who have made major advances in the understanding of psychology?

    A. Herodotus, Thucydides, Ptolemy

    B. Adam Smith, Milton Friedman, John Kenneth Galbraith

    C. Edward Hall, E.L. Thorndike, B.F. Skinner

    D. Thomas Jefferson, Karl Marx, Henry Kissinger

Answer: C

C.   Edward Hall, E.L. Thorndike, B.F. Skinner

Edward Hall wrote in the 1960s about the effects of overcrowding on humans, especially in large cities. E.L. Thorndike (1874-1949) was an early developer of an experimental approach to studying learning in animals and of educational psychology. B.F. Skinner (1904-1990) was a pioneer in behavioral psychology. (A) Herodotus, Thucydides, and Ptolemy were early historians. (B) Smith, Friedman, and Galbraith made significant contributions to the field of economics. (D) Jefferson, Marx, and Kissinger are figures in political science.

26. The writing of history is called:

    A. Public policy analysis

    B. Historiography

    C. Historical perspective

    D. Historical analysis

Answer: B

B.   Historiography

(B) Historiography is a term used to refer to the actual writing of history as well as the study of this type of writing. (A) Public policy analysis is part of political science. (C) Historical perspective refers to the prevailing viewpoint of a historical time, and (D) historical analysis concerns the interpretation of historical events.

MID. LEVEL HUMANITIES

27. **If geography is the study of how human beings live in relationship to the earth on which they live, why do geographers include physical geography within the discipline?**

    A. The physical environment serves as the location for the activities of human beings

    B. No other branch of the natural or social sciences studies the same topics

    C. The physical environment is more important than the activities carried out by human beings

    D. It is important to be able to subdue natural processes for the advancement of humankind

Answer: A

A. The physical environment serves as the location for the activities of human beings.

Cultures will develop different practices depending on the predominant geographical features of the area in which they live. Cultures that live along a river will have a different kind of relationship to the surrounding land than those who live in the mountains, for instance. Answer (A) best describes why physical geography is included in the social science of geography. Answer (B) is false, as physical geography is also studied under other natural sciences (such as geology.) Answers (C) and (D) are matters of opinion and do not pertain to the definition of geography as a social science.

28. A historian might compare the governmental systems of the Roman Empire and the twentieth century United States with regard to which of the following commonalities?

   A. Totalitarianism

   B. Technological development

   C. Constitutional similarities

   D. Federalism

Answer: D

D.   Federalism

(A) Totalitarianism is a form of government where citizens are completely subservient to the state. While this was sometimes the case during the reign of the Roman Empire, it was not common to 20th century America. (B) Technological development does not necessarily address similarities in governmental systems. (C) The Roman constitution applied to the republic of Rome but not directly to the empire as a whole. (D) Federalism is a type of governmental system where several separate states join under a common government. This describes both the United States and the Roman Empire and is the best answer.

29. Capitalism and communism are alike in that they are both:

   A. Organic systems

   B. Political systems

   C. Centrally planned systems

   D. Economic systems

Answer: D

D.   Economic systems

While economic and (B) political systems are often closely connected, capitalism and communism are primarily (D) economic systems. Capitalism is a system of economics that allows the open market to determine the relative value of goods and services. Communism is an economic system where the market is planned by a central state. While communism is a (C) centrally planned system, this is not true of capitalism. (A) Organic systems are studied in biology, a natural science.

MID. LEVEL HUMANITIES   415

TEACHER CERTIFICATION STUDY GUIDE

30. Which of the following demonstrates evidence of the interaction between physical and cultural anthropology?

   A. Tall Nilotic herdsmen are often expert warriors

   B. Until recent years the diet of most Asian peoples caused them to be shorter in stature than most other peoples

   C. Native South American peoples adopted potato production after invasion by Europeans

   D. Polynesians exhibit different skin coloration than Melanesians

Answer: B

B. Until recent years the diet of most Asian peoples caused them to be shorter in stature than most other peoples.

Cultural anthropology is the study of culture. Physical anthropology studies human evolution and other biologically related aspects of human culture. Answers (A) and (D) describe physical attributes of members of different cultures but make no connection between these attributes and the behaviors of these cultures. Answer (C) describes a cultural behavior of Native Americans but makes no connection to any physical attributes of the people of this culture. Answer (B) draws a connection between a cultural behavior (diet) and a physical attribute (height) and is the best example demonstrating the interaction between cultural and physical anthropology.

MID. LEVEL HUMANITIES

TEACHER CERTIFICATION STUDY GUIDE

31. A social scientist studies the behavior of four persons in a carpool. This is an example of:

  A. Developmental psychology

  B. Experimental psychology

  C. Social psychology

  D. Macroeconomics

Answer: C

C.   Social psychology

(A) Developmental psychology studies the mental development of humans as they mature. (B) Experimental psychology uses formal experimentation with control groups to examine human behavior. (C) Social psychology is a branch of the field that investigates people's behavior as they interact within society and is the type of project described in the question. (D) Macroeconomics is a field within economics and would not apply to this project.

32. Peace studies might include elements of all of the following disciplines except:

  A. Geography

  B. History

  C. Economics

  D. All of these might contribute to peace studies

Answer: D

D.   All of these might contribute to peace studies.

(D) All of these might contribute to peace studies. (A) Geography might examine the current and historical borders between two regions or nations, for instance. (B) History would contribute information on the origins of conflict and peace between peoples. Because scarcity of goods and differences in the relative wealth of nations are often factors in conflict and cooperation, (C) economics can be included in peace studies.

MID. LEVEL HUMANITIES

TEACHER CERTIFICATION STUDY GUIDE

33. Which of the following sets of terms relates to the Davisian erosion cycle?

    A. Youth, maturity, old age

    B. Atmospheric erosion, subsurface erosion, superficial erosion

    C. Fluvial, alluvial, estuarine

    D. Mississippian, Pennsylvanian, Illinoisian

Answer: A

A.   Youth, maturity, old age

The Davisian erosion cycle was developed by physical geographer William Morris Davis to describe three main stages in the life of a stream. Davis called these stages (A) Youth, maturity, and old age. In youth, a stream is forced into channels and cuts downward to a base level. In maturity, it begins to cut away at the sides of the channel and broaden. Finally, in old age, it develops into a wide flood plain. (B) Atmospheric erosion, subsurface erosion, and superficial erosion are types of soil erosion and do not describe the Davisian cycle. (C) Fluvial, alluvial, and estuarine are geological terms referring to rivers but not to erosion. (D) Mississippian and Pennsylvanian refer to geologic periods in North America. An Illinoisian is someone from Illinois

34. What is a drumlin?

    A. A narrow ridge of sand, gravel, and boulders deposited by a stream flowing on, in, or under a nonmoving glacier

    C. Accumulated earth, pebbles, and stones carried by and then deposited by a glacier

    C. The active front face of a non-stagnant glacier

    D. An elongated or oval hill formed by drift material of glaciers

Answer: D

D.   An elongated or oval hill formed by drift material of glaciers

Glacial material moving over land sometimes form long or oval hills, usually in groups, that are oriented in the direction of the ice flow. These hills, which can be of varying composition, are called drumlins.

MID. LEVEL HUMANITIES

35. A coral island or series of islands which consists of a reef which surrounds a lagoon describes a(n):

    A. Needle

    B. Key

    C. Atoll

    D. Mauna

Answer: C

C.   Atoll

An (C) atoll is a formation that occurs when a coral reef builds up around the top of a submerged volcanic peak, forming a ring or horseshoe of islands with a seawater lagoon in the center.

36. What type of cloud usually produces rain?

    A. Cirrus

    B. Cumulonimbus

    C. Altostratus

    D. Cirrostratus

Answer: B

B.   Cumulonimbus

(B) Cumulonimbus clouds reach high into the sky and are usually associated with instability and thundershowers. (A) Cirrus clouds are thin and wispy and are usually seen in fair weather. (C) Altostratus clouds are thin and spread out and can sometimes produce rain if they thicken. (D) Cirrostratus clouds are high, thin clouds that are nearly transparent and do not normally produce rain.

37. Which of the following is NOT a type of rainfall?

A. Convectional

B. Cyclonic

C. Adiabatic

D. Frontal

Answer: C

C. Adiabatic

(A) Convectional rain occurs when hot air rises quickly and is cooled and is usually accompanied by thunderstorms. (B) Cyclonic and (D) frontal rain occurs at the place where hot and cool air masses meet, called the "front." (C) Adiabatic is a term used in physics and is not a type of rainfall.

38. The Mediterranean type climate is characterized by:

A. Hot, dry summers and mild, relatively wet winters

B. Cool, relatively wet summers and cold winters

C. Mild summers and winters, with moisture throughout the year

D. Hot, wet summers and cool, dry winters

Answer: A

A. Hot, dry summers and mild, relatively wet winters

Westerly winds and nearby bodies of water create stable weather patterns along the west coasts of several continents and along the coast of the Mediterranean Sea, after which this type of climate is named. Temperatures rarely fall below the freezing point and have a mean between 70 and 80 degrees F in the summer. Stable conditions make for little rain during the summer months.

TEACHER CERTIFICATION STUDY GUIDE

39. The climate of Southern Florida is the _____ type.

    A. Humid subtropical

    B. Marine West Coast

    C. Humid continental

    D. Tropical wet-dry

Answer: A

A.   Humid subtropical

The (B) marine west coast climate is found on the western coasts of continents. Florida is on the eastern side of North America. The (C) humid continental climate is found over large land masses, such as Europe and the American Midwest, not along coasts such as where Florida is situated. The (D) tropical wet-dry climate occurs within about 15 degrees of the equator, in the tropics. Florida is sub-tropical. Florida is in a (A) humid subtropical climate, which extends along the East Coast of the United States to about Maryland, and along the gulf coast to northeastern Texas.

40. Which of the following is an island nation?

    A. Luxembourg

    B. Finland

    C. Monaco

    D. Nauru

Answer: D

D.   Nauru

(D) Nauru is located in Micronesia in the South Pacific and is the world's smallest island nation. (A) Luxembourg is a small principality in Europe, bordered by Belgium, France, and Germany. (B) Finland is a Scandinavian country on the Baltic Sea bordered by Norway, Sweden, and Russia. (C) Monaco is a small principality on the coast of the Mediterranean Sea that is bordered by France.

TEACHER CERTIFICATION STUDY GUIDE

41. Which location may be found in Canada?

    A. 27 N 93 W

    B. 41 N 93 E

    C. 50 N 111 W

    D. 18 N 120 W

Answer: C

C.   50 N 111 W

(A) 27 North latitude, 93 West longitude is located in the Gulf of Mexico. (B) 41 N 93 E is located in northwest China. (D) 18 N 120 W is in the Pacific Ocean, off the coast of Mexico. (C) 50 N 111 W is located near the town of Medicine Hat in the province of Alberta, in Canada.

42. The highest point on the North American continent is:

    A. Mt. St. Helen's

    B. Denali

    C. Mt. Everest

    D. Pike's Peak

Answer: B

B.   Denali

(B) Denali, also known as Mt. McKinley, has an elevation of 20,320 feet, and is in the Alaska Range of North America. It is the highest point on the continent. (A) Mt. St. Helen's, an active volcano located in the state of Washington, is 8,364 feet in elevation since its eruption in 1980. (D) Pike's Peak, located in Colorado, is 14,100 feet in elevation. (C) Mt. Everest, in the Himalayan Mountains between China and Tibet is the highest point on the earth at 29,035 feet but is not located in North America.

TEACHER CERTIFICATION STUDY GUIDE

43. Concerning the present political map of Africa, which statement most closely applies?

  A. The modern states reflect an effort to establish political units based on ethnic groupings

  B. The international community allowed for a period of elasticity with regard to boundaries, so that a condition of relative equilibrium could develop

  C. Africans were given the task of delineating the modern states, using whatever criteria they chose

  D. The modern states reflect imposed boundaries, without regard to ethnic groupings or other indigenous considerations

Answer: B

B. The international community allowed for a period of elasticity with regard to boundaries, so that a condition of relative equilibrium could develop.

Many African states were originally colonized by other countries and had borders drawn up (D) without regard to ethnic groupings or other indigenous considerations. With the relatively recent independence of colonial states, border disputes have arisen, but no complete delineation has taken place along ethnic or any other grounds, as described in answers (A) and (C). The international community has been involved individually and jointly, as members of the United Nations, providing diplomacy and refugee aid in some of the recent border disputes, as in that between Eritrea and Ethiopia, but has largely taken the stance that these issues should be worked out between the nations involved.

TEACHER CERTIFICATION STUDY GUIDE

44. Which of the following areas would NOT be a primary area of hog production?

    A. Midland England

    B. The Mekong delta of Vietnam

    C. Central Syria

    D. Northeast Iowa

Answer: C

C.   Central Syria

Pork is a common ingredient in the American, English, and Vietnamese cuisine, so one would reasonably expect to find hog production in (A) Midland England, (B) The Mekong Delta of Vietnam and (D) Northeast Iowa. The population of Syria is predominantly Islamic, and Islam prohibits the eating of pork. Therefore, one would be unlikely to find extensive hog production in (C) Central Syria.

45. Indo-European languages are native languages to each of the following EXCEPT:

    A. Germany

    B. India

    C. Italy

    D. Finland

Answer: D

D.   Finland

German, the native language of (A) Germany, Hindi, the official language of (B) India, and Italian, spoken in (C) Italy, are three of the hundreds of languages that are part of the Indo-European family, which also includes French, Greek, and Russian. Finnish, the language of (D) Finland, is part of the Uralic family of languages, which also includes Estonian. It developed independently of the Indo-European family.

46. A cultural geographer is investigating the implications of The Return of the Native by Thomas Hardy. He or she is most likely concentrating on:

   A. The reactions of British city-dwellers to the in-migration of French professionals

   B. The activities of persons in relation to poorly drained, coarse-soiled land with low-lying vegetation

   C. The capacity of riverine lands to sustain a population of edible amphibians

   D. The propagation of new crops introduced by settlers from North America

Answer: B

B.   The activities of persons in relation to poorly drained, coarse-soiled land with low-lying vegetation

Thomas Hardy's novel The Return of the Native takes place in England, in a fictional region based on Hardy's home area, Dorset. Hardy describes the people and landscape of this area, which is primarily heath. A heath is a poorly drained, coarse-soiled land with low-lying vegetation, as described in answer (B). This is the most likely concentration for a cultural geographer studying Hardy's novel.

47. Which of the following is NOT considered to be an economic need:

   A. Food

   B. Transportation

   C. Shelter

   D. Clothing

Answer: B

B.   Transportation

An economic need is something that a person absolutely must have to survive. (A) Food, (C) shelter and (D) clothing are examples of these needs. While an individual may also require (B) transportation to participate in an economy, it is not considered an absolute need.

48. **As your income rises, you tend to spend more money on entertainment. This is an expression of the:**

   A. Marginal propensity to consume

   B. Allocative efficiency

   C. Compensating differential

   D. Marginal propensity to save

Answer: A

A.   Marginal propensity to consume

The (A) marginal propensity to consume is a measurement of how much consumption changes compared to how much disposable income changes. Entertainment expenses are an example of disposable income. Dividing your change in entertainment spending by your total change in disposable income will give you your marginal propensity to consume.

49. **A student buys a candy bar at lunch. The decision to buy a second candy bar relates to the concept of:**

   A. Equilibrium pricing

   B. Surplus

   C. Utility

   D. Substitutability

Answer: C

C.   Utility

As used in the social science of economics, (C) utility is the measurement of happiness or satisfaction a person receives from consuming a good or service. The decision of the student to increase his satisfaction by buying a second candy bar relates to this concept because he is spending money to increase his happiness.

50. If the price of Good G increases, what is likely to happen with regard to comparable Good H?

    A. The demand for Good G will stay the same

    B. The demand for Good G will increase

    C. The demand for Good H will increase

    D. The demand for Good H will decrease

Answer: C

C. The demand for Good H will increase.

If Good G and Good H are viewed by consumers as equal in value but then the cost of Good G increases, it follows that consumers will now choose Good H at a higher rate, increasing the demand.

51. A teacher has an extra $1,000 which she wishes to invest and wants to minimize the risk. The best choice for investment, from the following, is:

    A. Money market account

    B. Treasury bills

    C. Stock in a new company

    D. Certificate of deposit

Answer: D

D. Certificate of deposit

(A) Money market funds will fluctuate in value based on international currency trading. (B) Treasury bills are issued by the federal government and carry very little risk but are available only at prices close to $10,000. The teacher does not have enough to invest. (C) Stock in a new company is very likely to change rapidly and carries a high degree of risk. A (D) Certificate of deposit is a certificate issued by a bank promising to pay a fixed amount of interest for a fixed period of time. Because most deposits are insured up to $100,000 by the federal government, there is little risk of losing money with this investment.

52. In a command economy:

A. The open market determines how much of a good is produced and distributed

B. The government determines how much of a good is produced and distributed

C. Individuals produce and consume a specified good as commanded by their needs

D. The open market determines the demand for a good, and then the government produces and distributes the good

Answer: B

B. The government determines how much of a good is produced and distributed.

A command economy is where (B) the government determines how much of a good is produced and distributed, as was the case in the Soviet Union and is still the case in Cuba and North Korea. A command economy is the opposite of a market economy, where (A) the open market determines how much of a good is produced and distributed.

53. In a barter economy, which of the following would not be an economic factor?

A. Time

B. Goods

C. Money

D. Services

Answer: C

C. Money

A barter economy is one where (B) goods and (D) services are exchanged for one another and not for money. Just as in an economy with currency, (A) time is a factor in determining the value of goods and services. Since no money changes hands in a barter economy, the correct answer is (C) money.

TEACHER CERTIFICATION STUDY GUIDE

54. Of the following, the best example of an oligopoly in the US is:

   A. Automobile industry

   B. Electric power provision

   C. Telephone service

   D. Clothing manufacturing

Answer: A

A.   Automobile industry

An oligopoly exists when a small group of companies controls an industry. In the United States at present, there are hundreds of (B) electric power providers, (C) telephone service providers and (D) clothing manufacturers. There are currently still just three major automobile manufacturers, however, making the (A) automobile industry an oligopoly.

55. Which best describes the economic system of the United States?

   A. Most decisions are the result of open markets, with little or no government modification or regulation

   B. Most decisions are made by the government, but there is some input by open market forces

   C. Most decisions are made by open market factors, with important regulatory functions and other market modifications the result of government activity

   D. There is joint decision making by government and private forces, with final decisions resting with the government

Answer: C

C.   Most decisions are made by open market factors, with important regulatory functions and other market modifications the result of government activity.

The United States does not have a planned economy, as described in answers (B) and (D) where the government makes major market decisions. Neither is the U.S. market completely free of regulation, as described in answer (A). Products are regulated for safety, and many services are regulated by certification requirements, for example. The best description of the U.S. economic system is therefore (C) Most decisions are made by open market factors, with important regulatory functions and other market modifications the result of government activity.

TEACHER CERTIFICATION STUDY GUIDE

56. An agreement in which a company allows a business to use its name and sell its products, usually for a fee, is called a:

   A. Sole proprietorship

   B. Partnership

   C. Corporation

   D. Franchise

Answer: D

D.   Franchise

A (A) sole proprietorship is where a person operates a company with his own resources. All income from this kind of business is considered income to the proprietor. A (B) partnership is an agreement between two or more people to operate a business and divide the proceeds in a specified way. A (C) corporation is a formal business arrangement where a company is considered a separate entity for tax purposes. In a (D) franchise, individuals can purchase the rights to use a company's name, designs, logos, etc., in exchange for a fee. Examples of franchise companies are McDonald's and Krispy Kreme.

TEACHER CERTIFICATION STUDY GUIDE

57. What is a major difference between monopolistic competition and perfect competition?

A. Perfect competition has many consumers and suppliers, while monopolistic competition does not

B. Perfect competition provides identical products, while monopolistic competition provides similar but not identical products

C. Entry to perfect competition is difficult, while entry to monopolistic competition is relatively easy

D. Monopolistic competition has many consumers and suppliers, while perfect competition does not

Answer: B

B. Perfect competition provides identical products, while monopolistic competition provides similar but not identical products.

A perfect market is a hypothetical market used in economics to discuss the underlying effects of supply and demand. To control for differences between products, it is assumed in perfect competition that all products are identical, with no differences, and the prices for these products will rise and fall based on a small number of factors. Monopolistic competition takes place in a market where each producer can act monopolistically and raise or lower the cost of its product, or change its product to make different from similar products. This is the primary difference between these two models; (B) perfect competition provides identical products, while monopolistic competition provides similar but not identical products.

58. Which concept is not embodied as a right in the First Amendment to the U.S. Constitution?

A. Peaceable assembly

B. Protection against unreasonable search and seizure

C. Freedom of speech

D. Petition for redress of grievances

Answer: B

B. Protection against unreasonable search and seizure

The first amendment to the Constitution reads, "Congress shall make no law respecting an establishment of religion, or prohibiting the free exercise thereof; or abridging the (C) freedom of speech, or of the press; or the right of the people (A) peaceably to assemble, and to (D) petition the government for a redress of grievances." The protection against (B) unreasonable search and seizure is a constitutional right, however it is found in the fourth amendment, not the first.

59. In the Constitutional system of checks and balances, a primary "check" which accrues to the President is the power of:

A. Executive privilege

B. Approval of judges nominated by the Senate

C. Veto of Congressional legislation

D. Approval of judged nominated by the House of Representatives

Answer: C

C. Veto of Congressional legislation

The power to (C) veto congressional legislation is granted to the U.S. President in Article I of the Constitution, which states that all legislation passed by both houses of the Congress must be given to the president for approval. This is a primary check on the power of the Congress by the President. The Congress may override a presidential veto by a two-thirds majority vote of both houses, however. (A) Executive privilege refers to the privilege of the president to keep certain documents private. Answers (B) and (D) are incorrect, as Congress does not nominate judges. This is a presidential power.

60. According to the Constitution any amendment must be ratified by _____ of the states to become a part of the Constitution:

   A. Three-fourths

   B. Two-thirds

   C. Three-fifths

   D. Five-sixths

Answer: A

A.   Three-fourths

Article V of the Constitution spells out how the document may be ratified. First, an amendment must be proposed by a two-thirds majority of both houses of Congress. Then it is passed to the state legislatures. If (A) three-fourths of the states pass the amendment, it is adopted as part of the constitution. The constitution currently has 27 amendments.

61. Collectively, the first ten Amendments to the Constitution are known as the:

   A. Articles of Confederation

   B. Mayflower Compact

   C. Bill of Rights

   D. Declaration of the Rights of Man

Answer: C

C.   Bill of Rights

The (A) Articles of Confederation was the document under which the thirteen colonies of the American Revolution came together and was the first governing document of the United States. The (B) Mayflower Compact was an agreement signed by several of the pilgrims aboard the Mayflower before establishing their colony at Plymouth in 1620. The (D) Declaration of the Rights of Man was the French document adopted after the French Revolution in 1789. The first ten amendments of the US Constitution, spelling out the limitations of the federal government, are referred to as (C) the Bill of Rights.

62. In the United States, if a person is accused of a crime and cannot afford a lawyer:

A. The person cannot be tried

B. A court will appoint a lawyer, but the person must pay the lawyer back when able to do so

C. The person must be tried without legal representation

D. A court will appoint a lawyer for the person free of charge

Answer: D

D. A court will appoint a lawyer for the person free of charge

The sixth amendment to the Constitution grants the right to a speedy and public jury trial in a criminal prosecution, as well as the right to "the assistance of counsel for his defense." This has been interpreted as the right to receive legal assistance at no charge if a defendant cannot afford one. (D) A court will appoint a lawyer for the person free of charge, is the correct answer.

TEACHER CERTIFICATION STUDY GUIDE

63. Which of the following lists elements usually considered responsibilities of citizenship under the American system of government?

   A. Serving in public office, voluntary government service, military duty

   B. Paying taxes, jury duty, upholding the Constitution

   C. Maintaining a job, giving to charity, turning in fugitives

   D. Quartering of soldiers, bearing arms, government service

Answer: B

B.   Paying taxes, jury duty, upholding the Constitution.

Only paying taxes, jury duty, and upholding the Constitution are responsibilities of citizens as a result of rights and commitments outlined in the Constitution – for example, the right of citizens to a jury trial in the Sixth and Seventh Amendments and the right of the federal government to collect taxes in Article 1, Section 8. (A) Serving in public office, voluntary government service, military duty and (C) maintaining a job, giving to charity, and turning in fugitives are all highly admirable actions undertaken by many exemplary citizens, but they are considered purely voluntary actions, even when officially recognized and compensated. The United States has none of the compulsory military or civil service requirements of many other countries. (D) The quartering of soldiers is an act, which, according to Amendment III of the Bill of Rights, requires a citizen's consent. Bearing arms is a right guaranteed under Amendment II of the Bill of Rights.

64. **Consider the following passage from the Mayflower Compact:
    "...covenant & combine ourselves together into a Civil body politick;"
    This demonstrates what theory of social organization?**

    A. Darwinian

    B. Naturalistic

    C. Nonconsensual

    D. Constitutional

Answer: D

D.   Constitutional

(D) Constitutional social organization requires at its heart clearly stated and mutually agreed on constitutional principles, which all involved parties promise to uphold. (B) A naturalistic theory of social organization is one freely chosen by its participants and not yet bound by a clear set of constitutional principles. A (A) Darwinian theory would reflect the "survival of the fittest" element of Darwin's theory of the evolution of natural life, as applied to the relationship of different groups within a society. (C) Nonconsensual theories compel participation in a system of social organization and thus would never be characterized by the word "covenant," which means an agreement entered into freely by both parties.

TEACHER CERTIFICATION STUDY GUIDE

65. Why is the system of government in the United States referred to as a federal system?

   A. There are different levels of government

   B. There is one central authority in which all governmental power is vested

   C. The national government cannot operate except with the consent of the governed

   D. Elections are held at stated periodic times, rather than as called by the head of the government

Answer: A

A. There are different levels of government

(A) The United States is composed of fifty states, each responsible for its own affairs but united under a federal government. (B) A centralized system is the opposite of a federal system. (C) That national government cannot operate except with the consent of the governed is a founding principle of American politics. It is not a political system like federalism. A centralized democracy could still be consensual but would not be federal. (D) This is a description of electoral procedure, not a political system like federalism

66. Which of the following are NOT local governments in the United States?

   A. Cities

   B. Townships

   C. School boards

   D. All of these are forms of local government

Answer: D

D. All of these are forms of local government

A local government is a body with the authority to make policy and enforce decisions on behalf of a local community. Cities and townships are by definition local, not statewide or federal, governments. A more central authority might make school policy in other countries, but, in the United States, school boards are local authorities. [However, according to the 2002 Census, several states run certain school districts themselves, without a local school board.]

MID. LEVEL HUMANITIES

TEACHER CERTIFICATION STUDY GUIDE

67. The major expenditures of state governments in the United States go toward:

A. Parks, education, and highways

B. Law enforcement, libraries and highways

C. Education, highways, and law enforcement

D. Recreation, business regulation, and education

Answer: C

C. Education, highways, and law enforcement

Education and highways are among the largest expenditures of state governments. Law enforcement is also significant, if much smaller than these other expenditures. Parks and recreation, business regulation, and libraries are all minor items by comparison

68. How does the government of France differ from that of the United States?

A. France is a direct democracy, while the United States is a representative democracy

B. France has a unitary form of national government, while the United States has a federal form of government

C. France is a representative democracy, while the United States is a direct democracy

D. France does not elect a President, whole the United States elects a President

Answer: B

B. France has a unitary form of national government, while the United States has a federal form of government.

The United States has a federal form of government, since its 50 states are responsible for their own affairs and do not have their governments appointed or supervised by a central government. France has a unitary form of national government, where the central government is responsible for regional as well as national affairs. Neither the U.S. nor France is a direct democracy, and both have an elected President.

MID. LEVEL HUMANITIES

69. In the Presidential Election of 1888, Grover Cleveland lost to Benjamin Harrison, although Cleveland received more popular votes. How is this possible?

   A. The votes of certain states (New York, Indiana) were thrown out because of voting irregularities

   B. Harrison received more electoral votes than Cleveland

   C. None of the party candidates received a majority of votes, and the House of Representatives elected Harrison according to Constitutional procedures

   D. Because of accusations of election law violations, Cleveland withdrew his name and Harrison became President

Answer: B

B.   Harrison received more electoral votes than Cleveland

Presidential elections, according to the United States Constitution, are decided in the Electoral College. This college mirrors the composition of the House of Representatives. The popular vote for each presidential candidate determines which slate of electors in each state is selected. Thus, while Cleveland won enough support in certain states to win a majority of the national popular vote, he did not win enough states to carry the Electoral College. If neither candidate had won the necessary majority, the House of Representatives would have made the final decision, but this did not occur in 1888. The other two answers are not envisioned by the Constitution and did not occur.

70. **How are major party candidates chosen to run for President in the United States?**

   A. Caucuses of major party officeholders meet to select a state's choice for the party, and the candidate selected by the most states becomes the nominee

   B. Potential Presidential nominees seek pledges from each state party's chair and co-chair, and the candidate with the most pledges becomes the nominee

   C. Nationwide primaries are held by each party, to select delegates to a national nominating convention

   D. Each state party decides how to select delegates to a nominating convention; these selection processes may be caucuses, primaries, or any other method chosen by the state party

Answer: D

D.   Each state party decides how to select delegates to a nominating convention; these selection processes may be caucuses, primaries, or any other method chosen by the state party.

A nominating convention selects each party nominee, and the delegates from each state are chosen as the state party sees fit. Caucuses are only one possible method. Pledges or nationwide primaries have never been a way of determining the nominee.

71. **A person who receives more votes than anyone else in an election is said to have a ____ of the votes cast; a person who has over 50% of the votes in an election is said to have a ____ of the votes cast.**

   A. Plurality; majority

   B. Majority; minority

   C. Plurality; minority

   D. Majority; plurality

Answer: A

A.   Plurality; majority

A majority means more than half of the whole. A plurality means the largest portion, when no one achieves a majority. A minority of the votes would be less than half of the votes.

TEACHER CERTIFICATION STUDY GUIDE

72. Which of the following developments is most closely associated with the Neolithic Age?

    A. Human use of fire

    B. First use of stone chipping instruments

    C. Domestication of plants

    D. Development of metallurgical alloys

Answer: C

C.   Domestication of plants

The Neolithic or "New Stone" Age, as its name implies, is characterized by the use of stone implements, but the first use of stone chipping instruments appears in the Paleolithic period. Human use of fire may go back still farther and certainly predates the Neolithic era. The Neolithic period is distinguished by the domestication of plants. The development of metallurgical alloys marks the conclusion of the Neolithic Age.

73. The Tigris-Euphrates Valley was the site of which two primary ancient civilizations?

    A. Babylonian and Assyrian

    B. Sumerian and Egyptian

    C. Hyksos and Hurrian

    D. Persian and Phoenician

Answer: A

A.   Babylonian and Assyrian

(B) While the Sumerians also lived in the southern Tigris-Euphrates valley, Egyptian civilization grew up in the Nile delta (3500BC-30 BC). (C) The Hyksos were an Asiatic people who controlled the Nile Delta during the 15th and 16th Dynasties (1674BC-1548BC). The Hurrians (2500BC-1000BC) came from the Khabur River Valley in northern Mesopotamia, where they spread out to establish various small kingdoms in the region. (D) The Persians (648BC- early 19th century AD) had a succession of empires based in the area known as modern-day Iran. The Phoenicians were a seafaring people who dominated the Mediterranean during the first century BC.

74. The politics of classical Athens is best described by which of the following?

    A. Limited democracy, including both slaves and free men

    B. One man dictatorial rule

    C. Universal democracy among free owners of property

    D. Oligarchy with a few families controlling all decisions

Answer: C

C. Universal democracy among free owners of property.

A citizen of Athens was a free man who owned property. Each had an equal vote in the governance of the city. All the other answers are thereby excluded by definition.

75. The _____ were fought between the Roman Empire and Carthage.

    A. Civil Wars

    B. Punic wars

    C. Caesarian Wars

    D. Persian Wars

Answer: B

B. Punic wars

The Punic Wars (264-146 BC) were fought between Rome and Carthage. (D) The Persian Wars were fought between Greece and Persia. (A) could refer to anything but doesn't apply to the Roman-Carthaginian conflicts. (C) is not a description of any series of conflicts.

76. What Holy Roman Emperor was forced to do public penance because of his conflict with Pope Gregory VII over lay investiture of the clergy?

   A. Charlemagne

   B. Henry IV

   C. Charles V

   D. Henry VIII

Answer: B

B.   Henry IV

Henry IV (1050-1106) clashed with Pope Gregory VII by insisting on the right of a ruler to appoint members of the clergy to their offices but repented in 1077. Charlemagne & Charles V were also Holy Roman Emperors but in the 9th and 16th centuries, respectively. Henry VIII, King of England, broke with the Roman Church over his right to divorce and remarry in 1534.

77. The _____ declared monophysitism (the belief that Jesus was completely divine with no admixture of humanity) to be a heresy?

   A. Council of Nicaea

   B. Diet of Worms

   C. Council of Trent

   D. Council of Chalcedon

Answer: D

D.   Council of Chalcedon

(A) In response to the Arian heresy asserting that Christ was a created being like other created beings, the Council of Nicaea (325 AD) established the divinity of Jesus Christ by declaring him to be of the same substance as God the Father, an article of faith then enshrined in the Nicene Creed. (B) At the Diet of Worms (1521 AD), the Holy Roman Empire tried and condemned Martin Luther and his writings. (C) The Council of Trent (1545 AD-1563 AD), an ecumenical council of the Roman Catholic Church, clarified many aspects of Catholic doctrine and liturgical life in an attempt to counter the Protestant Reformation. (D) The Council of Chalcedon (451 AD) confirmed the humanity of Christ by affirming that the Virgin Mary was indeed his human mother and therefore worthy of the Greek title Theotokos ("God-bearer").

78. The painter of the Sistine Ceiling was:

A. Raphael

B. Michelangelo

C. Leonardo da Vinci

D. Titian

Answer: B

B. Michelangelo

(A) Raphael (1483-1520 AD), (B) Michelangelo (1475-1564 AD), (C) Leonardo da Vinci (1452-1519 AD) and (D) Titian (1488-1576 AD) were all contemporary Italian Renaissance masters, but only Michelangelo painted the Sistine Chapel ceiling (1508-1512 AD).

79. Luther issued strong objection to all but which of the following practices of the 15th Century Roman Catholic Church?

A. The sacrament of baptism

B. Absolution of sins through the intermediation of a priest and through ceremony

C. The sale of indulgences, whereby the buyer may purchase purgation of sins

D. Imposed church control over the individual conscience

Answer: A

A. The sacrament of baptism

Absolution of sins by priests, the sale of indulgences and imposed church control over individual consciences were all practices which Martin Luther (1483-1546) and subsequent Protestants objected to on the basis that they required the Church to act as an intermediary between God and the individual believer. The sacrament of baptism, however, continues to be practiced in some form in most Protestant denominations, as the rite of initiation into the Christian community.

80. **The first explorer to reach India by sailing around the southern tip of Africa was:**

    A. Amerigo Vespucci

    B. Vasco da Gama

    C. Ferdinand Magellan

    D. John Cabot

Answer: B

B.   Vasco da Gama

(A) Amerigo Vespucci (1454-1512) was the Italian explorer to first assert that the lands to the west of Africa and Europe were actually part of a new continent and thus the name "America" was derived from his own "Amerigo." (B) Portuguese Vasco da Gama (1469-1524) built on the discoveries of previous explorers to finally round Africa's Cape of Good Hope and open a sea route for European trade with the east and the eventual Portuguese colonization of India. (C) Portuguese explorer Ferdinand Magellan (1480-1521), working for the Spanish crown, led the first successful expedition to circumnavigate the globe (1519-1522). Magellan himself actually died before the voyage was over, but his ship and 18 crewmembers did return safely to Spain. (D) John Cabot (1450-1499) was an Italian explorer working for the English crown and is thought to have been the first European to discover North America (1497) since the Vikings.

81. **Vasco Nunez de Balboa accomplished which of the following?**

    A. Sighting of the Pacific Ocean from lands discovered by Europeans in the 1500's

    B. The conquest of the Inca civilization through treachery and deceit

    C. The murder of the Aztec ruler and subsequent subjugation of the Empire

    D. None of the above

Answer: A

A.   Sighting of the Pacific Ocean from lands discovered by Europeans in the 1500's.

(A) Spanish explorer and conquistador Vasco Nunez de Balboa (1475-1519) was the first European known to have seen and sailed on the Pacific Ocean (1513) from newly discovered Panama. (B) The conquest of the Incas through treachery and deceit was carried out by Spanish conquistador Francisco Pizarro (1475-1541) in 1532. (C) The murder of Montezuma II, ruler of the Aztecs, and subsequent subjugation of the Empire was achieved by Spanish conquistador Hernan Cortez (1485-1547) between the years 1519 and 1521.

82. **Great Britain became the center of technological and industrial development during the nineteenth century chiefly on the basis of:**

   A. Central location relative to the population centers of Europe

   B. Colonial conquests and military victories over European powers

   C. Reliance on exterior sources of financing

   D. Resources of coal and production of steel

Answer: D

D.   Resources of coal and production of steel

Great Britain possessed a unique set of advantages in the 18th and 19th century, making it the perfect candidate for the technological advances of the Industrial Revolution. (A) Relative isolation from the population centers in Europe meant little to Great Britain, which benefited from its own relatively unified and large domestic market, enabling it to avoid the tariffs and inefficiencies of trading on the diverse (and complicated) continent. (B) Colonial conquests and military victories over European powers were fueled by Great Britain's industrial advances in transportation and weaponry, rather than being causes of them. (C) Reliance on exterior sources of funding – while Great Britain would enjoy an increasing influx of goods and capital from its colonies, the efficiency of its own domestic market consistently generated an impressive amount of capital for investment in the new technologies and industries of the age. (D) Great Britain's rich natural resources of coal and ore enabled steel production and, set alongside new factories in a Britain's landscape, allowed the production of goods quickly and efficiently.

83. **The years 1793-94 in France, characterized by numerous trials and executions of supposed enemies of the Revolutionary Convention, were known as the:**

   A. Reign of Terror

   B. Dark Ages

   C. French Inquisition

   D. Glorious Revolution

Answer: A

A.   Reign of Terror

(A) The period of the French Revolution known as the Reign of Terror (1793-94) is estimated to have led to the deaths of up to 40,000 people: aristocrats, clergy, political activists, and anyone else denounced as an enemy of the Revolutionary Convention, many falsely so. (B) The Dark Ages is the term commonly used for the Early Middle Ages in Europe, from the fall of Rome in 476 to 1000. (C) The French Inquisition was the Roman Catholic Church's attempts to codify into ecclesiastical and secular law the prosecution of heretics, most notably at the time, the Albigensians, in the 13th century. (D) The Glorious Revolution (1688-1689) is the title given to the overthrow of the last Catholic British monarch, James II, in favor of his Protestant daughter Mary and her husband, the Dutch prince William of Orange.

84. In the <u>first</u> aggression of World War II outside the Orient, identify the aggressor nation and the nation which was invaded:

   A. Germany; Sudetenland

   B. Italy; Abyssinia

   C. Germany; Poland

   D. Italy; Yugoslavia

Answer: B

B.   Italy; Abyssinia

(A) The Sudetenland (part of Czechoslovakia) was ceded to Nazi Germany in 1938 by the Munich Agreement of France, Britain, Italy, and Germany. The pretense for the annexation was the mistreatment of resident Germans by the Czechs. (B) Italy's invasion and annexation of Abyssinia in 1935-36 was condemned by the League of Nations but left unchallenged until the East African Campaign of World War II in 1941. Nazi Germany invaded Poland in 1939 and would occupy it until 1945. (D) After attempts to convince the Yugoslavians to join the Axis powers, Germany and Italy invaded Yugoslavia in 1941 and established the Independent State of Croatia.

85. In issuing an ultimatum for Soviet ships not to enter Cuban waters in October 1962, President John F. Kennedy, as part of his decision, used the provisions of the:

   A. Monroe Doctrine

   B. Declaration of the Rights of Man

   C. Geneva Convention

   D. Truman Doctrine

Answer: A

A.   Monroe Doctrine

(A) The Monroe Doctrine, initially formulated by Presidents James Monroe (1758-1831) and John Quincy Adams (1767-1848) and later enhanced by President Theodore Roosevelt (1858-1915), opposed European colonization or interference in the Americas, perceived any such attempts as a threat to US security, and promised U.S. neutrality in conflicts between European powers and/or their already established colonies. (B) The Declaration of the Rights of Man, widely adapted in future declarations about international human rights, was formulated in France during the French Revolution and adopted by the National Constituent Assembly in 1789 as the premise of any future French constitution. (C) The Geneva Conventions (1864, 1929, and 1949, with later additions and amendments) established humanitarian and ethical standards for conduct during times of war and has been widely accepted as international law. (D) The Truman Doctrine (1947), formulated by President Harry Truman (1884-1972), provided for the support of Greece and Turkey as a means of protecting them from Soviet influence. It thereby began the Cold War (1947-1991), a period in which the U.S. sought to contain the Soviet Union by limiting its influence in other countries.

86. In 1990, Alberto Fujimori was elected president of:

   A. Japan

   B. Okinawa

   C. South Korea

   D. Peru

Answer: D

D.   Peru

(A) Japan has a constitutional monarchy, symbolically led by an emperor, and has never elected presidents. (B) Okinawa is a part of Japan and as such does not elect a president. (C) With a modern history including 35 years of Japanese occupation, it is highly unlikely that South Korea would ever elect a Japanese citizen as President. (D) Alberto Fujimori, a dual citizen of Peru and Japan, was the first Asian to lead a Latin American country.

87. Which of the following most closely characterizes the geopolitical events of the USSR in 1991-92:

   A. The USSR established greater military and economic control over the fifteen Soviet republics

   B. The Baltic States (Estonia, Latvia, and Lithuania) declared independence, while the remainder of the USSR remained intact.

   C. Fourteen of fifteen Soviet republics declared some degree of autonomy; the USSR was officially dissolved; the Supreme Soviet rescinded the Soviet Treaty of 1922

   D. All fifteen Soviet republics simultaneously declared immediate and full independence from the USSR, with no provisions for a transitional form of government

Answer: C

C.   Fourteen of fifteen Soviet republics declared some degree of autonomy; the USSR was officially dissolved; the Supreme Soviet rescinded the Soviet Treaty of 1922.

The unraveling of the USSR in 1991-92 and the establishment of independent republics in its wake was a complex if relatively peaceful end to its existence. After a succession of declarations of autonomy by constituent states forced the dissolution of the central government, the Baltic States of Latvia, Lithuania, and Estonia immediately declared their independence. Other republics took longer to reconfigure their relationships to one another. There was no serious attempt by the central government to resist these changes militarily or economically.

88. **Chinese civilization is generally credited with the original development of which of the following sets of technologies:**

   A. Movable type and mass production of goods

   B. Wool processing and domestication of the horse

   C. Paper and gunpowder manufacture

   D. Leather processing and modern timekeeping

Answer: C

C.   Paper and gunpowder manufacture

(A) While China's Bi Sheng (d. 1052) is credited with the earliest forms of movable type (1041-48), mass production was spearheaded by America's Henry Ford (1863-1947) in his campaign to create the first truly affordable automobile, the Model T Ford. (B) While wool has been processed in many ways in many cultures, production on a scale beyond cottage industries was not possible without the many advances made in England during the Industrial Revolution (18th century). Various theories exist about the domestication of the horse, with estimates ranging from 4600 BC to 2000 BC in Eurasia. Recent DNA evidence suggests that the horse may actually have been domesticated in different cultures at independent points. (C) The earliest mention of gunpowder appears in ninth century Chinese documents. The earliest examples of paper made of wood pulp come from China and have been dated as early as the second century BC. (D) Leather processing and timekeeping have likewise seen different developments in different places at different times.

89. **Extensive exports of gold and copper; elaborate court and constitution; trade links on both the Atlantic and Indian Oceans; use of heavy stone architecture; these most closely characterize the civilization of:**

   A. Mwene Mutapa

   B. Chichen Itza

   C. Great Zimbabwe

   D. Muscat and Oman

Answer:

C. Great Zimbabwe

The medieval kingdom of Great Zimbabwe left the largest ruins in Africa from which archeologists have been able to discern the nature of their civilization. (B) Chichen Itza is a Mayan temple complex complete with other supporting buildings which has been excavated in Yucatan, Mexico, and is thought to date from 987 AD. (D) Muscat and Oman was an empire that dominated the southern Persian Gulf and Saudi peninsula and parts of the East African coast and Iranian Plateau. Its main export, however, was slaves.

90. **Which of the following is NOT one of the Pillars of Faith of Islam?**

   A. Alms-giving (zakah)

   B. Pilgrimage (hajj)

   C. Membership in a school of law (al-madhahib)

   D. Fasting (sawm)

Answer: C

C. Membership in a school of law (al-madhahib)

The Five Pillars of Islam are the faith profession that there is no God but Allah and Muhammad is his prophet, prayer (salah), pilgrimage to Mecca (hajj), alms-giving (zakah), and fasting during the holy month of Ramadan (sawm).

MID. LEVEL HUMANITIES

91. The native metaphysical outlook of Japan, usually characterized as a religion, is:

   A. Tao

   B. Shinto

   C. Nichiren Shoju

   D. Shaolin

Answer: B

B.   Shinto

(A) Tao is the Chinese philosophical work that inspired Taoism, the religious tradition sourced in China. (B) Shinto is the system of rituals and beliefs honoring the deities and spirits believed to be native to the landscape and inhabitants of Japan. (C) Nichiren Shoju is a strand of Nichiren Buddhism, a tradition started by a Japanese Buddhist monk, Nichiren (1222-1282). (D) The Shaolin temple (originally built in 497 AD) is the Chinese Buddhist monastery considered to be the source of Zen Buddhism and its subsequent martial arts.

92. The Native Americans of the Eastern Woodlands lived on:

   A. Buffalo and crops such as corn, beans, and sunflowers

   B. Chiefly farming of squash, beans, and corn

   C. A variety of game (deer, bear, moose) and crops (squash, pumpkins, corn)

   D. Wolves, foxes, polar bears, walruses, and fish

Answer: C

C.   A variety of game (deer, bear, moose) and crops (squash, pumpkins, corn)

(A) Buffalo live in the plains habitat found in Western and Midwestern North America. (B) & (C) While the Native Americans did farm the "Three Sisters" of corn, squash and beans, the woods of the East also meant that a variety of game (deer, bear, moose) were widely available for them to hunt. (D) However, wolves, foxes, walruses, polar bears, and fish are found together only within the Arctic Circle, not in eastern woodlands.

93. **Apartments built out of cliff faces; shared government by adult citizens; absence of aggression toward other groups. These factors characterize the Native American group known as:**

   A. Pueblos

   B. Comanches

   C. Seminoles

   D. Sioux

Answer: A

A.   Pueblos

(B) The Comanches were a nomadic Native American group that emerged around 1700 AD in the North American Plains and were decidedly aggressive towards their neighbors. (C) The Seminoles are a native American group which originally emerged in Florida in the mid-18th century and was made up of refugees from other Native tribes and escaped slaves. (D) The Sioux were a Native American people who originally lived in the Dakotas, Nebraska and Minnesota and clashed extensively with white settlers.

94. **Columbus first reached Western Hemisphere lands in what is now:**

   A. Florida

   B. Bermuda

   C. Puerto Rico

   D. Bahamas

Answer: D

D.   Bahamas

Christopher Columbus (1451-1506) visited the Bahamas in 1492 and Puerto Rico in 1493 but never landed on either Bermuda or Florida.

95. **The "Trail of Tears" relates to:**

    A. The removal of the Cherokees from their native lands to Oklahoma Territory

    B. The revolt and subsequent migration of the Massachusetts Pilgrims under pressure from the Iroquois

    C. The journey of the Nez Perce under Chief Joseph before their capture by the U.S. Army

    D. The 1973 standoff between federal marshals and Native Americans at Wounded Knee, S.D.

Answer: A

A. The removal of the Cherokees from their native lands to Oklahoma Territory (1838-39).

(B) There never was a revolt and migration of the Massachusetts Pilgrims under pressure from the Iroquois. (C) The 1877 journey of the Nez Perce under Chief Joseph was a strategically impressive attempt to retreat from an oncoming U.S. Army into Canada. (D) The 1973 Wounded Knee incident was the occupation of the town of Wounded Knee, South Dakota, by the American Indian Movement to call attention to issues of Native American civil rights. Their action led to a 71-day standoff with U.S. Marshals, which was eventually resolved peacefully.

97. **Bartholomeu Dias, in seeking a route around the tip of Africa, was forced to turn back. Nevertheless, the cape he discovered near the southern tip of Africa became known as:**

    A. Cape Horn

    B. Cabo Bojador

    C. Cape of Good Hope

    D. Cape Hatteras

Answer: C

C. Cape of Good Hope

(A) Cape Horn is located at the southern tip of Chile, and therefore South America. It was discovered by Sir Francis Drake as he sailed around the globe in 1578. (B) Cajo Bojador, on the Western coast of northern Africa, was first successfully navigated by a European, Portuguese Gil Eanes, in 1434. (D) Cape Hatteras is located on the U.S. Atlantic coast, at North Carolina.

97. The Middle Colonies of the Americas were:

    A. Maryland, Virginia, North Carolina

    B. New York, New Jersey, Pennsylvania, Delaware

    C. Rhode Island, Connecticut, New York, New Jersey

    D. Vermont and New Hampshire

Answer: B

B.   New York, New Jersey, Pennsylvania, Delaware

(A), (C) & (D). Maryland, Virginia, and North Carolina were Southern colonies, Rhode Island, Connecticut, and New Hampshire were New England colonies and Vermont was not one of the 13 original colonies.

98. Slavery arose in the Southern Colonies partly as a perceived economical way to:

    A. Increase the owner's wealth through human beings used as a source of exchange

    B. Cultivate large plantations of cotton, tobacco, rice, indigo, and other crops

    C. Provide Africans with humanitarian aid, such as health care, Christianity, and literacy

    D. Keep ships' holds full of cargo on two out of three legs of the "triangular trade" voyage

Answer: B

B.   Cultivate large plantations of cotton, tobacco, rice, indigo, and other crops.

The Southern states, with their smaller populations, were heavily dependent on slave labor as a means of being able to fulfill their role and remain competitive in the greater U.S. economy. (A) When slaves arrived in the South, the vast majority would become permanent fixtures on plantations, intended for work, not as a source of exchange. (C) While some slave owners instructed their slaves in Christianity, provided health care or some level of education, such attention was not their primary reason for owning slaves – a cheap and ready labor force was. (D) Whether or not ships' holds were full on two or three legs of the triangular journey was not the concern of Southerners as the final purchasers of slaves. Such details would have concerned the slave traders.

99. **Of the following, which contributed most to penetration of western areas by colonial Americans?**

    A. Development of large ships capable of sailing upstream in rivers such as the Hudson, Susquehanna, and Delaware

    B. The invention of the steamboat

    C. Improved relations with Native Americans, who invited colonial Americans to travel west to settle

    D. Improved roads, mail service, and communications

Answer: D

D.   Improved roads, mail service and communications

(A) Because the Susquehanna, Delaware, and Hudson are limited to the northeast, they would not have helped the colonists penetrate any further West. (B) Since these were the waterways that they had immediate access to, the development of the steamboat was similarly unhelpful in this regard. (C) In general, colonist-Native American relations got worse, not better as colonists moved West, so colonists were unlikely to have been invited yet further west. (D) Improved roads, mail service, and communications made traveling west easier and more attractive because they meant not being completely cut off from news and family in the east.

100. **A major quarrel between colonial Americans and the British concerned a series of British Acts of Parliament dealing with:**

   A. Taxes

   B. Slavery

   C. Native Americans

   D. Shipbuilding

Answer: A

A.   Taxes

Acts of Parliament imposing taxes on the colonists always provoked resentment. Because the colonies had no direct representation in Parliament, they felt it unjust that that body should impose taxes on them, with so little knowledge of their very different situation in America and no real concern for the consequences of such taxes. (B) While slavery continued to exist in the colonies long after it had been completely abolished in Britain, it never was a source of serious debate between Britain and the colonies. By the time Britain outlawed slavery in its colonies in 1833, the American Revolution had already taken place and the United States were free of British control. (C) There was no series of British Acts of Parliament passed concerning Native Americans. (D) Colonial shipbuilding was an industry that received little interference from the British.

101. **The first shots in what was to become the American Revolution were fired in:**

   A. Florida

   B. Massachusetts

   D. New York

   D. Virginia

Answer: B

B.   Massachusetts

(A) At the time of the American Revolution, Florida, while a British possession, was not directly involved in the Revolutionary War. (B) The American Revolution began with the battles of Lexington and Concord in 1775. (C) There would be no fighting in New York until 1776 and none in Virginia until 1781.

102. The U.S. Constitution, adopted in 1789, provided for:

    A. Direct election of the President by all citizens

    B. Direct election of the President by citizens meeting a standard of wealth

    C. Indirect election of the President by electors

    D. Indirect election of the President by the U.S. Senate

Answer: C

C.   Indirect election of the President by electors

The United States Constitution has always arranged for the indirect election of the President by electors. The question, by mentioning the original date of adoption, might mislead someone to choose B, but while standards of citizenship have been changed by amendment, the President has never been directly elected. Nor does the Senate have anything to do with presidential elections. The House of Representatives, not the Senate, settles cases where neither candidate wins in the Electoral College.

103. The area of the United States was effectively doubled through purchase of the Louisiana Territory under which President?

    A. John Adams

    B. Thomas Jefferson

    C. James Madison

    D. James Monroe

Answer: B

B.   Thomas Jefferson

(B) The Louisiana Purchase, an acquisition of territory from France, in 1803 occurred under Thomas Jefferson. (A) John Adams (1735-1826) was president from 1797-1801, before the purchase, and (C) James Madison, (1751-1836) after the Purchase (1809-1817). (D) James Monroe (1758-1831) was actually a signatory on the Purchase but also did not become President until 1817.

104. **What was a major source of contention between American settlers in Texas and the Mexican government in the 1830s and 1840s?**

   A. The Americans wished to retain slavery, which had been outlawed in Mexico

   B. The Americans had agreed to learn Spanish and become Roman Catholic, but failed to do so

   C. The Americans retained ties to the United States, and Santa Anna feared the power of the U.S.

   D. All of the above were contentious issues between American settlers and the Mexican government

Answer: D

D. All of the above were contentious issues between American settlers and the Mexican government.

The American settlers simply were not willing to assimilate into Mexican society but maintained their prior commitments to slave holding, the English language, Protestantism, and the United States government.

105. **"Fifty-four Forty or Fight" refers to the desire of some nineteenth century Americans to:**

   A. Explore the entire Missouri River valley to its source in the Oregon Territory

   B. Insist that Mexico cede all of Texas to the U.S. or face war

   C. Demand that American territory reaches to the border of Russian America

   D. Pay only $54,040,000 for all of the Oregon Territory

Answer: C

C. Demand that American territory reaches to the border of Russian America.

"Fifty-four Forty or Fight" refers to the latitude of the northern border of the Oregon Territory with Russian Alaska. Britain and the United States were negotiating a division of the Territory, but some Americans used this slogan to campaign for demanding all of it for the United States. (A) Has the merit of speaking of Oregon Territory, although it has nothing to do with the controversy, while (B) speaks of threatening war, although the wrong one. (D) Might be tempting only because it recalls the famous Louisiana Purchase.

106. Which President helped postpone a civil war by supporting the Compromise of 1850?

   A. Henry Clay

   B. Franklin Pierce

   C. Millard Fillmore

   D. James Buchanan

Answer: C

C.   Millard Fillmore

Millard Fillmore was the President who signed the Compromise of 1850. Henry Clay was instrumental in negotiating the compromise but was never President. Presidents Franklin Pierce and James Buchanan were later involved in the 1854 Kansas-Nebraska Act, which undid this Compromise.

107. Which American Secretary of War oversaw the purchase of present-day southern Arizona (the Gadsden Purchase) for the purpose of building a railroad to connect California to the rest of the United States?

   A. Henry Clay

   B. William Seward

   C. Franklin Pierce

   D. Jefferson Davis

Answer: D

D.   Jefferson Davis

Jefferson Davis was the Secretary of War in question. Franklin Pierce was President at the time. Neither Henry Clay nor William Seward was ever Secretary of War.

108. A consequence of the Gold Rush of Americans to California in 1848 and 1849 was that:

A. California spent the minimum amount of time as a territory, and was admitted as a slave state

B. California was denied admission on its first application, since most Americans felt that the settlers were too "uncivilized" to deserve statehood

C. California was purchased from Mexico for the express purpose of gaining immediate statehood

D. California did not go through the normal territorial stage but applied directly for statehood as a free state

Answer: D

D. California did not go through the normal territorial stage but applied directly for statehood as a free state.

California, suddenly undergoing a massive increase in population and wealth and desiring orderly government, found it had little recourse but to claim status as a free state and appeal directly for statehood. Congress had moved too slowly on the question of making California United States Territory. California was never a territory but only a military district. California was not denied admission to the Union but was an essential part of the Compromise of 1850. Immediate statehood was definitely not an express policy of the U.S. in acquiring California, but the Gold Rush changed attitudes quickly.

109. Of the following groups of states, which were slave states?

    A. Delaware, Maryland, Missouri

    B. California, Texas, Florida

    C. Kansas, Missouri, Kentucky

    D. Virginia, West Virginia, Indiana

Answer: A

A.   Delaware, Maryland, Missouri.

(A) Delaware, Maryland and Missouri were all slave states at the time of the Civil War. (B) Florida and Texas were slave states, while California was a free state. (C) Kansas, Missouri, and Kentucky were all originally slave territories, and Missouri and Kentucky were admitted to the Union as such. However, Kansas' petition to join the union in 1858 was blocked in order to preserve the balance between slave and free states. Kansas was admitted as a free state in 1861. (D) Indiana was a free state.

110. In the American Civil War, who was the first commander of the forces of the United States?

    A. Gen. Ulysses S. Grant

    B. Gen. Robert E. Lee

    C. Gen. Irwin McDowell

    D. Gen. George Meade

Answer: C

C.   General Irwin McDowell

(A) Gen. Ulysses S. Grant was the final commander of the Union army during the Civil War. (B) Gen. Robert E. Lee was the commander of the Confederate army. (D) Gen. George Meade was the Union commander at the Battle of Gettysburg in 1863.

111. Abraham Lincoln won re-election in 1864 chiefly through:

    A. His overwhelming force of personality and appeal to all segments of the electorate

    B. His reputation as the Great Emancipator

    C. The fact that people felt sorry for him because of his difficulties

    D. His shrewd political manipulation, clever use of patronage jobs, and wide-appeal selection of cabinet members

Answer: D

D.   His shrewd political manipulation, clever use of patronage jobs, and wide-appeal selection of cabinet members

President Lincoln in his own lifetime was a hugely divisive figure, even in the North. He did not appeal to all segments of the electorate, his reputation as the Great Emancipator really developed after the war, and few felt sorry for him for his personal and political difficulties. Rather, Lincoln constantly maneuvered to maintain the advantage, using all the powers of the Presidency to win re-election despite his own unpopularity.

112. How many states re-entered the Union before 1868?

State	Date of Readmission
Alabama	1868
Arkansas	1868
Florida	1868
Georgia	1870
Louisiana	1868
Mississippi	1870
North Carolina	1868
South Carolina	1868
Tennessee	1866
Texas	1870
Virginia	1870

  A. 0 states

  B. 1 state

  C. 2 states

  D. 3 states

Answer: B

B. 1 state

Only Tennessee was readmitted before 1868, as the above table indicates.

113. **The Interstate Commerce Commission (ICC) was established in reaction to abuses and corruption in what industry?**

    A. Textile

    B. Railroad

    C. Steel

    D. Banking

Answer: B

B.   Railroad

The ICC was established to fight abuses in the railroad industry.

114. **Which of the following sets of inventors is correctly matched with the area in which they primarily worked?**

    A. Thomas Edison and George Westinghouse: transportation

    B. Cyrus McCormick and George Washington Carver: household appliances

    C. Alexander Graham Bell and Samuel F. B. Morse: communications

    D. Isaac Singer and John Gorrie: agriculture

Answer: C

C.   Alexander Graham Bell and Samuel F. B. Morse: communications

Bell, inventor of the telephone, and Morse, inventor of the telegraph and Morse code, were both working in the area of communications. While Westinghouse did invent various technologies crucial to the railroads and thus transportation, Edison did not; both are strongly linked to electrical inventions. McCormick and Carver specialized in agricultural inventions, while Singer, an inventor of the sewing machine, and Gorrie, the inventor of air conditioning and refrigeration, were best known for their household appliances.

115. The Teapot Dome scandal related to:

A. The improper taxing of tea surpluses in Boston

B. The improper awarding of building contracts in Washington, D.C.

C. The improper sale of policy decisions by various Harding administration officials

D. The improper sale of oil reserves in Wyoming

Answer: D

D.   The improper sale of oil reserves in Wyoming

This scandal refers to the improper sale of federal oil reserves in Teapot Dome, Wyoming, an infamous event in the Harding Administration (1921-25). C would be tempting, especially since the Secretary of the Interior personally benefited from the sale, but no significant policy decisions were involved. No building of a dome or tea to put in the Teapot were involved in the making of this scandal.

116. Which of the following was NOT a factor in the United States' entry into World War I?

A. The closeness of the Presidential Election of 1916

B. The German threat to sink all allied ships, including merchant ships

C. The desire to preserve democracy as practiced in Britain and France as compared to the totalitarianism of Germany

D. The sinking of the Lusitania and the Sussex

Answer: A

A.   The closeness of the Presidential Election of 1916

Not sure where the facts are on this one: Wilson won re-election in 1916! Since there was no presidential election of 1916, this could not have been a factor the United States' entry into the war; the last election had been in 1914. All the other answers were indeed factors.

117. What 1924 Act of Congress severely restricted immigration in the United States?

   A. Taft-Hartley Act

   B. Smoot-Hawley Act

   C. Fordney-McCumber Act

   D. Johnson-Reed Act

Answer: D

D.   Johnson-Reed Act

(A) The Taft-Harley Act (1947) prohibited unfair labor practices by labor unions. (B) The Smoot-Hawley Act (1930) raised U.S. tariffs on imported goods to negative effect on the U.S. economy and world trade as (C) the Fordney-McCumber Act (1922) had done before it.

118. The first territorial governor of Florida after Florida's purchase by the United States was:

   A. Napoleon B. Broward

   B. William P. Duval

   C. Andrew Jackson

   D. Davy Crockett

Answer: C

C.   Andrew Jackson

119. **President Truman suspended Gen. Douglas MacArthur from command of Allied forces in Korea because of:**

   A. MacArthur's inability to make any progress against North Korea

   B. MacArthur's criticism of Truman, claiming that the President would not allow him to pursue aggressive tactics against the Communists

   C. The harsh treatment MacArthur exhibited toward the Japanese after World War II

   D. The ability of the U.S. Navy to continue the conflict without the presence of MacArthur

Answer: B

B. MacArthur's criticism of Truman, claiming that the President would not allow him to pursue aggressive tactics against the Communists

Truman suspended MacArthur because of clear insubordination: MacArthur had publicly criticized the President, his Commander in Chief, and had openly undermined his policy of negotiating a settlement with the Communists. MacArthur was a general of proven effectiveness; so, (A) cannot be correct. MacArthur was actually rather lenient to the Japanese after World War II, and he was a general, not an admiral of the Navy.

120. Which of the following most closely characterizes the Supreme Court's decision in Brown v. Board of Education?

   A. Chief Justice Warren had to cast the deciding vote in a sharply divided Court

   B. The decision was rendered along sectional lines, with northerners voting for integration and southerners voting for continued segregation

   C. The decision was 7-2, with dissenting justices not even preparing a written dissent

   D. Chief Justice Warren was able to persuade the Court to render a unanimous decision

Answer: D

D. Chief Justice Warren was able to persuade the Court to render a unanimous decision. The Supreme Court decided 9-0 against segregated educational facilities.

121. The economic practices under President Ronald Reagan ("Reaganomics") were characterized by:

   A. Low inflation, high unemployment, high interest rates, high national debt

   B. High inflation, low unemployment, low interest rates, low national debt

   C. Low inflation, high unemployment, low interest rates, depletion of national debt

   D. High inflation, low unemployment, high interest rates, low national debt

Answer: A

A. High inflation, low unemployment, high interest rates, high national debt.

122. The Harlem Renaissance of the 1920s refers to:

A. The migration of black Americans out of Harlem, and its resettlement by white Americans

B. A movement whereby the residents of Harlem were urged to "Return to Africa"

C. A proliferation in the arts among black Americans, centered on Harlem

D. The discovery of lost 15th century Italian paintings in a Harlem warehouse

Answer: C

C. A proliferation in the arts among black Americans, centered on Harlem.

(C) During the Harlem Renaissance (1919-1930s), America's black community expressed itself in art, literature, and music with new fervor and creativity. (A) Harlem's continues to enjoy Black Americans as the majority of its population. (B) & (D) are fictitious events.

123. Which of the following is most descriptive of the conflict between the U.S. government and the Seminoles between 1818 and 1858?

A. There was constant armed conflict between the Seminoles and the U.S. during these years

B. Historians discern three separate phases of hostilities (1818, 1835-42, 1855-58), known collectively as the Seminole Wars

C. On May 7, 1858, the Seminoles admitted defeat, signed a peace treaty with the U.S., and left for Oklahoma, except for fifty-one individuals

D. The former Seminole chief Osceola helped the U.S. defeat the Seminoles and effect their removal to Oklahoma

Answer: B

B. Historians discern three separate phases of hostilities (1818, 1835-42, 1855-58), known collectively as the Seminole Wars.

(A) Intermittent conflicts between the U.S. government and the Seminole Native Americans can be classified into (B) three separate phases of hostilities. (C)

124. Match the railroad entrepreneur with the correct area of development:

    A. Henry Plant: Tampa and the West Coast

    B. Cornelius Vanderbilt: Jacksonville and the Northeast

    C. Henry Flagler: Orlando and the Central Highlands

    D. J.P. Morgan: Pensacola and the Northwest

Answer: A

A. Henry Plant: Tampa and the West Coast

(A) Henry Plant (1819-1899) was responsible for building railroad along the West Coast of Florida, making Tampa the end of the line. (B) Cornelius Vanderbilt (1794-1877), transportation mogul, concentrated his efforts in the Northeast of the country and was largely uninvolved in Florida. (C) Henry Flagler (1830-1913) was a Floridian involved in railways and oil production but is more closely associated with Miami than Orlando. (D) J.P. Morgan (1837-1913) was a New York-based banker.

125. Florida's space exploration industry is centered in:

    A. Baker County

    B. Broward County

    C. Brevard County

    D. Bradford County

Answer: C

C. Brevard County

(C) Florida's Kennedy Space complex is on Cape Canaveral in Brevard County.

XAMonline, INC. 21 Orient Ave. Melrose, MA 02176

Toll Free number 800-509-4128

TO ORDER Fax 781-662-9268 OR www.XAMonline.com

<u>WEST-E/B PRAXIS   - WEST - 2007</u>

PO#   Store/School:

Address 1:

Address 2 (Ship to other):

City, State Zip

Credit card number_____-_____-_____-_____   expiration_____

EMAIL _____

PHONE   FAX

13# ISBN 2007	TITLE	Qty	Retail	Total
978-1-58197-550-5	WEST-B Reading, Mathematics, Writing			
978-1-58197-564-2	WEST-E/PRAXIS II™ Biology 0235			
978-1-58197-565-9	WEST-E/PRAXIS II™ Chemistry 0245			
978-1-58197-566-6	WEST-E/PRAXIS II™ Designated World Language: French Sample Test 0173			
978-1-58197-557-4	WEST-E/PRAXIS II™ Designated World Language: Spanish 0191			
978-1-58197-558-1	WEST-E/PRAXIS II™ Elementary Education 0014			
978-1-58197-554-3	WEST-E/PRAXIS II™ English Language Arts 0041			
978-1-58197-551-2	WEST-E/PRAXIS II™ General Science 0435			
978-1-58197-559-8	WEST-E/PRAXIS II™ Health & Fitness 0856			
978-1-58197-560-4	WEST-E/PRAXIS II™ Library Media 0310			
978-1-58197-555-0	WEST-E/PRAXIS II™ Mathematics 0061			
978-1-58197-556-7	WEST-E/PRAXIS II™ Middle Level Humanities 0049, 0089			
978-1-58197-561-1	WEST-E/PRAXIS II™ Middle Level Math/Science 0439, 0069			
978-1-58197-568-0	WEST-E/PRAXIS II™ Physics 0265			
978-1-58197-563-5	WEST-E/PRAXIS II™ Reading/Literacy 0300			
978-1-58197-552-9	WEST-E/PRAXIS II™ Social Studies 0081			
978-1-58197-553-6	WEST-E/PRAXIS II™ Special Education 0353			
978-1-58197-567-3	WEST-E/PRAXIS II™ Visual Arts Sample Test 0133			
	SUBTOTAL		Ship	$8.25
	FOR PRODUCT PRICES VISIT **WWW.XAMONLINE.COM**		**TOTAL**	